T0022567

ULTIMATE GUIDE SERIES

ULTIMATE GUIDE TO HEAVEN AND HELL

BY E. RAY CLENDENEN

Ultimate Guide to Heaven and Hell
© 2024 by Holman Bible Publishers
Brentwood, Tennessee
All rights reserved

978-1-0877-8831-9

Dewey Decimal Classification: 236.2
Subject Heading: DEATH \ HEAVEN \ HELL

Unless otherwise noted, Scripture passages are taken from the Christian Standard
Bible® (CSB), copyright © 2017 by Holman Bible Publishers. All rights reserved.

The interior of the *Ultimate Guide to Heaven and Hell* was designed and typeset by 2K/
DENMARK, using Bible Serif created by 2K/DENMARK, Højbjerg, Denmark.

Printed in China
1 2 3 4 5 6 7 8 9 10 · 30 29 28 27 26 25 24
RRD

TABLE OF CONTENTS

To all my fellow travelers who have shown me the love of Christ,
encouraged me, prayed with and for me, taught me
the ways of the Lord, and given me hope.
Thank you!

PREFACE

I may be one of the few who almost always reads the preface of a book. I love to know the rest of the story. How did a book come about? Why does it exist? Is there something I need to know in order to fully appreciate what it says? Might there be a funny story behind it? Or a sad one? As my wife Gigi can attest, I am plagued by insatiable curiosity.

In high school I came to love plays and musicals and was in a few. I even love opera—though again, perhaps, that makes me one of a few. (So does my love of fruitcake.) As will become apparent, I love humor whenever possible. Anyway, in some book prefaces, the author takes his or her shoes off and lets us into their lives. But in other cases, like this one, the preface might be compared to "breaking the fourth wall" as they say in theater language. Between the world of the actors on stage and the audience is an imaginary wall that keeps the actors from seeing or hearing the audience. But sometimes an actor will look through the wall directly at the audience and gesture to them or even address them directly, and the other actors are not supposed to notice. Thornton Wilder's play *Our Town* (1938) uses this device continually, allowing the main character, the stage manager, to serve as narrator and also to play some of the minor parts. I recently watched a wonderful 2003 performance in which Paul Newman played the stage manager.[1]

Throughout this book, I play the part of a tour guide who is trying to show the reader around the afterlife—heaven and hell. I chose that approach for several reasons. One is to hide the fact that I was trained as a Bible scholar rather than a journalist or writer. The pedantic and esoteric comes naturally to me, and as Professor Hendricks would warn us at Dallas Seminary, it is a sin to bore people with the Word of God. Besides, I want readers to keep reading instead of falling asleep.

Another reason for adopting the guidebook genre is the name of the series: "Ultimate Guides." The approach seemed perfect. Gigi and I love to travel, and I have a bookshelf full of guidebooks. These cover Cape Cod, the Alaska Highway, Norway, diving in Indonesia, Olympic National Park, North and South Dakota, and lots of other topics, some of which we have not yet used. Regardless, the most important reason for the guidebook approach is that I found the title itself embarrassingly presumptuous. The only thing that is ultimate is God, and I am not him. The idea that I could write an ultimate guide to anything seemed ludicrous. So, I needed a more lighthearted approach to avoid (more) accusations of being a pompous know-it-all.

About the time I turned seventy in 2019, I decided it was time to see what I could learn about death and the afterlife. So naturally I started reading. While in seminary back in the seventies, I encountered Richard Baxter's book, *The Saints' Everlasting Rest* (1650) and decided that when I got closer to the end of my life, I would read it. But when I got a copy and started reading, it was not my cup of tea. Unperturbed, I got lots of other books (such fun!) and started my investigation with them and with relevant passages of Scripture. When my boss at Lifeway suggested I might write one of their Ultimate Guides books and showed me a prospective list of subject ideas for them, I was immediately drawn to this one. So that's how this particular project happened.

My first step was to list all the questions I could think of about death and its aftermath. Then I put them into what seemed like logical order and began studying and writing. That was a long time ago, and I am *amazed* at how much fun it has been digging into one Bible passage after another, trying to answer as many questions as possible. Since I have been studying the Bible over fifty years and have several degrees in biblical studies, you might think that I could just sit down and write out most of the answers. Not so. I found that I did not know all the answers. And even after much study, I cannot affirm that this book is really the "ultimate" source on these topics.

In the first place, I soon realized I had more questions than I had the time or energy or expertise to answer. Alan W. Gomes, theology professor at Biola University, has written the highly recommendable book, *40 Questions about Heaven and Hell*.[2] While I either did not tackle or only hit with a glancing blow many of his questions, I think I have provided reasonable answers to the most important ones. (And in many cases, more than one reasonable answer is possible.) My hope and prayer are that I have provided significant information and a perspective that readers will find encouraging, comforting, and motivating to pursue their own answers as they pursue the God of ultimate answers and ultimate delight. The ultimate answer, perhaps, is as Henri Nouwen puts it: "I believe that God, who has given me my life, loves me with an everlasting love. I believe that this everlasting love is stronger than death, and I believe that everything that happens during my life offers me an opportunity to let my death become a rebirth."[3] I hope readers will choose to take this particular ultimate answer to heart.

Unfortunately, by this project's deadline I still had not read all the books I accumulated, and I look forward to reading the rest soon. One book I read too late to incorporate is Dale Allison's *Night Comes: Death, Imagination, and the Last Things*. He has an interesting survey of eight different views on the nature of heaven, one of which is that at least redeemed people become angels at death. We neglected to address this issue because it seems more mythological than real, and the evidence for this viewpoint is not substantial. Allison, however, not only shows how prevalent this view is in the broader culture, but what a historical pedigree it has—one going back to ancient Jewish and Christian texts. The view was held by Tertullian, Clement of Alexandria, and Origen.[4] Allison notes that in Jesus's statement in Luke 20:36 that those in the new age will not marry, the word translated "like angels" (CSB, NIV, NRSV, NASB, NLT) can also be rendered "equal to angels" (ESV, RSV, NET, KJV).[5] The Roman Catholic New Jerusalem Bible renders it "the same as the angels." The sense, Allison says, could be that "human beings will be like angels and therefore won't marry." However misguided the view may be, it is helpful to know where it comes from.

Most Christians assume we will recognize each other in heaven, so I chose not to discuss the question in this book. Allison, however, has a helpful survey of the issue and the evidence for it. He points, for example, to the phrase "gathered to their people" as implying it (see the section "Idioms for Death," in this book's chapter 10). Another indication is the eschatological banquet with the patriarchs mentioned by Jesus (Matt 8:11) and the reunion of living and deceased believers when Christ returns (1 Thess 4:16–17). In fact, one difference between immortality and the Bible's emphasis on resurrection is that it always portrays resurrection as a communal affair.[6] Surely mutual recognition must be assumed. Allison also points out, "We're all social beings socially formed. We are who we are because of our continual interactions with others."[7] If our individual identities are preserved beyond death, so should be our social identities. He also mentions some Christian writers who have unwisely made claims like this one: "If there were but one soul enjoying God, it would be happy, even though it had no neighbor."[8] I must say here that in view of God's statement, "It is not good for the man to be alone" (Gen 2:18) and the stress on connectedness throughout Scripture, Aquinas was wrong.[9]

One last item Allison mentions is important for us to bear in mind. No one could have taken the Old Testament promises of the Messiah and written the account of Jesus's life we find in the four Gospels, even though many Gospel texts point back to the Old Testament.[10] Likewise, the Bible's portrayal of the afterlife is in broad strokes. I have pointed elsewhere to the old TV show, "Alfred Hitchcock Presents" (1955–1965), which always began with a life-sized line drawing of a man in profile, into which the rotund Alfred Hitchcock walked. The sketch fit him perfectly. Nevertheless, no one could paint an exact likeness of Mr. Hitchcock based only on the drawing. Just as the profile of Jesus in the Old Testament left out much that was filled in by the reality of our Savior when He came, much of our individual and corporate future as God's people after death is only hinted at in the New Testament. I therefore agree with my wife Gigi, who likes to say that whatever our views are regarding what happens after our deaths or at and beyond Christ's return, we are going to be wonderfully surprised. Allison helpfully calls attention to this by citing 1 John 3:2, the first part of which I usually do not fully appreciate. John said, "What we will be has not yet been revealed."[11] I think that is important for us to remember.

One last thing I would like to do is express my appreciation for my loving wife Gigi: for her prayers, for listening to every chapter of this book, and for giving me honest feedback. She always makes me feel that she believes in me and is my greatest fan. I am also grateful to my many Christian friends who have prayed for me during this project and have sounding boards to my questions and ideas. (An upheaval in my life a little over ten years ago and the subsequent healing and recovery process has exponentially raised my appreciation for and dependence on the love of God and of my Christian brothers and sisters.) Many of these are members of the Christ-focused, grace-focused Seventh Day Adventist church Gigi and I attend. Despite my contrary views on some of the denomination's stances, I have never felt so loved and valued as I do in fellowship there. They have patiently, graciously, and lovingly interacted with my non-Adventist views and given me a deeper understanding of the issues involved. (I apologize to them for often using Adventist views as a foil to present my own views in this book. I hope I have done it with love and respect.) I am also grateful to my editor, Jason Kees, for making this a better book.

> Look, God's dwelling is with humanity, and he will live with them. They will be his peoples, and God himself will be with them and will be their God. He will wipe away every tear from their eyes. Death will be no more; grief, crying, and pain will be no more, because the previous things have passed away. (Rev 21:3–4)

NOTES

[1] "Our Town 2003 Broadway Production Paul Newman as Stage Manager." https://www.youtube.com/watch?v=gc109cGQ9_Q.

[2] Alan W. Gomes, *40 Questions about Heaven and Hell* (Grand Rapids: Kregel, 2018).

[3] Henri Nouwen, *Beyond the Mirror: Reflections on Life and Death* (NY: Crossroad, 1990), 93.

[4] Dale C. Allison Jr., *Night Comes: Death, Imagination, and the Last Things* (Grand Rapids: Eerdmans, 2016), 129–31.

[5] Allison, *Night Comes*, 128–29.

[6] Allison, *Night Comes*, 41.

[7] Allison, *Night Comes*, 136.

[8] Allison, *Night Comes*, 137.

[9] Allison, *Night Comes*, 42.

[10] See Allison, *Night Comes*, 148.

[11] See Allison, *Night Comes*, 149.

ORIENTATION

The Roman Colosseum

PREPARING TO MOVE

Your company has just told you that you are being assigned to work in a foreign country that you've never visited, and you have agreed to move with the job. You will be moving one year from today. And you expect to stay there until you retire or die.

What are you going to do? If it were me, I would Google the new location and begin to learn everything I could about it. I also would look for books about it on Amazon and at my local library. I'd read everything I could about the history and culture of the place. I would watch all the travel videos about it I could find. I would ask all my friends if they or their friends had ever been there. Then I would meet with anyone I could find and ask hundreds of questions. Meanwhile, I'd make lists of other things I needed to do to prepare, then I would begin to do those things. If a different language was spoken there, I'd begin learning it. Preparing for my move would be my prime directive.

PHILIPPIANS AND HEAVENLY CITIZENSHIP

> Our citizenship is in heaven, and we eagerly wait for a Savior from there, the Lord Jesus Christ. He will transform the body of our humble condition into the likeness of his glorious body, by the power that enables him to subject everything to himself. (Phil 3:20–21)

According to the Bible, Christians will someday find themselves living in territory unlike anything we have ever seen with a closeness to God we have never had before. That territory is often called *heaven*, simply defined as "the place where God uniquely dwells." Discovering more about it will be largely the occupation of this book. But first, it is helpful to recognize that the Bible says we believers currently hold a dual citizenship there.

To grasp what that means, let's begin with a corresponding example. The people of first-century Philippi, in what today is Greece, lived in a Roman colony, which amounted to a "little Rome." A remarkably high percentage of these Macedonians proudly claimed Roman citizenship, even though Rome was 800 miles away, and most of them had never seen it.

In the apostle Paul's letter to the Christians there, he tells them that just as Philippi in the province of Macedonia was a colony of the Roman empire, with Roman culture, language, and government, so Christians there (and everywhere on earth) constitute a colony of heaven on earth. They are citizens of it, although they have not yet been there (see Phil 3:20–21). Consequently, the Philippian believers were to maintain ultimate loyalty to their heavenly homeland, pursuing heavenly goals, and following heavenly behavioral guidelines.[1] In fact, because Christians are citizens of heaven, we should "pay careful attention to" people like Paul and other Christians who are loyal to their heavenly citizenship and know heavenly culture (Phil 3:17).

> Just as Philippi in the province of Macedonia was a colony of the Roman empire, with Roman culture, language, and government, so Christians there (and everywhere on earth) constitute a colony of heaven on earth. They are citizens of it, although they have not yet been there.

We might expect Paul to motivate attentiveness by assuring us that we will someday go to heaven. Instead, he points out that Christians "eagerly wait for a Savior *from there*, the Lord Jesus Christ," who will come and "transform the body of our humble condition into the likeness of his glorious body, by the power that enables him to subject everything to himself" (Phil 3:20–21; emphasis mine). What happened to "Christians go to heaven when they die"? It appears that heaven will come here to earth in time. But we'll dig into that in later chapters.

Earlier in his letter, in Philippians 1:27, Paul had given them a prime directive. "Just one thing: As citizens of heaven, live your life worthy of the gospel of Christ." The verse begins in Greek with the word *monon*, which means "only." Paul uses it here to

The Via Egnatia (Egnatian Way) that runs alongside the Roman forum at Philippi. Chariot ruts are visible in the stone.

stress the importance of what he's about to say to them. The CSB translates it "just one thing." Other translations use "whatever happens" (NIV) or "above all" (NLT). One commentary on Philippians suggests, "Now, the important thing is this."[2] What Paul tells the Philippian Christians (and us), then, is that whatever happens, the one thing above all else that should concern us, what really matters, what we should make the top priority, is to remember that we are citizens of heaven and that "the gospel of Christ" is to set the standard for our behavior. He then specifies the kind of behavior he has in mind: "standing firm in one spirit, in one accord, contending together for the faith of the gospel." We must stand our ground with firm convictions against those who "live as enemies of the cross of Christ" (3:18). But it's not just "me against the world." We believers must zealously guard our unity of purpose, relying on other faithful Christians and depending on the Holy Spirit. We must also be willing to suffer for Christ (Phil 1:27–30). So now, as people who will one day live in "heaven," our prime directive is to get to know all we can of heaven and to allow that knowledge to govern our hearts and our behavior. That, I hope, is the main reason you are reading this book.

> *The one thing above all else that should concern us, what really matters, what we should make the top priority, is to remember that we are citizens of heaven and that "the gospel of Christ" is to set the standard for our behavior.*

Just knowing and doing the truth, however, is not enough. We will find that the main thing we know about heaven is that God our Creator is there. So, learning about heaven mostly has to do with getting to know God. This includes gaining familiarity with his nature, character, and attributes, or—as Bible students used to say—his "perfections." This is what we call *theology*. A Jesuit theologian named Leonardus Lessius (1554–1623) wrote something we would be wise to bear in mind: "Although all Theology teaches what is conducive to a pious and holy life, nothing draws us so powerfully away from the love of perishable things and influences our heart[s] with the desire of what is celestial and eternal as the meditation of the divine perfections."[3]

Getting to know God, however, also means experiencing him—not just individually, but in community with others. Paul therefore urged the Colossians, "Let the word of Christ dwell richly among you, in all wisdom teaching and admonishing *one another*" (Col 3:16; emphasis mine). And how were they to do that? Through giving and listening to sermons and attending seminars and study groups? Those are certainly important, but Paul does not go there. What especially causes the word of Christ to "dwell richly" in and among us, he says, is to teach and admonish one another with "psalms, hymns, and spiritual songs, singing to God with gratitude in [our] hearts." Learning to live wholeheartedly as citizens of heaven, then, requires the nurturing of relational love and joy.[4]

MOVING CAN BE SCARY

But you may have another reason for reading this book. There is an elephant in the room. It's the inescapable fact that between here and there stands a barrier—a door. You have seen many people go through this door but never seen them return. It's a scary door called *death*. There may be wonderful things on the other side.

But even if that's the case, the thought of going through it is scary to you. When you see someone heading toward the door, you are like an audience member in a movie theater showing an old, black-and-white horror movie about a haunted house. One of the characters reaches toward the door, and you want to yell, "Don't open that door!" We have all heard stories and may have talked to someone whose heart stopped, who had a "near-death experience," and who revived to tell us about it. But they did not actually die like Lazarus who was in the tomb for three days. What did he experience? We don't know. And that ups the tension.

We have all heard stories and may have talked to someone whose heart stopped, who had a "near-death experience," and who revived to tell us about it. But they did not actually die like Lazarus who was in the tomb for three days. What did he experience? We don't know.

I grew up with an overwhelming fear of death. Even into my young teens, if I began thinking about the topic, which I often did, I would become gripped with terror worse than the fear of any monster. To me, death meant dissipating into nonexistence, and the thought of that prompted uncontrollable sobs. It also meant that my life, which hung by a bare thread in my imagination, was meaningless. Soon everything and everyone I cared about, I believed, would be gone, and I would be nothing.

I can pinpoint when this fear started. When I was five years old, my grandmother woke me to say my father had a heart attack during the night and died. I immediately cried and ran to my bedridden mother to cry some more. The next thing I remember was playing outside with my cousins when my aunt drove up and told me to get in the car. She took me to the funeral home and walked me into the parlor where my father's body rested. She picked me up and showed

me his body in the casket. I am pretty sure I screamed, cried, and soon ran from the room. I have no more memories until long afterward. I also have no memory of anyone talking to me about death or heaven or God or Jesus. All I had was my imagination. And as a result, I grew up thinking a lot about dying.

This study of the afterlife is not just an academic exercise to me. Perhaps it isn't to you either. It is something we all have a *vital* interest in. So, what is it that lies beyond the door? How can we know for sure anything does? Our first chapter will wrestle with that last question.

GUIDEBOOK TO THE AFTERLIFE

The Bible often presents the afterlife—heaven and hell—in terms of a destination that all human beings will experience (one or the other). This reality opens up the possibility of considering our topic of investigation like the hypothetical emigrant portrayed in the opening paragraph, one who pores over travel guides to learn all he can about the possibilities ahead.

Traditional guidebooks help us plan a trip by introducing us to things like the geography, history, and culture of a region. They also provide other helpful information such as things to see and do, the people, nightlife, currency, transportation, flora and fauna, places to stay and eat, and may even touch on high-risk areas to avoid. They usually end with a more detailed look at the various sections or subregions of the country or city. Although we cannot research heaven and hell in these literal terms, they may provide a figurative itinerary for our travels through the various biblical passages dealing with the afterlife.

NOTES

[1] See Gordon D. Fee, *Paul's Letter to the Philippians,* New International Commentary on the New Testament (Grand Rapids: Eerdmans, 1995), 379; Joseph H. Hellerman, *Philippians,* Exegetical Guide to the Greek New Testament (Nashville: B&H, 2015), 221–22.

[2] Peter T. O'Brien, *The Epistle to the Philippians,* New International Greek Testament Commentary (Grand Rapids: Eerdmans, 1991), 144.

[3] Cited in Michael P. Knowles, *The Unfolding Mystery of the Divine Name: The God of Sinai in Our Midst* (Downers Grove, IL: InterVarsity, 2012), 41.

[4] See Jim Wilder and Michel Hendricks, *The Other Half of Church: Christian Community, Brain Science, and Overcoming Spiritual Stagnation* (Chicago: Moody, 2020), 198.

CHAPTER 1

TRAVEL BROCHURES: IS IT JUST HYPE?

WHO DO YOU BELIEVE?

We have all seen travel brochures and promotional videos that picture and describe a luxurious Shangri-La where one can escape the pressures and frustrations of daily life with a visit to paradise. Or perhaps we should invest in "economical" time-share plans that will allow us to experience "very cheaply" all the Shangri-Las on earth—a different one or two each year. Sound good? Yeah, right! You want to go somewhere nice, but how do you know whom or what to believe? You can read reviews, but they are usually mixed. Which reviews should you believe?

Perhaps you opened this book thinking you already know all about heaven. You have watched movies and TV shows related to the topic, a documentary about near-death experiences, and maybe even read a book by or about someone who claims to have been there. Amazon, after all, offers hundreds of them. In one, the prosperity gospel preacher Jessie Duplantis claims to have gone there in "something like a cable car." When he reached out to an apparently distressed Jesus there, he was told, "I need you, Jesse."[1] (Shudder!)

Of such resources a postmodern Pilate who asks, "What is truth? Did he really go to heaven?" may conclude, "Well, why not? Anything is possible." But if where I spend eternity depends even in part on decisions I make now, I might want more to go on. When I put the lives of my family and me on an airplane, I depend on the knowledge, technical expertise, skill, and experience of thousands of people who built and serviced and tested and supervised and supported and flew that

plane. If I were to ask them, "Is this plane capable of getting us where we want to go?," I do not want to hear, "Why not? Anything is possible." In fact, I want evidence and sound reasons why I should trust the claims that a particular plane and captain can get us somewhere safely. I am not like the title character in the movie *Elf*, who goes into a dingy café and excitedly congratulates the personnel for having "the best coffee in the world," as their sign claims. Where's the proof?

JESUS OUR AUTHORITY

Am I asking too much? Are the truth claims of people calling themselves eyewitnesses to the afterlife all we have to go on? Definitely not. New Testament scholar N. T. Wright admits that "all language about the future, as any economist or politician will tell you, is simply a set of signposts pointing into a fog. . . . But that doesn't

Are the truth claims of people calling themselves eyewitnesses to the afterlife all we have to go on? Definitely not.

mean it's anybody's guess or that every opinion is as good as every other one. And—supposing someone came forward out of the fog to meet us? That, of course, is the central though often ignored Christian belief."[2] There was a man who lived a little over two thousand years ago who said, "I have come into the world for this: to testify to the truth" (John 18:37). Was Jesus of Nazareth just a fraud, a fool, a lunatic? Or is it reasonable to believe his claims?

The disciple Matthew tells us in his Gospel about the voice from heaven that declared at Jesus's baptism, "This is my beloved Son, with whom I am well-pleased" (Matt 3:17). He writes that when Jesus finished preaching his great sermon on the mountain, "The crowds were astonished . . . because he was teaching them like one who had authority, and not like their scribes" (Matt 7:28–29). Matthew also tells us of a Roman centurion who had come to believe Jesus had authority simply to command disease to depart and it would—even if Jesus was not there (Matt 8:5–9)! He tells us how he and the other apostles were amazed when Jesus simply "rebuked the winds and the sea." They asked in astonishment, "What kind of man is this? Even the winds and the sea obey him!" (Matt 8:26–27). Moreover, Jesus proved by healing a paralyzed man that He "has authority on earth to forgive sins." And "when the crowds saw [that], they were awestruck and gave glory to God, who had given such authority to men" (9:6–8), that is, to the man Jesus Christ (who even had the authority to share his authority with his disciples; see Matt 10:1).

For these reasons and others, I believe Jesus is the eternal Son of God who became a perfect man and died and rose again to rescue people from the domination of sin and death. But I did not always believe that. I grew up attending church often, praying to God when I needed help, listening to Bible stories, and even reading the Bible a few times when I was feeling bad. But in high school, I thought myself too sophisticated for all that stuff and decided the Bible was just an old book written hundreds of years ago (I did not know how long) by lots of old guys with irrelevant, antiquated ideas. I virtually threw it in the trash. But I couldn't get away from the idea that there was a God who really might care about me and who was certainly not happy with some of the things I did. The idea was nurtured by my occasional encounters with spiritual TV broadcasts like those of the Billy Graham crusades. Over time, I grew full of thoughts and feelings of fear, shame, and longing in spite of my efforts to dismiss Scripture. Then late one night during my senior year, while watching an old movie, I became gripped with the fear that someday all my sins would be exposed for all to see. And on a trip to the bathroom, I fell on my knees, declared my faith in Jesus, and asked Him to forgive me and enter my life. I did not see or hear him, but I know He was there and that He forgave me and made me His child that night.

After that, something changed in me—not everything, but something. I wanted to find out what God has to say in the Bible, so I started reading it every day. I have missed very few days since 1967, in fact, because I mysteriously came to believe that my spiritual life depends on me taking in Scripture as much as my

physical life depends on eating food. Through Christian friends and mentors in college and the ministry of InterVarsity Christian Fellowship, I grew in understanding who Christ is and what the Bible says. While I continued to sin sometimes, I believed God would help me and would never leave me, and I believe that even more (including the part about my continuing to sin) today.

I mysteriously came to believe that my spiritual life depends on me taking in Scripture as much as my physical life depends on eating food.

So what? Along the way, as God's hidden but powerful Spirit guided me, I came to believe not only that Christ was God and Savior, but that the Bible was His authoritative Word. The more I came toward deeper knowledge of and love for Christ, I came to treasure the Bible as His Word to me and to any who would read it in faith. Jesus said to His Jewish opponents in John 7:17, "If anyone wants to do [God's] will, he will know whether [my] teaching is from God or whether I am speaking on my own." And since I began to see that what Jesus taught aligned with God's teachings presented earlier in Scripture, I came to believe the Bible is the only source of ultimate truth and grew interested in the writings of those who felt the same.

In college I read with great interest the 1958 book *Basic Christianity* by John Stott. In it, I learned that Christianity *is* Christ and that it is "the only religion in the world which rests on the Person of its Founder."[3] I learned too that Jesus claimed to be the one and only divine Messiah and also the Son of God. These claims he backed consistently with His teaching, His moral character, His miracles, His prophecies, and especially His life-changing, sacrificial death and resurrection. I came to see that these claims are unavoidable and what Jesus said and did is unexplainable unless He is who he claims. I also encountered this compelling argument by C. S. Lewis concerning Christ's identity, which he first made on British radio in the turbulent 1940s:

> A man who was merely a man and said the sort of things Jesus said would not be a great moral teacher. He would either be a lunatic—on the level with the man who says he is a poached egg—or else he would be the Devil of Hell. You must make your choice. Either this man was, and is, the Son of God, or else a madman or something worse. You can shut him up for a fool, you can spit at him and kill him as a demon or you can fall at his feet and call him Lord and God, but let us not come with any patronizing nonsense about his being a great human teacher. He has not left that open to us.[4]

This Jesus, Messiah and Son of God, who came "to testify to the truth" (John 18:37), is the eyewitness to the heavenly realms that we have been looking for. It is pointless to expect anyone to ascend to heaven and then return and report to us what he found. But Jesus Himself came from there and can tell us. The Pharisee Nicodemus could not accept at first Jesus's testimony regarding new birth and the heavenly kingdom, so Jesus replied in John 3:11–13,

"Truly I tell you, we speak what we know and we testify to what we have seen, but you do not accept our testimony. If I have told you about earthly things and you don't believe, how will you believe if I tell you about heavenly things? *No one has ascended into heaven except the one who descended from heaven—the Son of Man*" (John 3:13, emphasis mine)

Jesus accuses Nicodemus of speaking in ignorance because no one has "ascended into heaven" to discover heavenly truth. But standing in front of Nicodemus is the only one who can be a source of heavenly truth, the Son of Man, who has "descended from heaven." Even Nicodemus claimed to "know" from Jesus's miracles that he was "a teacher who has come from God" (John 3:2), and Jesus acknowledged to his heavenly Father that his disciples "have known for certain that I came from you" (John 17:8). Indeed, He is the only qualified and authorized guide to the beauty and wonder of the heavenly realm.

BIBLICAL RELIABILITY

You and I do not have the privilege of face-to-face encounters with Jesus. So where can we go for answers concerning the afterlife? The answer came to me from my third hero of the Christian faith when I was in college, theologian J. I. Packer. In his 1958 book, "*Fundamentalism" and the Word of God*, Packer declared that "the problem of authority is the most fundamental problem that the Christian Church ever faces" (notice his prophetic use of the phrase "ever faces").[5] He elaborated by stating, "The Christian's most pressing need in every age is to have a reliable principle by which he may test the conflicting voices that claim to speak for Christianity and so make out amid their discordant clamour what he ought to believe and do."[6] In other words, we need to know what Jesus really said on our topics—distinguishing it from anything else that people might claim.

> *"The problem of authority is the most fundamental problem that the Christian Church ever faces."*

Many proposals have been made as to where we might encounter an authoritative word from God, such as Scripture, church tradition, experience, or reason. But the venue in which I encountered our Savior Jesus Christ was the New Testament documents, which I had come to see as a historically reliable guide to what he taught (through F. F. Bruce's 1954 book, *The New Testament Documents: Are They Reliable?*). And in the New Testament I found that Jesus never based His teaching on any human authority, but only on His own divine authority as God's Son from heaven and also on the Old Testament, which He regarded as the Word of God in all its parts and in every detail. For Jesus, as well as for the New Testament writers, then, an argument could be settled with a quote from the Old Testament; such are often introduced by the phrase, "It is written."[7] As British New Testament scholar John Wenham stated, "Indeed, it is probable that if we cannot know Jesus' teaching about [the authority of the Old Testament], we cannot know His teaching about anything."[8] We cannot claim to trust Jesus and to welcome him into our lives, accepting as true and reliable His promises about our salvation, and then refuse to believe everything He says, including what He says about the Bible, and about heaven, hell, the afterlife, and everything else.

One of the last things Jesus said to his disciples, according to the eyewitness Matthew, was that "all authority has been given to [Him] in heaven and on earth" (Matt 28:18). That means Jesus has authority *everywhere* about *everything*! On that authority, he entrusted His disciples with the task of making disciples of the nations and of "teaching them to observe everything [He had] commanded [them]"

(Matt 28:20). In order to do that, he bestowed on them the Holy Spirit, who would "teach [them] all things and remind [them] of everything [He had] told [them]" (John 14:26). It would be with the authority and power of this

"All authority has been given to Jesus in heaven and on earth."

"Spirit of truth," in fact, that they would testify about Jesus (John 15:26). And everything else Jesus wanted to teach his disciples would be taught to them by the same Spirit of truth, who would guide them "into all the truth" (John 16:12–15). We might state the end result of this in Jesus's own words: "Heaven and earth will pass away, but [His] words will never pass away" (Matt 24:35). Jesus, then, passed along the truth and shared His authority with the apostles who wrote the New Testament, which therefore holds the same authoritative status as the Old Testament; it is the Word of God.[9]

The point is our source of reliable knowledge and the final authority about things pertaining to God and the place where he dwells is His written Word, the Old and New Testaments. Truth can be found elsewhere—as in the case of Einstein's formula for the relationship of matter and energy. But anything that contradicts the Bible is not truth. I can know, for example, that the Ten Commandments were not left on earth by aliens visiting from another planet because such a claim contradicts the Bible.

Our source of reliable knowledge and the final authority about things pertaining to God and the place where he dwells is His written Word, the Old and New Testaments.

With this idea of Scripture's trustworthiness in mind, let us consider one interesting passage Jesus shared on the afterlife. Because of its genre, Jesus's parable about the rich man and Lazarus (Luke 16:19–31) need not be treated as a historical account.[10] Nevertheless, Jesus told the parable for a reason, and truth can be derived from it. The rich man is pleading from Hades with Abraham, who is can be seen "a long way off" with Lazarus, who is being comforted after his own death. Still considering Lazarus's station in life as well beneath his own, the rich man pleads that Abraham will send him Lazarus to Hades to comfort him. Abraham tells him such a thing is impossible, since there can be no transport between Hades and Abraham's pleasant location. So, the rich man pleads that he at least send Lazarus "to warn" his brothers. He is told that not only is that too impossible, but that such a visitation from "heaven" to earth would be pointless and redundant. The brothers in view already have the Scriptures. And thus it is the Scriptures, the Bible, that we must look to for information, warning, and comfort regarding the afterlife. Returning spirits would have nothing to add to the discussion. One point of this parable is that the Bible is Jesus's answer to our curiosity and our desperate pleas for information about it.

More broadly than that, in 2 Timothy 3:15–17 the apostle Paul told his protégé Timothy that for all issues relating to God's dealing with humanity, "the sacred Scriptures" are the final authority because they are from God's own mouth (that's the meaning of the word "inspired" here). As we open our minds and hearts to God's training through engaging with the Bible, we can become "complete, equipped for every good work." Again, the message comes across that for answers to questions related to the afterlife and human destiny, we need not—indeed, we must not—look any further than the Bible.

The same point can be made from the little book we call Jude, named for its author who was the "brother of James" and the half-brother of Jesus (Jude 1). The purpose for his letter was to press the urgency of defending the truth of the Christian faith against some "ungodly" people who had infiltrated the church and were "turning the grace of our God into sensuality and denying Jesus Christ, our only Master and Lord" (v. 4). They rejected authority and instead relied on "their dreams" (v. 8). Against these malicious intruders, Jude urged the Christians to "contend for the faith that was delivered to the saints once for all" (v. 3). By "the faith" Jude was referring to "all the truth" that Jesus and the Holy Spirit had definitively taught the apostles (John 14:26; 16:12–15) and that they had "delivered" to believers after them (Jude 3).

> *Jude urged the Christians to "contend for the faith that was delivered to the saints once for all."*

Thus again, this body of truth is the benchmark to which all Christian teaching must adhere. It cannot change or be revised or amended because it was delivered "once for all." According to New Testament scholar Tom Schreiner, "No supplements or corrections will be tolerated. The gospel of Jesus Christ has received its full explication through the apostles." From statements such as this and Hebrews 1:2 ("In these last days, he has spoken to us by his Son"), "early Christians rightly concluded that the canon of Scripture [the twenty-seven books of the New Testament] should be restricted to those early writings that explicated the ministry, death, and resurrection of Jesus Christ."[11]

It was in elementary school that I first heard this scientific principle usually attributed to Aristotle: "Nature abhors a vacuum." This concept also applies to knowledge. When we do not know about something or someone, when we have unanswered questions, it is difficult for people to let it go. Inevitably, it seems, someone will start a rumor or imagine what might be the case, or will make some assumptions, or will take giant leaps over tall buildings into unfounded or even impossible conclusions. This is especially the case when the conclusions support some pet belief or prejudice we have. This is even true in matters of religion. Theological questions that are difficult or even impossible to answer tend to generate multiple views and opinions, which are often argued arrogantly with malice, vehemence, and sarcasm, or just pontificated. Matters God did not see fit to explain clearly in the Bible have invariably invited speculation through the centuries, as have matters about which we have nothing whatsoever to go on. What was Jesus like as a five-year-old? Various people have come up with answers to that question that God did not choose to tell us about. Similarly, much about heaven and hell has also invited wild speculation over the centuries.

As we work through this summary guidebook to the afterlife, we will run into various urban legends or modern fairytales we must examine. (For example, birds will not really explode if they eat wedding rice, and most people actually use 100% of their brains). So how are we going to determine what is true or false about the afterlife, heaven, hell, the new heaven and the new earth, resurrection, angels, heavenly choirs, marriage in heaven, reincarnation, purgatory, near-death experiences, and more? We will investigate what the Bible says, tentatively make inferences where we can, and respect that God has not yet chosen to speak about some topics.

CHRISTIAN TESTIMONY

One last topic to consider before we move forward is the importance of Christian testimony. To claim that Christians can be guides to the wonders of heaven may seem absurd to some, who point to Christian hypocrisy as the reason they turned their backs on the church. Some might reasonably object that using Christian testimony as a guide to heavenly truth is too biased and subjective to be helpful—especially given what I have said about Scripture. Nevertheless, we need to recognize a testimony's role in helping us grasp certain aspects of eternity. Previously we saw that Jesus, our source and standard of truth (John 3:11–13; 18:37), shared with his disciples the authority to make more disciples (see Matt 28:18–20). He also empowered them to be his witnesses (those who testify to the truth). He said, "You will receive power when the Holy Spirit has come on you, and you will be my witnesses in Jerusalem, in all Judea and Samaria, and to the ends of the earth" (Acts 1:8).

The first disciples, then, could testify to what they had seen and heard of Jesus. For instance, John writes,

> What was from the beginning, what we have heard, what we have seen with our eyes, what we have observed and have touched with our hands, concerning the word of life—that life was revealed, and we have seen it and we testify and declare to you the eternal life that was with

the Father and was revealed to us—what we have seen and heard we also declare to you, so that you may also have fellowship with us; and indeed our fellowship is with the Father and with his Son, Jesus Christ. (1 John 1:1–3)

Jesus remains the final authority and Master Guide to the heavenly realities of the present and the future, the divine plan is for his children by faith—those who know and belong to him and possess his Spirit—to serve as apprentice guides to those realities. We should be able to testify about the revealed, eternal word of life as part of giving an invitation to others to have a share in that life (the meaning of "fellowship") as we all share the life of our Father and his Son, Jesus Christ. And that testimony has been passed on to others, as the apostle Paul instructed Timothy: "What you have heard from me in the presence of many witnesses, commit to faithful men who will be able to teach others also" (2 Tim. 2:2; see also John 17:20).

Jesus remains the final authority and Master Guide to the heavenly realities of the present and the future, the divine plan is for his children by faith—those who know and belong to him and possess his Spirit—to serve as apprentice guides to those realities.

But, as we have seen, only Jesus is the Master Guide, and only the Bible can be trusted completely, without hesitation, as his master guidebook, conveying to us his words. Despite our efforts to be faithful to Jesus and his Word, we are imperfect vessels, whose testimony must always be tested against the biblical standard of truth (see 1 Thess 5:21).

Furthermore, not everyone claiming to follow Jesus and to know the truth can be trusted. Jesus warned us that there would be weeds, pretenders, among the wheat in his heavenly kingdom on earth before his return (Matt 13:24–30). He also explained,

"Not everyone who says to me, 'Lord, Lord,' will enter the kingdom of heaven, but only the one who does the will of my Father in heaven. On that day many will say to me, 'Lord, Lord, didn't we prophesy in your name, drive out demons in your name, and do many miracles in your name?' Then I will announce to them, 'I never knew you. **Depart from me, you lawbreakers!**'" Matthew 7:21–23

My point here is that some claiming to speak for God may be "blind guides" (Matt 15:14; 23:16, 24), and some may be false teachers (2 Pet 2:1), who "come in by stealth," but are "ungodly," having turned "the grace of our God into sensuality and denying Jesus Christ, our ... Lord" (Jude 4).

Some claiming to speak for God may be "blind guides"

These caveats do not negate, however, the important role Jesus assigned individual Christian testimony. Those who truly belong to him and know him are "not of this world," just as Jesus was not of this world (John 15:19; 17:14–18). But in what way is this true since our feet are firmly planted on the earth? And if we are not "of this world," to what world do we belong?

Key here is realizing that when Jesus says in John 16:11, "The ruler of this world has been judged," he is talking about the devil, that is, Satan, the evil one (see John 13:2, 27; 17:15). So, to be "of this world" would mean, in effect, to follow (whether knowingly or not) the agenda, values, and practices of "the ruler of this world." The alternative is to follow Jesus, the Creator and King of heaven and earth, who came into the world "to testify to the truth" (John 18:37). To what "world" do genuine Christ followers belong, then? To the heavenly world, the kingdom from which Christ came, where God's will is consistently and perfectly done—even if we fail to reflect that reality perfectly (see Matt 6:9–10).

In the Introduction, we saw from Philippians 1:27 that Christians already are "citizens of heaven," just as the Philippians were citizens of Rome. Therefore, we are to know the God of heaven and to live in this world according to heavenly principles. That includes, Paul says, living "in one spirit, in one accord" with other believers. Jesus told his disciples that by showing our loving unity with one another, "everyone will know that [we] are [His] disciples" (John 13:35). Furthermore, our unity even extends to oneness with God, which verifies Christ's mission and is the basis for our unity with one another. We believers possess and display to the world God's glory, which is His nature and presence at work. This reality led Jesus to pray,

"May they all be one, as you, Father, are in me and I am in you. *May they also be in us, so that the world may believe you sent me.* I have given them the *glory* you have given me, so that they may be one as we are one. *I am in them and you are in me*, so that they may be made completely one, that the world may know you have sent me and have loved them as you have loved me." John 17:21–23, emphasis mine

Christian testimony is imperfect and inconsistent, but God uses it. My infantile spiritual life received a jumpstart when I spent a week in the mountains of Colorado at InterVarsity's Christian camp for college students. One activity was a small group overnight backpacking trip, which I loved. But a couple of days into it, the leader got sick and asked me to fill in. He showed me where to turn off the trail and climb the ridge into a valley where we should camp. But I missed the turn and took my group over the highest rather than the lowest part of the ridge, and we missed the prepared campsite. We passed it as we trudged up the valley the next day on our way back to our cabins. We returned back safely, and there was no lasting harm done except to my pride. I proved myself a faulty guide, as I have been again throughout the years of my Christian ministry and testimony. But Jesus's first disciples were not faultless either. And God's servants listed in Hebrews 11 are commended not for their faultlessness but for their persevering faith.

Our ministry is effective to the extent that believers live in the world without belonging to it, that is, in loving unity and in submission to and dependence on God. We often fail and even then serve as examples of God's grace, loving mercy, and power in our weakness (see 2 Cor 12:9). But when we live as citizens of heaven, we validate the truth of the gospel and Christ's witness to heavenly realities. In this way, we can serve as "ambassadors for Christ, since God is making his appeal through us" (2 Cor 5:20). The way of the witness is not just using persuasive words but living in light of eternity while still in the world. We believers have the freedom to do that because, like Jesus, we do not need the world's approval or acceptance. We already have the complete, unconditional, and eternal acceptance of our Father, to whom we belong.[12]

> *When we live as citizens of heaven, we validate the truth of the gospel and Christ's witness to heavenly realities.*

NOTES

[1] Recounted in John Blanchard, *The Hitch-hiker's Guide to Heaven* (Faverdale North Darlington, UK: EP Books, 2013), 81.

[2] N. T. Wright, *Surprised by Hope: Rethinking Heaven, the Resurrection, and the Mission of the Church* (New York: HarperOne, 2008), xiii–xiv.

[3] John R. W. Stott, *Basic Christianity* (Chicago: Inter-Varsity, 1958), 20.

[4] C. S. Lewis, *Mere Christianity* rev. ed. (New York: HarperOne, 2001), 52.

[5] J. I. Packer, *"Fundamentalism" and the Word of God* (Grand Rapids: Eerdmans, 1958), 42.

[6] Packer, 44.

[7] See Matt 4:4, 10; 11:10; 21:13; 26:24, 31; Mark 7:6; 9:13; 14:21, 27; and John 6:45. The phrase "it is written" is also used about ten times in the Old Testament to express trust in a reliable written authority.

[8] John W. Wenham, "Christ's View of Scripture," in *Inerrancy*, ed. Norman L. Geisler (Grand Rapids: Zondervan, 1979), 5.

[9] See 1 Cor 2:13; 14:37; 2 Cor 13:3; Col 4:16; 1 Thess 2:13; 2 Thess 3:14; 1 Tim 5:18; 1 Pet 1:12; 2 Pet 3:14–18; Rev 1:1–3, 11; 22:18–19.

[10] Considering the context of parables in 15:3–16:9 and the initial words, "Now a certain man . . .", we may consider the story of the rich man and Lazarus as a parable, not a historical account. Lazarus having a name indicates his importance, not his historicity.

[11] Thomas R. Schreiner, *1 & 2 Peter and Jude*, Christian Standard Commentary (Nashville: Holman, 2020), 525.

[12] See Henri J. M. Nouwen, *Beyond the Mirror: Reflections on Death and Life* (New York: Crossroad, 1990), 68–73.

CHAPTER 2

GEOGRAPHY OF HEAVEN AND EARTH

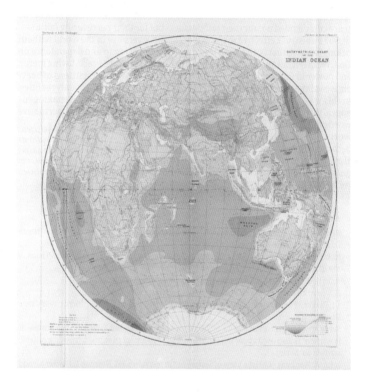

Our topical tour begins with the various regions of the afterlife. This requires a look at the geography of the visible and invisible universe as revealed in the Bible. Many scholars believe the Bible assumes a triple-decker universe borrowed from the surrounding peoples in Egypt and Mesopotamia. They picture it in this way:

Heaven
Earth
Realm of the Dead /Sheol/Hell

WHAT IS MEANT BY *HEAVEN*?

Before we can evaluate this understanding of cosmic geography, we must look more closely at the slippery term "heaven" or "heavens." According to Merriam-Webster, the word we typically associate with the night sky as well as the place of the righteous dead is "Middle English *heven, hevene,* from Old English *heofon.*" But since our concern revolves around what the Bible teaches, we are more interested in the Old Testament Hebrew and Aramaic words and the New Testament Greek word for "heaven," which are *shamayim* (Aramaic *shemayin*) and *ouranos,* respectively.[1]

The Hebrew and Aramaic words for *heaven,* which occur 458 times in the Old Testament, are always grammatically plural (hence the *-im/-in* ending). That word "grammatically" means that just because a word is plural in form does not mean it refers to more than one of something. When I go buy a "pair of pants," someone just learning English might wonder why I come back with only one item. The same is true of eyeglasses and scissors, which have two parts, though these items are technically singular as well. But what about molasses, news, billiards, and politics? They all use a singular verb. For instance, the news *is* [not *are*] always bad.

People have different theories as to why the Hebrew word translated *heavens* is plural, but the bottom line is that no one knows. Our best guess is that it is because of the boundless vastness of what it refers to.[2] The Hebrew word for "water" (*mayim*) is also always plural in form (even when referring to "a little water in a cup," as in 1 Kgs 17:10), and no one knows the reason for that either.

The Greek word for *heaven* I mentioned occurs in the New Testament 273 times and is plural only a third of the time. But we will talk about that later.

Now, the main reason the Bible's words for "heaven" are troublesome, however, is that they refer to different things in different contexts. Even the English phrase "the heavens" is used poetically of the biosphere or of the realm of the "stars," and "heaven" can be a state of utter happiness and contentment. The CSB translates the Hebrew word mentioned as "sky" or "skies" about 130 times. About 125 times it's rendered "the heavens," and about 170 times it appears simply as "heaven." Even when the Greek word is plural, it's usually rendered as "heaven."

The Russian cosmonaut, Yuri Gagarin, trained as a steelworker in industrial college, learned to fly in his spare time, then graduated from air force cadet school in 1957. Four years later the Russians launched the 27-year-old into space. He spent an hour and a half orbiting at an altitude of 187 miles and is reported by some as having become an expert on the existence of God as a result. He supposedly claimed, "I looked and looked but I didn't see God."[3] Whoever said or wrote this did not understand that "heaven" in the Bible means different things in different contexts, as do many words in various languages. The word *run,* for example, means something different when applied to a race, a line, a nose, a car engine, an advertisement, or an election. The word *heaven* can refer directly to the physical realm above the earth that is occupied by air, birds, clouds, and beyond that the sun, moon, and stars. (These, by the way,

The word heaven *can refer directly to the physical realm above the earth that is occupied by air, birds, clouds, and beyond that the sun, moon, and stars.*

are almost always listed in that order in the Bible).[4] With that sense, "heaven" could be combined with "earth" to refer to God's material creation, as in Genesis 1:1. This is what the Greeks referred to as the *kosmos*.

But the word translated *heaven* can also refer indirectly or symbolically to the supernatural or spiritual realm of God's dwelling—a realm invisible to space explorers. At times, the terms *heaven* and *earth*, instead of being combined, could be contrasted, as in the case of *oil* and *water*. In these instances, the terms took on their symbolic meanings. "Heaven" referred to the invisible, nonmaterial, supernatural, or spiritual realm, as opposed to "earth," the physical creation occupied by people and other creatures. Psalm 115:16 serves as an example of this use: "The *heavens* are the LORD's, but the *earth* he has given to the human race." The preacher in Ecclesiastes instructs, "God is in heaven and you are on earth, so let your words be few" (Eccl 5:2). When the terms are used in such a way, "heaven" refers to the invisible realm and "earth" refers to all of creation, including the sky and the heavenly bodies.

The word translated heaven can ... refer indirectly or symbolically to the supernatural or spiritual realm of God's dwelling—a realm invisible to space explorers.

In the New Testament as well, heaven and earth could be combined to refer to all of creation, as in Matthew 24:35: "Heaven and earth will pass away, but my words will never pass away." Here the verb translated "pass away" is grammatically singular in Greek, indicating that "heaven and earth" is indeed seen as one. But the word pair could also refer to the spiritual realm versus the earthly one, as in John 3:31: "The one who is from the earth is earthly and speaks in earthly terms. The one who comes from heaven is above all." The apostle Paul also contrasts Adam and Christ as the earthly man versus the heavenly man: "The first man was from the earth, a man of dust; the second man is from heaven" (1 Cor 15:47). Jesus instructed his listeners in Matthew 6:19–20 not to be fooled by tangible, socially impressive bling: "Don't store up for yourselves treasures on earth ... But store up for yourselves treasures in heaven." In these cases, the contrast between heaven and earth emphasizes how far apart they are.

In the first half of the Lord's Prayer in Matthew 6:9–10, Jesus instructs His disciples to bring before God three petitions. They are to say, "Our Father in heaven," and then follow that with, "*your name be honored as holy. / Your kingdom come. / Your will be done / on earth* as it is in heaven." The last request and concluding phrase could be rendered more literally: "Let your will be accomplished, / as in heaven, also on earth." That final phrase is probably to be understood as applying to all three petitions. As the Father's name is honored as holy in heaven, as His kingdom exists in heaven, and as His will is perfectly accomplished in heaven, may that also become true on earth. So, Jesus contrasts the current situation in the two realms. Unlike the situation in heaven, on earth the Father's name is seldom honored, His kingdom is not fully realized, and His will is often opposed. Yet we believers are to live in anticipation of the day when the heavenly realm will invade the earthly and establish God's authority and worship here as it is already established there. Other passages make clear that Jesus's death and resurrection made this future situation certain, but it will not be realized until Jesus

Unlike the situation in heaven, on earth the Father's name is seldom honored, His kingdom is not fully realized, and His will is often opposed.

returns.[5] We will come back to this topic later and look more closely at how heaven and earth and our own lives will change when Jesus returns.

One interesting indication that "heaven" could have two meanings is found in the Gospel of Matthew, which has a special interest in heaven. This is clear from the unusually high number of times the word occurs there: it features 82 out of the 273 uses in the New Testament as a whole. That's more than twice as many as in any other book except Revelation, where it is still only found 52 times. While the book of Revelation might be the first place we expect to find information about heaven, Matthew's Gospel is equally rich in sublime truth about the spiritual realm.

Whereas only about one-third of the uses of the word *heaven* in the New Testament are plural, with very little difference in meaning from the singular, Matthew uses the plural twice as often as the singular (more than all the other New Testament books combined), and the two forms have clearly different uses. New Testament scholar Jonathan Pennington has shown that the standard explanations for Matthew's affinity for the word *heaven*, especially in the plural (that is, Jewish squeamishness about speaking directly of "God," and a belief in multiple heavens) are inadequate. He demonstrates that Matthew uses the singular to refer to the skies and when combined in the pair "heaven and earth." He uses the plural, on the other hand, to refer to the invisible, divine realm, usually in the expression "kingdom of heaven" in contrast to the kingdoms of the earth.[6]

> *Matthew uses the singular to refer to the skies and when combined in the pair "heaven and earth." He uses the plural, on the other hand, to refer to the invisible, divine realm, usually in the expression "kingdom of heaven" in contrast to the kingdoms of the earth.*

The Egyptian goddess of heaven/sky Nut pictured as bending over the earth god Geb and being upheld by the god of air/wind Shu.

TRIPLE-DECKER UNIVERSE?

Now back to the question of whether or not the Bible assumes a triple-decker universe. There are at least two problems with this picture. The first is that it's a simplistic understanding of how the cosmos was understood by people in the ancient Near East. They actually spoke and drew pictures of it in conflicting ways rather than having a consistent viewpoint of the world as a unified system with distinct parts and clearly defined relationships. Through his study of the religious images and symbols of ancient cultures, Othmar Keel, professor emeritus of Old Testament at the University of Fribourg, demonstrated the multitude of ways the cosmos was viewed—in terms of symbols rather than explanations. The sky, for example, could be represented as a fixed cover over the earth, the protective wings of a giant bird, the uplifted body of a woman, or a celestial ocean. Each picture revealed different aspects of what people believed was above the earth.[7]

Many images "show the world as a composite of earth and sky, with the sky protectively spreading its wings over the earth and ensuring its prosperity."[8] In ancient Sumer in the third-millennium BC town of Nippur, the world was said to have begun with the union of the god An (heaven) and the goddess Ki (earth).[9] Keel points out that when the realm of the dead is included in a description of the cosmos, "it can be placed . . . in the earth or (like the Duat in early Egypt) in the sky." When portrayed as a subterranean ocean, he says, it is often viewed as a threat to the earth rather than as part of the cosmos.[10]

A dualistic formula like "heaven and earth," according to Keel, is at least as common in the ancient Near East as a threefold division. In Akkadian texts (those of Mesopotamia in the second millennium BC), "The world is almost always described" by the phrase "heaven and earth" and represented by the gods Anu (sky) and Enlil/Ea (earth). In Egypt the dualistic formula is found in texts from the older Pyramid age, with earth as the region of living humanity and the ordinary dead, while heaven is the region of the gods and dead kings. There a separate region of the dead does not appear until the Middle Kingdom (2040–1782 BC). Keel concludes that the formula of heaven and earth "illuminates very well the conception and perception of the world in the ancient Near East and in the [Old Testament]."[11]

The other problem with the idea the Bible's writers had in mind a triple-decker universe is that, as Pennington demonstrates, the Bible portrays the universe in dualist terms, with no distinct third realm.[12] Heaven and earth are paired at least 185 times in the Old Testament. About 31 times they are side-by-side like flesh and blood, salt and pepper, bread and butter, food and drink, black and white, shoes and socks, and flora and fauna. The phrase "heaven and earth" or "the heavens and the earth" refers to the entire creation, as we have seen. More frequently, the pair occurs with other words in between, as in Psalm 73:25: "Who do I have *in heaven* but you? / And I desire nothing *on earth* but you." A third kind of pairing places one of the terms opposite a synonym like "the heights" or "the depths." Although the order of terms is almost always set, like *up and down* or *flesh and blood*, a few times the terms are reversed for poetic effect: "These

> *The Bible portrays the universe in dualist terms, with no distinct third realm.*

are the records of the *heavens* and the *earth*, concerning their creation. At the time that the LORD God made the *earth* and the *heavens*" (Gen 2:4, emphasis mine; also Jer 10:11).

Word pairs often form the building blocks of Hebrew poetry, as in Isaiah 53:5:

> But he was *pierced*
> > because of our *rebellion*,
> *crushed*
> > because of our *iniquities*.

Here, and below, I have added formatting and emphasis to highlight effects mentioned. The pairs are almost synonyms (pierced/crushed, rebellion/iniquities), but antonyms are also used. Heaven and earth are set against each other in Psalm 33:13–14:

> The LORD looks down from *heaven*;
> he observes everyone.
> He gazes on all the inhabitants of the *earth*
> from his dwelling place.

Other word pairs rely on a general-specific relationship,[13] such as parent-father, in which the first word includes the second, as in Isaiah 48:13:

> My own *hand* founded the earth,
> and my *right hand* spread out the heavens.

The same relationship is found in Psalm 8:3, in which "heavens" includes "the moon and the stars."

> When I observe your *heavens*,
> > the work of your fingers,
> *the moon and the stars*,
> > which you set in place

This kind of word pair is important to recognize because some scholars claim that Psalm 148:7 speaks not of the earth but of a third level in the biblical universe, the netherworld or realm of the dead, in which the "sea monsters" are mythological subterranean monsters and "ocean depths" refers to the "primeval waters" of chaos.[14] That passage says,

> Praise the LORD from the *earth*,
> all *sea monsters* and *ocean depths*.

Besides that idea being pure speculation, the structure of Psalm 148 shows this is not the case. The psalm calls on all creation to praise the Lord. Verses 1–6 call on the invisible and visible "heavens" to praise him, including all the entities in the heavens. In the invisible heavens are the angels and heavenly armies (v. 2); in the visible heavens are the sun, moon, and stars (v. 3), and the "highest heavens" and "waters above the heavens" (v. 4). Then verses 7–14 call on the earth and everything associated with it to praise God, including sea creatures (v. 7), meteorological forces (v. 8), mountains and trees (v. 9), animals, crawling things, and birds (v. 10), and earthly leaders and common people on the earth (vv. 11–12). The psalm recognizes several levels or parts of creation, yet all are within the dual structure of heaven and earth. The realm of the "sea monsters and ocean depths" is clearly part of the earth.[15] As Old Testament scholar David Tsumura concludes, "The Psalmist's understanding of the world is bipartite, rather than tripartite."[16]

[Psalm 148] recognizes several levels or parts of creation, yet all are within the dual structure of heaven and earth.

A few passages, however, do seem to go against this. Deuteronomy 5:8 instructs not to make idols of anything in "the heavens above or on the earth below or in the waters under the earth." Pennington shows, however, that in passages listing other elements alongside heaven and earth, such as the sea, water under the earth, the depths, and so forth,[17] the other elements are considered part of either the heavenly or the earthly realms.[18] He then explains that the place of the dead, Sheol or Hades, represents "an undeveloped thought" that is "fundamentally a part of the earth."[19] Therefore, a more accurate biblical picture of the universe would look like this:

Heaven:
Invisible: Realm of God & angels
Visible: Cloudy skies // Starry skies

Earth:
Invisible: Place of the dead
Visible: Place of the living

What the Bible says, though, is often just not enough for us. Desperate to fill the void in our understanding of the physical and spiritual universe, people in the Middle Ages let speculation run rampant. One of the most popular portrayals (see below) was offered in 1493 by Hartmann Schedel (1440–1514) in his illustrated book referred to as the *Nuremberg Chronicle.* One of the nearly two thousand woodcuts inside it is called "The Sanctification of the Seventh Day" and shows God resting after creation. It also depicts the earth in the center of 13 concentric, revolving spheres. The first three, together with the earth, constitute the classical elements: earth, water, air, and fire. Then come the seven planetary spheres: the moon, Mercury, Venus, the sun, Mars, Jupiter, and Saturn. Beyond that are the Zodiac of fixed stars, the crystalline ceiling, and Aristotle's prime force believed to keep the universe in motion. Above and around the spheres is the infinite realm inhabited by God, the angelic hierarchy (named on the side), and the saints. The four winds appear in the corners.[20] Copernicus and Kepler certainly had their work cut out for them in trying to overcome the influence of such vivid and attractive mass media.

Copernicus and Kepler certainly had their work cut out for them in trying to overcome the influence of such vivid and attractive mass media.

De sanctificatione septime diei

Onsummato igitur mundo: per fabricam diuine solercie sex dierum. Creati em dispositi z ornati tande pfecti sunt celi z terra. Complecut de gliosus opus sui: z requieuit die septimo ab operib[us] manuum suarum: post q[uam] cuctum mundi: z omnia que in eo sunt creauit: no quasi operando lassus: sed nouam creaturam facere cessauit: cuius materia vel similitudo non precesserit. Opus enim propagationis operari non desunt. Et dominus eidem diei benedixit: z sanctificauit illu: vocautq[ue] ipsum Sabati quod nomen hebraica lingua requiem significat. Eo q[uod] in ipso cessauerat ab oim opere q[uod] patrarat. Un z Iudei eo die a laboribus propriis vacare dignoscutur. Quem z ante leges certe gentes celebrem obseruarunt. Iamq[ue] ad calcem venium et operum diuinorum. Illum ergo timeamus: amemus: veneremur. In quo sunt omnia siue visibilia siue inuisibilia. Et a domino celi: domino bono: omniu. Cui data oims potestas in celo z in terra. Et presentia bona: quatenus bona sint. Et veram eterne vite felicitatem queram[us].

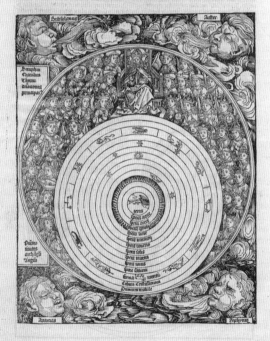

"The Sanctification of the Seventh Day"

WHAT'S UNDER THE EARTH?

We must not take lightly, however, what the New Testament says about a demonic realm that is sometimes associated with the heavens and sometimes with the earth. The apostle Paul declared that a time is coming when all of God's creation will submit to the exalted Christ: "At the name of Jesus / every knee will bow— / in heaven and on earth / and under the earth" (Phil 2:10; cf. Rev 5:3, 13). That last phrase, "under the earth," may refer to the realm of demonic forces spoken of in Ephesians 6:12 as "rulers, . . . authorities, . . . cosmic powers of this darkness, . . . evil, spiritual forces in the heavens." We will look more closely at this later.

The Bible portrays all of reality in multi-dimensional, dualistic terms: heaven and earth, the invisible heavenly realm where God is said to "dwell" and the visible earthly realm occupied by humanity, where God's authority and presence are less clear. The physical universe is also portrayed in dualistic terms, as we have seen (that is, heaven and earth). But the invisible realm itself is also multi-dimensional. As Pennington expresses it, those who encounter Jesus find themselves at a fork in the road that leads eventually to different "regions" of the afterlife.[21] One path leads by way of faith and righteousness to the heavenly dwelling of God and to eternal reward. Because "heaven" can refer to the physical regions above the earth, God's dwelling and the path to it are sometimes portrayed symbolically as "up," as when Jesus ascended at Pentecost in Acts 1:9–11.

> *The Bible portrays all of reality in multi-dimensional, dualistic terms: heaven and earth, the invisible heavenly realm where God is said to "dwell" and the visible earthly realm occupied by humanity, where God's authority and presence are less clear.*

> [Jesus] was taken up as they were watching, and a cloud took him out of their sight. While he was going, they were gazing into heaven, and suddenly two men in white clothes stood by them. They said, "Men of Galilee, why do you stand looking up into heaven? This same Jesus, who has been taken from you into heaven, will come in the same way that you have seen him going into heaven."

But if God's dwelling is not literally *up*, why did Jesus depart the physical, earthly world by ascending? And where, then, did he really go?

In the prescientific world of the Bible before Galileo, which was bound by what people could see, we imagined being limited by the horizons and by the "firmament" or "ceiling" of the sky, where the sun traveled each day from east to west. Since they could see that *down* was the direction of death and the grave, they reasoned the pathway to the God of life had to be up beyond what could be seen. The nature of the Bible as divine communication to humanity led to the use of many earthly, visual assumptions, such as the idea that the sun rises and sets when, in fact, it is the earth that moves. So, when Jesus departed the earthly, visible world for the heavenly, invisible one, he went *up* in part because that is where everyone assumed God dwelt.

The Bible's two realms—an invisible, supernatural realm in which God and spiritual beings typically operate, on the one hand, and the visible, earthly realm of God's creation, on the other hand—may perhaps best be imagined in terms of two *dimensions*. We often speak of the three dimensions of length, width, and breadth (x, y, and z), but mathematicians in the eighteenth and nineteenth centuries began to envision higher dimensions or levels of reality. In geometry, for example, a *two*-dimensional square becomes a cube in *three* dimensions, but then a *tesseract* (or "hypercube") in *four* dimensions. (This shape is neither a cube nor a power source in the Marvel universe).[22] By analogy, it may be useful to speak of invisible heaven and visible earth as the two *dimensions* or levels of reality. Though we describe them, with the Bible, as symbolically up and down, we could equally well think of them as side-by-side.

Represention of a tesseract. By Brooklyn Sluder. Used by permission.

The destinies of believers and unbelievers are not the same. Speaking of those destinies in terms of heaven and hell, however, is an oversimplification. For example, the Bible describes "a new heaven and a new earth" (Rev 21:1) that will come into being at the return of Christ following a general resurrection. There God will forever dwell with his people. Before going there, however, our tour will take us to the invisible realm of the dwelling place of God and the angels to see what the Bible will show us.

> *The destinies of believers and unbelievers are not the same. Speaking of those destinies in terms of heaven and hell, however, is an oversimplification.*

NOTES

[1] A small percentage of the Old Testament is written in the later language of Aramaic. Aramaic is closely related to Hebrew, so their words for "heaven" are similar, like the Latin and Greek word for "father," pater, and the Spanish padre and the French papa.

[2] Jonathan T. Pennington, Heaven and Earth in the Gospel of Matthew (Grand Rapids: Baker, 2007), 41, says, "[A] sense of the innumerable heights above could reasonably result in a preference for the plural."

[3] This quote by the cosmonaut is disputed and may have been credited to him by Russian leader Nikita Khrushchev.

[4] The terms occur together in seventeen verses, including Gen 37:9; Deut 4:19; Ps 148:3; Jer 8:2; Joel 2:10; Matt 24:29; Rev 8:12.

[5] See Pennington, *Heaven and Earth,* 205.

[6] See Pennington, *Heaven and Earth,* 125–61.

[7] Othmar Keel, *Symbolism of the Biblical World: Ancient Near Eastern Iconography and the Book of Psalms*, trans. Timothy J. Hallet (London: SPCK, 1978), 10.

[8] Keel, *Symbolism*, 29.

[9]   E. C. Lucas, "Cosmology," in *DOTP,* 132.

[10] Keel, *Symbolism,* 30.

[11] Keel, *Symbolism,* 30.

[12] See Pennington, *Heaven and Earth,* 172–79.

[13] See David Tsumura, "A 'hyponymous' word pair, *'rs* and *thm(t),* in Hebrew and Ugaritic," *Biblica* 69 (1988): 258–69.

[14] See Hans-Joachim Kraus, *Psalms 60–150, trans.* Hilton C. Oswald (Minneapolis: Fortress, 1993), 563; M. J. Dahood, *Psalms III (101–150),* Anchor Bible 17A (New York: Doubleday, 1970), 353.

[15] See Pennington, *Heaven and Earth,* 178.

[16] Tsumura, "A 'hyponymous' word pair," 264–65.

[17] See also Gen 2:1; Exod 20:11; Deut 5:8; Neh 9:6; Ps 135:6; Hag 2:6.

[18] See Pennington, Heaven and Earth, 171.

[19] Pennington, Heaven and Earth, 181.

[20] See https://digital.library.cornell.edu/catalog/ss:19343151 (accessed 6/20/19). Also see Alister E. McGrath, *A Brief History of Heaven* (Malden, MA: Blackwell, 2003), 55.

[21] See Pennington, *Heaven and Earth,* 209.

[22] See, for example, Carl Sagan's explanation of the fourth dimension. Carl Sagan, "4th Dimension," YouTube March 24, 2009, video, https://youtu.be/UnURElCzGco.

CHAPTER 3

HEAVEN: THE CELESTIAL FIRE

Perhaps you've made a list of several places you "MUST SEE BEFORE YOU DIE." We begin our travel guide to the various regions of the afterlife with a look at the number one site there "NOT TO BE MISSED!" This is the Grand Canyon, Niagara Falls, Yellowstone, Giza, the Taj Mahal, Machu Picchu, and Victoria Falls of the afterlife all rolled into one—HEAVEN: THE LAND OF THE CELESTIAL FIRE.

Christian glimpsing the Celestial City from afar. Pilgrim's Progress by John Bunyan

DANTE AND THE EMPYREAN

The fifteenth-century work by Hartmann Schedel that we discussed in the previous chapter named the realm beyond the stars the "Empyrean." It was the realm of paradise, God, angels, and the saints. The term *empyrean* comes from a Greek word that means "in the fire" and is an appropriate term for the invisible, heavenly realm of God. The Lord our God, after all, "is a consuming fire" (Deut 4:24; Heb 12:29).

An earlier portrayal of the regions of the afterlife, including the Empyrean, came from the Italian poet Dante Alighieri (1265–1321), who in the fourteenth century wrote an allegorical, visionary account of his journey beyond the grave. It was called *The Divine Comedy*—that last word meaning it does not have a tragic ending. Borrowing from the Christian teaching of his day but also from Greek and Latin mythology, he produced a poem of a hundred cantos and over fourteen thousand lines.

In it, Dante, having become spiritually lost in midlife at age thirty-five and desiring peace with God, finds that he must journey through Hell and Purgatory to reach the divine Presence. He is guided through Hell and Purgatory by the Latin poet Virgil (representing reason), then into Paradise by his beloved Beatrice (symbolizing theology), then finally into God's Presence by the Cistercian monk and mystic, Bernard of Clairvaux (1090–1153). In the last part of Dante's journey, he describes the divine realm beyond the nine spheres of heaven (the moon, Mercury, Venus, the Sun, Mars, Jupiter, Saturn, the stars, and the angels) as a place engulfed in "living light," a "veil of radiance." He writes,

> From matter's largest sphere,
> we now have reached the heaven of pure light,
> light of the intellect, light filled with love,
> love of true good, love filled with happiness,
> a happiness surpassing every sweetness.[1]

Then (in canto 31) he sees an enormous rose, whose petals consist of the glorified saints. The host of angels flies around it like a swarm of bees, which "flying, sees and sings the glory of the One who draws its love." Dante describes them:

> Their faces were all living flame; their wings
> were gold; and for the rest, their white was so
> intense, no snow can match the white they showed.

After that Dante sees Mary, "the Queen," seated prominently in her "loveliness" on her throne, "to whom this realm is subject and devoted." Although returning several times to Mary, the mother of Jesus, the pilgrim sees other godly women like Rachel, Sarah, Rebecca, and Judith there. He also encounters John the Baptist, Francis, Benedict, Augustine, and others. Finally, he sees "the Primal Love" and his radiance, represented by three reflecting circles of different colors, "and the third seemed fire breathed equally" by the other two circles, one of which represented Christ (canto 33). The idea of Dante and Beatrice gazing on the highest heaven, the Empyrean, was illustrated by Gustave Duré (1832–1883).

I present Dante's vision of the afterlife not because of its reliability but because of its captivating influence on the human imagination.

FIRE AND LIGHT IN HUMAN IMAGINATION

That God's presence should be represented by fire and light is not unbiblical, but the significance of both is also known outside the Bible. The ancient Asians reduced everything to five elements: wood, earth, water, fire, and metal. The Pre-Socratic Greek philosophers, who lived before the close of the fifth century BC, and who were also concerned about the material substance of the universe, favored only four elements: earth, water, air, and fire. These corresponded to solid, liquid, gas, and heat. Heraclitus of Ephesus (who lived about 500 BC) argued that fire is the basic substance and that, rather than being created, the world is ultimately an eternal, undying fire, which is constantly changing.[2]

Moreover, fire has always played a vital role in religions all over the world. Agni, representing fire, for example, was one of the chief deities in ancient India. In ancient Egypt the Eye of the god Horus was a flame,

Moreover, fire has always played a vital role in religions all over the world.

which he used to defeat his enemies. The dead even aspired to be transformed into a flame, "the glowing Eye of Horus." And of Marduk, the god of Babylon, the song of creation says that "when he moved his lips, a fire was kindled."[3] It is not difficult to see why fire captured the imagination of ancient peoples, as its discovery and many uses caused it to be treasured and guarded as a vital source of heat and light. One of the most popular Greek myths was of the Titan Prometheus

A Gustave Doré illustration of the Empyrean in Dante's *The Divine Comedy*.

who stole fire from the workshop of Hephaistos and Athena on Mount Olympus and gave it to man to ease the burdens of life.

GOD'S APPEARANCES IN FIRE

Fire from God always either destroys or purifies.

The Hebrew word for "fire," *'esh,* and related words are found almost 400 times in the Old Testament, and the uses are frequently of tremendous significance. Fire from God always either destroys or purifies. Although the word does not occur in the Bible before the time of Abraham in Genesis 15, fire was evidently a gift of God to Adam and Eve since it would have been involved in Abel's offering of the "firstborn of his flock and their fat portions" (Gen 4:4). Even before that, the animals that furnished clothing for Adam and Eve may also have become food for them, as God taught them the principle of animal sacrifice (Gen 3:21; more on this later).

Our interest, however, is the important part that fire plays in many of the biblical theophanies. In order to gain an understanding of what God's eternal dwelling place is like, a look at the ways he has revealed himself on earth is not a bad place to start. The term *theophany* refers to an appearance or manifestation of God, often in dreams or visions. It may involve a human form, some element of nature, or something more fantastic and impossible to describe adequately. It may involve a poetic description of an experience or a literal description of something that was seen. As Old Testament scholar Doug Stuart points out, however, God's infiniteness means that a divine "appearance" can never be anything but a partial revelation of his character to finite humans. Other phenomena God has used to reveal his presence are storms, wind, clouds, smoke, and blazing light.[4]

> *A divine "appearance" can never be anything but a partial revelation of his character to finite humans.*

To Abraham

Although not God's first appearance in the Bible or even his first appearance to Abraham, the first use of the word *fire* appears as God makes a covenant with Abraham in Canaan. In answer to Abraham's request for a sign like Noah's rainbow to strengthen his faith in God's promise of a future land, God provided one while he slept. He affirmed and sealed the promise by appearing symbolically as "a smoking fire pot and a flaming torch," that is, "a torch of *fire*," passing between the sacrificial animals that Abraham had prepared (Gen 15:8–21). Here is the first use of fire as a symbol for God.

Most scholars recognize the significance of this ritual as summoning destruction on one who failed to keep his word, just as the life of the animals had been taken (see Jer 34:18).[5] Therefore, in this case, if God failed to fulfill His promise to provide a future land for His people, He would cease to exist. The term for "fire pot" elsewhere usually refers to an oven for baking bread (see Lev 26:26). The Hebrew term for "smoke" occurs 25 times, almost always in a context either of judgment or of a manifestation of God. The term translated "torch" here is used of the lightning that occurs with the "smoke" at Sinai (Exod 20:18), and it also signifies God's presence in Isaiah 62:1; Ezekiel 1:13; and Daniel 10:6. "Smoke," "fire," and "lightning" occur together at Mount Sinai (see Exod 19:16–18), indicating God's presence and causing fear and trembling in the Israelites.

> *If God failed to fulfill His promise to provide a future land for His people, He would cease to exist.*

The "birds of prey" that swoop down to eat the animal carcasses Abraham prepared perhaps signify that Israel will have enemies, although they will be unsuccessful in opposing God's purposes (see Ps 2:1–6). "If God is for us," after all, "who is against us?" (Rom 8:31).

To Moses

We find the word *fire* again as a symbol of God's presence in an incident from the life of Moses, a fugitive in exile from Egypt. As a young man he'd wanted to help his people, the Hebrews, but failed miserably in his first attempts. Nevertheless, at age 80 and while shepherding west of Midian in the Sinai boondocks, where he led his flock in search of pasture, he reached a hill called Horeb (or Sinai); it was later known as "the mountain of God." One evening he noticed a bush on fire that would not stop burning. When Moses went to investigate, he found that the Lord was in that "flame of fire within a bush" (the word for "bush," by the way, is similar to the word for "Sinai"). From it, God called to him: "Moses, Moses!" (Exod 3:1–4).

Since that incident, many have discovered that God's nearness is more often found not in the heights of our spirituality but in the depths, "at points of failure."[6]

> *God's nearness is more often found not in the heights of our spirituality but in the depths, "at points of failure."*

If you were to travel to Sinai today, you would find Saint Catherine's Monastery, known officially as the Sacred Monastery of the God-Trodden Mount Sinai, located at its base of what many believe to be Mount Sinai—Jebel Musa, in Egypt.) It is the oldest functioning monastery in the world, having been built in the sixth century AD, and it's operated by the Greek Orthodox Church. In the heart of this monastery is Saint Helen's Chapel, also known as the Chapel of the Burning Bush. Next to it is a very old, large bush of the rose family called *Rubus sanctus* ("holy bush"); this is believed by some to be the very bush from which God spoke. Many believe the bush's presence is the main reason the monastery was built.[7]

Centuries after Moses, another exile, named John, a prisoner on the island of Patmos, would hear a divine voice coming from one who looked like a man but who had "eyes like a *fiery flame*," a description that uses the same words as Exodus 3:2 in the Greek Old Testament (Rev 1:14). He saw the figure with the fiery eyes again, whom he had come to know as the Son of God, the Lamb, and the King of Kings. But this time he was seen riding a white horse and leading an army of angels (Rev 19:12). The phrase is also found describing the "Ancient of Days" in Daniel 7:9; his "throne was *flaming fire*; its wheels were blazing fire."

Doug Stuart points out that in the ancient Semitic culture, addressing someone by saying their name twice, as God did to Moses in Exodus 3:4, expressed endearment, affection, and friendship.[8] The God who spoke to Moses, then, made it clear that he loved and cared about Moses, as well as his people. When God tells Moses in Exodus 3:7, "I have observed the misery of my people in Egypt,"

Saint Catherine's Monastery

He does not mean only that he noticed it. He uses a verb phrase (literally, "seeing I have seen" that also occurs in Gen 26:28 as "clearly seen" and in 1 Sam 1:11 as "take notice") that means He paid very close attention to His people's painful experience.[9] Now, at the right moment and in the right way He would launch his rescue plan.

While expressing such affection, however, God told Moses not to come any closer and to remove his sandals (Exod 3:5; see Josh 5:15), since he was essentially standing in the living room of holy God, hence the description "holy ground." Wherever God is—even within a person's life—that place is holy. God's instruction not to "come closer" (literally, "do not come near here") uses the Hebrew verb *qarab*, "to come near or approach," a word often used in connection to human relations with God. Later, after God had made his presence dwell in the tabernacle, one of the functions of the Levites was to camp around the tabernacle and guard it. Any "unauthorized person" who came "near" was to be killed, so that "no wrath [would] fall on the Israelite community" (Num 1:50–53). Similar "boundaries" were placed around Mount Sinai before God appeared there in order that neither man nor beast might "go up on the mountain or touch its base" and thereby lose his or her life (see Exod 19:12–13).

As in the case of great kings of antiquity and even modern times, nearness to God was a treasured privilege available to only a select few, which only the King could grant (see, for example, Esth 5:1–2). It involved personal relationship and honored service. But whereas even a royal person was still a flesh-and-blood human being, who had earned his or her status by military prowess, royal birth, or human ingenuity, the nature of God was entirely different. The Westminster Shorter Catechism's definition of God is hard to improve: "God is a spirit, infinite, eternal, and unchangeable in his being, wisdom, power, holiness, justice, goodness, and truth." As a result, earthbound creatures need divine protection just to enter His presence without being destroyed. Following a strict protocol was absolutely required in the Old Testament era. And to look at His face could be deadly. Moses knew this somehow, and thus "hid his face" from God in fear (Exod 3:6).

Nearness to God was a treasured privilege available to only a select few, which only the King could grant.

Now, unlike the human face, the "face" of God—which should not be confused with the face of Jesus, who took on flesh and thus shielded humanity from the deadly divine effect warned about in the Old Testament—is a cloudless window into the total essence of his glory. An encounter with God's infinite purity and splendor, we must understand, could blast a person right off the planet with more force than launches a NASA shuttle. Later in Exodus, Moses later asked to see God's glory and was shown God's goodness. God told Moses in 33:20, "You cannot see my face, for humans cannot see me and live." In verse 23 He added, "[Y]ou will see my back, but my face will not be seen." Then God hid Moses while His glory passed by so that Moses only got to glimpse God's "afterglow" (Exod 33:18–23).[10] At least we assume that is what happened. Moses only recounts God's promise, not the actual event. Exodus 33 ends abruptly without a description of Moses's experience, leading Brennan Manning to wonder, "What happens in the wordless, empty, but shattering collision with the glory of God that such a glimpse entails?

Can we gaze even momentarily into the precipitous depths of the crushing majesty and unapproachable holiness of the living God?"[11]

Can we gaze even momentarily into the precipitous depths of the crushing majesty and unapproachable holiness of the living God?"

Later, in Numbers 12:8, God would tell Moses's jealous siblings, Aaron and Miriam, that he spoke to Moses "directly, / openly, and not in riddles." He added, "[H]e sees the form of the LORD." The term translated "form" is used of visual images, so God would let Moses see a depiction of Him. In a few places, an encounter with God is described as being "face to face."[12] But we must understand this is an idiom, a phrase having a meaning all its own, like "mouth to mouth"; the former means "directly" or "personally," as opposed to in a dream. These only describe, then, "limited-scale" encounters with a *manifestation* of God rather than with His full glorious splendor, that is, His "face."[13] Nevertheless, having seen such a manifestation, the "angel of the LORD," Samson's father panicked. He said, "We're certainly going to die because we have seen God!" (Judg 13:22). Even the angelic seraphim of the prophet Isaiah's vision, in fact, hid their faces in the presence of the Lord in the temple "seated on a high and lofty throne" (Isa 6:1–2),[14] and Isaiah cried, "Woe is me for I am ruined . . . because my eyes have seen the King, the LORD of Armies" (6:5).

Nevertheless, nearness to the sublime Being is the greatest gift of all. As the psalmist declared, "But as for me, God's presence [that is, his "nearness"] is my good" (Ps 73:28). It is, in fact, as biblical scholar Derek Kidner wrote, "The chief and only *good*."[15] Even God's stiff-necked people "seek me day after day and delight to know my ways, like a nation that does what is right and does not abandon the justice of their God. They ask me for righteous judgments; they delight in the nearness of God" (Isa 58:2). Human beings are attracted by the idea of God, yet encountering the real God can be as deadly as a candle to a moth.

Human beings are attracted by the idea of God, yet encountering the real God can be as deadly as a candle to a moth.

Annie Dillard vividly describes such an encounter she observed while reading by candlelight:

> A golden female moth, a biggish one with a two-inch wingspan, flapped into the fire, dropped her abdomen into the wet wax, stuck, flamed, frazzled and fried in a second.[16]

With such a picture fresh in mind, you may now have second thoughts about taking a trip to heaven, the land of the Celestial Fire. But rather than discourage you, I hope merely to remind you that no fallen human will ever be able to enter God's presence in heaven "as is." Therefore, preparations must be made, and I am not talking about packing a flame-resistant suit alongside your toothbrush. We will talk in a later chapter about how one can travel to heaven without getting incinerated. But first, let's look at a few more glimpses of heaven by way of fire theophanies.

Through Fire and Lightning

In Moses's encounter with the Egyptians, he discovered that the God who had appeared to him as a flame of fire in a bush could also be fiery lightning working against their enemies (see Exod 9:23–24, where "lightning" translates the Hebrew word for "fire"). The psalmist declares, "Fire goes before [God] / and burns up his foes on every side. / His lightning lights up the world; / the earth sees and trembles" (Ps 97:3–4). Then after securing the Hebrews' release from Egypt, God led them toward the land He had prepared for them, illuminating their way by means of a "pillar of fire" (appearing in daylight only as "a pillar of cloud"; Exod 13:21–22; Neh 9:12). When the Egyptian army appeared at their heels beside the Red (or Reed) Sea, the pillar moved behind Israel to protect them. Exodus 14:24 makes clear that the pillar of fire was an appearance of none other than God himself: "During the morning watch, *the Lord looked down* at the Egyptian forces *from the pillar of fire and cloud*" and routed the Egyptian forces, protecting his people (emphasis mine). As verse 28 tells us, "Not even one of [the Egyptians] survived." Nor was one Israelite lost.[17]

This pillar of fire and cloud, representing God's presence, guided Israel throughout their wilderness journeys, often in directions that challenged their faith. But as Doug Stuart explains, "It was necessary for Israel to learn faith while confused, while afraid, while desperate—not just in theory but under pressure of actual conditions where survival was uncertain and faith was tested to the limit."[18] Nevertheless, even amid their complaints (see Exod 16:9–10), they saw this supernatural manifestation of fire and cloud every day, assuring them of God's presence, care, and protection.

When Israel arrived at Sinai, Moses met with God on the mountain and was told that God would come to him "in a dense cloud" (lit. "in a cloud of the cloud") to show the people that Moses was His spokesman (Exod 19:9). After the people prepared themselves for three days, God indeed showed up in a heavy cloud—along with thunder and lightning and even "a very loud blast from a ram's horn, so that all the people in the camp shuddered" (v. 16). Then Moses summoned the people to the foot of the mountain "to meet God" (v. 17) in a terrifying experience emphasized in verses 18–19:

> Mount Sinai was completely enveloped in smoke because the LORD came down on it in fire. Its smoke went up like the smoke of a furnace, and the

whole mountain shook violently. As the sound of the trumpet grew louder and louder, Moses spoke and God answered him in the thunder.[19]

The mention of "the smoke of a furnace" (v. 18) that covered the whole mountain echoes an earlier passage describing the scene after God rained burning sulfur down on Sodom and Gomorrah. In it, Abraham had seen "smoke was going up from the land like the smoke of a furnace" (Gen 19:28, using a word for "furnace" that only occurs four times in the Old Testament). The reason for the smoke in Moses's day was that God had descended on the mountain in the form of fire. And as the people shook with fear (Exod 19:16), so the mountain shook at God's presence in the fire. And the people could see and hear that Moses and God were talking to one another, although God's voice sounded like thunder. After Moses courageously went up the mountain to receive further instructions from God, he came back down (vv. 20–25), and then everyone heard God's thunderous but comprehensible proclamation of what has come to be called the "Ten Commandments" in Exod 20:1–17 (referred to literally as "the ten words" in Exod 34:28; Deut 4:13; 10:4).

When Moses addressed Israel's second generation not long before his death, he recalled these events and asked them, "Has anything like this great event ever happened, or has anything like it been heard of? Has a people heard God's voice speaking from the fire as you have, and lived?" (Deut 4:32–33). Yet the whole thing was an experience the people of Israel did not want repeated. They believed, in fact, that if God continued to speak directly to them, they would "die." Therefore, they would be satisfied after this for God to deliver his messages to them through Moses (Exod 20:18–21; also see Deut 5:24–26).

> *"Has a people heard God's voice speaking from the fire as you have, and lived?"*

APPROACHING THE HOLY GOD

I must repeat that as terrifying and deadly as is this divine, celestial fire, our situation is not hopeless. My point is not that "you can't get there from here, and even if you could you'd be sorry you went." Some verses in the Bible suggest otherwise. Old Testament scholar Ken Mathews declares that the divine fire creates not only fear but awe, not only flight but attraction, not only curse but blessing.[20] Even after the incarnation of the Son of God (see John 1:14), the apostle John could write in John 1:18 and 1 John 4:12, "No one has ever seen God." Nevertheless,

> *The divine fire creates not only fear but awe, not only flight but attraction, not only curse but blessing.*

he wrote in 1 John 3:2, "We know that when he appears, we will be like him because we will see him as he is." Jesus said in the Sermon on the Mount, "Blessed are the pure in heart, / for they will see God" (Matt 5:8), and the author of Hebrews wrote, "Pursue peace with everyone, and holiness—without it no one will see the Lord" (Heb 12:14). And just before the cross Jesus prayed, "Father, I want those you have given me to be with me where I am, so that they will see my glory" (John 17:24). And when one of the criminals hanging beside Jesus on the cross rebuked the other and asked Jesus to remember Him in his coming kingdom, Jesus solemnly swore that on that very day he would be with Jesus, not in terrifying fire, but in "paradise" (Luke 23:43).

We will look more closely in a later chapter at this term *paradise* (Gk. *paradeisos*), which translated the Hebrew word for "garden" in Genesis 2–3. But here we must recognize that Jesus was relying on this man's knowledge, hope, and longing for a future place and experience of peace with God. Perhaps there is an obscure, almost hidden memory in the human psyche of a place and time in the remote past when such a thing was a reality. The concept is certainly there in the Hebrew Scriptures. It is perhaps not totally unlike the glimpses I retain of a few times with my father, who died when I was five: a hand, a smile, a voice, a whistle. We long for a return to that tranquility, security, contentment, and rest, walking with our divine Father in the garden (see Gen 3:8). Perhaps this is part of what motivated Moses to ask to see God's glory in Exod 33:18. Surely it is part of what worshipers of God desire and what the psalmists longed for as they waited in distress for God. Psalm 42:1–2, for instance, says,

> As a deer longs for flowing streams,
> so I long for you, God.
> I thirst for God, the living God.
> When can I come and appear before [you]?

Are there dangers in approaching God? Oh, yes. But there are also delights. That is how the psalmist can declare,

> How lovely is your dwelling place,
> LORD of Armies.
> I long and yearn
> for the courts of the LORD;
> my heart and flesh cry out for the living God. . . .
> Better a day in your courts
> than a thousand anywhere else.
> I would rather stand at the threshold of the house of my God
> than live in the tents of wicked people.
> For the LORD God is a sun and shield.
> The LORD grants favor and honor;
> he does not withhold the good
> from those who live with integrity.
> Happy is the person who trusts in you,
> LORD of Armies! (Ps 84:1–2, 10–12)

Those of us who like to play it safe rather than taking risks like mountain climbing or diving into the depths perhaps will never know the exhilaration of such accomplishments.[21] But there could never be greater exhilaration than daring to approach the holy God who is a consuming fire and finding his smiling face and welcoming arms forever (see Num 6:22–27). How that is possible is the subject of the next chapter.

There could never be greater exhilaration than daring to approach the holy God who is a consuming fire and finding his smiling face and welcoming arms forever.

NOTES

[1] Paul MacKendrick and Herbert M. Howe, eds. *Classics in Translation, Volume I: Greek Literature* (Madison, WI: University of Wisconsin Press, 1952), 106–8.

[2] MacKendrick and Howe, *Classics*, 106–8.

[3] G. Johannes Botterweck and Helmer Ringgren, eds., *Theological Dictionary of the Old Testament* (Grand Rapids: Eerdmans, 1974), 1:420, 423.

[4] Douglas K. Stuart, *Exodus: An Exegetical and Theological Exposition of Holy Scripture,* New American Commentary (Nashville: B&H, 2006), 113.

[5] Richard S. Hess, "The Slaughter of the Animals in Genesis 15," in *He Swore an Oath: Biblical Themes from Genesis 12–50,* ed. R. S. Hess, P. E. Satterthwaite, and G. J. Wenham (Cambridge: Cambridge University Press, 1993), 55–65.

[6] Michael P. Knowles, *The Unfolding Mystery of the Divine Name: The God of Sinai in Our Midst* (Downers Grove, IL: InterVarsity, 2012), 45.

[7] See "Chapel of the Burning Bush" Geographia, accessed February 23, 2003, http://www.geographia.com/egypt/sinai/burningbush.htm.

[8] See Stuart, Exodus, 113. Other examples of this practice are in Gen 22:11; 1 Sam 3:10; 2 Sam 18:33; 2 Kgs 2:12; Luke 10:41; 22:31; and Acts 9:4.

[9] See Stuart, *Exodus*, 113–15.

[10] Stuart (*Exodus,* 709) points to several passages that speak of not seeing someone's face in the sense of not seeing them at all (Gen 43:3, 5; 44:23; Exod 10:28; 2 Sam 14:24). In Jer 18:17 God pronounces judgment on Israel: "I will show them my back and not my face / on the day of their calamity," meaning he won't be there to help them. It seems that Moses, however, did see something, though not much.

[11] Brennan Manning, *Ruthless Trust: The Ragamuffin's Path to God* (New York: HarperCollins, 2000), 58.

[12] See Gen 32:30; Exod 33:11; Num 14:14; Deut 5:4; 34:10; Judg 6:22; Ezek 20:35.

[13] See Stuart, *Exodus,* 709.

[14] This is not to say that angels could not look at God. Jesus tells his disciples in Matt 18:10, "Angels continually view the face of my Father in heaven."

[15] Derek Kidner, *Psalms 73–150* (London: Inter-Varsity, 1975), 264.

[16] Annie Dillard, *Holy the Firm* (New York: Harper & Row, 1977), 16.

[17] Victor P. Hamilton, *Exodus: An Exegetical Commentary* (Grand Rapids: Baker, 2011), 219.

[18] Stuart, *Exodus,* 374–75.

[19] Although some would see a volcanic eruption described in these verses, this does not really fit the description.

[20] Kenneth A. Mathews, *Genesis 11:27–50:26,* New American Commentary (Nashville: B&H, 2005), 176.

[21] For interesting thoughts on what drives mountaineers, see David Lavender, *One Man's West: New Edition* (Lincoln, NE: University of Nebraska Press, 1977), 87–93.

CHAPTER 4

HEAVEN: AVOIDING THE FIRE

HANDLING FIRE WITH CARE

The alternative afterlife destinations of heaven and hell are often portrayed in terms of a land of harps and clouds versus one of fire and smoke. As we saw in the last chapter, however, the Bible often uses fire as a symbol of God's very presence.

Of course, we know that fire has many useful purposes. For instance, fire usually at the center of any camp in the wilderness and may be kept burning to some degree, especially when the weather is cool. It warms us on a cold night or morning, helps us prepare food, dries wet clothing, burns trash, purifies and disinfects, and provides light for our evening at the campsite.

Nevertheless, as every wise camper knows, certain rules must be followed to avoid serious harm or even disaster related to one. The campfire must be properly located and kept under control at all times. Anything flammable must be kept a safe distance away from it, including clothing and skin. And even embers must be totally extinguished before leaving campsite is vacated.

My point is that much as a campfire—a good thing—must be approached and treated with great care, God must be approached on His own terms. The Bible often portrays the positive attributes of fire in

Much as a campfire—a good thing—must be approached and treated with great care, God must be approached on His own terms.

eliminating impurity through the refining process (see Zech 13:9; Mal 3:2; 1 Pet 1:7) and the destruction of unclean refuse, such as the golden calf in Exodus 32:20 or the waste from sacrifices (Exod 29:14; Lev 4:12, 21; 16:27; Heb 13:11). But this brings us back to the negative effects of fire from a holy God on things or even individuals who are a source of contamination of his world and especially of his people.

A British arctic expedition led by Captain Sir John Franklin left in two ships, the *Erebus* and *Terror*, on May 19, 1845, with a crew of 138 officers and men. Its mission was to explore the Northwest Passage in the Canadian arctic. The ships became icebound in Victoria Strait near King William Island in 1846, however. Within a few years all aboard had died of cold, starvation, or disease. Not one survived. It turned out that only six of the men had any experience in the arctic. Thus, for a projected two- or three-year voyage, they carried only a 12-day supply of coal for the steam engines and no arctic clothing. Instead, the ships were laden with a 1,200-volume library, a hand organ, "china place settings for officers and men, cut-glass wine goblets, and sterling silver flatware."[1] All this to say, presumptive arrogance compounded with ignorance is a deadly combination with which to approach an expedition—whether to the arctic or the heavenly realms. We can't go to heaven where God dwells as we are, any way that we please. Heaven will make no compromises with us.

Heaven will make no compromises with us.

JUDGMENT BY FIRE

In the previous chapter, I established that the word translated "fire" in English first appears in the Bible in Genesis 15 as a symbol of God. Its second occurrence is in God's judgment against the people of Sodom (and Gomorrah) who were "evil, sinning immensely" (Gen 13:13). Suddenly, "out of the sky [or heaven] the LORD rained on Sodom and Gomorrah burning sulfur" (Gen 19:24), so that the cities and all their inhabitants were "demolished" (v. 25). We have already mentioned the Lord sending the seventh plague of hail and fiery lightning against the Egyptians (Exod 9:13–26).

The next instance of fire linked to God's judgment is in Leviticus 10:1–2. There two of Aaron's sons tried to offer incense to the Lord with "unauthorized fire," that is, they made an offering contrary to God's laws (see Exod 30:9). While the two were in the very act of illicit "worship," "fire came from the LORD and consumed them" (Lev 10:2). The later mention of this event, when God gave instructions about the ceremony of the Day of Atonement in Leviticus 16:1–2, suggests the reason for God's heated response. Nadab and Abihu had decided to take a field trip to the mercy seat behind the curtain in the most holy place, the very throne room of the Lord—perhaps to practice or show off their priestly skills.[2] Like the bad guy in *Indiana Jones and the Last Crusade,* they failed to "choose wisely." God, after all, had appeared to Israel at Mount Sinai so that it was "completely enveloped in smoke" like that of a furnace "because the LORD came down on it in fire" and "the whole mountain shook violently" (Exod 19:18). This same God, they knew, was now appearing in the cloud above the mercy seat (Exod 40:34–38; Lev 16:2, 13), and He is to be honored and obeyed and not disrespected or trifled with.

[God] is to be honored and obeyed and not disrespected or trifled with.

The next time the Bible tells of the fire of judgment coming out from the Lord is set in the wilderness, too. There many of the people rebelled and threw a temper tantrum against the Lord, complaining about the food he was providing. As a result, "his anger burned, and fire ... blazed among them and consumed the outskirts of the camp" (Num 11:1; also v. 33).

A few chapters later, Korah and 250 other Levites, whom God "let come near" (using the Hebrew verb *qarab*) to serve Him, rebelled and went on strike. Dissatisfied with their role of serving under the direction of Moses and Aaron, they demanded equal status as priests (see Num 16:1–5). In response, Moses set up an Elijah-like contest (see 1 Kings 18) at the entrance to the tent of meeting to see whose incense offering the Lord would accept. Suddenly "the glory of the LORD" showed up at the event and told Moses and Aaron to stand back "so [God could] consume them [that is, the *whole* community] instantly" (Num 16:19–21). Yet having heard Moses and Aaron's pleas for mercy for the people, God had them tell all those who were not followers of Korah to stand back. Suddenly "the earth opened its mouth and swallowed them and their households, all Korah's people, and all their possessions" (v. 31). Then as the rest of the people fled in terror, "fire also came out from the LORD and consumed the 250 men who were presenting the incense" (Num 16:16–35). Thus, once again, the Lord made a statement that dealings with Him will be on His terms or not at all.

A similar incident occurred later when the king of Samaria twice sent a captain and 50 soldiers to arrest the prophet Elijah in 2 Kings 1:9–14, and both times "a divine fire came down from heaven and consumed [the captain] and his fifty men" (v. 12). Lest we mistakenly think it is just the Old Testament-era God who does such things, the apostle Paul tells us in 2 Thessalonians 1:6–9 about what will happen to those who persecute the followers of Christ:

> [I]t is just for God to repay with affliction those who afflict you and to give relief to you who are afflicted, along with us. This will take place at the revelation of the Lord Jesus from heaven with his powerful angels, when he takes vengeance with flaming fire on those who don't know God and on those who don't obey the gospel of our Lord Jesus. They will pay the penalty of eternal destruction from the Lord's presence and from his glorious strength.

"They will pay the penalty of eternal destruction from the Lord's presence and from His glorious strength."

Clearly fire can have devasting effects, especially in the hands of a holy God.

THE FRIGHTENING CHARACTER OF FIRE

Fire frequently originates in the terrifying phenomenon of lightning and often results in uncontrollable and devastating fires. Nowhere do we see fire and lightning as instruments of divine judgment more vividly than in the book of Revelation.

4:5 Flashes of *lightning* and rumblings and peals of thunder came from [God's] throne. Seven *fiery torches* were burning before the throne, which are the seven spirits of God.

8:5, 7 The angel took the incense burner, filled it with *fire* from the altar, and hurled it to the earth; there were peals of thunder, rumblings, flashes of *lightning*, and an earthquake. . . . The first angel blew his trumpet, and hail and fire, mixed with blood, were hurled to the earth. So a third of the earth was burned up, a third of the trees were burned up, and all the green grass was burned up.

11:19 Then the temple of God in heaven was opened, and the ark of his covenant appeared in his temple. There were flashes of *lightning*, rumblings and peals of thunder, an earthquake, and severe hail.

16:18 There were flashes of *lightning*, rumblings, and peals of thunder. And a severe earthquake occurred like no other since people have been on the earth.

Not as frequent as lightning but much more devastating in scope is the phenomenon of volcanic eruptions. These too share similar features with some of God's judgments as described in Scripture. Known volcanic eruptions, like that of Italy's Mount Vesuvius in AD 79, have taken the lives of tens of thousands and obliterated entire cities. Fiery eruptions in Indonesia alone are estimated to have been responsible for the deaths of at least 137,409 people in the modern era, with the highest toll coming not from Krakatoa (where over 36,000 died in 1883 and over 400 more in 2018) but from Mount Tambora (over 71,000 in 1815).[3]

HOLY FEAR

What better symbol than fire could show that our awesome God must be approached with holy fear? As C. S. Lewis put it, He is "not a tame lion."[4] With good reasons, the term "fear" is found in modern English Bibles about half as often as it was at first. Nevertheless, Presbyterian minister Donald McCullough points out that "in our eagerness to make known the approachability of God, we often overlook astonishment over the approachability of *God*."[5] The poet Annie Dillard once remarked that the ministers in many churches tend to "come at God with an unwarranted air of professionalism, with authority and pomp, as though they knew what they were doing, as though people in themselves were an appropriate set of creatures to have dealings with God."[6] She writes, "I often think of the set pieces of liturgy as certain words which people have success-fully addressed to God without their getting killed. . . . If God were to blast such a service to bits, the congre-gation would be, I believe, genuinely shocked."[7] Elsewhere Dillard comments, "It is madness to wear ladies' straw hats and velvet hats to church; we should all be wearing crash helmets. Ushers should issue life preservers and signal flares; they should lash us to our pews. For the sleeping [G]od may wake some day and take offense, or the waking [G]od may draw us out to where we can never return."[8]

"In our eagerness to make known the approachability of God, we often overlook astonishment over the approachability of God."

It is madness to wear ladies' straw hats and velvet hats to church; we should all be wearing crash helmets.

Attempts to domesticate and manipulate God with human words, rituals, music, impressive buildings, and kneeling benches are useless and ludicrous. He has provided means for us to approach and enjoy Him, and religiosity is not it. In the end He will not tolerate our refusal to follow our agendas instead of His own. As McCullough wrote, even "all our theological systems are but moons, dim reflec-tions of a blazing Sun."[9]

"All our theological systems are but moons, dim reflections of a blazing Sun."

THE ACCESS ROAD OF VICARIOUS SACRIFICE

The means God established to circumvent the barrier between the darkness of human weakness and corruption and the blinding light and consuming fire of divine infiniteness and holiness is vicarious sacrifice. The catalyst between human darkness and divine light is death. Just as a bolt of lightning cannot be extinguished before it strikes, but can only be diverted by a lightning rod, so the fires of divine wrath cannot be extinguished before bringing condemnation and death—either to the sinner or to a vicarious substitute. As Old Testament scholar Gordon Wenham notes, "Sacrifice is the appointed means whereby peaceful coexistence between a holy God and sinful man becomes a possibility."[10] Only in the shadow of vicarious sacrifice can we find the tranquility, security, contentment, and rest with our holy, Creator God that we long for.

The catalyst between human darkness and divine light is death.

Only in the shadow of vicarious sacrifice can we find the tranquility, security, contentment, and rest with our holy, Creator God that we long for.

"Fire" is first applied explicitly to the practice of animal sacrifices when Abraham carried "the fire and the knife" up the mountain to offer his son Isaac but was gratefully ordered by God to substitute a ram instead (Gen 22:6–13). We already saw the principle of animal sacrifice appears in Genesis 3 and 4, with God providing animal clothing for Adam and Eve and then later when Abel offers the life of a lamb in faith. Surely an altar was involved in the latter scene at least, but the term itself appears for the first time in Genesis 8:20. There Noah offered burnt offerings to the Lord for delivering him and his family from the flood.

Noah's offerings are followed by God's promise (spoken literally "to [Noah's] heart") in Genesis 8:21b–22. God said he would "never again curse the ground because of human beings, even though the inclination of the human heart is evil from youth onward." He also promised, "I will never again strike down every living thing as I have done. As long as the earth endures, / seedtime and harvest, cold and heat, / summer and winter, and day and night will not cease."

Was there a logical connection between Noah's offerings and God's promise? Yes! It is found in the first part of verse 21. The occasion for God's gracious promise was "when the LORD smelled the pleasing aroma" of Noah's sacrifices. Few of us have failed to experience the delight and sense of peace and contentment that certain scents can bring us. Consider, for example, the aroma of a flowery meadow after a rain, clean mountain air scented with evergreens and aspen, or the fragrant breeze that meets you as you approach the ocean for a much-needed vacation. Suddenly the cares of the world seem to melt away. Many scents awaken delightful memories of the past, too. such as a barn full of hay, of clean sheets dried in the sunshine, of freshly ground coffee, of old books, or Grandma's kitchen. The Hebrew root of the word for "pleasing" used in Genesis 8:21 means "to rest," and the term is probably better rendered "soothing."

God had sent the flood because of extensive and incorrigible human wickedness. In fact, according to Genesis 6:5, "Every inclination of the human mind [lit., "of the thoughts of (humanity's) heart"] was nothing but evil all the time" before it. Although the waters of the flood had cleansed the earth, the human heart had not changed; thus, God's heart remained "deeply grieved" over mankind's wickedness (Gen 6:6). As Old Testament scholar Ken Mathews explains, "Noah's worship soothed the broken 'heart' (v. 21) of God, which had been injured by man's wickedness."[11]

"Noah's worship soothed the broken 'heart' of God, which had been injured by man's wickedness."

The phrase "pleasing/soothing aroma" is found 45 times in the Old Testament, mostly in Leviticus and Numbers. It almost always describes an offering to God.[12] My point is not that God literally inhales the scent of an offering and feels better as a result or even that he needs food or anything else that worshipers can provide. Expressions that describe God in human terms are called *anthropomorphisms* (think, God in human form) or *anthropopathisms* (think, God with human emotions). These help us better understand God's actions by comparing them to human actions and their causes. Thus, when the Bible says that God sees or hears or smells, the point is that God *knows* and acts based on that knowledge. Most theologians affirm that God has feelings such as affection, loathing, and anger, but not in a way identical to ours either. Most importantly, his feelings are subject to his sovereign purposes. Whereas humans often proceed from emotion to will to action, divine action always has its source in the divine will, then in divine emotion. For this reason, as Gordon Wenham explains, "Every sacrifice [thus] declares the gospel of hope, that the God who so hates sin that he contemplates destroying all mankind has through sacrifice provided a way of salvation."[13]

The nations around Israel knew nothing of a divinely ordained means to bring about a relationship between the infinite and holy God and his helpless and

Egyptian falcon god Horus from the Oriental Institute Museum, University of Chicago

Winged lion from Babylon from the Oriental Institute Museum, University of Chicago

wayward people. What started out as post-flood humanity's shared memory of the interaction between God and Noah that Moses recorded in Genesis, after all, had been largely forgotten. Followers of Marduk and of the other high gods of Babylon, as well as the other minor deities and spirits, thus were like children of alcoholic parents. These people lived in fearful dependence on their petulant gods, who required being tended and fed. People constantly dreaded unintentionally or unknowingly displeasing them and as a result experiencing misfortune, illness, or even death. They had to exert great effort and expense to court the gods' favor by trying to satisfy their desires and needs—even though the gods seldom made their wishes clear, and pleasing one god might displease another. The Lord speaking through the psalmist, however, declares in Psalm 50:12–13:

> If I were hungry, I would not tell you,
> for the world and everything in it is mine.
> Do I eat the flesh of bulls
> or drink the blood of goats?

In the case of sacrifices offered to Israel's God, he is not literally calmed or pacified from anger just because he received certain offerings that changed his behavior toward the offeror. Rather, from the time that sin entered human experience, God graciously instituted animal sacrifice as the means by which he can forgive the penalty of death and thus maintain a relationship with sinful people of faith. He chooses to forgive in response to such sacrifice.

[God] chooses to forgive in response to such sacrifice.

In most of the divinely ordained sacrifices described in the Old Testament, a life was given (symbolized by blood) and a portion of the offered creature was burned on the fires of the altar. As God explains in Leviticus 17:11, "[T]he life of a creature is in the blood, and I have appointed it to you to make atonement on the altar for your lives, since it is the lifeblood that makes atonement." Old Testament scholar Jay Sklar explains the matter this way: the blood "served as a ransom payment for the guilty," delivering the sinner from the Lord's just penalty of death for his sin (see Gen 2:17; Rom 6:23). He also explains that the *atonement* offered to those making sacrifices in faith involved not only rescue from death by payment of a ransom, but also removal of sin's spiritual contamination, which violates God's holiness and cuts us off from him.[14] When God received Noah's prototypical offerings, he accepted them as atonement for mankind, thus allowing us to continue living on the earth. English Bible translator William Tyndale (1494–1536) invented the term *atonement*, meaning *at-one-ment*, (used in Lev 5:10 and elsewhere) to summarize the Bible's teaching on God's determination to reconcile us to Himself; that is, to make peace between our holy God and sinful people. As Wenham explains, ultimately, "the acceptance of every sacrifice depends on God's antecedent gracious purpose, whereby he appointed the sacrificial system as a means of atonement for reconciliation between [himself] and man."[15]

For an individual to bring an animal sacrifice involved several steps. The first was to choose an animal, which had to be "unblemished;" that is, it could have no defects. Coming before God, after all, requires perfection. It was therefore required in a vicarious substitute. When applied to a person, the term meant "blameless." The worshiper had to present the animal at the altar for a priest to examine and accept it. Then the worshiper "laid" his or her hand on the animal's head in confessional prayer, symbolizing the transference of the guilt of the individual to the animal. This understanding is suggested by the verb translated "laid," which meant more precisely to "lean" or "press" (see Lev 1:3–4; 16:21).[16] Even in the New Testament, laying on of hands involved transference of something (see Acts 8:18).[17]

The next step was for the worshiper to kill the animal as a symbolic act representing the offering of his or her own life. According to Wenham, "What [the offeror] does to the animal, he does symbolically to himself. The death of the animal portrays the death of himself."[18] This is clearly the function of the ram Abraham offered "as a burnt offering in place of his son" Isaac (Gen 22:13).

After the animal's death, the priest involved would pour the animal's blood at the foot of the altar or smear it on the altar's horns, or sprinkle it before the veil inside the tabernacle. This symbolized cleansing—removing of defilement caused by sin, which made it possible for God to continuing dwelling with his people. Finally, all or part of the animal was burned on the altar. Some sacrifices, called fellowship offerings, were shared by the priest and the offeror, his family, and friends as a celebration of communal joy.[19]

So, fire gains special prominence in the book of Leviticus because of its essential role in the sacrifices that brought reconciliation and peace between God and his covenant people. During the ordination of Aaron and his sons as priests, "fire came from the LORD and consumed the burnt offering . . . on the altar" (Lev 9:24; see also Judg 6:21), so initiating and giving God's seal of approval to Israel's sacrificial system and Aaron's priesthood. The same thing occurred later after King Solomon dedicated the newly built temple in Jerusalem (see 2 Chr 7:1–3). Wenham makes a fitting point to conclude this section: "Sin and uncleanness lead a person from the realm of life into the realm of death. Sacrifice stops this process, indeed reverses it. It gives life to those doomed to die."[20]

> "Sin and uncleanness lead a person from the realm of life into the realm of death. Sacrifice stops this process, indeed reverses it. It gives life to those doomed to die."

JESUS OUR COMPLETE AND ULTIMATE ACCESS

As wonderful and as full of grace, mercy, and hope as the sacrificial system was, it was not the final answer to humanity's sin problem, as the author of Hebrews 9 explains. The grace and truth found in the old covenant and the law of Moses was only a foretaste, a shadow, an opening or warm-up act to the solution that would be embodied in Jesus the Messiah. God intended that the Old Testament priesthood, animal sacrifices, and tabernacle/temple, while being effective in the short-term, would have a predetermined obsolescence.

Whereas the old covenant offered provisional blessing, Jesus brought eschatological, eternal blessing. Whereas the old covenant provided external, ritual cleansing (Heb 9:13–14), Jesus brought moral and spiritual cleansing of the heart, as well as eternal life through the Spirit; moreover, this Spirit serves as a spring of life-giving water flowing in the heart of each believer (see John 4:14; 7:38).

> The grace and truth found in the old covenant and the law of Moses was only a foretaste, a shadow, an opening or warm-up act to the solution that would be embodied in Jesus the Messiah.

Although under the old covenant it was possible for a believer to draw near to God through the sacrifices, it was far from easy. There was a strict, divinely determined protocol involving washings and temple personnel and blood. And even then, the average believer could get only so close. Only the priests could penetrate the walls and enter the holy place in the temple. And only the high priest could move beyond the doors and smoke and veil and enter the holiest place where the symbolic ark of the covenant was located. And he could only do that once a year and only by bringing sacrificial blood.

According to Hebrews 9:8, by these restrictions associated with the earthly sanctuary, "The Holy Spirit was making it clear that the way into the most holy place had not yet been disclosed while the first tabernacle was still standing." As New Testament scholar Tom Schreiner explains, "Access to God's presence was not yet freely available."[21] The problem was that, ultimately, "it is impossible for the blood of bulls and goats to take away sins" (Heb 10:4). Schreiner suggests a reason for this: "Animals could scarcely provide atonement. They didn't realize why they were slain and had no consciousness of the significance of their death. They certainly didn't give their life voluntarily for the sake of sinners but were coerced to die against their will."[22] So, from the beginning, the old covenant sacrifices provided only a provisional solution that pointed forward to the work of Christ, the ultimate solution.

> *The way into the most holy place had not yet been disclosed while the first tabernacle was still standing.*

The coming and life of Jesus, the Son of God, climaxing in his death, resurrection, and ascension, thus proved to be a historical and spiritual continental divide. It was the crucial event; in fact, the term *crucial* comes from the Latin word *crux*, "cross." The world's spiritual terrain changed radically. Jesus, then, was not only the "good shepherd," as he is often called (John 10:11). He is also "the Lamb of God, who takes away the sin of the world" (John 1:29). It was as the good shepherd, however, that Jesus declared his intention to "lay down [his] life for the sheep" (John 10:15), that is, for all who "will listen to [his] voice" (10:16). But far from being a sacrificial lamb in the Old Testament sense, Jesus offered his life voluntarily. He said, "No one takes it from me, but I lay it down on my own. I have the right to lay it down, and I have the right to take it up again. I have received this command from my Father" (John 10:18).

> *The old covenant sacrifices provided only a provisional solution that pointed forward to the work of Christ, the ultimate solution.*

As D. A. Carson explains, the "moral significance" of this "God-ordained sacrifice . . . is bound up with the willingness of the sacrifice to submit to God's will."[23] The cross, then, rather than being a surprise to God, was not even a hiccup in his plan. It was his predetermined purpose from the very beginning. The early Christians knew that Jesus "was delivered up according to God's determined plan and foreknowledge" (Acts 2:23). They acknowledged in prayer that the hateful people who put Jesus on the cross were only allowed to "do whatever [God's] hand and [God's] will had predestined" (Acts 4:28).

In Jesus the ultimate atonement was accomplished. As the author of Hebrews puts it in 9:11–12, "In the greater and more perfect tabernacle not made with hands (that is, not of this creation), he entered the most holy place once for all

SOLOMON'S TEMPLE, EXTERIOR VIEW (LOOKING WEST)

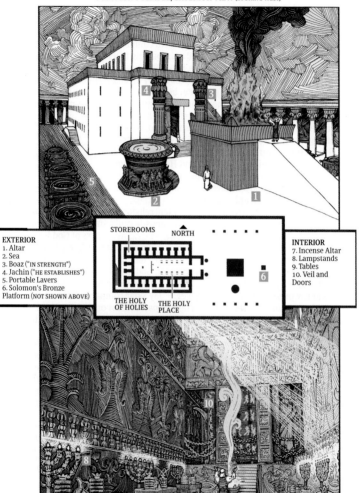

EXTERIOR
1. Altar
2. Sea
3. Boaz ("IN STRENGTH")
4. Jachin ("HE ESTABLISHES")
5. Portable Lavers
6. Solomon's Bronze
Platform (NOT SHOWN ABOVE)

STOREROOMS NORTH
THE HOLY OF HOLIES
THE HOLY PLACE

INTERIOR
7. Incense Altar
8. Lampstands
9. Tables
10. Veil and Doors

SOLOMON'S TEMPLE, INTERIOR VIEW (LOOKING WEST)

time, not by the blood of goats and calves, but by his own blood, having obtained eternal redemption."

There is no suggestion here that Jesus brought His literal blood into a heavenly sanctuary. The point here is that Jesus's dying a sacrificial death on the cross was the way He was able to provide us with complete, once-for-all cleansing of sin from our hearts and lives, as well as imparting to us eternal redemption and bringing us into God's very presence. Because Jesus paved the way for us, we who trust in Him can boldly enter God's presence by means of His blood (Heb 10:19)—something no ordinary Old Testament believer would ever dare to hope for![24]

Now, the "tabernacle" and "most holy place" spoken of above is not likely a literal structure in heaven but heaven itself, which is God's throne room (see Isa 66:1). With this in mind, we can better grasp that Jesus, our great high priest "has passed through the heavens" (Heb 4:14) into the very presence of the God who reigns and rules, and He has already brought with Him all who have placed their trust in Him and become God's children, that is, all who are "in Christ" (Rom 3:24; 8:1; Eph 2:6; etc.).

Now, the "tabernacle" and "most holy place" spoken of above is not likely a literal structure in heaven but heaven itself, which is God's throne room.

We might ask, then, whether Old Testament religion was simply a sham that gave people a false sense of security. To that the apostle Paul's answer would be, "By no means!" As he explains in Romans 3:22, 24, "The righteousness of God is through faith in Jesus Christ to *all* who believe. . . . They are justified freely by his grace through the redemption that is in Christ Jesus" (emphasis mine). That means that because of the sacrifice Christ would provide, God "passed over the sins previously committed" (v. 25) and authentically declared in response to animal sacrifices previously presented, "You are forgiven."[25] Jay Sklar compares atonement under the old covenant to God accepting a check in payment for one's debts, but then not cashing it until He Himself put money into the person's account. Sklar writes,

> In the grand scheme of things, it is not possible for the lifeblood of an animal to fully ransom the lifeblood of a human. To return to the analogy, the [check] would have bounced. So why did the Lord receive it as payment at the time? Because he knew that there would one day be money in the account to cover the debt: namely, when Jesus gave his lifeblood as the perfect and final ransom for the lifeblood of sinners (Heb 10:10, 12–14).[26]

Jesus, our blameless Savior, took the fiery judgment of God on Himself at the cross that was our due because of sin. Because of Him, we believers can enter boldly into the holy presence of our heavenly Father who loves us. The fires of divine wrath have burned themselves out on Christ for all who are incorporated into Him by faith. As a result, like Shadrach, Meshach, and Abednego, we can walk around with Jesus unharmed by celestial fire with no effect on us (see Dan 3:24–27) except warmth and light and joy and in the beautiful presence of our glorious God.

The fires of divine wrath have burned themselves out on Christ for all who are incorporated into Him by faith.

McCullough suggests that, like Thor Heyerdahl, who sailed across the Atlantic in a reed boat, in worship "we leave the shore—the narrow inlets of selfish desires, the shoals of disappointments, the jagged rocks of personal pain—and sail into the vastness of God."[27]

So is heaven the ultimate destination of all whose sins are covered by Jesus's blood, who have escaped God's fiery wrath? The next chapter will address this question.

NOTES

[1] Annie Dillard, *Teaching a Stone to Talk: Expeditions and Encounters* (New York: Harper Collins, 1982), 42–43.

[2] Jay Sklar, *Leviticus*, Tyndale Old Testament Commentaries (Downers Grove, IL: InterVarsity, 2014), 157.

[3] "List of Volcanic Eruptions by Death Toll," Wikipedia, accessed February 24, 2023, https://en.wikipedia.org/wiki/List_of_volcanic_eruptions_by_death_toll.

[4] C. S. Lewis, *The Lion, the witch, and the Wardrobe* (New York: Macmillan, 1950), 4.

[5] Donald W. McCullough, *Waking from the American Dream: Growing through Your Disappointments* (Downers Grove, IL: InterVarsity, 1988), 90.

[6] Annie Dillard, *Holy the Firm* (New York: Harper & Rowe, 1977), 59.

[7] Dillard, *Holy the Firm, 59.*

[8] Dillard, *Teaching a Stone to Talk,* 58–59.

[9] McCullough, *Waking,* 92.

[10] Gordon J. Wenham, *The Book of Leviticus,* New International Commentary on the Old Testament (Grand Rapids: Eerdmans, 1979), 56.

[11] Kenneth A. Mathews, *Genesis 1–11,* New American Commentary (Nashville: B&H, 2005), 392–93.

[12] Exceptions are Ezek 6:13; 16:19; 20:28; and Dan 2:46.

[13] Gordon J. Wenham, "The Theology of Old Testament Sacrifice," in *Sacrifice in the Bible,* ed. Roger T. Beckwith and Martin J. Selman (Eugene, OR: Wipf & Stock, 1995), 85.

[14] Sklar, *Leviticus,* 50–53.

[15] Wenham, "The Theology of Old Testament Sacrifice," 81.

[16] Wenham demonstrates this sense at work in Isa 59:16; Ezek 24:2; 30:6; and Amos 5:19. See Wenham, "The Theology of Old Testament Sacrifice," 79.

[17] Stuart, *Exodus,* 622.

[18] Wenham, "The Theology of Old Testament Sacrifice," 77.

[19] ??

[20] Wenham, "The Theology of Old Testament Sacrifice," 82.

[21] Thomas R. Schreiner, *Commentary on Hebrews,* Biblical Theology for Christian Proclamation (Nashville: B&H, 2015), 262.

[22] Schreiner, *Commentary on Hebrews,* 292.

[23] D. A. Carson, *The Gospel According to John,* Pillar New Testament Commentary (Grand Rapids: Eerdmans, 1991), 389.

[24] See E. Ray Clendenen, *Jesus's Opening Week: A Deep Exegesis of John 1:1–2:11* (Eugene, OR: Wipf & Stock, 2019), 150.

[25] See Lev 4:20, 26, 31, 35; 5:10, 13, 16, 18; 6:7.

[26] Sklar, *Leviticus,* 72.

[27] McCullough, *Waking,* 96.

CHAPTER 5

IS HEAVEN OUR FOREVER HOME?

Heaven, the supernatural realm and dwelling place of God, is a location most of us have been building an understanding of since childhood. Particularly if you grew up in church, you have sung songs about it, songs involving a stairway, knocking on a door, or the day of rejoicing that's ahead when "we all get" to "glory land." You might even recall joyously singing about your coming move "way beyond the blue," or imagining what it will be like to stroll over heaven with the people we love.

Most everybody—at least those who believe in the existence of such a place—wants to go to "the seventh heaven" or "hog heaven" or get "pennies from heaven." They think "heaven knows." They hope heaven "can wait" or that heaven will "help" them. Some wonder (based on popular songs and theories too) whether they'll be allowed to take their guns or dogs "up there" (yes, it's a real song). Others are quick to say an experience "feels like heaven"—though what they base that on I don't know. (Come to think of it, I don't know where songwriters got a lot of their above-mentioned ideas either.)

My point is that many people assume heaven, much as it's popularly imagined, is the last stop to which the train of life delivers all its passengers—well, at least all who managed to get on the right train. But is it? Does the Bible present heaven the way people typically do? And, more importantly for this chapter, is heaven really God's final reward for the righteous?

There are Bible verses that seem to suggest this last understanding. But what I hope you'll see in the paragraphs ahead is that while many passages are taken to speak about heaven being our final destination, most of them point forward to realities far richer than that.

A CLOSER LOOK AT KEY PASSAGES BELIEVED TO REFER TO HEAVEN
John 14:1–3

As Jesus's last Passover approached, he sent Peter and John to prepare for him and the disciples to eat the feast in Jerusalem. They were led by a man to "a large, furnished room upstairs" in his house (Luke 22:7–13). The apostle John is the one who gives us in John 13–17 the most complete record of what was said and done there. After washing his disciples' feet, at the supper Jesus predicted Judas's betrayal and Peter's denial (13:1–38). Then, with the meal done, Jesus began to preach what came to be called "the upper room discourse" in chapters 14–16; it's followed by Jesus's "high priestly prayer" in chapter 17. Since he knew the emotional state of his disciples at this time as well as the disturbing events that would occur within hours, Jesus began his sermon in John 14:1 this way: "Don't let your heart be troubled. Believe in God; believe also in me." (It's no wonder this particular passage is quoted at Christian funerals, for in the face of the great enemy, death, our hearts are naturally "troubled.")

Next, knowing he was on the verge of departure, Jesus told his disciples to "believe" or "trust" (v. 1). Then he offered them this assurance (John 14:2–3): "In my Father's house are many rooms. If it were not so, would I have told you that I am going to prepare a place for you? If I go away and prepare a place for you, I will come again and take you to myself, so that where I am you may be also."

> *"I will come again and take you to myself, so that where I am you may be also."*

One thing we should notice is that Jesus doesn't specify here the timing or setting of his coming for us. Will this occur at the believer's death, or at Jesus's second coming? Most scholars seem to favor the latter.

Regardless, the familiar term "mansions" taken by the KJV from the Latin Vulgate (*mansiones*), seems absurd in view of their stated location "in [His] Father's house." New Testament scholar F. D. Bruner therefore suggests rendering the statement, "On my Father's estate there are many homes"[1]; but although *oikos*, "house," occasionally means "household,"[2] the meaning "estate" is not found elsewhere. So, it makes more sense to render the plural of the Greek word *monē*, "dwelling place," as "rooms." If that strikes you as rather confining, understanding it as "suites" would be just as correct. The singular of the word is just as accurately rendered in John 14:23 as "home." Therefore, we might say that in the Father's house are many "suites/homes," and thus there is ample room for us all.

The heretical idea sometimes heard that Jesus is currently building us a house whose style and level of comfort is determined by the amount of money each of us gives to God's work is ridiculous and nowhere found in Scripture. Jesus is speaking of a place that already exists within the "Father's house" and will have ample room for all. As D. A. Carson points out, it is Jesus's cross and resurrection that prepares the place for his disciples, not their stewardship.[3]

Now, the phrase "Father's house" is generally taken to refer to heaven, where Jesus went after his ascension to "the right hand of God" (1 Pet 3:22; also Rom 8:34; Col 3:1; Heb 1:3). This is not explicitly stated, however, nor is the location of "where I am you may be also" in John 14:3. So, what else could it mean? Jesus speaks of the "Father's house" elsewhere only in John 2:16, and there He refers to the Jerusalem temple ("Stop turning my Father's house into a marketplace!"). But consider the young Jesus's explanation to his parents: "Didn't you know that it was necessary for me to be in my Father's house?" (Luke 2:49) does not actually use the word for "house" and could be rendered "my Father's place/presence"; nevertheless, it still refers to the temple, which we know the Romans destroyed in AD 70. My point is that in John 14:2–3 Jesus is not so much referring to a real place where God dwells. For centuries, the physical temple had been where people met with God, but it had been defiled and would be replaced. The "Father's house," by contrast, will stand and become a place for all nations (see Isa 2:2; 56:7; Mark 11:17; Rev 15:4). According to John 2:13–22, in fact, Jesus was about to allow the temple of His body to be consumed in his zeal to provide for God's people a new place in which to live forever in the joy of God's presence.

Jesus was about to allow the temple of His body to be consumed in his zeal to provide for God's people a new place in which to live forever in the joy of God's presence.

New Testament Theologian Greg Beale has pointed to an interesting parallel passage in Revelation 12:5–6. In that chapter the people of God are portrayed as a woman clothed in splendor and wearing a glorious crown. She is persecuted by a dragon, representing the kingdoms of this world and the devil. Yet she gives birth to her deliverer, who will "rule all nations with an iron rod" but is (temporarily) "caught up to God and to his throne," referring to Christ's resurrection and ascension (12:5). After that, the woman flees into the wilderness "where she had a *place prepared* [cp. John 14:2–3] by God, to be nourished there for 1,260 days" (that is, three and a half years). Here she seems to represent the current people of God—protected, cared for, and empowered to witness despite persecution until the Messiah returns.[4] Beale proposes that the "place" in the wilderness "where Christians are kept safe from the devil is none other than God's invisible spiritual sanctuary."[5] Of the parallel passage in John 14:2–3, he argues, "Jesus explains that 'the Father's house' and the 'place' are anywhere that he and the Father come in the Spirit to abide with the disciples (14:16–24; 15:26–27; 16:7, 13–16). . . . It is by being in the place of the Spirit that they are enabled to persevere and overcome temptations to compromise because of persecution."[6] Although this is true, and Jesus speaks of the "place" as God's presence, I am inclined to think that Jesus had in mind primarily the new creation and His return (see Rev 21–22).

As theologian Stephen Bryan explains, "The Father and the Son are united in their action to make the dwelling place of God the eternal dwelling place of the followers of Jesus."[7] However, Jesus's words

> are not so much concerned with the removal of his followers from earth to heaven as they are about the dissolution of the divide between heaven and earth; God's earthly house is no longer separate from his heavenly house. Jesus displaces the earthly dwelling place of God and also goes to the Father to prepare the heavenly dwelling of God to be the dwelling place of his people. It is thus through union with Jesus that the followers of Jesus ultimately enjoy the continual experience of God's presence.[8]

Jesus's main point, then, is that He will come for us, and then we will live and be cared for in God's presence. As Jesus had said in John 12:26, "Where I am, there my servant also will be." The idea is found again at the end of Jesus's upper room or farewell discourse, when he prays for "those [God has] given [Him] to be with [Him] where [He is]" (17:24). Here we learn that He will take us there himself.

> *Jesus's main point . . . is that He will come for us, and then we will live and be cared for in God's presence.*

Our desire to know more about where that is may be foreshadowed by the first disciples' question to Jesus in John 1:38: "Where are you staying?" The verb translated "stay" is the Greek word *menō*, related to the noun *monē*, "dwelling." Jesus's reply to them might be his reply to us as well: "Come and you'll see" (John 1:39). We have only limited knowledge of what lies behind "the final curtain." As Leslie Newbigin has helpfully said, "What is made available to us through Jesus . . . is not a sketch of what lies beyond the curtain but a firmly marked way through the curtain," which is "I am the way."[9]

> *"What is made available to us through Jesus . . . is not a sketch of what lies beyond the curtain but a firmly marked way through the curtain," which is "I am the way."*

2 Corinthians 5:1–5

In 2 Corinthians 3–4, the apostle Paul explains the basis for his confidence and faithful endurance in the face of persecution. Interestingly, it is not the thought of entering heaven itself but of future resurrection in Jesus and a subsequent "eternal weight of glory" (4:14–18). New Testament scholar David Garland is right, in fact, that Paul did not write 5:1–10 to answer questions about the afterlife but only to affirm "his confidence in the Christian's transformation in the life after death,"[10] an aspect of future glory. Paul's afflicted body (described in 4:7 as a

Bedouin tent.

"clay jar") is illustrated in 5:1–5 as an "earthly tent" that will be dismantled ("destroyed") at death and replaced by "a building from God." This building is further described as "an eternal dwelling in the heavens, not made with hands." Our earthly body will be replaced by our resurrection body. But when will this happen (at death or at Christ's return) and where (in heaven or on earth)?

New Testament scholar Gordon Fee considers it a certainty that 2 Corinthians 5:1 teaches the believer's final destiny is in heaven.[11] But there are problems with this interpretation. The phrase "our earthly tent" (more literally, "our earthly house [*oikia*] that is a tent") refers to our current physical bodies by way of an allusion to the Old Testament tabernacle. First Chronicles 9:23 tells us that before Solomon built the temple, Levites were assigned to guard (literally) "the gates of the house of Yahweh, the house of the tent."[12] To a Jewish tentmaker this image would suggest "travel and transitoriness, nomadic existence and pilgrimage" as well as Israel's wanderings with God's tabernacle in the wilderness, somewhat like our Christian pilgrimage now in which we have the indwelling of God's Spirit.[13] As in 1 Corinthians 15 (see vv. 38, 42–44, 52–54), Paul contrasts a temporary, decaying body with a permanent, indestructible, resurrection body, pictured as a "building" that is "from God" (2 Cor 5:1) but also as a garment that each will "put on" (2 Cor 5:2).

Paul contrasts a temporary, decaying body with a permanent, indestructible, resurrection body, pictured as a "building" that is "from God."

"An eternal dwelling in the heavens, not made with hands" in verse 1 is literally "a house [*oikia*] made without hands eternal in the heavens." The earthly house, then, is contrasted with the eternal house. Our heavenly, permanent house-body, which is not just a "house" but a "building," will replace our earthly, temporary house-body. "In the heavens" does not refer to where we will live forever, which is not Paul's concern here. It speaks not of location but of quality (something "heavenly" as opposed to "earthly"[14]) or source. If I promise my dinner guests I have homemade ice cream in the freezer, I am not suggesting we go to the freezer to enjoy it.[15] Similarly, when Jesus promised, "Your reward is great in heaven," he did not mean that was necessarily where we would receive it (Matt 5:12; 6:1; Luke 18:22; Col 1:5).

Elsewhere Paul shows that the believer's new body will appear on earth at the resurrection when Jesus returns (see 1 Cor 15:22–23; 1 Thess 4:16). In the meantime, life in these current bodies comes with lots of groaning (2 Cor 5:2, 4), the sound of pain and grief as we long for deliverance (Pss 6:6; 31:10; 38:8; 102:5). In Romans Paul says we groan for a specific reason, because we are "eagerly waiting for adoption, the redemption of our bodies" (8:23). Similarly, in 2 Corinthians 5:2, our groaning expresses our longing to "put on" our resurrection bodies. The phrase usually rendered "our heavenly dwelling" (CSB, ESV, NIV, NRSV) is better and more literally "our dwelling which is *from heaven*" (KJV, NKJV), as it is "from God" in verse 1. Since verse 2 says our new bodies will come *from* heaven, we should not press verse 1 to say that these will remain *in* heaven.

The believer's new body will appear on earth at the resurrection when Jesus returns

In 1 Corinthians 15:40, Paul contrasts "heavenly bodies and earthly bodies." The latter type he also calls the "natural body," belonging to the temporal world, and the former is described as the "spiritual body," in that the resurrection body is energized and guided by God's Spirit in a way that the natural body is not, thus belonging to the eternal world (15:44). One's "spiritual" body will not lack physical substance but will be like Christ's resurrected body, which is by nature "of heaven" or "heavenly" (15:48–49).[16] Jesus's resurrected body had physicality, just as ours will.

One's "spiritual" body will not lack physical substance but will be like Christ's resurrected body, which is by nature "of heaven" or "heavenly" (15:48–49).

The parallels between this passage and 1 Corinthians 15:50–58 suggest the time and circumstances of our receiving these new bodies. Paul's reference at the end of 2 Corinthians 5:4 to being "clothed, so that mortality may be swallowed up by life," for example, echoes 1 Corinthians 15:54: "When this corruptible body is clothed with incorruptibility, and this mortal body is clothed with immortality, then the saying that is written will take place: **Death has been swallowed up in victory.**" This end state will only take place at Christ's return, "at the last trumpet. For the trumpet will sound, and the dead will be raised incorruptible, and we will be changed" (1 Cor 15:52). Paul's confidence and faithful endurance, then, come from recognizing that this life is a cardboard box.

While we focus on what is seen, and we feel "at home" in this shabby box of a body, we are in a real sense "away from the Lord" (2 Cor 5:6). We are to walk by faith in the unseen and eternal and to long to be away from this tent of a body and to dwell with God in our "building," our permanent body from him. This passage says nothing about where we will reside after death. On the issue of an "intermediate body," see chapter 11 ("Is This a Direct Flight?").

Philippians 3:20–21

Paul's words, "Our citizenship is in heaven, and we eagerly wait for a Savior from there, the Lord Jesus Christ. He will transform the body of our humble condition into the likeness of his glorious body, by the power that enables him to subject everything to himself," provide another passage that's often taken to imply the believer's future residence must be up in heaven (Phil 3:20–21). Since "our citizenship is in heaven," from which our Savior will come, the assumption is often made that He will transport us there when we die. But this passage only speaks of Jesus coming to us rather than our going to Him, and of His coming to take over ("subject everything to himself") as well as to "transform" our bodies from humiliation to glory (3:21). Paul's point was that we believers, unlike people whose focus is on "earthly things" and whose "end is destruction" (3:19), should be focused on the heavenly realm to which we belong and from which our Savior is coming.

We believers . . . should be focused on the heavenly realm to which we belong and from which our Savior is coming.

Philippi was proud to be a Roman colony by decree of Octavius Caesar. Andrew Lincoln explains it was "governed as if it was on Italian soil and its administration reflected that of Rome in almost every respect."[17] Paul used that political reality to suggest that the church is, as it were, a heavenly colony, whose ultimate loyalty is to the commonwealth of heaven, whose laws and values are to govern our daily lives as we await our King's return (see Phil 1:27: "As citizens of heaven, live your life worthy of the gospel of Christ.").[18] Rather than speaking of a Rescuer who is coming to free us from imprisonment in enemy territory and take us home, then, this passage speaks of a King who is coming to conquer the enemy's territory and incorporate it into His own. According to New Testament scholar N. T. Wright, "The idea of the emperor coming from the mother city" for the sake of "the beleaguered colony" had explicit resonances in the Philippians' own experience."[19] Against this background, Paul's point in Philippians is that . . .

> *Rather than speaking of a Rescuer who is coming to free us from imprisonment in enemy territory and take us home, then, [Philippians 3:20–21] speaks of a King who is coming to conquer the enemy's territory and incorporate it into his own.*

Christians should live in the present as members, already, of the world that is yet to be. This new-age reality was inaugurated at Easter, and will be completed, through the powerful return of Jesus, in and through the final resurrection of all his people. The future resurrection thus provides and undergirds the present status, the present political stance, and the present ethical life of Christians.[20]

Colossians 1:4–5

In Colossians 1:4–5 Paul writes, "[W]e have heard of your faith in Christ Jesus and of the love you have for all the saints because of the hope reserved for you in heaven." At a glance, Paul's reference to "the hope reserved for [us] in heaven" might suggest that is where we will be. But we need to look at this more closely.

Having heard from his friend Epaphras about the Colossian Christians' faith and love, Paul tells them in 1:3–8 how grateful he is for them. The "hope" he speaks of in verse 5 furnishes the grounds for their faith and love, as brought out by the expanded translation of the NIV: "the faith and love that spring from the hope stored up for you in heaven." "Hope" here is not an attitude of confidence or expectation but is the substance of divine blessing that will be ours. It's an essential aspect of the gospel of truth, described in Colossians 1:23 as "the hope of the gospel that you heard." So, does this verse speak of the Christian's future as if it were a gift stored for us in heaven to be opened when we get there?

A bicycle "kept safe."

Well, the Greek word for "stored up" (NIV) or "reserved" (CSB; *apokeimai*) in verse 5 can refer to something that is kept safe, as the fearful servant "kept [his mina] safe in a cloth" in Luke 19:20–21. It can also refer to something simply set aside "in layaway," to be given later (2 Tim 4:8). The first sense is probably in view here, making the passage synonymous with Peter's assurance that our "inheritance" is being "kept" (*tēreō*), that is, watched over and protected in heaven for us (1 Pet 1:4). One commentator notes, it "even now exists in the transcendent realm of God's person and purposes."[21]

But what is this "hope" being kept safe for us? In Colossians 1:22–23 Paul says "the hope of the gospel" involves our being "present[ed]" before God "holy, faultless, and blameless" as a result of our having been "reconciled" to God by Christ's death (1:22). But where, when, and how will that occur? New Testament scholar Doug Moo argues from biblical parallels that Paul is referring here to *the final judgment*.[22] The verb for "present," after all, can describe one's appearance before a ruler or judge (see Acts 23:33). Romans 14:10 says, "[W]e will all *stand before* the judgment seat of God" (emphasis mine). As Paul states in 2 Corinthians 4:14, "For we know that the one who raised the Lord Jesus will also raise us with Jesus and present us."

How can Paul claim the believer will be raised "with Jesus"? As Harris explains, "with" here does not mean "at the same time as." Paul's point is that "Christ's resurrection formed the guarantee of believers' resurrection." We could say that our resurrection will be "in the wake of" or "by virtue of" Christ's.[23] And by "present us with you" Paul is saying that at the resurrection God will bring all believers, including Paul, safely into the divine presence. Just as the chief eunuch presented young Daniel and his three friends to Nebuchadnezzar (Dan 1:18), we will be presented for vindication "before the judgment seat of Christ" (2 Cor 5:10). So our "hope," mentioned in Colossians 1:22–23, will be realized at Christ's return when all believers are raised.

> *Our "hope," mentioned in Colossians 1:22–23, will be realized at Christ's return when all believers are raised.*

In Colossians 1:27, then, Paul appropriately describes the believer's hope as a "hope of glory" that is founded on the present reality of the indwelling Christ, "Christ in [us]." He describes the gospel he preached among the Gentiles as "the glorious wealth of this mystery, which is Christ in [us], the hope of glory." This is the "absolutely incomparable eternal weight of glory" Paul spoke of in 2 Corinthians 4:17, which will certainly be ours at Christ's return because we are united with him.

On the other hand, although our bodily resurrections await Christ's return, we have already been *spiritually* raised with Him (see Eph 1:3; 2:4–6; Col 2:12–13). Therefore, Paul can say in Colossians 3:1, "So if you have been raised with Christ, seek the things above, where Christ is, seated at the right hand of God." In other words, that is where our hope is. Like hikers dependent on a compass, we should constantly be orienting ourselves to these heavenly realities and heavenly values.[24]

This present evil world offers no hope. Not real hope. Rather, it is like a derelict ship that is hopelessly falling apart. Nevertheless, by God's grace we believers have "died" to this doomed world (see 2:20), and our lives are now "hidden with Christ in God" (Col 3:3), suggesting lack of visibility but also safety. This does not mean

our hope lies in being taken out of this fallen world. Rather, our hope is in "Christ, who is [our] life," who is going to "appear." And when He does, then we "also will appear with him in glory" (3:4). Who we really are in Christ, which is now hidden from the world, will become clear in glorious light when Christ returns (see 1 John 3:2). As New Testament scholar Michael Bird says, "The mystery of heaven is not found in visionary ascents to the heavenly throne, but it consists in the life of heaven coming down and falling upon Jews and Gentiles through the indwelling of the Messiah."[25] Our hope ultimately consists in the return of Christ. He has our lives firmly in his grip.

> *"The mystery of heaven is not found in visionary ascents to the heavenly throne, but it consists in the life of heaven coming down and falling upon Jews and Gentiles through the indwelling of the Messiah."*

Hebrews 11:13–16

In chapter 11 the writer of Hebrews presents the testimonies of Old Testament believers who won God's approval and pleased him by faith in his promises (v. 2). Verses 13 through 16 say,

> These all died in faith, although they had not received the things that were promised. But they saw them from a distance, greeted them, and confessed that they were foreigners and temporary residents on the earth. Now those who say such things make it clear that they are seeking a homeland. If they were thinking about where they came from, they would have had an opportunity to return. But they now desire a better place—a heavenly one. Therefore, God is not ashamed to be called their God, for he has prepared a city for them.

The people in view oriented their lives by an inheritance they could not see because they believed their God was true to his word. Living as "foreigners and temporary residents on the earth" (v. 13), they looked forward to "the city ... whose architect and builder is God" (v. 10), "a homeland" (v. 14, that is, "a place where they are citizens"[26]), "a better place—a heavenly one" (v. 16a). "Therefore, God is not ashamed to be called their God, for he has prepared a city for them" (v. 16b). These four verses seem to suggest that their inheritance, the city they sought, would not be on the earth but in heaven. So, is this a correct interpretation?

Theologian Richard Middleton points out that several New Testament passages tell us of what God either has prepared or is preparing for his children's future. These use the same verb, *hetoimazō*, "to prepare," that is used in Hebrews 11:16 and in several of the passages already discussed (like John 14:2; Rev 12:6). Jesus also tells His disciples about "the kingdom prepared for [them] from the foundation of the world" (Matt 25:34). In 1 Corinthians 2:9 Paul does not specify what God **has prepared . . . for those who love him**"—only that it is something so remarkable that "no human heart has conceived it." But we saw in Colossians that what is being kept safe for us or "reserved" (a synonym for "prepared") is the "hope of glory," our assurance that we will be vindicated before the judgment seat of Christ at the resurrection, when we will "appear with him in glory" (Col 3:4). Not until the last book of the Bible does John tell us that what has been "prepared like a bride adorned for her husband" is "a new heaven and a new earth" and "the holy city, the new Jerusalem." This is pictured "coming down out of heaven from God" (Rev 21:1–2).

Consequently, the "city" that the author of Hebrews describes as "a heavenly dwelling" is "heavenly" in that it will come "down out of heaven," just as we saw that our new bodies are described as "our heavenly dwelling" in 2 Corinthians 5:2 because they are our dwelling that is *from heaven*. Hebrews 13:14 also speaks of seeking "an enduring city" that is "to come." In the same way, I have a bowl in my study that I refer to as "my African bowl" because it was made in Africa, not because Africa is where it resides. This is why the author of Hebrews can later describe this city which God has prepared as "the city of the living God (the heavenly Jerusalem)" (Heb 12:22). The anticipated city, one scholar proposes, "lies not so much above . . . but ahead."[27] We will look further at Hebrews 11 in chapter 11 of this book: "Is This a Direct Flight?"

> *The anticipated city, one scholar proposes, "lies not so much above . . . but ahead."*

1 Peter 1:3–5

Let us now turn to what the apostle Peter's writings can contribute to this discussion. First Peter 1:3–5 says,

> Blessed be the God and Father of our Lord Jesus Christ. Because of his great mercy he has given us new birth into a living hope through the resurrection of Jesus Christ from the dead and into an inheritance that is imperishable, undefiled, and unfading, kept in heaven for you. You are being guarded by God's power through faith for a salvation that is ready to be revealed in the last time.

As we have seen in Paul's writings, Peter assures his Christian readers that God has given believers "new birth into a living hope through the resurrection of Jesus Christ from the dead" (1 Pet 1:3). As a result, we have an "imperishable, undefiled, and unfading" inheritance that is being "kept," that is, watched over and protected in heaven for us (1:4). Not only is our inheritance being kept safe, but our own faith is "being guarded by God's power . . . for a salvation that is ready to be revealed in the last time" (1:5).

This unveiling of our salvation "in the last time" will occur "at the revelation of Jesus Christ;" that is, when he returns from heaven, accompanied by "praise, glory, and honor" (1:7). The Greek words for "revealed" (*apokaluptō*) and "revelation" (*apokalupsis*) are more concentrated here (six times in 1,684 words) than in any other New Testament book except 2 Thessalonians. (It's found only twice in Revelation). Regardless, these words refer to uncovering what was previously hidden. Used in a theological way, they speak of God revealing his word and will to people in visions or, most vividly, in Jesus Christ.

The phrase "the revelation of [the Lord] Jesus [Christ]," in fact, occurs several times in the New Testament and twice in 1 Peter, referring to Christ's second coming. Paul urges us to "eagerly wait for the revelation of our Lord Jesus" (1 Cor 1:7). He also comforts us with the assurance of relief from suffering when God's kingdom comes "at the revelation of the Lord Jesus from heaven with his powerful angels . . . when he comes to be glorified by his saints and to be marveled at by all those who have believed" (2 Thess 1:7, 10). Peter uses the phrase in reference to Christ's return not only in 1 Peter 1:7 but also in 1:13, where he tells us to "set [our] hope completely on the grace to be brought to [us] at the revelation of Jesus." So again, the point is not that we are going to heaven to enjoy God's gift and glory. Rather, Jesus will bring the gift of God's glory to us! Peter and the other New Testament writers are urging us to watch for it.

The point is not that we are going to heaven to enjoy God's gift and glory. Rather, Jesus will bring the gift of God's glory to us!

The Greek noun *doxa*, translated "glory," and the verb *doxazō*, "glorify," occur 14 times in 1 Peter, more often than in any other New Testament book relative to its size. Whereas the noun in classical Greek was a 90-pound weakling of a word, meaning only "expectation" or "opinion," it was filled with power by its use in the Greek Old Testament to render the Hebrew *kavod*, "glory, majesty, splendor." Likewise, the classical Greek verb *doxazō*, meaning only "to think, suppose," was given steroids in the Old Testament and came to mean "to praise, honor, glorify, clothe in splendor." The concept of "glory" applies most naturally to the majestic, dazzling, jaw-dropping nature of God as He manifests Himself in multiple ways—most especially in the person and works of Jesus Christ.

The Old Testament speaks of a future time when the kingdoms of this world are bankrupt and desolate and God Himself will step in and shake the foundations and bring judgment. Isaiah tells us how God will gather all the redeemed from "all nations and languages" of the earth to see His glory (Isa 66:18). And He will "display his glory / in the presence of his elders" (Isa 24:23; see Rev 4–5). Yes, as commentator John Oswalt says, the glory of the Lord will come "like the moment of sunrise after a long and anxious night" and will shine over his people (Isa 60:1).[28]

His glory will be such that the two lights He created, the brightest things on earth, the sun and the moon, will be put to shame and disgraced at the coronation of the Lord of Armies as King on Mount Zion in Jerusalem (see Isa 24:23). Then the desert will become a garden, and "they will see the glory of the Lord, / the splendor of our God" (Isa 35:2). Isaiah 40 speaks of the Lord's coming, too, when "the glory of the Lord will appear, / and all humanity [lit. "all flesh"] together will see it" (v. 5). That "all flesh" will see it indicates this is an eschatological coming, with all the divine majesty of power and grace.[29] As Habakkuk reports, "The earth will be filled / with the knowledge of the Lord's glory, / as the water covers the sea" (Hab 2:14; see Ps 102:15–16).

Although the human lifespan has greatly increased due to advances in science and medicine, the death rate remains the same, even for God's children. But death looks different to a child of God than to a nonbeliever. When I was a pastor in a farm community in Illinois, I was outside a farmer's home with a group from church. Suddenly the wind shifted and the unpleasant smell of cow manure from a nearby pen inundated the gathering. One of the farmers said, "I know some people don't like that smell, but to me it's the smell of money." Death is an unpleasant experience for everyone; but for the child of God, for whom death does not have the last word, it should nevertheless be the smell of glory, of which we are assured "through the resurrection of Jesus Christ, who has gone into heaven and is at the right hand of God" (1 Pet 3:21–22). Christ has triumphed over all the forces hostile to his rule and to his children, even death.

> *Death is an unpleasant experience for everyone; but for the child of God, for whom death does not have the last word, it should nevertheless be the smell of glory.*

New Testament scholar Tom Schreiner points to a related implication that "believers will reign together with [Jesus]" one day.[30] Our sharing in Christ's victory, after all, is suggested in Peter's call in 1 Peter 4:13–14 for us to rejoice when we share in Christ's sufferings because it means we will "also rejoice with great joy when his glory is revealed . . . because the Spirit of glory and of God rests on [us]" (see Matt 5:12; Acts 5:41). In 1 Peter 5:1 Peter makes it explicit that those who rejoice in their suffering with Christ will also share in His glory, which is "about to be revealed" when Christ returns.[31] At that time, "when the chief Shepherd appears, [we who trust in him] will receive the unfading crown of glory" (5:4; see Col 3:4; 1 John 2:28; 3:2).[32] Unlike the athletic or military crowns awarded in Peter's day or the achievement awards we receive in life that often end up in a box or even the trash, the glory Christ earned for us and will bring us when He returns will radiate his splendor over us forever (see 1 Pet 5:10).

Old Testament scholar John Oswalt finds a foreshadowing of this where Isaiah announces a day when "the LORD will shine over you, / and his glory will appear over you. / Nations will come to your light, / and kings to your shining brightness" (Isa 60:1–3). Oswalt asserts, "The wonder of this chapter is that the glory of the Lord is to be reflected from Israel." Israel had sought glory from the nations but received humiliation because . . .

> glory belongs to God alone. . . . Nevertheless, God promised that He would somehow share his glory with them. . . . He will not share his glory with an idol . . . but he does intend to share it with his people. . . . How will God do it? According to [Isaiah] 49:3, he will do it through his Servant [Jesus]. This is exactly the way in which the NT writers understood these passages, as indicated by such references as John 1:14; 17:4, 22; Rom. 8:17; and 1 Pet. 4:13–14.[33]

WHAT ABOUT THE RAPTURE?
1 THESSALONIANS 4:13-18

Many Christians understand the next main event in God's plan of redemption to be something called "the rapture." They base the rapture theory on Paul's teaching in 1 Thessalonians 4:13–18. He writes,

> We do not want you to be uninformed, brothers and sisters, concerning those who are asleep, so that you will not grieve like the rest, who have no hope. For if we believe that Jesus died and rose again, in the same way, through Jesus, God will bring with him those who have fallen asleep. For we say this to you by a word from the Lord: We who are still alive at the Lord's coming will certainly not precede those who have fallen asleep. For the Lord himself will descend from heaven with a shout, with the archangel's voice, and with the trumpet of God, and the dead in Christ will rise first. Then we who are still alive, who are left, will be caught up together with them in the clouds to meet the Lord in the air, and so we will always be with the Lord. Therefore encourage one another with these words.

The term "rapture" comes from the Latin Vulgate's rendering of "caught up" in verse 17 (Greek *harpazō*) by the verb *rapio*, meaning "to sieze, carry off." Many believe this event will amount to Jesus bringing the souls of departed Christians with Him from heaven to be reunited with their risen bodies at his return. At the

The Sanctuary of Christ the King, a monument in Almada, Portugal

same time, living believers will be "*caught up* together with them in the clouds to meet the Lord in the air," before Jesus takes the whole party back to heaven. Some believe that in this way the church will be spared the terrible events to take place on the earth known as "the tribulation" (see Mark 13:19, 24; Rev 7:14).[34]

Based on all we have seen already, though, Middleton is justified in asserting that "heaven is meant to be manifested on earth in the present (ethics) and will be manifested on earth in the future (eschatology); in no case is heaven the final destination of the righteous."[35] Rather than God's final salvation involving taking His followers from earth to heaven; instead, He will bring heaven down to earth.

Rather than God's final salvation involving taking His followers from earth to heaven; instead, He will bring heaven down to earth.

An obvious question at this point is, "Well, what about 1 Thessalonians 4:13–17, then?" Indeed, at a glance it describes Jesus *bringing* deceased believers *with Him* from heaven when he returns. Yet in context, this passage is intended to offer hope to grieving friends and family members of Christians who had died (v. 8). New Testament scholar Jeff Weima contrasts the substantial hope Christians have with the kind of hopelessness commonly offered by non-Christians ("the rest, who have no hope," in v. 13). He points out that in a second-century letter, a woman named Irene, having recently lost a loved one, tries to console a couple who have lost a son by pointing out simply that "one is able to do nothing against such things [that is, death]. Therefore, they should "comfort [themselves.]"[36] In Homer's *Iliad*, Achilles tells a grief-stricken father, "You must endure, and not be broken-hearted. Lamenting for your son will do no good at all."[37] The Bible affirms those who "grieve hopefully," as can be seen in Jesus's interactions at Lazarus's tomb (John 11:33, 38) and as Paul urges here (1 Thess 4:13–18).[38]

That section appears to teach that Christians who have died (1 Thess 4:14), also referred to as those who've merely "fallen asleep," are now with Jesus, presumably in heaven. The figurative use of "sleep" for death is common in the New Testament (Matt 27:52; Acts 7:60; 13:36; 2 Pet 3:4), and Paul consistently uses the verb *koimaō*, meaning "to sleep," in this way (1 Cor 11:30; 15:6, 18, 20, 51). It is found three times here in our passage. Weima shows that just as we use euphemisms for death today, the practice was common in the ancient world, in the Old Testament, and in literature penned between the Testaments.[39] This is strong evidence against understanding the Bible to teach that people literally fall asleep when they die, awaiting Christ's return.

Paul does describe Christians as "dead" in v. 16. The reason the metaphor of sleep is used of death so often in the Bible is that the latter is so often associated with finality, and the death of a believer is far from final. In Matthew 8:24, during a storm, Jesus was "sleeping" (Gk. *katheudo*) in the disciples' boat. But the disciples were able to "wake" him, and he calmed the storm (v. 25–26). Then in Matthew 9:24, when presented with a girl known by her parents and everyone else to be dead (Mark 5:35), Jesus said, "The girl is not dead but asleep [*katheudō*]." In this instance He used these words metaphorically and prophetically, as the one who held "the keys of death and Hades" (Rev 1:18). Jesus did not come to wake the sleeping but to "raise the dead" (Matt 10:8; 11:5; John 5:21), as He would "the dead man" Lazarus (John 11:44; 12:1).

A common view of the Thessalonians passage is that when Christ returns, He will bring all the deceased believers with Him to be united with surviving Christians on the earth. Then He will take the whole group back to heaven. This is commentator Charles Wanamaker's view, based on the imagery of the clouds in 1 Thessalonians 4:17.[40] There are two initial cracks in this explanation, however. First, why would Jesus bring with him Christians who have died and already been with Him in heaven, only to take them back immediately along with the living ones He retrieves from the earth? This, of course, is not an insurmountable problem, since God does many things without explaining them to us. We might suppose, then, that these people come with him because Christ is their head[41] and they are his body or to be joined to their raised bodies. Nevertheless, it's puzzling.

The second crack is more troublesome. In verse 14 Paul describes "those who have fallen asleep" that *God* will bring *through Jesus*. (Why not say that Jesus will bring them?) Yet in verse 16 he describes apparently the same ones as "the dead in Christ" rising. We might suppose that God/Christ brings the *spirits* of believers who have "fallen asleep" to be reunited with their *bodies* that have died and will now rise. But Paul does not say that.

Have these people been in heaven without bodies (either consciously or unconsciously), or with only temporary bodies (an interpretation of 2 Cor 5:1–5 that I have judged unsatisfactory previously)?[42] New Testament scholar Gordon Fee observes that Paul does not offer comfort to surviving Christians based simply on their loved ones' presence with God in heaven, as contemporary Christians commonly do. Only the certainty of their coming resurrection will suffice for Paul. Fee supposes that "for Paul this being present with the Lord is not the real thing, as it were; that will happen only at the Eschaton."[43] This suggested tension between "resurrection" and "being present with the Lord," however, plays havoc with Paul's longing in 2 Corinthians 5:8 to be "away from the body and at home with the Lord." How can being "at home with the Lord" be less than "the real thing"?

> *Paul does not offer comfort to surviving Christians based simply on their loved ones' presence with God in heaven.*

A better answer would be that the comfort these grieving Christians are seeking is that their lost loved ones will not be excluded from the festive gathering with the Lord when He returns. Paul offers this comfort in 1 Thessalonians 4:16 by assuring the remaining Christians that "the dead in Christ will rise first." That is why they will all be celebrating the Lord's return together.

> *The comfort these grieving Christians are seeking is that their lost loved ones will not be excluded from the festive gathering with the Lord when He returns.*

Additional confusion is caused by difficulties in interpreting and translating the second half of verse 14. The main question is whether the phrase "through Jesus" modifies the verb "will bring" or the participle rendered "those who have fallen asleep." In Greek it occurs between the two and could modify either one or both. The CSB and ESV imply that it modifies "will bring," understanding Jesus as the instrument by which God will bring them. Several translations have something like NASB's wording: "those who have fallen asleep through Jesus" (also KJV, NKJV, NIV, NET). What makes the latter view difficult is that instead of speaking of falling asleep *in* Jesus (as in 1 Cor 15:18, using the Gk. preposition *en*), here we have *through* (Gk. *dia*), that is, *by means of* Jesus (1 Cor 15:21). Paul is not likely to be saying that Jesus caused them to die.

The phrase translated "in the same way" (CSB), "even so" (ESV), or "so also" (NASB) joins the two halves of 1 Thessalonians 4:14, suggesting that "God" is the actor in both halves. Paul's point, I believe, is that just as God raised Jesus from the dead, God will also bring up from the dead, with and by means of Jesus, those (believers) who have fallen asleep.[44] The verse does not explicitly say that Jesus will bring anyone with Him *from heaven* when He comes. It says that God will bring deceased believers back from the dead. Weima agrees that "will bring" means that God "will resurrect these deceased believers and cause them to be present at Christ's return, such that they will be 'with him'."[45]

> *Just as God raised Jesus from the dead, God will also bring up from the dead, with and by means of Jesus, those (believers) who have fallen asleep.*

When such things are discussed, another verse is sometimes suggested from the previous chapter. In 1 Thessalonians 3:13, Paul writes of "the coming of our Lord Jesus *with all his saints*." The Greek term for "saints" is the Greek plural adjective *hagioi*, translated "holy ones"; this is used many times of believers, especially in Paul's writings. Most commentators, however, think the word here refers to holy angels. Fee, for example, thinks that Paul's language is too close to Zechariah 14:5 ("the LORD my God will come and all the holy ones with him") to be accidental, and that the phrase there "can only refer to angels."[46] Fee also sees Paul as echoing Jesus in Mark 8:38, where Jesus says the Son of Man will come "in the glory of his Father with the holy angels" (also Matt 25:31). Next, Fee points to Paul's assurance in 2 Thessalonians 1:7 that "relief" will come to the afflicted "at the revelation of the Lord Jesus from heaven with his powerful angels." Fee thinks these are referred to as "his saints" in 1:10, since the Lord's coming "to be glorified by his saints" is followed by "and to be marveled at by all those who have believed," which is evidently a group not included in the phrase "his saints."[47] Also, commentator Gary Shogren cites Jude 14–15: "Look! The Lord comes with tens of thousands of his holy ones to execute judgment on all and to convict all the ungodly." Here the holy ones are clearly angels, especially since Jude is alluding to the apocryphal book of 1 Enoch, where there is no doubt (see 1 Enoch 1:9; 60:4; 61:10). According to Shogren, "The breadth of the evidence shows that 1 Thess 3:13 refers to angels, as does 2 Thess 1:7."[48]

On the other hand, Weima, whose interpretation of 1 Thessalonians 4:13–18 I follow, thinks 3:13 refers to all believers. "Not only the living Christians in Thessalonica but also 'those who have fallen asleep,' over whom the church is grieving—will be present and reunited at Christ's return," he says. In this understanding, Jesus has to bring no one but angels with Him from heaven. Nevertheless, with hearts "blameless in holiness," we will all be with the Lord at his coming. "Once all believers are reunited with one another and with Jesus in the air [4:17], they proceed ... to escort the descending and reigning Christ to earth in a manner by which he does come 'with all his holy ones' (3:13)."[49]

Another possible verse pointing to Christ bringing believers with Him from heaven, however, is Revelation 19:14. After John hears "a vast multitude" celebrating God's victory in heaven and announcing the "marriage feast of the Lamb"

(19:1, 9), he sees someone riding a white horse in heaven. This rider is called "Faithful and True" and also "the Word of God"; he is wearing "a robe dipped in blood" (19:11–13). Then verse 14 says, "The armies that were in heaven followed him on white horses, wearing pure white linen." While we would probably think these armies were angels, their wearing "pure white linen" may echo the description of the bride (the church) in 19:8, who is given "fine linen to wear, bright and pure. For the fine linen represents the righteous acts of the saints [*hagioi*]." Therefore, the armies coming from heaven in 19:14 could be believers, although in 15:6 John also describes the seven angels coming from the temple "dressed in pure, bright linen." Besides, none of these verses about holy ones coming from heaven with Jesus sound like Paul's reference to "those who have fallen asleep" (1 Thess 4:14).

Now back to 1 Thessalonians. After 4:14 Paul extends his encouragement to those who are grieving with "a word from the Lord" (4:15; perhaps referring to Jesus's words in Matt 24:29–33, 40–41). Since Christians who have died physically were united with Christ in His death and resurrection, those Christians still living when Christ returns "will certainly not precede those who have fallen asleep" (1 Thess 4:15). Rather, Paul says in verse 16, at Jesus's tumultuous return from heaven "the dead in Christ will rise first." Only after that, according to verse 17, will those remaining alive be "caught up" by clouds "together with them" (that is, at the same time) for a meeting with the Lord "in the air." Weima points out that the many texts in the Bible associating clouds with the appearance of God show that the clouds here signify God's presence.[50] One obvious parallel is in Daniel 7:13, which is quoted or alluded to several times in the New Testament (see Matt 24:30; 26:64; Mark 13:26; 14:62; Luke 21:27; Rev 14:14).

While we want to know what happens next and where the Lord takes us—surely we will not remain in the air—all Paul tells us is that "we will always be with the Lord." As he assures us in 1 Thessalonians 5:10, Christ "died for us, so that whether we are awake or asleep, we may live together with him." This is our ultimate hope and our source of courage in the face of death.

As many have pointed out, however, the use of the noun *apantesis,* "meeting," used in 1 Thessalonians 4:17 (usually rendered by the infinitive "to meet"), may offer us a clue as to what happens next. As New Testament scholar Helmut Koester explains,

> *Apantesis* is a technical term describing the festive and formal meeting of a king or other dignitary who arrives for a visit of a city. It is the crucial term for Paul's description of the festive reception of the Lord at his coming. The united community, those who are alive and those who have died and have been raised, will meet the Lord like a delegation of a city that goes out to meet and greet an emperor when he comes to visit.[51]

This is the sense in the two other New Testament passages using the term. The five wise virgins in Jesus's parable in Matthew 25:6 went out "to meet" the groom and then "went in with him to the wedding banquet" (v. 10). Similarly, when Paul and his fellow travelers finally approached Rome, Christians there "heard the news about [them] and had come *to meet* [them] as far as the Forum of Appius and the Three Taverns," which was about 30 miles from Rome![52] Then they all proceeded to enter Rome together (Acts 28:15–16). The word also perfectly fits the scene at Jesus's triumphal entry into Jerusalem described in the Gospels. Although *apantesis* is not found there, John 12:12-13 uses a synonym, *hupantesis*: "The next day, when the large crowd that had come to the festival heard that Jesus was coming to Jerusalem, they took palm branches and went out *to meet* him" (emphasis mine).

The agenda of the Lord's meeting with believers in the air after descending from heaven with such fanfare would not seem to include taking them away to heaven but escorting them back to earth. In light of all the passages we have examined, Koester may not exaggerate when he concludes, "It is not possible to understand this passage as a statement about the 'rapture' of the believers *into heaven*."[53] Middleton suggests that the initial statement in verse 14 of what will happen at Jesus's return, that "God will bring *with him* those who have fallen asleep," means that "those raised from the graves, who have met the returning Lord, will then enter the city with him."[54] This seems to be a reasonable understanding of the passage.

> *The agenda of the Lord's meeting with believers in the air after descending from heaven with such fanfare would not seem to include taking them away to heaven but escorting them back to earth.*

CONCLUSION

We have looked in this chapter at several New Testament passages commonly used to support the view that heaven is the destiny of believers when they die. We found that this is not exactly what these particular passages present.

In answer to the question of whether believers go to heaven when they die, we must answer yes, and no. We have suggested that the biblical picture of the afterlife" is not of believers being caught up to heaven but of Jesus bringing heaven down to earth, or rather to a "new earth" (see Rev 21–22). The expression

"new earth," in fact, is always found with "new heaven(s)." But it is only used in the Bible in two passages in the New Testament (2 Pet 3:13; Rev 21:1) and two passages in the Old (Isa 65:17; 66:22). Does the Bible really present a consistent view of such an end for God's people and God's creation? We will consider this in the next chapter, as well as what this does to our "guidebook."

NOTES

1   Frederick Dale Bruner, *The Gospel of John: A Commentary* (Grand Rapids: Eerdmans, 2012), 810.

2   See Matt 10:12–13; 12:25; 13:57; Mark 3:25; John 4:53; 1 Cor 16:15; and Phil 4:22.

3   D. A. Carson, *The Gospel According to John*, The Pillar New Testament Commentary (Grand Rapids: Eerdmans, 1991), 489.

4   See G. K. Beale, *Revelation*, The New International Greek Testament Commentary (Grand Rapids: Eerdmans, 1999), 624–47.

5   Beale, *Revelation*, 648.

6   Beale, *Revelation*, 649.

7   Stephen M. Bryan, "The Eschatological Temple in John 14," *Bulletin of Biblical Research* 15 (2005): 195.

8   Bryan, "Eschatological Temple," 198.

9   Quoted in Bruner, *The Gospel of John*, 822.

10 David E. Garland, *2 Corinthians*, Christian Standard Commentary (Nashville: Holman, 2021), 276.

11 Gordon D. Fee, *The First and Second Letters to the Thessalonians*, New International Commentary on the New Testament (Grand Rapids: Eerdmans, 2009), 181. Kindle.

12 See James M. Scott, *2 Corinthians*, New International Biblical Commentary (Peabody, MA: Hendrickson, 1998), 110.

13 Murray J. Harris, *The Second Epistle to the Corinthians: A Commentary on the Greek Text*, The New International Greek Testament Commentary (Grand Rapids: Eerdmans, 2005), 370.

14 Harris, *The Second Epistle to the Corinthians*, 373.

15 See N. T. Wright, *The Resurrection of the Son of God*, Christian Origins and the Question of God (Minneapolis: Fortress, 2003), 368.

16 See Wright, *The Resurrection of the Son of God*, 350–52.

17 A. T. Lincoln, *Paradise Now and Not Yet* (Cambridge: Cambridge University Press, 1981), 100.

18 See J. Richard Middleton, *A New Heaven and a New Earth: Reclaiming Biblical Eschatology* (Grand Rapids: Baker, 2014), 218.

19 See Wright, *The Resurrection of the Son of God*, 231–32.

20 Wright, *The Resurrection of the Son of God*, 235.

21 Douglas J. Moo, *The Letters to the Colossians and to Philemon*, The Pillar New Testament Commentary (Grand Rapids: Eerdmans, 2008), 86. See also Wright, *The Resurrection of the Son of God*, 238.

22 Moo, *Colossians*, 142–43.

23 Harris, *Second Epistle to the Corinthians*, 353–55.

24 See Moo, *Colossians*, 246.

25 Michael Bird, *Colossians and Philemon*, New Covenant Commentary (Eugene, OR: Cascade, 2009), 68. See also p. 99.

26 Gareth Lee Cockerill, *The Epistle to the Hebrews*, The New International Commentary on the New Testament (Grand Rapids: Eerdmans, 2012), 551.

[27] Anthony Thiselton, *Life after Death: A New Approach to the Last Things* (Grand Rapids: Eerdmans, 2001), 105.

[28] John N. Oswalt, *The Book of Isaiah, Chapters 40–66*, The New International Commentary on the Old Testament (Grand Rapids: Eerdmans, 1998), 536.

[29] Edward J. Young, *The Book of Isaiah, Volume 3* (Grand Rapids: Eerdmans, 1972), 30.

[30] Thomas R. Schreiner, *1&2 Peter and Jude*, Christian Standard Commentary (Nashville: Holman, 2020), 225.

[31] See Schreiner, *1&2 Peter and Jude*, 269.

[32] Schreiner (*1&2 Peter and Jude*, 272) also points out that the verb translated "receive" here (*komizō*) is used six out of ten times of reward or punishment received on the last day (Cp. 2 Cor 5:10; Eph 6:8; Col 3:25; Heb 10:36; 1 Pet 1:9).

[33] Oswalt, *The Book of Isaiah, Chapters 40–66*, 537–38.

[34] For a brief survey of views regarding the tribulation and rapture, see Millard J. Erickson, *Christian Theology* (Grand Rapids: Baker, 1985), 1217–24; R. G. Clouse, "Rapture of the Church," in *Evangelical Dictionary of Theology, Second Edition*, ed. W. A. Elwell (Grand Rapids: Baker, 2001), 983–85. Also see Anthony A. Hoekema, *The Bible and the Future* (Grand Rapids: Eerdmans, 1979), 164–72; Thomas R. Schreiner, *New Testament Theology: Magnifying God in Christ* (Grand Rapids: Eerdmans, 2008), 816–21.

[35] Middleton, *A New Heaven and a New Earth*, 211.

[36] Jeffrey A. D. Weima, *1–2 Thessalonians*, Baker Exegetical Commentary on the New Testament (Grand Rapids: Baker, 2014), 334. Kindle. He points out that many inscriptions from Thessalonica "illustrate how little expectation for a life after death existed among the general population" (p. 333).

[37] Wright, *The Resurrection of the Son of God*, 32.

[38] See Timothy Keller, *On Death* (New York: Penguin, 2020), 35–40.

[39] Weima, *1–2 Thessalonians*, 326–27.

[40] Charles A. Wanamaker, *The Epistles to the Thessalonians*, The New International Greek Testament Commentary (Grand Rapids: Eerdmans, 1990), 170, 175–76.

[41] See D. Edmond Hiebert, *The Thessalonian Epistles: A Call to Readiness* (Chicago: Moody, 1971), 192–93.

[42] Hiebert's view is that believers are in heaven in a disembodied state, but that appears to contradict Paul's statement in 2 Cor 5:3 that "we will not be found naked." Hiebert, *The Thessalonian Epistles*, 201.

[43] Fee, *Thessalonians*, 170.

[44] The two prepositional phrases on either side of the verb for "bring" make two related points: (1) by means of, and (2) along with Jesus. Trying to connect the first option to "those who have fallen asleep" makes little sense. Having a verb modified by two prepositional phrases is not "dubious on grammatical grounds," as Wanamaker claims (*The Epistles to the Thessalonians*, 169). Wanamaker admits that interpreting "by means of Jesus" as indicating relationship to him is an "unusual" way of saying the same thing as "in Christ." Fee points out (*Thessalonians*, 170) that "one can find no parallel in Paul where the preposition *dia*, which ordinarily expresses secondary agency (i.e., God does something "through" Jesus), is used in a locative sense ("in" Him). Weima, however, correctly sees Christ's resurrection as "the means by which believers are resurrected [see 1 Cor. 15:21] and able to be with Jesus at his return" (*1–2 Thessalonians*, 318).

[45] Weima, *1–2 Thessalonians*, 319.

[46] Not all Old Testament scholars agree, but see Carol L. Meyers and Eric M. Meyers, *Zechariah 9–14*, Anchor Bible (New York: Doubleday, 1993), 429–30; Eugene H. Merrill, *Haggai, Zechariah, Malachi: An Exegetical Commentary* (Chicago: Moody, 1994), 350; Pamela J. Scalise, "Zechariah," in *Minor Prophets II*, by John Goldingay and Pamela J. Scalise, Understanding the Bible Commentary (Grand Rapids: Baker, 2009), 309.

[47] This is not the case, however, if 1:10 echoes Hebrew parallelism in which "saints" is defined by "all those who have believed." See the comments under 1 Thess 3:13 in Gary S. Shogren, *1 & 2 Thessalonians*, Zondervan Exegetical Commentary on the New Testament (Grand Rapids: Zondervan, 2012). He nevertheless interprets "holy ones" as angels.

[48] Shogren, *1 & 2 Thessalonians*.

[49] Weima, *1–2 Thessalonians*, 243.

[50] Weima, *1–2 Thessalonians*, 332.

[51] Helmut Koester, "Imperial Ideology and Paul's Eschatology in 1 Thessalonians," in *Paul and Empire: Religion and Power in Roman Imperial Society,* ed. Richard A. Horsley (Harrisburg, PA: Trinity Press International, 1997), 160. This point was also made long ago in James Hope Moulton and George Milligan, *The Vocabulary of the Greek Testament Illustrated from the Papyri and Other Non-literary Sources* (Grand Rapids: Eerdmans, 1930), 53. Their study of New Testament words found in the Greek papyri notes that "the word seems to have been a kind of [technical term] for the official welcome of a newly arrived dignitary—a usage which accords excellently with its NT usage."

[52] Craig S. Keener, *The IVP Bible Background Commentary: New Testament* 2nd ed. (Downers Grove, IL: InterVarsity, 2014), 416.

[53] Emphasis added. Koester, "Imperial Ideology and Paul's Eschatology in 1 Thessalonians," 160.

[54] Middleton, *A New Heaven and a New Earth,* 224. Also Green, *Thessalonians,* 228.

CHAPTER 6

NEW CREATION

In the previous chapter, I attempted to show that the simplistic idea that "Christians go to heaven at death" might not be quite right. Our destination in the afterlife is, in fact, far better than most assume.

Maria Shriver's 1999 children's book called *What's Heaven?* teaches children that "if you're good throughout your life," you get to go to "a beautiful place where you can sit on soft clouds." She says our grandmas are "watching over us from up there."[1] Although many would agree this is what's in store for travelers to the afterlife, the only credible source of information we have, the Bible, says something different.

The most important difference, of course, involves Shriver's entry requirement. The be "good throughout your life" and you'll get in idea is found nowhere in Scripture. As we saw in an earlier chapter, the key that opens the door to pleasant, eternal life with God is not something we have done (or not done) but a person, Jesus Christ. Anyone who has a relationship with Him based on faith (trust) already has a non-expiring passport and visa to God's kingdom signed and stamped by the Son of God (see John 3:15–16).

Anyone who has a relationship with Him based on faith (trust) already has a non-expiring passport and visa to God's kingdom signed and stamped by the Son of God.

Another major difference between what Shriver describes and the Bible's description appears in the

Lord's Prayer; there Jesus speaks of God's "kingdom" as something coming *here*, resulting in God's will being done on *earth* as it is currently done in heaven (Matt 6:10). Even earlier, in Jesus's Sermon on the Mount, He declared that "the poor in spirit" and "the humble" would be blessed not only with "the kingdom of heaven," but that they would "inherit the earth" (Matt 5:1–5). We can observe this difference in the last chapters of the Bible, too; they tell us where everything is headed. The book of Revelation is the apostle John's record of a vision (or series of visions) that God showed him near the end of his life while in exile on the island of Patmos in the Aegean Sea off the coast of Turkey. In the first four verses of chapter 21, John tells us this:

> I saw a new heaven and a new earth; for the first heaven and the first earth had passed away, and the sea was no more. I also saw the holy city, the new Jerusalem, coming down out of heaven from God, prepared like a bride adorned for her husband.
>
> Then I heard a loud voice from the throne: Look, God's dwelling is with humanity, and he will live with them. They will be his peoples, and God himself will be with them and will be their God. He will wipe away every tear from their eyes. Death will be no more; grief, crying, and pain will be no more, because the previous things have passed away.

We all know what disaster may await us if we try to drive the wrong way on a one-way street. My son Jon used to love to go the wrong way on his video racing games and crash into the other cars. Thankfully, he does not do that now that he drives a real car. And if we try to rise up into an eternity in the clouds when Jesus and the new world are headed down, the outcome will not be pretty. This is why, as theologians Gentry and Wellum state, "It must be emphasized that the final state is not heaven, but rather life in a new creation.... The final goal is not to get away from this world, full of evil and completely ruined by our poor stewardship, but to live in a new creation where we have a brand-new start."[2] Indeed, as we saw in the last chapter, the Bible does not portray Christians taken up to dwell with God, but God bringing heaven down to us for a reuniting of heaven and earth to be our home with Him. To understand this incredibly exciting reality, however, we need to start at the beginning. That means turning attention to the book of Genesis.

> *"It must be emphasized that the final state is not heaven, but rather life in a new creation.... The final goal is not to get away from this world, full of evil and completely ruined by our poor stewardship, but to live in a new creation where we have a brand-start."*

BIBLICAL TRAJECTORY: CREATION TO NEW CREATION

Back in Sunday school I was introduced to the books of the Bible by means of a picture of books sitting on a shelf. Each biblical book was represented by a different volume, and these were grouped in traditional categories, each category being represented by a different color. On the left, the Old Testament was divided into Law, History, Poetry, Major Prophets, and Minor Prophets. On the right, the New Testament was divided into Gospels, History, Paul's Epistles

LAW

HISTORY

POETRY & WISDOM

MAJOR PROPHETS

MINOR PROPHETS

GOSPELS

HISTORY

PAUL'S LETTERS

GENERAL LETTERS

PROPHECY

("epistle" being an old word for *letter*, not the wife of an apostle), General Epistles, and the Book of Revelation (another one-book category). It looked like the Bible was evenly divided between Old and New Testaments, although we later learned in "sword drills" that if you opened the Bible in the middle, you found the Psalms. As I've explained previously, I eventually decided the Bible was just a collection written by a lot of people a long time ago and therefore irrelevant to my life. As a teenager, I virtually threw it away. But then I met Jesus and discovered the Bible is really about Him. That caused me to take it out of the trash and begin to read it. Although I started with Paul's "letters," that's not where the story begins.

Great epic series spanning many years and involving many characters have been around a long time and remain all the rage. Popular examples from film and literature include *The Lord of the Rings*, *The Chronicles of Narnia*, *Harry Potter*, *Star Wars*, *Hunger Games*, *Little House on the Prairie*, *Outlander*, *The Avengers*, *Star Trek*, *The Bourne Trilogy*, *Terminator*, *Rocky*, and *The Godfather*—and those are just some of my favorites. Some of the most popular epic TV series I remember are *Roots*, *The Sopranos*, *Band of Brothers*, *Downton Abbey*, *Mr. Selfridge*, *I, Claudius*, and *Upstairs, Downstairs*. To a certain extent, any of these can be entered and enjoyed at any point—even if the reader or viewer doesn't know the whole story from the beginning. Nevertheless, any series is better if its books or episodes are read or seen in order. (In fact, whenever a new episode in a film series is available, my wife and I try to watch or re-watch the previous film(s) before seeing the new one to ensure we have the storyline down.) The Bible is very much like that. It was fine for me to begin with Paul's letters, but I am certain I would've understood and appreciated their messages much better had I patiently and methodically started back at the Bible's beginning. But I was an eighteen-year-old boy without much patience.

Besides, I still thought of the Bible as a collection of sixty-six books, or at least eight to ten sets of books, until a visiting lecturer in seminary showed us how to view the Bible as a whole, with an overriding story. I was an adult by the time I was taught to "walk through the Bible." In the last several decades, the idea has grown in popularity that the Bible is held together by "one great story" having a beginning, a middle, and an end. This powerful concept is now taught by many Bible teachers and preachers and is explained in many books.[3] It even became the basis for a new area of study called *biblical theology*, which examines how all the parts of the Bible are related.[4] All this to say, we should not be surprised to discover the Bible contains an overarching trajectory that reaches from the first book of the Bible, even the first verse about God creating "the heavens and the earth," to the end of the book of Revelation and the appearance of "a new heaven and a new earth." All 66 books in the case work together.

Now, whereas in ancient treaties from the Middle East the gods were summoned as witnesses, in Deuteronomy—the fifth book of the Bible—God calls on heaven and earth, that is, His whole created order, to witness His covenant with Israel (4:26; 30:19). The song of Moses (Deut 32) and the entire Torah (Deut 31:19–28) do the same. In fact, Moses's song is even addressed to the heavens and earth (Deut 32:1). All this shows that God's creation has a permanent place of honor in His eternal purposes.

Perhaps the most obvious link between the ends of the Bible's trajectory is Isaiah 1:2, which, echoing Deuteronomy 32:1, opens with an address to the heavens and earth, which as Barry Webb points out, "foreshadows the climax towards which the whole vision of Isaiah moves."[5] In Isaiah God promises to "create a new heaven and a new earth," also referred to as Jerusalem, the mountain of the Lord, and Mount Zion (Isa 65:17–18; see 2:2–3; 4:5; 24:23; 56:7; 57:13; 65:25; 66:20–22). As T. Desmond Alexander explains, the Lord will dwell in "a temple-city that will fill the whole earth" and become a new Eden.[6] Through Moses, God had warned Israel of the disastrous consequences of ignoring His laws and abandoning the God who had created them,

The Lord will dwell in "a temple-city that will fill the whole earth" and become a new Eden.

rescued them from slavery, and blessed them lavishly. Their refusal to "serve the LORD [their] God with joy . . ., even though [they] had an abundance of everything" (Deut 28:47) only put them in a nosedive into stubborn and adulterous idolatry—at the bottom of which would be the Lord's burning anger and the nation's destruction (see Deut 29:16–28). The land that God intended to be a source of blessing would be cursed as in Adam's day (v. 27; see Gen 3:17–19) and would become a source of pestilence, disease, drought, and starvation (see Deut 28:15–67). God would also leave them defenseless against nations who would oppress them and finally rip them out of the land and scatter them across the earth, where they would be "an object of . . . ridicule" (28:37) with "no resting place . . . . There the LORD [would] give [them] a trembling heart, failing eyes, and a despondent spirit. [Their lives would] hang in doubt before [them. They would] be in dread night and day, never certain of survival" (28:65–66).

Indeed, by the days of Isaiah and the other prophets, Israel was starting to reap those very consequences. Nevertheless, amid decadence and devastation, God assured the faithful few and any who would repent that eventually "through the judgment [would] come an eschatological salvation for God's people so saturated with the glory of God that mere words cannot bear the weight of the tremendous majesty."[7] This glorious, eschatological salvation is pictured not only in spiritual but in physical, earthly, and cosmic terms. Isaiah tells us "the Lord GOD will wipe away the tears / from every face / and remove his people's disgrace / from the whole earth" (Isa 25:8). And we should not allow the perspective inherited from Plato and the Greeks to deconstruct or divert us from the biblical perspective. The Bible nowhere says that matter itself is to be discarded and that real life is to be experienced by our "immortal souls." God created a *physical* universe inhabited by *physical* creatures. Human beings in particular have bodies shaped by the very hands of the divine Potter (see Gen 2:7). They are bodies destined by sin to decay and die, but they are even more certainly destined by our sovereign God through Christ to be redeemed and glorified (see Rom 8:23, 28–30).

Now, it's not insignificant or merely figurative that God speaks through the prophets in picturing of our ultimate salvation in terms of Zion, the city of Jerusalem, the mountains and land of Israel, and also the entire earth and heaven as the setting for his redemptive work.

Now, it's not insignificant or merely figurative that God speaks through the prophets in picturing of our ultimate salvation in terms of Zion, the city of Jerusalem, the mountains and land of Israel, and also the entire earth and heaven as the setting for his redemptive work.

Isaiah 24 describes devastating judgment from God, after which God's splendor will exceed that of the sun and moon: "The moon will be put to shame / and the sun disgraced, / because the LORD of Armies will reign as king / on Mount Zion in Jerusalem, / and he will display his glory / in the presence of his elders" (v. 23). Isaiah 2:2–3 also declares,

> In the last days / the mountain of the LORD's house will be established / at the top of the mountains / and will be raised above the hills. / All nations will stream to it, / and many peoples will come and say, / "Come, let's go up to the mountain of the LORD, / to the house of the God of Jacob. / He will teach us about his ways / so that we may walk in his paths." / For instruction will go out of Zion / and the word of the LORD from Jerusalem.

This particular piece of land proves dear to God's heart throughout the biblical story.

In chapter 11 the prophet tells of a coming "shoot" from the "stump of Jesse," that is, a Davidic Messiah, who will bring about an era of righteousness and peace in which wolf, lamb, leopard, goat, calf, lion, child, and cobra will "lie down together" (11:1, 5–8). David, it should be noted, grew up in Bethlehem of Israel and was Jerusalem's greatest king. He would become the ancestor to *the world's* greatest King, the Messiah, also born in Bethlehem. "They will not harm or destroy each other / on [God's] entire holy mountain," Isaiah writes of that great day ahead, "for the land will be as full / of the knowledge of the LORD / as the sea is filled with water" (11:9). As Old Testament scholar Stephen Dempster says, "It would be hard to imagine a clearer description of the restoration of the original conditions of Edenic paradise."[8] And yet, as Paul Williamson, another scholar of the Old Testament, points out, this will be "not simply Eden restored, but Eden perfected."[9] Adam and Eve had one way to mess up Eden, but there will be no way to mess up what is to come.

This will be "not simply Eden restored, but Eden perfected.

In Isaiah the Lord also speaks of the Messiah as His servant, who "will not grow weak or be discouraged until he has established justice on earth. The coasts and islands will wait for his instruction" (42:4). Isaiah repeatedly points out, too, that the Lord is Creator; the heavens and the earth are His handiwork, and He has a purpose for them (see 37:16; 40:26, 28; 42:5; 44:24; 45:8, 12; 48:13; 51:13; 66:1–2). In 45:18 he says, "The God who formed the earth and made it, / the one who established it / (he did not create it to be a wasteland, / but formed it to be inhabited)—/ he says, 'I am the LORD, / and there is no other.'" In Isaiah 51 the Lord rebukes His people for their fear of men, declaring, "I am the LORD your God / . . . his name is the LORD of Armies. / I have put my words in your mouth, / and covered you in the shadow of my hand, / in order to plant the heavens, / to found the earth, / and to say to Zion, 'You are my people'" (51:15–16). Shall the Lord who created the heavens and the earth abandon it because of the deplorable failure of those to whom he entrusted it? Old Testament scholar Christopher Wright answers with a triumphant No! He adds, "There is a serious 'earthiness' about the Old

"There is a serious 'earthiness' about the Old Testament hope. God will not just abandon his creation, but will redeem it."

Testament hope. God will not just abandon his creation, but will redeem it."[10] As another scholar, Donald Gowan, declares, "The [Old Testament] does not imagine the redemption of humanity apart from a correspondingly redeemed world."[11]

HEAVEN AND EARTH PASSING AWAY

What do we do, then, with biblical passages that seem to suggest the universe is headed for a massive conflagration in which all that we know will be annihilated? Not only does Jesus say that before his return the sun and moon will turn dark and "heaven and earth will pass away" (Matt 24:29–35; see Ps 102:25–28), but 2 Peter 3:7 says "the present heavens and earth are stored up for fire, being kept for the day of judgment and destruction of the ungodly." And verses 10–12 warn that on the day of the Lord "the elements will burn and be dissolved, and the earth and the works on it will be disclosed. . . . [T]he heavens will be dissolved with fire and the elements will melt with heat." Finally, in John's vision described in Revelation, he sees the sun turn black, the stars fall to earth, and the sky "split apart like a scroll being rolled up" (Rev 6:12–14). Then in a passage previously quoted, he tells us "the first heaven and the first earth . . . passed away" (21:1; Perhaps this is similar to 20:11: "Earth and heaven fled from his presence, and no place was found for them").

Some people give great emphasis to the importance of taking the Bible literally. But this plays havoc with the nature of normal communication, which uses both literal and figurative language. If I describe an argument at the office as "fireworks," for example, few people would fail to apprehend that I am not speaking literally. Nineteenth-century British clergyman E. W. Bullinger wrote a massive tome on *Figures of Speech Used in the Bible* that is still unsurpassed and widely used. He explains that figurative language gives "additional force, more life, intensified feeling, and greater emphasis" to what is said. It also captures an audience's attention and makes a message more memorable.[12]

As N. T. Wright explains, "All Christian language about the future is a set of signposts pointing into a mist. Signposts do not normally provide you with advance photographs of what you'll find at the end of the road, but that does not mean they aren't pointing in the right direction."[13] As so often happens with exploration, when we get to the end of

> *All Christian language about the future is a set of signposts pointing into a mist.*

the road, we will be awestruck with surprise. With such language of cosmic destruction as is quoted above, Jesus and the New Testament writers were drawing on common Old Testament images that speak of the necessity for radical, foundational change, transformation, and even cosmic upheaval (see Deut 32:22; Isa 13:9–13; 24:1–20; 64:1–3; Jer 4:23–28; Ezek 32:4–7; Zeph 1:2–3, 14–18). We might compare Jesus's extreme language in Mark 9:43 that calls for radical seriousness in avoiding sin ("if your hand causes you to fall away, cut it off").

One reason to suspect these particular end times passages should be understood figuratively is that a literal interpretation cannot be consistently maintained, even within the passages themselves. For example, Exodus 14 recounts God's drowning the Egyptian army and delivering Israel through the Red Sea. Yet Exodus 15:7 speaks of God consuming the army "like stubble," as if they were burned to death (see the similar combination of judgment fire and flood in Isa 30:27–28). In Exodus 15:7, God says he would draw his sword and destroy them with his hand, which was also not necessary. Therefore, vv. 7 and 9 cannot be taken literally in light of the fuller historical account.

Likewise, according to 2 Peter 3:6 the world of Noah's time is said to have "perished," a word that in the active voice is often rendered "destroy."[14] Yet it was not obliterated but purged and then renewed. Second Peter's next verse compares what happened then to what will happen by fire in the last days, at "the day of judgment and destruction [noun form of the word in v. 6] of the ungodly." This suggests it is the ungodly, not the universe itself, that will be "destroyed." (The destiny of the ungodly, by the way, is discussed in a later chapter).

> *It is the ungodly, not the universe itself, that will be "destroyed."*

At the end of 2 Peter 3:10 all contemporary translations have something like "the earth and the works on it will be disclosed" (as opposed to NKJV, "will be burned up"[15]). If the earth were literally burned up, how could there still be anything left to "disclose"? The imagery, then, may point to the process of purification or refining by fire, that is, redemption and transformation rather than obliteration (see Mal 3:2–4).[16] For there will be some who remain after "the heavens [are] dissolved with fire and the elements . . . melt with heat," who in "holy conduct and godliness" have waited for "the day of God," when God will bring "new heavens and a new earth, where righteousness dwells"

(2 Pet 3:10–13). The prophet Isaiah put it this way: Whoever remains in Zion and whoever is left in Jerusalem will be called holy—all in Jerusalem written in the book of life—when the Lord has washed away the filth of the daughters of Zion and cleansed the bloodguilt from the heart of Jerusalem by a spirit of judgment and a spirit of burning. Then the LORD will create a cloud of smoke by day and a glowing flame of fire by night over the entire site of Mount Zion and over its assemblies. For there will be a canopy over all the glory, and there will be a shelter for shade from heat by day, and a refuge and shelter from storm and rain (Isa 4:3–6).As Paul says, "This world in its current form is passing away" (1 Cor 7:31). And John agrees: "The world with its lust is passing away, but the one who does the will of God remains forever" (1 John 2:17). The substance of the world is not passing away but will remain.

When Jesus, John, and Peter speak of the heavens and the earth "passing away," they do not necessarily

This world in its current form is passing away.

mean that they will finally be destroyed to be replaced by something entirely new. After all, as Doug Moo explains, in Revelation 21:5, God proclaims, "I am making everything new!" He does not proclaim, "I am making new things." "The language here suggests renewal, not destruction and recreation."[17] The image of clothing wearing out is also used (see Ps 102:26; Isa 51:6; Heb 1:11), but there is no "destruction of substance"[18] (see Isa 51:11). I could say that as I watched my children grow up, with mixed emotions I saw the little girl and boy that they were gradually passing away.

On the spiritual plane, according to Paul, "If anyone is in Christ, he is a new creation; the old has passed away, and see, the new has come" (2 Cor 5:17). Here we speak of sudden, radical transformation without necessarily any immediate external manifestation.[19] Jesus, John, and Peter refer to it as "new birth," or being "born again/from above" (see John 1:13; 3:3–8; Jas 1:18; 1 Pet 1:3, 23; 1 John 5:1–4). In Titus 3:5 Paul uses the term "regeneration," which renders the Greek word *palingenesia,* whose etymology suggests the idea "becoming again." Whereas in Titus

3:5 it has to do with spiritual rebirth through the Holy Spirit, the other New Testament use of the word appears when Jesus refers to a cosmic rebirth, a "renewal of all things" (Matt 19:28), which will happen "when the Son of Man sits on his glorious throne." Peter echoes the same idea with a different word in his temple sermon in Acts 3 when he refers to the return of Christ bringing about "the time of the restoration of all things" (Acts 3:21) in the coming age (see Mark 10:30; Luke 18:30). Paul describes this coming age as the time when creation is "set free" (Rom 8:21).

THE RECYCLING OF HEAVEN AND

EARTH

What God will do to his creation might be compared to recycling, "the process of collecting and processing materials that would otherwise be thrown away . . . and turning them into new products."[20] Most of us have seen amazing works of art made from things like bottlecaps or other trash.

My grandmother used to make her shoes out of discarded Kleenex boxes and clothing scraps, and we used to laugh at her (shamelessly). What God will do with this present creation, though, will be more on the order of taking the materials found in a typical garbage dump and building a rocket to the moon. But even that picture does not do justice to God's overhaul plan. He will take this deteriorating universe that is slowing down and rebuild it into an improved creation that is "better than it was before—better, faster, stronger."[21] The cost of this project has already been paid: it's the precious blood of Christ. But will be more beautiful, amazing, and glorious than the first one. And, oh yes, it will be eternal (Isa 66:22).

In his perfect timing, God will provide for his people not a cloud but a place, a land, a restored earth and cosmos. He redeemed Israel from Egypt to give them the land he had promised Abraham (see Exod 33:1; Lev 25:38). Later, before God sent wayward Israel into Babylonian exile, seemingly ending the nation's rela-

> *In his perfect timing, God will provide for his people not a cloud but a place, a land, a restored earth and cosmos.*

tionship to the promised land for good, he instructed Jeremiah to redeem some family property in Anathoth. This symbolized that God would redeem His people and restore them to the land one day, since "nothing is too difficult" for the God who "made the heavens and earth by [his] great power" (Jer 32:17) and "gave [his people] this land [he] swore to give" (32:22).

Yet God would not only rescue the Israelites from captivity and bring them home to the land He had given them. He would also "give them integrity of heart and action so that they will fear [him] always, for their good and for the good of their descendants after them. [God would] make a permanent covenant with them: [He would] never turn away from doing good to them, and [he would] put fear of [himself] in their hearts so they [would] never again turn away" (32:39–40). When was this promise fulfilled? Well, although God brought Israel back provisionally to their homeland, the promise continues to hang in the air. God began its true fulfillment in Christ at the cross and at the empty tomb and by the Spirit at Pentecost. Yet its consummation will follow the return of Christ and the resurrection of the saints.

Just as believers in Christ "groan . . ., eagerly waiting for . . . the redemption of our bodies," so God's "creation," his entire created universe,[22] "has been groaning" and "eagerly waits with anticipation for God's sons to be revealed" at the resurrection because then "creation itself will also be set free from the bondage to decay" (8:19–25). Thus, heaven and earth will not be excluded from the celebration on that great day of final redemption. As Isaiah puts it, they will, "Break out into singing . . . / For the LORD has redeemed Jacob, / and glorifies himself through Israel" (44:23; see also 49:13; 55:12).

The Bible consistently affirms the goodness of creation.[23] That is God's evaluation six times in Genesis 1, with a seventh climactic "very good" appearing in 1:31. Although God cursed his creation so that it became a source of pain and frustration to disobedient humanity (Gen 3:16–18; 5:29), it is never said to have lost its inherent, God-given goodness. In fact, Paul says that "everything created by God is good" (1 Tim 4:4).

We in modern America have been appropriately described as a "throwaway culture." But God is not a throwaway God. He is a redeemer God. I have never been a farmer, but I came from farmers, and I pastored in farm country. One thing I admire about farmers is their resourcefulness and the priority they place on fixing what is broken rather than getting rid of it. God is like that. When God's initial creation and the garden of Eden got sabotaged by the rebels God put in charge, He did not just throw everything away and start over. Even when things were at their very worst and God had to clean house with a flood, He nevertheless kept the heavens and the earth, one family of Adam's descendants, and an ark full of animals Adam had named. Since then, the Lord has been directing an even greater reclamation project and has spared no expense to ensure that it will succeed.

God is not a throwaway God. He is a redeemer God.

Someday we will enjoy a new creation—one built out of the old, just as Jesus's resurrection body was built out of the old (his burial clothes were empty), and as our bodies will come from the seed of the old (see 1 Cor 15:38, 42–44). And as N. T. Wright tells us, "What God did for Jesus at Easter he will do not only for all those who are 'in Christ' but also for the entire cosmos."[24] Just as God took a part of humanity, brought it through the flood, and began rebuilding, He did it again with Abraham, Isaac, and Jacob, making from them a new people. Then He did it again with a new remnant after the exile. Then with a divine infusion of life involving Christ's incarnation, crucifixion, and resurrection, God began a spiritual chain reaction that is producing a countless multitude of children for him from all nations. They will inhabit a new, renovated garden, expanded to cover the earth, with mountains and rivers and forests and lakes and valleys and oceans, all full of God's creatures. I agree, by the way, with Old Testament scholar Paul Williamson that John's statement that "the sea was no more" in Revelation 21:1 must be figurative, since the sea image is regularly used in Scripture to connote chaos, evil, and opposition to God's people (see Pss 74:12–14; 89:9–10; Isa 27:1; Jer 5:22; Dan 7:2–3; Rev 13:1). It can be viewed as a "murky, unruly part of God's creation" that separates nations. The sea can be dangerous, terrifying, and deadly. Nevertheless, it is these things—chaos, evil, rebellion, separation, threat, fear, sorrow, and death—that certainly will be no more in the new world, rather than the sea itself.[25] When European travelers first observed Polynesians surfing in Hawaii at the end of the nineteenth century, the local residents of the small city of Los Angeles didn't even go to the beaches. There was no easy way to get there, and they viewed the sea as "a wild and dangerous place, with enormous waves that could break a man to pieces."[26] But those attitudes quickly changed.

They will inhabit a new, renovated garden, expanded to cover the earth, with mountains and rivers and forests and lakes and valleys and oceans, all full of God's creatures.

Isaiah's assurance that in the coming age "the land will be as full of the knowledge of the LORD as the sea is filled with water" (Isa 11:9) would sound rather odd if in that age there were no sea.

What is more, even the skies and the heavens beyond will be renovated and made brilliantly visible again, "things on earth" and "things in heaven" having been reconciled to God and pacified through Christ (see Col 1:20). And God's children will reign and work and play and worship our Creator in resurrected bodies that will never wear out or decay or die or have to struggle against evil (see Isa 40:29–31). And our Savior will "have first place in everything" (Col 1:18). When I talk about heaven, that final state of things is what I am talking about when I speak of heaven.

> *God's children will reign and work and play and worship our Creator in resurrected bodies that will never wear out or decay or die or have to struggle against evil.*

When Jeremiah and the rest of God's people who believed his promise of restoration were dragged by the Babylonians into exile, they clutched God's promise to their chests with confidence that they would see their God-given land again. In a similar way, when Christians who believe Christ's promise of restoration feel themselves being dragged from this world by death's approach, we can nevertheless know that death has no more power over us than Pilate had over Jesus, who said to him, "You would have no authority over me at all . . . if it hadn't been given you from above" (John 19:11). Christ, in fact, has disarmed death so that it does not harm us as much as it releases us. By God's grace, it has become only our victorious, transforming passage into real life. Our lives now and forever are in God's hands, and He has promised to redeem our bodies and restore us to an earth that will be glorified to match our glorified bodies (1 Cor 15:35–58). As Doug Moo says, "The glory that humans will experience, involving as it does the resurrection of the body . . . necessarily requires an appropriate environment for their embodiment."[27] The most important thing about the new creation is that God will be here (see Ezek 37:27; 43:7, 9; 48:35; Rev 21:3; 22:3).

So, what will occupy our time in this new world? With mountains and rivers and forests and lakes and valleys and (I hope) oceans full of God's creatures, I can think of a few things I might like to do. Will there be libraries and verandas where I can have time finally to read for pleasure? Will there be discussion groups? Lectures by Jesus and the biblical authors? Games to play? Stories to tell and to listen to around campfires? Williamson's assurance provides a fitting conclusion to our chapter. He writes,

> Some readers may be relieved to see no mention of endless singing or perpetual harp-playing. The [biblical] text neglects to say exactly how we will occupy ourselves in this new creation, but we can rule out the possibility of boredom in a perfected physical realm filled with all the majesty and splendor of God.[28]

NOTES

1   Maria Shriver, *What's Heaven?* (New York: St. Martin's, 1999), as quoted in N. T. Wright, *Surprised by Hope: Rethinking Heaven, the Resurrection, and the Mission of the Church* (New York: HarperOne, 2008), 17.

2   Peter J. Gentry and Stephen J. Wellum, *Kingdom through Covenant: A Biblical-Theological Understanding of the Covenants* (Wheaton, IL: Crossway, 2012), 467.

3   For example, T. Desmond Alexander, *From Eden to the New Jerusalem: An Introduction to Biblical Theology* (Grand Rapids: Kregel, 2008); G. K. Beale, *A New Testament Biblical Theology: The Unfolding of the Old Testament in the New* (Grand Rapids: Baker, 2011); Thomas R. Schreiner, *The King in His Beauty: A Biblical Theology of the Old and New Testaments* (Grand Rapids: Baker, 2013); Craig G. Bartholomew and Michael W. Goheen, *The Drama of Scripture: Finding Our Place in the Biblical Story* 2nd ed. (Grand Rapids: Baker, 2014).

4   See Scott J. Hafemann, ed., *Biblical Theology: Retrospect and Prospect* (Downers Grove, IL: InterVarsity, 2002); Edward W. Klink III and Darian R. Lockett, *Understanding Biblical Theology: A Comparison of Theory and Practice* (Grand Rapids: Zondervan, 2012).

5   Barry G. Webb, *The Message of Isaiah*, The Bible Speaks Today (Downers Grove, IL: InterVarsity, 1996), 42.

6   Alexander, *From Eden to the New Jerusalem*, 52 (see 52–54); Gentry and Wellum, *Kingdom through Covenant*, 467.

7   James M. Hamilton, Jr., *God's Glory in Salvation through Judgment: A Biblical Theology* (Wheaton, IL: Crossway, 2010), 190.

8   Stephen G. Dempster, *Dominion and Dynasty: A Theology of the Hebrew Bible*, New Studies in Biblical Theology (Downers Grove, IL: InterVarsity, 2003), 175.

9   Paul R. Williamson, *Death and the Afterlife: Biblical Perspectives on Ultimate Questions*, New Studies in Biblical Theology (Downers Grove, IL: InterVarsity, 2018), 189.

10 Christopher J. H. Wright, *An Eye for an Eye: The Place of Old Testament Ethics Today* (Downers Grove, IL: InterVarsity, 1983), 90.

11 Donald E. Gowan, *Eschatology in the Old Testament* (Philadelphia: Fortress, 1986), 118.

12 E. W. Bullinger, *Figures of Speech Used in the Bible Explained and Illustrated* (1898; reprint, Grand Rapids: Baker, 1968), v, xii. See also D. Brent Sandy, *Plowshares and Pruning Hooks: Rethinking the Language of Biblical Prophecy and Apocalyptic* (Downers Grove, IL: InterVarsity, 2002), 75–102.

13 Wright, *Surprised by Hope*, xiii.

14 See Matt 10:28; 21:41; Mark 1:24; 9:22; Luke 6:9; 17:27, 29; John 10:10; Rom 14:15; 1 Cor 1:19; 10:9; 2 Cor 4:9; Jas 4:12; and Jude 5.

15 Greek manuscripts differ here, but most scholars agree that the original probably had "found, disclosed."

16 See J. Richard Middleton, *A New Heaven and a New Earth: Reclaiming Biblical Eschatology* (Grand Rapids: Baker, 2014), 189–200; Williamson, *Death and the Afterlife*, 181; Al Wolters, "Worldview and Textual Criticism in 2 Peter 3:10," *Westminster Theological Journal* 49 (1987): 405–13.

17 Douglas J. Moo, "Nature in the New Creation: New Testament Eschatology and the Environment," *Journal of the Evangelical Theological Society* 49.3 (2006): 466.

18 See Herman Bavinck, *The Last Things: Hope for This World and the Next*, ed. John Bolt; trans. John Vriend (Grand Rapids: Baker, 1996), 157.

19 See Middleton, *A New Heaven and a New Earth*, 205–6.

20 "The U.S. Recycling System," United States Environmental Protection Agency, updated November 15, 2022, https://www.epa.gov/circulareconomy/us-recycling-system#:~:text=In%20the%20United%20States%2C%20recycling,remanufacturing%20them%20into%20new%20products.

21 This phrase come from the 1970s TV show, *The Six Million Dollar Man*, starring Lee Majors as the "bionic man."

22 See Moo, "Nature in the New Creation," 460.

23 See Wright, *Surprised by Hope*, 94.

24 Wright, *Surprised by Hope*, 99.

25 See Williamson, *Death and the Afterlife*, 181–82; G. K. Beale, *The Book of Revelation*, New International Greek Testament Commentary (Grand Rapids: Eerdmans, 1999), 1041–43.

26 Simon Winchester, *The Pacific* (New York: Harper Perennial, 2015), 134.

27 Moo, "Nature in the New Creation," 462 (see also 469).

28 Williamson, *Death and the Afterlife*, 189.

CHAPTER 7

JESUS: THE SOLAR EXPRESS

Now that we have seen what a wonderful, exciting place awaits us in the new creation, we need to answer the question, how do I get there? In our chapter, "Atonement: Avoiding the Fire," we saw that the vicarious sacrifice of Jesus Christ is the only vehicle that can tke us from the world of spiritual darkness into the world of the light of God's fiery presence. We are saved by the blood of the cross. But releasing the damsel-in-distress from certain disaster in the old melodramas was only one side of the coin. The other side was to get her back home. Similarly, rescuing Israel from Egyptian bondage was just the beginning of getting them to the promised land. Is there another essential aspect to our salvation?

Many decades ago, when I was a spiritual infant beginning to understand the new birth I had just experienced, I argued with a couple of friends that, although I believed Jesus rose from the dead, it was the cross, not the resurrection, that was essential to my salvation. I was immediately shelled by my companions with a full broadside of Scriptural cannonballs. I finally had to surrender. If the cross of Christ is the vehicle, the power of his resurrection is the fuel.

In Greek mythology the River Styx formed the boundary between the world of the living and the underworld. It was the job of Cheron to ferry the dead across the river in his boat. The price was a coin placed in the mouth of the dead person before burial.

And, lo ! toward us in a bark
Comes on an old man, hoary white with eld,
Crying, " Woe to you, wicked spirits ! "

Canto III., lines 76-78.

Gustave Doré engraving from Dante's Divine Comedy. Here Cheron is bringing souls across the river Acheron to Hell.

If we were to borrow the idea of a coin from this fanciful story, we might say that Jesus is that coin. On one side is his vicarious death on the cross; on the other side is his resurrection and ascension to the right hand of the Father in heaven. Of course, we would be left with the boat and the ferryman, which would also have to be Jesus. Sometimes illustrations die of creativity.

The point is that we are not saved by the cross alone. We are saved by Jesus: His life, His vicarious death, His resurrection and ascension, and His ongoing intercession at the right hand of the Father. Finally, we will be saved at His return, at the last trumpet, when He will raise from the dead all who belong to Him (1 Cor 15:50–58). In this chapter we will be looking at how Christ's resurrection empowers us to face with confidence not only the afterlife but also our present life of trials, challenges, and failures. The focus, of course, will be on His resurrection as the power source that will shuttle us from this life into our glorious, eternal future with God. But first, we will step back and observe what the Bible says about its necessity.

> *We are saved by Jesus: His life, His vicarious death, His resurrection and ascension, and His ongoing intercession at the right hand of the Father.*

THE NECESSITY OF JESUS'S RESURRECTION

Several New Testament passages declare the salvific requirement value not only of the cross but also of the resurrection. They begin when Jesus first informs his disciples about His approaching suffering. Matthew 16:21 says, "From then on Jesus began to point out to his disciples that *it was necessary* for him to go to Jerusalem and suffer many things from the elders, chief priests, and scribes, be killed, and be raised the third day" (see the parallels in Mark 8:31; Luke 9:22). These words are echoed after Jesus's crucifixion, when some women from Galilee come to His tomb and find it empty. They are met by two men (angels), who tell them, "He is not here, but he has risen! Remember how he spoke to you . . ., saying, '*It is necessary* that the Son of Man be betrayed into the hands of sinful men, be crucified, and rise on the third day'?" (Luke 24:7; see the parallels in Matt 28:5–7; Mark 16:5–7). Then, when the resurrected Jesus meets two men on the road to Emmaus, who are discussing reports that He is alive again, He says to them, "How foolish you are, and how slow to believe all that the prophets have spoken! Wasn't it *necessary* for the Messiah to suffer these things and enter into his glory?" (Luke 24:25–26).[1] In the apostle John's account of his and Peter's race to Jesus's tomb following the women's report, he admits, "[We] did not yet understand the Scripture that *he must* [the same Gk. word also translated "it is necessary"] rise from the dead" (John 20:9).

> *Wasn't it necessary for the Messiah to suffer these things and enter into his glory?*

The apostle Paul continued this message when he preached in the synagogue in Thessalonica. He explained the prophecies and proved that the Messiah *must* "suffer and rise from the dead" (Acts 17:3). Paul later had the opportunity to speak in the presence of King Herod Agrippa II, a Roman ruler descended from Herod the Great. He concluded by saying, "To this very day . . . I stand and testify to both small and great, saying nothing other than what the prophets and Moses said would take place—that the Messiah *would* suffer, and that, as the first to rise

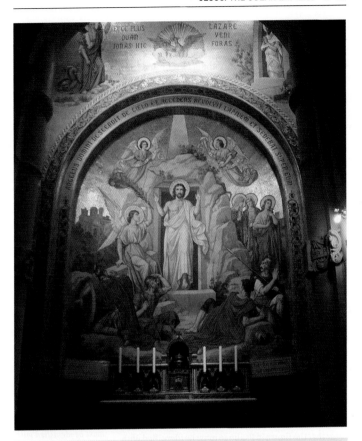

A colorful depiction of the resurrection. Rosary Basilica, Lourdes, 19th century, mosaic

from the dead, he would proclaim light to our people and to the Gentiles" (emphasis mine; Acts 26:22–23).

But why was it *necessary* for Jesus to rise from the dead? Several answers can be given, but the first is that the Old Testament prophesied it. This is made explicit *The Old Testament prophesied it.*

in John 20:9 and in Acts 17:3, which I've cited. But Jesus also makes the point when he uses the language of necessity in his appearance to the startled disciples in the upper room. There he says, "These are my words that I spoke to you while I was still with you—that everything written about me in the Law of Moses, the

Prophets, and the Psalms *must* be fulfilled.... This is what is written: The Messiah will suffer and rise from the dead the third day" (emphasis mine; Luke 24:44, 46). As New Testament scholar Craig Evans explains, "The main point that Jesus makes in v. 44 is that there really is nothing new or unexpected in his resurrection on the third day.... (1) While he was still with them he had told them of these things. ... (2) [D]isciples should understand the events of Jesus' passion and resurrection because they are foretold in Scripture (i.e., the OT)."[2]

Now, on the day of Pentecost mentioned in Acts 2 Peter uses what he learned from the resurrected Christ to preach the gospel. He tells his international Jewish audience that the "lawless people" who murdered Jesus by nailing Him to a cross did not surprise God or foil His plans. Rather, it happened "according to God's determined plan and foreknowledge" (v. 23). Likewise, raising Jesus from the dead was not quick thinking on God's part, but the fulfillment of prophecies made many centuries earlier. Peter, borrowing from the Greek translation of Psalm 18:4 ("ending the pains of death"), explains that "it was not possible for [Jesus] to be held by death" (Acts 2:24). Although the Hebrew version of Psalm 18:4 has "the ropes of death," the Greek translator read it as "the labor pains of death,"[3] creating a different metaphor. As one writer proposes, "The abyss cannot hold Christ any more than the womb can hold the child."[4]

Raising Jesus from the dead was not quick thinking on God's part, but the fulfillment of prophecies made many centuries earlier.

We might suppose that Jesus's being the sinless Son of God and the Creator of all things is the reason death could not hold him. But Peter explains it by quoting from Psalm 16:8–11, which, he says, is about David's promised messianic son (Acts 2:25a). Speaking in the voice of this son, according to Peter, David says in Psalm 16:10, **"[Y]ou will not abandon me in Hades / or allow your holy one to see decay"** (quoted in Acts 2:27).[5] This, then, is why Jesus could speak in confidence on the cross that His death would take Him not to Hades, "the place where the dead are gathered for judgment,"[6] but to "paradise" that very day (Luke 23:43). It was David's prophecy of the Messiah's resurrection in Psalm 16 that best explained Jesus's resurrection to Peter and also at least partly explained Jesus's words to the co-suffering criminal.[7] Old Testament scholar Seth Postell shows that in the context of Psalms 15–24 we must reach the same conclusion as Peter that the figure in Psalm 16 must be identified with the messianic King, who would die and rise from the dead.[8] David could not be speaking of himself, Peter says in Acts 2:29–31:

The figure in Psalm 16 must be identified with the messianic King, who would die and rise from the dead.

[T]he patriarch David ... is both dead and buried, and his tomb is with us to this day.[9] Since he was a prophet, he knew that God had sworn an oath to him to seat one of his descendants on his throne. Seeing what was to come, he spoke concerning the resurrection of the Messiah: **He was not abandoned in ["into"] Hades, and** his flesh **did not experience decay.**

The accounts of Jesus's resurrection are not the result of a spin placed on current events by his disciples in order to protect their hides or make a power grab. Nor are they accounts of a "spiritual," that is, a non-literal or non-physical resurrection of some kind. Novelist Marilynne Robinson says that Jesus wasn't just "so powerfully remembered that his friends felt Him beside them as they walked along the road, and saw someone cooking fish on the shore and knew it to be Him, and sat down to supper with Him, all wounded as He was."[10] Indeed, it takes a novelist's imagination to read the Gospel accounts in that way. Jesus's followers really were witnesses of the fulfillment of an ancient divine promise of the Messiah's bodily resurrection, that is, of "his flesh." In fact, Peter points out, the miracle of the overflow of God's Spirit just witnessed on the day of Pentecost further demonstrated that Jesus was not only raised from the dead but had "been exalted to the right hand of God and has received from the Father the promised Holy Spirit" (Acts 2:33). So his supreme authority as messianic King-Priest on the throne of David has been demonstrated (see Luke 1:32; Acts 2:30; Heb 8:1).[11] As Peter concludes in Acts 2:36, "Therefore let all the house of Israel know with certainty that God has made this Jesus, whom [they] crucified, both Lord and Messiah."

As a result of the resurrection Jesus could go again to the right hand of God—this time in his risen body.

New Testament scholar Simon Gathercole points out that Jesus did not "become" Lord and Christ at the resurrection. According to Luke 2:11 He was already that when He was less than a day old. Rather, as a result of the resurrection Jesus could go again to the right hand of God—this time in His risen body (see John 17:5") and having received and gifted the Spirit to the church. In this way He stepped into "a new role in salvation history, in relation to a new entity (the church), which [had] not previously existed." Jesus now occupies a new position with respect to the world.[12] Having "conquered [it]" (John 16:33), casting out and condemning "the ruler of this world" (John 12:31; 14:30–31; 16:11), Jesus has become "Lord of all" (Acts 10:36; Rom 10:12), including being "Lord over both the dead and the living" in his future role as Judge (Rom 14:9).[13]

As New Testament scholar David Peterson spells out, "God's promise to King David that he would establish the throne of his descendant forever (2 Sam 7:12–16) became the basis of messianic expectation in the Old Testament (e.g., Isa 9:6–7; 11:1–10; Jer 23:5–6; Ezek 34:23–24; Zech 9:9–10; 12:7–13:1) and in later Jewish writings."[14]

Ivory cover c. 400, already with sleeping soldiers; Ascension above

According to the apostle Paul in Romans 1:1–4, the gospel God promised through the prophets involved not only the incarnation of Christ from the seed of David "according to the flesh," but also his "resurrection." Jesus our Lord "was appointed to be the powerful Son of God according to the Spirit of holiness by the resurrection of the dead" (v. 4). It was the eternal Son of God who became the human descendant of David in Bethlehem, but He was qualified to be the messianic Son of God, having power to save, by his resurrection.

It was the eternal Son of God who became the human descendant of David in Bethlehem, but he was qualified to be the messianic Son of God, having power to save, by his resurrection.

Peter's sermon in Acts 2 is largely echoed by Paul when he preaches in a synagogue in Asia Minor. He points out Jesus's descent from David, His unlawful but prophesied death, His resurrection, and His appearances to witnesses (Acts 13:22–31). Elsewhere Paul makes clear that God promised David more than a descendant. In verses 32 and 33 Paul notes that God also promised him "good news," and that promise has been fulfilled not only through the cross, but also "by [God's] raising up Jesus" from the dead, and so inaugurating Him (as Paul also says in Rom 1:4) as the messianic Son of God. This fulfills Psalm 2:7, which Paul quotes here. In this psalm, the Lord, "the one enthroned in heaven" (2:4), laughs at earthly rulers who think they can disregard Him and pursue their own self-serving agendas. Then God's wrath thunders down when He announces prophetically, "I have installed my king / on Zion, my holy mountain" (2:6). Finally, the messianic King Himself declares what the Lord has decreed about Him: "He said to me, 'You are my Son; / today I have become your Father. / Ask of me, / and I will make the nations your inheritance / and the ends of the earth your possession" (2:7–8).

Who is the installed king? He is the Lord Jesus Christ. When is "today"? It is the day of Jesus's resurrection. The psalm echoes God's promise to King David regarding a descendant whose everlasting throne and kingdom God would establish (2 Sam 7:12–13, 15–16; also see Ps 89:3–4). This descendant would even be declared by God to be His own son: "I will be his father, and he will be my son" (2 Sam 7:14). God had created Adam and appointed him as His "son" (Gen 5:1–3; Luke 3:38) to serve as priest and king in Eden, displaying God's righteous character and spreading God's kingdom of righteousness throughout "the whole earth" (Gen 1:26–28).[15] But Adam failed. Then Israel, God's "firstborn son" (see Exod 4:22), was to take Adam's place as royal priest (a "kingdom of priests" in Exod 19:6), representing God to the other nations. Old Testament scholar Peter Gentry explains that Israel had a threefold purpose as God's son: "[It would] show the nations how to have a right relationship to God, how to treat each other in a truly human way, and how to be faithful stewards of the earth's resources."[16] But Israel failed. Nevertheless, God raised up King David, whose royal descendants were to be God's sons to display God's righteous character and spread God's kingdom of righteousness throughout the earth. But all the Davidic descendants failed—until Jesus, who pleased the Father in every respect and truly carried out "all [his] will" (Acts 13:22; see Matt 3:17; 17:5; 27:54; Mark 1:11; 9:7; Luke 3:22; 9:35).[17] His resurrection day was the date of his coronation and the inauguration of his kingdom, which Psalm 2 and other Old Testament texts assure us will be worldwide in scope and eternal in duration. As Isaiah, for example, prophesied, the child who is the Son born for us and given to us will have a vast and everlasting dominion. "He will reign on the throne of David / and over his kingdom, / to establish and sustain it / with justice and righteousness from now on and forever. / The zeal of the LORD of Armies will accomplish this" (Isa 9:6–7; see Amos 9:11–12; Mic 5:2–4; Zech 9:9–10).

His resurrection day was the date of his coronation and the inauguration of his kingdom, which Psalm 2 and other Old Testament texts assure us will be worldwide in scope and eternal in duration.

Finally, by citing Isa 55:3 ("I will give you the holy and sure promises of David") Paul makes the point that Jesus's resurrection was the distribution center from which all the blessings come to us, which David's faithful descendant earned through His obedient life and vicarious death on the cross (note "**I will give you**" in Acts 13:34; it's a reference to Isa 55:3).[18] I suspect this explains Paul's later charge to Timothy to "Remember Jesus Christ, risen from the dead and descended from David, according to [Paul's] gospel" (2 Tim 2:8). Indeed, the promises earned and received by the son of David, the Son of God, including forgiveness of sins (Acts 13:38), are given to all who join themselves to Him by faith. As Paul explains, "Everyone who believes is justified through him from everything that [he or she] could not be justified from through the law of Moses" (v. 39).

We finish our look at the necessity of Jesus's resurrection with a glance at the critical passage on resurrection in 1 Corinthians 15. Here I only need to call

Church window in Kruiskerk, Dordrecht, The Netherlands

attention to Paul's argument that Jesus's resurrection plays an indispensable part in the very workings of the gospel. What Paul declares when he preaches the gospel, he says, are the essential ingredients of our salvation. They are as necessary to our rescue from the darkness, bondage, and death caused by sin as the sun itself is necessary to a sunrise. He gives those ingredients in verses 3–8: (1) Christ's death "for our sins according to the Scriptures," (2) His physical burial, (3) His being "raised on the third day according to the Scriptures," and (4) His appearances to Cephas (Peter), the Twelve disciples, "over five hundred brothers and sisters at one time," and to James the half-brother of Jesus and the rest of the apostles, including Paul.

> *Jesus's resurrection plays an indispensable part in the very workings of the gospel.*

Paul's declaration that Christ's resurrection was "according to the Scriptures," that is, that it was prophesied in the Old Testament, is confirmed by the passages we have seen. But the inclusion of "on the third day" is less clear (see also Matt 16:21; Mark 8:31; Luke 9:22; 13:32; 24:46). He was probably thinking of Hosea 6:1–2 (as Jesus surely was in the Gospel passages). It assures Israel that the Lord would "heal" their body, torn to pieces by His punishment for their rebellion (see Hos 5:14), if they would repent. He would even restore life to them "after two days / and on the third day he [would] raise [them] up / so [they could] live in his presence" (Hos 6:2). As we saw in our chapter discussing the atonement, this would not be possible apart from the bloody death of the Suffering Servant on the cross, who "bore our sicknesses" and "carried our pains," who was "struck down by God and afflicted" because of Israel's (and our) rebellion. "Punishment for our peace was on him, / and we are healed by his wounds" (Isa 53:4–5). But, as we have seen, His death alone was not enough. "Because he had done no violence / and had not spoken deceitfully" (v. 9), He would be raised. And according to Isaiah 53:11–12,

> After his anguish, / he [would] see light and be satisfied. / By his knowledge, / [God's] righteous servant [would] justify many, / and he [would] carry their iniquities. / Therefore [God would] give him the many as a portion, / and he will receive the mighty as spoil, / because he willingly submitted to death, / and was counted among the rebels; / yet he bore the sin of many / and interceded [or "will intercede"] for the rebels.

As New Testament scholar Greg Beale claims, these verses are "best read to refer to the Servant's recovery from death." And "his seed," mentioned just before this passage in verse 10 and as Isa 66:22–23 shows, "is God's new people, who will live forever in the new creation."[19]

Beale further explains, "Paul sees the resurrection prophecy applied to Israel to have begun in Jesus," who was the firstfruits of "those who belong to Christ" (see 1 Cor 15:23).[20] In Acts 26:23 Paul also calls Jesus "the first to rise from the dead." If you tie tin cans securely to the car of newlyweds, the tin cans will follow them when they race off to their honeymoon. The same principle would apply if you attached your hamster's cage to a huge bunch of helium balloons and then let go of the balloons. Beale comments, "The additional future resurrections *must necessarily come* because they actually belong to Christ's resurrection itself."[21]

In fact, in the course of arguing against spiritualists who denied that people would be physically, that is, bodily raised from the dead, Paul includes making the case that if *Christ* has not been raised, then Christian preaching is a waste of time, and worse, preachers of the gospel are liars (1 Cor 15:12–15). Christian faith would be pointless, and there would be no hope for the world of lost sinners. We would necessarily remain condemned in the darkness and bondage of sin. And when someone died, whether Christian or not, he or she would be eternally lost (vv. 17–18). Under such circumstances, anyone persisting in following a Christ who urges self-denial in this life but offers nothing beyond the grave is pathetic (v. 19). If Christ is raised, Paul argues, there is a resurrection; but if Christ is not raised, there is no gospel. In Romans, he says that the kind of faith that opens our spiritual bank accounts to the divine deposit of unlimited righteousness and gives us spiritual security both now and forever is faith "in him who raised Jesus our Lord from the dead. He was delivered up [or "because of"; see NASB, NKJV] our trespasses and raised for [or "because of"] our justification" (Rom 4:24–25). As New Testament scholar Tom Schreiner explains, "The cross and resurrection of Jesus cannot finally be separated from one another."[22] As I've pointed out, they are two sides of the same salvation-bearing coin.

Interestingly, the earliest crucifixion in an illuminated manuscript to date, from the Rabbula Gospels, also shows the resurrection.

If Christ is raised, Paul argues, there is a resurrection; but if Christ is not raised, there is no gospel.

Jesus lived an amazing life and did many extraordinary things; He drove out demons and performed many healings "today and tomorrow," as he told the Pharisees. Yet, He said, "on the third day I will complete my work" (Luke 13:32). We must not absolutize Jesus's statement made on the cross: "It is finished" (John 19:30). Certainly, not *everything* was finished that day. God's purposes and work, in fact, will continue until "the end," when "[Christ] hands over the kingdom to God the Father, when he abolishes all [other] rule and all authority and power" (1 Cor 15:24). At the cross, the Son laid down His life and thus *completed His mission* in the world, which His Father had given Him. Even shortly before His arrest, Jesus said to His Father, "I have glorified you on the earth by completing the work you gave me to do" (John 17:4). Unquestionably, then, it was at the cross that the definitive sacrifice was offered, sin was atoned for, and the rulers and authorities were disarmed and disgraced (see Col 2:15). All that Christ was to do actively for our atonement, He had done. Yet the inevitable other side of the coin was also essential to the atonement. The misguided college student was wrong. Christ's bodily resurrection is the fuel without which the vehicle of the cross will not take us into the "abundant joy" and "eternal pleasures" of God's presence both now and, even more, in the afterlife (Ps 16:11).

Christ's bodily resurrection is the fuel without which the vehicle of the cross will not take us into the "abundant joy" and "eternal pleasures" of God's presence both now and, even more, in the afterlife.

THE POWER OF JESUS'S RESURRECTION

Although the possibility of bodily resurrection was "ardently denied" in Greek and Roman culture,[23] many Jews accepted it, as is apparent in the controversy between the Pharisees and Sadducees in the New Testament (see Luke 20:27–40; Acts 23:6–8). The idea that being raised from the dead might carry with it extraordinary powers was also evidently a superstition held by some in Jesus's day. Herod, the Roman ruler of Galilee, for instance, gave some credence to the possibility that Jesus's wondrous works might be explained if he were actually John the Baptist come back to life (See Matt 14:2; Mark 6:14–15). His entertaining such a preposterous idea may have resulted from a guilty conscience over having John beheaded (see Matt 14:3–12).

Nevertheless, there is some truth in associating resurrection with power. Not only does resurrection require "power" (1 Cor 6:14; Eph 1:20), but the Bible shows that Jesus's resurrection results in His power being made available to those who believe in Him. As New Testament scholar Clinton Arnold explains, "The power of God is one of the central themes of Ephesians."[24] Paul reports in his wonderful prayer for believers in Ephesus and elsewhere that the Spirit we have received because of Jesus's resurrection (see the previous discussion of Acts 2:33) would do several things for us. He prays that the Spirit will lead us into a closer relationship with God (1:17) and a deeper understanding of three things: the blessings God has bestowed on us, how much He cherishes us, and "the immeasurable greatness of his power toward us who believe, according to the mighty working of his strength" (Eph 1:17–19).[25]

Verse 19 uses four synonyms, almost all the words in the Greek language for *power*. Paul's word translated "immeasurable" here is made from two other words that usually mean "to throw beyond." The Greek lexicon gives the meaning as to "go beyond, surpass, outdo."[26] All power on earth or in the heavens—whether military, political, financial, psychological, biological, electrical, meteorological, gravitational, magnetic, volcanic, tectonic, hydraulic, nuclear, solar, stellar, angelic, demonic—is limited. God's power, we must remember, surpasses all other powers, whether they are sources of our pride or of our terror. The Puritans are said wisely to have feared nothing but God, and they loved Him because His power is "toward us who believe," that is, He is "for us."

As I can personally testify, human beings have an uncanny and immense capacity to fear. Several years ago, I read Ed Welch's book, *Running Scared: Fear, Worry, and the God of Rest,* because of my interest in the topic of God's rest. I remember thinking when I first opened it that fear was one issue I did not have a problem with. But the more I honestly examined my own thoughts and feelings, the clearer it became that I struggle with fear as much as anyone.

God's power, we must remember, surpasses all other powers, whether they are sources of our pride or of our terror.

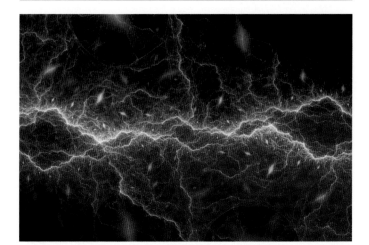

In fact, I recently noticed in myself twinges of resurfacing depression and suspected the problem might be caused by some underlying worry. I decided to take Paul's advice to pray rather than worry (Phil 4:6). I began by making a list of all the big or little things I was worrying about, and I ended up with a list 43 items long! Then I began to pray about them. How can Christians, having access to God's limitless power, ever fear or worry? Yet, we must remind ourselves daily that God is "for us."

Consider these verses. I've added the italics for emphasis.

> **Romans 5:8:** "God proves his own love *for us* in that while we were still sinners, Christ died *for us.*"
>
> **Romans 8:26:** "In the same way the Spirit also helps us in our weakness, because we do not know what to pray for as we should, but the Spirit himself intercedes *for us.*"
>
> **Romans 8:31, 32, 34:** "What, then, are we to say about these things? If God is *for us*, who is against us? He did not even spare his own Son but gave him up *for us* all. How will he not also with him grant us everything? . . . Who is the one who condemns? Christ Jesus is the one who died, but even more, has been raised; he also is at the right hand of God and intercedes *for us.*"
>
> **Ephesians 5:2:** "Christ also loved us and gave himself *for us*, a sacrificial and fragrant offering to God."
>
> **1 John 3:16:** "This is how we have come to know love: He laid down his life *for us.*"

Paul goes on to say in Ephesians 1 that God demonstrated the limitless reservoir of His power by raising Christ from the dead and seating Him at His right hand as ruler over all—including all spiritual forces and His spiritual body, the church (1:20–23). Then in chapter 2 Paul shows that God also demonstrated His power, as well as His loving mercy, by freeing us from spiritual death and bondage. He "made us alive with Christ" and "raised us up with him and seated us with him in the heavens in Christ Jesus, so that in the coming ages he might display the immeasurable [same word as in 1:19] riches of his grace through his kindness to us in Christ Jesus" (2:5–7). Just as there is no limit to his power, there is also no limit to the gracious kindness God lavishes on His children.

We saw earlier that one day the power of Jesus's resurrection will raise our bodies to live together with Him forever. As Jesus says in John 11:25, "I am the resurrection and the life. The one who believes in me, even if he dies, will live." But what is our condition now? Well, we have been rescued, bought and set free, purified and accepted by God, even adopted as His children. And all that is extraordinarily wonderful. We were poor, helpless, hopeless orphans, but now someone immensely wealthy and kind has adopted us and promised that He will come for us. So, do we now just wait at the train station or on the roof of a tall building with our arms raised? No. Because as the Bible tells us here in Ephesians and elsewhere, Jesus's resurrection provides us with more than hope for the future. It furnishes us with power for the present. This is what it means to "have eternal life" (1 John 5:13).

Jesus's resurrection provides us with more than hope for the future. It furnishes us with power for the present.

How does Christ's resurrection do that? The answer in Ephesians 2:6–7 involves the key term "with." It turns out we believers were not just made alive and raised spiritually *by* Christ but *with* Him. And the word "with" is not just a preposition Paul adds to show that somehow, when Christ was raised, we were there. He added the Greek preposition *sun*, "with," as a prefix on the verbs "make alive," "raise up," and "seat" to create a whole new concept. In fact, he liked that concept so much that he did the same thing in Colossians 2:12–13, where he says we were "buried with [Jesus], . . . raised with him, . . . and made . . . alive with him." This means that when Jesus was bodily raised from the dead, *He was not alone!* We were spiritually attached to Him. It was a "package deal." The

When Jesus was bodily raised from the dead, He was not alone!

reason we can be sure of bodily resurrection, then, is that we are already joined to Him spiritually just as a linked-up train's cars are pulled along by its engine. Thus, we could say that where our spirits are, our bodies will physically follow. This is why Beale can call Christ "the bridgehead of the new creation."[27]

Our union with Him, though, is even tighter than that of train engine and cars. In Ephesians 1:3–14 Paul repeatedly uses a phrase found many times in his writings (first in Rom 3:24), noting that all our spiritual riches come to us from God because we are "in Christ."[28] In Romans 6 Paul says that we are "alive to God in Christ Jesus," that is, "alive from the dead" (vv. 11, 13). Paul also writes that our union with Christ means that the crucified and resurrected "Christ lives in" us (Gal 2:19–20). To quote Beale again, "Saints (that is, living believers) are not merely *like* resurrected beings; rather, they actually have begun to experience the end-time resurrection that Christ experienced because they are identified with him by faith."[29] The apostle John also testifies in 1 John 5:11–12, "God has given us eternal life, and this life is in his Son. The one who has the Son has life. The one who does not have the Son of God does not have life" (see John 3:15–16, 36; 5:24; 6:40, 47, 54). Because of Christ's death and resurrection, the reborn child of God will receive a new kind of life—"God's own kind of life, divine life." Jesus said, "The Father has life in himself" and "has granted" that the Son might be a dispenser of

Because of Christ's death and resurrection, the reborn child of God will receive a new kind of life—"God's own kind of life, divine life."

that life (John 5:26). Jesus Himself is "the eternal life that was with the Father and was revealed to us" (1 John 1:2). This is not the kind of life we know in this world, which will end; it is the kind of life that will define life in the age to come, in the new heavens and earth. The crucified and resurrected Christ has rescued us from "this present evil age" (Gal 1:4), and the life "of the coming age," together with its "powers" (Heb 6:5), have invaded the present age.[30]

Paul also explains in Ephesians 1:22–23 (also in Rom 12:4–8; 1 Cor 12:12–31) that Christ is the head, and we believers are his body, "the fullness of the one who fills

all things in every way." As Arnold explains, the head was used in Greek culture as a metaphor for the command and supply center for the body.[31] Having Christ as our individual and corporate head is what supplies us with "the immeasurable greatness of his power toward us who believe" (Eph 1:19). Knowing this, in fact, is what gives us the confidence to pray to Him "who is able to do above and beyond all that we ask or think according to the power that works in us" (Eph 3:20). And we have this power because of Jesus's resurrection and our spiritual resurrection with Him. We have certainty about the future and power for the present. So why should we ever worry or be afraid? Let us conclude our look at the necessity and present significance of Jesus's resurrection by observing Beale's warning:

> Not taking seriously enough the resurrection language applied to the Christian's present experience to designate real eschatological resurrection existence, albeit on the spiritual level, has unintentionally eviscerated the ethical power of church teaching and preaching, since Christians must be aware that they presently have resurrection power to please and obey God.[32]

Christians must be aware that they presently have resurrection power to please and obey God.

Someone might draw back from all this wonderful news about resurrection life, however, and ask, "How can I know it's true?" Especially when my time comes and I am lying on my deathbed, I might ask, When I arrive at God's airport or train station that is supposed to take me to the afterlife with Jesus, will the solar express really be there? How can I know that it is not just a fairy story invented to get me through life without panic or despair? How can I know there is really something beyond the grave, an afterlife to go to? The answer, as we have seen, is the resurrection of Jesus Christ. But how do I know that Jesus was really raised from the dead? How do I know there is a train at all? That question will be addressed in the next chapter.

NOTES

[1] Although "enter into his glory" does not explicitly refer to Jesus's resurrection, it assumes it. The emphasis appearing in passages throughout this paragraph is my own.

[2] Craig A. Evans, *Luke,* Understanding the Bible Commentary Series (Grand Rapids: Baker, 1990), 357.

[3] The Hebrew for "rope, cord" is *chebel,* while the word for "labor pain" is *chēbel* (with a long *e*).

[4] G. Bertram, "*ōdín* [birthpang]," *Theological Dictionary of the New Testament,* ed. G. Kittel and G. Friedrich, abridged by G. W. Bromiley (Grand Rapids: Eerdmans, 1985), 1354.

[5] While some modern versions render the Hebrew word *shāchat* in Ps 16:10 as "the pit" rather than "corruption/decay," see the case for the latter in Seth D. Postell, "Psalm 16: The Resurrected Messiah" in *The Moody Handbook of Messianic Prophecy: Studies and Expositions of the Messiah in the Old Testament,* ed. Michael Rydelnik and Edwin Blum (Chicago: Moody, 2019), 522–25.

[6] Darrell L. Bock, *Acts,* Baker Exegetical Commentary on the New Testament (Grand Rapids: Baker, 2007), 124.

[7] Postell makes a persuasive case that in book one of Psalms (Pss 1–41), and especially Pss 15–24, the historical David represents figuratively and prophetically the future Davidic/

messianic King ("Psalm 16: The Resurrected Messiah," 513–21. Also see Bock, *Acts*, 125. Postell (p. 521) argues that "the numerous lexical and thematic links" between the concentric Pss 15–24 and the "royal (messianic) psalms (Pss 18; 20–21) strategically placed around the central psalm, Ps 19, suggests that the figure in Ps 16 must be identified as the messianic King" of Psalm 2.

[8] Postell, "Psalm 16," 524–25. Also see Postell's case for the messianic message of the book of Psalms in "Messianism in the Psalms," in Rydelnik and Blum, 457–75.

[9] According to John Polhill, "The site of David's tomb mentioned in v. 29 is no longer certain but was probably on the south side of the southeast hill of Jerusalem near the pool of Siloam" (*Acts*, New American Commentary [Nashville: B&H, 1992], 114).

[10] Marilynne Robinson, *Housekeeping* (New York: Picador, 1980), 194.

[11] See the discussion of these verses in Bock, *Acts*, 128–29.

[12] Simon J. Gathercole, "What Did the First Christians Think about Jesus?" in *How God Became Man: The Real Origins of Belief in Jesus' Divine Nature* (Grand Rapids: Zondervan, 2014), 110. Gathercole also speaks of an "intensification" of Jesus's authority in his risen and exalted state (see Matt 28:18), including taking on "the role of final judge" (p. 113).

[13] Gathercole, "What Did the First Christians Think about Jesus?" 114.

[14] David G. Peterson, *Commentary on Romans*, Biblical Theology for Christian Proclamation (Nashville: Holman, 2017), 86.

[15] Stephen G. Dempster, *Dominion and Dynasty: A Theology of the Hebrew Bible*, New Studies in Biblical Theology (Downers Grove, IL: InterVarsity, 2003), 58–65.

[16] Peter J. Gentry and Stephen J. Wellum, *Kingdom through Covenant* (Wheaton, IL: Crossway, 2012), 399 (see pp. 395–401).

[17] See Gordon Wenham's explanation of the "interruption of the [Davidic] dynasty" in the conditional clause in Ps 132:11–12. *The Psalter Reclaimed: Praying and Praising with the Psalms* (Wheaton, Crossway, 2013), 95.

[18] See Gentry and Wellum, *Kingdom through Covenant*, 418–21.

[19] G. K. Beale, *A New Testament Biblical Theology: The Unfolding of the Old Testament in the New* (Grand Rapids: Baker, 2011), 232.

[20] Beale, *A New Testament Biblical Theology*, 261.

[21] Emphasis mine. Beale, *A New Testament Biblical Theology*, 261. Also see Duane A. Garrett, *Hosea, Joel*, The New American Commentary (Nashville: B&H, 1997), 158–59: "The 'two days' are for Israel metaphorical for a relatively short captivity but have a literal fulfillment in the resurrection of Christ. Similarly, the raising to life is literal in the case of Christ, but in the case of Israel it is a metaphor for restoration. On the other hand, there is also a literal fulfillment for the Israel of God, when all who are Christ's shall be raised at his coming (1 Thess 4:13–17)."

[22] Thomas R. Schreiner, *Romans*, Baker Exegetical Commentary on the New Testament (Grand Rapids: Baker, 1998), 243.

[23] Paul R. Williamson, *Death and the Afterlife: Biblical Perspectives on Ultimate Questions*, New Studies in Biblical Theology (Downers Grove, IL: InterVarsity, 2018), 66.

[24] Clinton E. Arnold, *Ephesians*, Zondervan Exegetical Commentary on the New Testament (Grand Rapids: Zondervan, 2010), 121.

[25] See the discussion of this passage in Arnold, *Ephesians*, 99–110.

[26] *A Greek-English Lexicon of the New Testament and other Early Christian Literature*, rev. and ed. F. W. Danker, 3rd edition (Chicago: University of Chicago Press, 2000).

[27] Beale, *A New Testament Biblical Theology*, 257.

[28] This concept of union with Christ deserves much more attention than I can give it here. See J. Todd Billings, *Union with Christ: Reframing Theology and Ministry for the Church* (Grand Rapids: Baker, 2011); Constantine R. Campbell, *Paul and Union with Christ: An Exegetical and Theological Study* (Grand Rapids: Zondervan, 2012); Marcus Peter Johnson, *One with Christ: An Evangelical Theology of Salvation* (Wheaton, IL: Crossway, 2013); and Robert Letham, *Union with Christ: In Scripture, History, and Theology* (Phillipsburg, NJ: P&R, 2011).

[29] Emphasis added. Beale, *A New Testament Biblical Theology,* 250.

[30] See Thomas R. Schreiner, *New Testament Theology: Magnifying God in Christ* (Grand Rapids: Baker, 2008), 84–90.

[31] Arnold, *Ephesians,* 115.

[32] Beale, *A New Testament Biblical Theology, 251.*

CHAPTER 8

RESURRECTION: NOT A FAIRY STORY

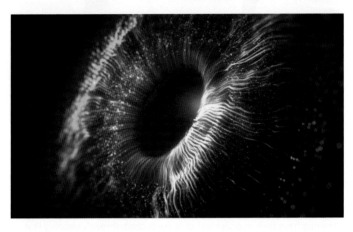

As we look back over the ground we have covered so far in our guidebook to the afterlife, we see first the discussion of what the Bible means by "heaven" as opposed to "earth." Then there was the nature of heaven as God's dwelling place, which is a dangerous place for careless travelers, though a place of infinite delight for those who belong there. Then we learned that although many destinations can be reached by many modes of transportation—plane, train, automobile, boat, bicycle, or on foot—there is only one option for travel to heaven. Entrance is only granted through use of the vehicle of Christ's vicarious sacrifice. Then we dispelled the myth about heaven being the final destination for followers of Jesus, and we sketched the new world Christ will establish for us at His return, where heaven and earth will be united. In the previous chapter we discovered that the vehicle of the cross is incomplete without the power of Jesus's resurrection, which not only fuels our journey to the new world but also our preparatory lives now as God's children who will be immigrating there.

How can any intelligent person in the modern world entertain even the possibility of such an outrageous claim that Jesus's thoroughly dead and buried body could have risen from the dead, even gloriously and eternally transformed?

His resurrection is so important that we are devoting a chapter now to answer the question: How can any intelligent person in the modern world entertain even the possibility of such an outrageous claim that Jesus's thoroughly dead and buried body could have risen from the dead, even gloriously and eternally transformed? Because of its importance and the difficulty many

people have of believing it, there is an amazing number of books on the credibility of Jesus's resurrection, and some of my favorites are listed in the note.[1] We can only skate over the surface, so I urge anyone who has never read any of these to obtain and read several carefully and even periodically.

THE WORLD'S ULTIMATE HERO

People have always loved fanciful stories about heroes doing the impossible and escaping from their enemies and even from death through amazing feats of resourcefulness, ingenuity, skill, strength, and luck. Greek mythology, for instance, has the legend of the brilliant craftsman Daedalus, who, with the help of his son Icarus, creates the Labyrinth on the island of Crete for King Minos to imprison the monster Minotaur. The Labyrinth, supposedly so complicated a maze of passages that no one can escape being killed by the invincible monster within it, is the perfect place for Minos to imprison his enemies. But the Athenian hero Theseus does the impossible. He enters the Labyrinth, slays the Minotaur, and escapes alive, although his father Aegeus thinks he died and so drowns himself in the Aegean Sea, which thereby came to bear his name.

Meanwhile, Minos had imprisoned Daedalus and Icarus in an inescapable tower to preserve the secret of the Labyrinth. But resourceful Daedalus makes wings for himself and his son out of bird feathers attached to wooden frames with wax. They succeed in escaping, but Icarus ignores his father's warning and flies so high that the sun melts the wax, and he falls to his death.

The twists and turns of such stories entertained and inspired Greek children for centuries, as we in modern times are entertained by stories of such heroes as Pecos Bill, Robin Hood, Flash Gordon, Superman, Batman, Ironman, Captain Kirk, Captain America, Black Panther, Bilbo Baggins, Luke Skywalker, and innumerable others. Some legendary heroes like Davy Crockett began as real people, whose admirable feats on behalf of others against almost impossible odds, were embellished over time. But the life of the world's ultimate and very real Hero needs no embellishment. He actually did the impossible and literally escaped the

Tornabuoni frescoes chapel in Florence. Announcement of the angel in the Church of San Zaccaria.

prison of death for the sake of others. His life did much more than inspire. His amazing accomplishments even did more than deliver others from physical death. People like Albert Einstein carried us into the atomic age. But Jesus's heroic and cosmically epoch-making act of sacrificially dying for others and victoriously rising from the dead marks the turn from darkness, bondage, and death to eternal light, freedom, and life for anyone who will look to Him in faith. In Jesus is immeasurable power, not only for achieving transport into God's delightful presence, but also for living meaningfully, abundantly, joyfully, and victoriously even now.

GULLIBILITY IN ANTIQUITY?

Modernists often speak of the ancient world in which the Bible originated as one populated by gullible, pre-scientific simpletons who didn't know the word "impossible." Today they are perceived to be people like *Alice in Wonderland*, who even at the beginning of her adventure, because "so many out-of-the-way things had happened lately . . . had begun to think that very few things indeed were really impossible."[2] In *Through the Looking Glass, writer* Lewis Carroll has the rather confused and unstable White Queen tell seven-and-a half-year-old Alice that with practice one can believe impossible things. She says, "When I was your age, I always did it for half-an-hour a day. Why, sometimes I've believed as many as six impossible things before breakfast."[3] Modernists boast about how our knowledge has delivered us from such naïve thinking, which they are certain led to traditional but outdated beliefs like the virgin birth of Christ, His nature as both God and man, the atoning power of His cross, His bodily resurrection and ascension, and the expectation of His return.

Children still often think that anything is possible through enough determination, hard work, and persistence. There is plenty of anecdotal evidence for this. Annie Dillard, who grew up in Pittsburgh in the 1950s, describes the successful efforts of turning "the old grim city" of Pittsburgh with its dirty air into "a sparkling new one" with clean air. She also points to Jonas Salk's ending the polio epidemic by isolating seventy-four strains of polio virus, then selecting three to be grown in tissues cultured from monkey kidneys in a "broth" containing "sixty-two ingredients in careful proportion." Then there was the building of the Panama Canal by moving 240 million cubic yards of dirt in ten years at the cost of $336,650,000 and 21,000 lives. As a girl, she believed no task was impossible. The word "never entered my reckoning." And yet when a physicist from Bell Laboratories spoke at her school about lasers, "you could not reasonably believe a word he said, but you could see that he believed it."[4] Although even children have credibility limits, those of adults are narrower. When George Westinghouse figured out how to make air brakes, Cornelius Vanderbilt the railroad magnate was incredulous: "Do you mean to tell me with a straight face that a moving train can be stopped with wind?"[5]

Dillard recounts how as her life experience increased, her credibility limits narrowed. Especially after the death of her beloved grandfather from a brain tumor, she came to know that no willpower could prevent someone's dying. And no willpower could restore someone dead, breathe life into that frame and set it going again in the room with you to meet your eyes. That was the fact of it. The strongest men and women who had ever lived had presumably tried to resist their own deaths, and now they were dead. It was on this fact that all the stirring biographies coincided, concurred, and culminated.[6]

The strongest men and women who had ever lived had presumably tried to resist their own deaths, and now they were dead.

She came to trust this fairly early, not because she was a child of the Enlightenment, but because she had seen death. And the people in the days of Jesus had more experience with death than young Annie Dillard.

When John the Baptist told the Jewish hypocrites that "God is able to raise up children for Abraham from these stones" (Matt 3:9), He was using a ridiculous example of something everyone would regard as impossible. Jesus was doing the same when He compared the likelihood of a rich man entering God's kingdom to a camel going through the eye of a needle. Recognizing the impossibility of the latter, His disciples asked, "Then who can be saved?" to which Jesus replied, "With man this is impossible, but with God all things are possible" (Matt 19:24–26). In a book titled *The Myth of God Incarnate*, Frances Young, a former British professor of New Testament and theology, made the absurd claim that "the Christians of the early church lived in a world in which supernatural causation was accepted without question, and divine or spiritual visitants were not unexpected."[7] This would be news to elderly Zechariah, the priest when the Lord's angel appeared to him inside the temple: "He was terrified and overcome with fear" (Luke 1:12). And when the angel told him he and his elderly wife would have a son, he did not believe it (vv. 18–20). He had plenty of cause for doubt. Luke tells us in verse 7 that the couple "had no children because Elizabeth could not conceive, and both of them were well along in years." Instead of "could not conceive," several translations say that Elizabeth "was barren," which many may think means that she had not produced a child. But that would be redundant. The Greek text says she was *steira,* which one Greek lexicon appropriately renders "sterile, incapable of bearing children."[8] Lest we think this a temporary condition, Luke tells us they were both "well along in years." It was too late. Zechariah did not have many sperm left, and Elizabeth had probably already passed through menopause. As New Testament scholar Joel Green explains, "The situation is impossible . . . both she and her husband are too old for childbearing." It is "hopeless, apart from miraculous intervention."[9] We should not be too hard on Zechariah for his unbelief, then.

And when Zechariah came out of the temple literally speechless, the people did not say, "Oh, he must've seen an angel." Rather, they thought he had a vision (v. 22). Visions were not entirely out of the question.
Angels were. Mary, though, was more trusting of the angel's message to her, but she was still terrified and dumbfounded at the impossible idea she could have a baby without sexual relations (Luke 1:29–38).

Fear and astonishment were consistent responses of Jesus's followers to news of his resurrection, often joined by unbelief.

Even the brave Roman soldiers guarding Jesus's tomb were terrified and "became like dead men" when the Lord's angel descended from heaven with an earthquake and rolled away the stone (Matt 28:2–4). In fact, fear and astonishment were consistent responses of Jesus's followers to news of His resurrection, often joined by unbelief (Matt 28:5; Mark 16:5–8; Luke 24:5, 11, 22–24, 37–43; John 20:24–28).

Supernatural visitation and bodily resurrection were just as foreign to the ancient worldview as they are to ours. Many scholars have shown that although belief in a shadowy, ethereal, but rather gloomy existence beyond death was common in the ancient world, the possibility of bodily resurrection was consistently excluded within Greek and Roman culture and almost everywhere else.[10] This is why when Paul declared in Athens that God had raised Jesus from the dead he was

Persian Zoroastrianism and Pharisaical Judaism held that both the righteous and wicked would be raised at the end of history to receive their just rewards, but no such event was expected before that.

ridiculed (Acts 17:32). Such an idea seemed to deserve nothing but laughter and sarcasm. Persian Zoroastrianism and Pharisaical Judaism held that both the righteous and wicked would be raised at the end of history to receive their just rewards, but no such event was expected before that.

REASONS FOR UNBELIEF

So, people in Jesus's time were no more likely to believe the reports about Jesus's resurrection—or anyone else's—than people are today. The response of any reasonable person is the same, and, as Annie Dillard put it, "That was the fact of it." Then why did so many

So, people in Jesus's time were no more likely to believe the reports about Jesus's resurrection—or anyone else's—than people are today.

people believe the reports, especially to the extent that Jesus's bodily resurrection became foundational to virtually every form of early Christianity?[11] And why do so many otherwise seemingly reasonable people today believe it? Some Christian *apologists* (scholars who specialize in defending the Christian faith) would say there are two factors that keep people from accepting that Jesus rose from the dead: (1) ignorance, that is, a lack of knowledge and understanding of the facts, or (2) prejudice, that is, a closed-minded commitment to the view that everything that happens in the physical universe consistently obeys the laws of nature.

But not all Christian apologists agree that unbelief can be explained so simply. Refusing to accept the right of someone to evaluate the evidence differently is disrespectful, intolerant, and unkind. People are complex, and the reasons for our opinions and convictions are complex. Christian faith is, after all, according to the apostle Paul, God's gift (Phil 1:29; also Acts 16:14). Therefore, I agree with those who simply attempt to demonstrate that it is not irrational (historically, philosophically, or theologically), in view of the evidence, to conclude that God raised Jesus physically from the dead with a gloriously transformed body. Only if one is already unmovably committed to the view that bodily resurrection cannot occur is such belief impossible.[12] In that case, the presentation of evidence would seem to be pointless (apart from God changing the heart).[13] Many historians argue that a unique event in space and time cannot be evaluated using historical methods, any more than temperature can be measured with a voltmeter. Other historians reject such a narrow view of the historical method, while acknowledging that it is never possible to prove scientifically the occurrence of an event in the past, since it is by nature unrepeatable. As someone said, we would not deny that the death of the last dinosaur was a historical event even if no one was there to record it.

> *It is not irrational (historically, philosophically, or theologically), in view of the evidence, to conclude that God raised Jesus physically from the dead with a gloriously transformed body.*

What we are saying, then, is that Jesus's resurrection is a miracle, and accepting it requires your allowing the possibility that God may in rare moments choose to intervene in His creation and violate His usual way of running the universe. Philosopher Stephen Davis defines a miracle like this: "A miracle is an event E that (1) is brought about by God and (2) is contrary to the prediction of a law of nature that we have compelling reason to believe is true." That is, circumstances preceding E would cause anyone, based on the universally accepted laws of nature, necessarily to predict a result other than E. The believer in God can only conclude that God caused event E to occur. The skeptic, on the other hand, may accept the facts of the event while refusing to accept it as a miracle, that is, an act of God, even though he may not have another reasonable explanation.[14] Or he or she may dispute that the event occurred at all.

> *Jesus's resurrection is a miracle, and accepting it requires your allowing the possibility that God may in rare moments choose to intervene in his creation and violate his usual way of running the universe.*

Unfortunately, many of these skeptics call themselves "Christian" and are often leaders in churches and institutions that continue to claim that name, even though these individuals may refuse to accept as literally true many or most of the traditional teachings of the Christian faith, such as the trinitarian nature of

God, the substitutionary nature of Christ's atonement, his bodily resurrection, and the expectation of his literal return. This would be the case, for example, with the contributors to the previously mentioned book, *The Myth of God Incarnate*, edited in 1977 by former professor of theology at the University of Birmingham, John Hick. Gerd Lüdemann, professor of New Testament studies in the theological faculty of the University of Göttingen in Germany from 1983 to 1999, taught that the so-called reports of Jesus's resurrection were only hallucinations and fantasies.[15]

WHY WE BELIEVE
The Certainty of Belief

Now, finally, drawing on the work of the scholars mentioned at the beginning of this chapter, and others, I will attempt to outline why we can be confident that Jesus actually, literally, and bodily rose from the dead. In approaching this topic, I can't help recalling an incident from my college days. After entering Rice University in Houston, Texas, to major in electrical engineering, I became more and more hungry to better understand the Christian faith I had adopted just before leaving high school. In my sophomore year at Rice I registered for an introductory religious studies course, in which we studied the major religions of the world, ending up with a look at Christianity from a relatively liberal (Barthian or neo-orthodox) perspective. My professor, Niels C. Nielsen Jr., a graduate of Yale University, had just founded the department of religious studies the year before in 1968, and he would chair the department until his retirement. The man was an outstanding scholar, and the author of nine books by the time of his death in 2018 at the age of 97. He was also a kind and humble man as well as an interesting lecturer, who responded graciously and patiently to my fundamentalist zeal.

I had just handed out to the class copies of an article I had recently discovered, which creatively described how liberal theologians were destroying the church (John Warwick Montgomery's "Parable of the Engineers"). During class, contrary to the professor's more subjective interpretation, I declared that I believed Jesus's resurrection was a demonstrably historical event. Dr. Nielsen responded by inviting me to stand up and explain the basis for my conclusion. As I recall, I talked about the empty tomb, the disciples' transformation, the founding of the Christian movement, and the change of worship from the Jewish Sabbath to the first day of the week, Sunday, in commemoration of the day Jesus rose. When I finished, Dr. Nielsen pointed out that all I had proven was that the disciples, or at least those who wrote the New Testament and other early Christian documents, had a religious experience that led them to *believe* that Jesus had risen. Reginald Fuller, for example, a skeptical New Testament scholar, wrote concerning Jesus's resurrection that however one explains the disciples' experiences, "Within a few weeks after the crucifixion Jesus' disciples *came to believe* this is one of the indisputable facts of history," a fact "upon which both believer and unbeliever may agree."[16] So Dr. Nielsen was essentially correct, except that I am convinced there are good reasons to conclude that the disciples' experience was more than subjective, private, or mystical.

There are good reasons to conclude that the disciples' experience was more than subjective, private, or mystical.

Resurrection of Jesus Christ (Kinnaird Resurrection) by Raphael, 1502

Alternative Explanations

Presentations of the evidence for Jesus's resurrection inevitably respond to the various alternative explanations that skeptics have offered over the centuries to the resurrection accounts, since all of them are still heard today. I know of no one who has claimed Jesus was not crucified. Even skeptic John Dominic Crossan writes, "That he was crucified is as sure as anything historical can ever be."[17] However, some skeptics have claimed Jesus did not *die* on the cross, that He was not buried in a tomb, or that the tomb's location was forgotten. Some have claimed Jesus's body was stolen, either by his disciples or by someone else (see Matt 27:64; 28:13). Many have argued that we do not know what happened to Jesus's body, but that He was clearly not raised from the dead, since death is final. After hearing a debate between Antony Flew, former British philosopher of religion and noted atheist, and Christian philosopher Gary Habermas, secular philosopher Charles Hartshorne admitted his inability to "explain away the evidences to which Habermas appeals." Nevertheless, he said, "[M]y metaphysical bias is against resurrections."[18]

> *"[M]y metaphysical bias is against resurrections."*

Many skeptics of Jesus's bodily resurrection have continued using traditional Christian language about Jesus being raised by claiming that Jesus's followers eventually came to believe he had ascended and was alive in heaven, and they began speaking of this in terms of his having "risen." Stories of his body having been seen were either based on hallucination or just rumors and legends, some propose. Liberal theologian Gordon Kaufman, who taught for 30 years at Harvard Divinity School, interpreted Jesus's resurrection as simply meaning that "God's act begun in Jesus still continues."[19] The proponents of these alternative views are often highly intelligent and competent historians, philosophers, and even theologians, and they should not be carelessly dismissed. However, their conclusions often appear highly unlikely, and the sheer variety of them may render them suspect, besides the fact that accepting the biblical accounts is so much simpler. In some cases, like Hartshorne, they offer no alternative view of the evidence at all.

Testimony of the Apostle Paul

Our earliest written account that something unusual happened after Jesus's crucifixion is in the ancient letter the apostle Paul wrote in about AD 50 to the church in the Greek city of Thessalonica on the Aegean Sea. In it he praises their spreading of the gospel throughout the Greek world and how they were testifying about their own conversion from idols "to serve the living and true God" and how they were living in anticipation of the return of God's Son "whom he raised from the dead" (1 Thess 1:6–10). As New Testament scholar Paul Barnett notes, Paul is not arguing the point of resurrection here. He is simply mentioning in passing their common belief in something long held to be true.[20]

Paul wrote more about what happened to Jesus in his letter to the church in the southern Greek city of Corinth in about AD 54/55.[21] The gospel he had preached to them, he says, included the following facts:

> I passed on to you as most important what I also received: that Christ died for our sins according to the Scriptures, that he was buried, that he was raised on the third day according to the Scriptures, and that he appeared to Cephas, then to the Twelve. Then he appeared to over five hundred brothers and sisters at one time; most of them are still alive, but some have fallen asleep. Then he appeared to James, then to all the apostles. Last of all, as to one born at the wrong time, he also appeared to me. (1 Cor 15:3–8)

Paul must have encountered these facts about Jesus's resurrection in the early to mid-30s, just after his conversion. He not only believed them but based the rest of his life on them, resulting in his execution in about AD 65, probably by beheading. As New Testament scholar Ben Witherington explains, "Without question, the period A.D. 63–68 was one of the most turbulent in early Christian history. Christianity endured the loss not only of two of its greatest missionaries and apostles, Peter and Paul, but also of many others tortured and killed in the Neronian crackdown."[22]

Paul must have encountered these facts about Jesus's resurrection in the early to mid-30s, just after his conversion. He not only believed them but based the rest of his life on them, resulting in his execution in about AD 65, probably by beheading.

Paul already knew about Jesus's crucifixion, of course, before his conversion, as well as the claims that Jesus was alive again. That, in fact, is why he was hunting down Christians. Paul then would have learned the details of Jesus's last days on earth from Christians in Damascus and Jerusalem just a few short years after the events happened (Acts 9:17–18; Gal 1:18).[23] Jesus is believed to have died in either AD 30 or 33.[24] So, by the time Paul wrote to the Corinthians he had had plenty of time and opportunity to verify the facts with many eyewitnesses. Against the imagined "mass hallucination" theory is the evidence from Paul and others that "multiple people, individually and in groups, saw Jesus in diverse locations, in distinct contexts, and when they were in different frames of mind."[25]

"Multiple people, individually and in groups, saw Jesus in diverse locations, in distinct contexts, and when they were in different frames of mind."

Paul's account in Corinthians calls attention to several facts critical for our purposes. The first is the reference to Jesus's literal body and the allusion to the empty tomb: Jesus really "died" and was "buried," though His body was apparently no longer available, since he "was raised." These were the critical facts for Paul, substantiated by Jesus's many appearances. Next, Jesus's *transformed* (not just resuscitated) body (1 Cor 15:42–44, 50–53) was seen *by hundreds* of people, who testified to having seen Jesus alive after His death, and many of these were still alive for questioning. Paul himself also could testify to having seen the risen Jesus just as Peter (Cephas) and the others had seen Him, and he was the last person to have done so (see the accounts in Acts 9:1–9; 22:6–16; 26:12–18). This last bit of information is especially important because it points to the fact that Jesus's appearances evidently ceased, which we would not expect to be the case if the witnesses were only talking about subjective visionary experiences.

Jesus's appearances evidently ceased, which we would not expect to be the case if the witnesses were only talking about subjective visionary experiences.

One more item of interest is Paul's reference to Jesus's appearance to his half-brother James, who, although an unbeliever up to the time of Jesus's death (Mark 3:21, 31; 6:3–4; John 7:5), was converted afterward and became a leader in the Jerusalem church (Acts 12:17; 15:12–21; Gal 1:19) until his own martyrdom.[26] Some skeptics have claimed that the resurrection accounts were invented to support the authority of church leaders. N. T. Wright asks, if that were the case, why is there no story of Jesus appearing to James?[27] The reference here in Paul's letter is the only thing we have to explain James's conversion before his sudden appearance as a believer in Acts. Without Paul's notation here, we'd have nothing.

Portrait of Wittgenstein on being awarded a scholarship from Trinity College, Cambridge, 1929

Karl Popper in the 1980s

Conflicting Testimonies in the Gospels?

Besides the philosophical issue regarding miracles, the biggest obstacle, perhaps, to accepting the biblical accounts found mainly in the Gospels of Matthew, Mark, Luke, and John (but also in Acts and the apostle Paul's writings), is their variation in detail. We must ask ourselves, however, if we had only one account, would the gospel narrative be any easier to accept? Or if the different accounts were exactly the same, would they be more believable? There would be serious doubts in either of those cases. Thus, we would be wise to consider contemporary situations in which several independent eyewitnesses to an event report to us what happened.[28]

> *We must ask ourselves, however, if we had only one account, would the gospel narrative be any easier to accept? Or if the different accounts were exactly the same, would they be more believable?*

    N. T. Wright offers an entertaining and enlightening example. An argument between two of the most famous twentieth-century philosophers occurred in a room at Cambridge University on Friday, October 25, 1946.[29] The philosophers were Ludwig Wittgenstein and Karl Popper. As a group of academics, including other philosophers, all sat around a fireplace, Popper delivered a paper critical of Wittgenstein. The famous philosopher Bertrand Russell served as moderator. Evidently Wittgenstein interrupted Popper, a heated argument ensued, and Wittgenstein grabbed a poker from the fireplace and waved it around, then he left. Some of the academics are still living and remember the event well—"or so they say." After the explosive exchange, as Wright says, "When those present compared notes, they could not quite agree on what exactly had happened." Was the poker red-hot or cool? Did he just wave it around, or threaten Popper with it? Did he slam the door when he left or leave quietly? Did Popper state the moral principle "not to threaten visiting speakers with pokers" before or after Wittgenstein left? The point (pun intended) is that . . .

> everybody disagrees on the precise details. But nobody doubts that the meeting took place. Nobody doubts that Wittgenstein and Popper were the two main adversaries, with Russell as a kind of senior umpire. Nobody doubts that Wittgenstein did at least wave a poker around and that he left quite abruptly. . . . It is a commonplace among lawyers that eyewitnesses disagree but that this doesn't mean nothing happened.[30]

Wright and others make the point persuasively that the various accounts of events in Matthew, Mark, Luke, John, Acts, and Paul's writings overlap enough and yet differ enough to indicate they are all reacting independently to the same shocking events. Theirs are not "tales artfully told by people eager to sustain a fiction and therefore anxious to make everything look right." Rather, they are "the hurried, puzzled accounts of those who have seen with their own eyes something which took them horribly by surprise and with which they have not yet fully come to terms."[31]

Christian philosopher Stephen Davis points out that "few of the discrepancies among the Gospel accounts of the empty tomb present serious problems; plausible harmonizations . . . can be suggested without great difficulty." He does admit, however, that "some of the discrepancies are difficult if not impossible sensibly to harmonize—such as the location of the stone when the women arrived . . . and the reaction of the women."[32] Davis then summarizes the essential facts on which the accounts agree:

"Few of the discrepancies among the Gospel accounts of the empty tomb present serious problems; plausible harmonizations . . . can be suggested without great difficulty."

> All unite in proclaiming that *early on the first day of the week certain women, among them Mary Magdalene, went to the tomb; they found it empty; they met an angel or angels; and they were either told or else discovered* (Mary Magdalene in the fourth Gospel) *that Jesus was alive.* There is also striking agreement between John and at least one of the Synoptics [Matthew, Mark, and Luke] on each of these points: *the women* [at least Mary] *informed Peter and/or other disciples of their discovery, Peter went to the tomb and found it empty, the risen Jesus appeared to the women, and he gave them instructions for the disciples.*[33]

We might add that the accounts agree on Jesus rising on the third day after His crucifixion, that the obstacle of the stone was moved for the women, and Luke and John agree that Peter and another disciple went to the tomb to check on the women's story.

An interesting case of an apparent discrepancy is described by Wright. According to Luke 24:12, when Peter ran to the tomb and "stooped to look in, he saw only the linen cloths. So he went away, amazed at what had happened." Luke mentions no other disciple with him. However, just a few verses later in verse 24 he records the words of the Emmaus Road disciples to Jesus: "Some of those who were with us went to the tomb and found it just as the women had said, but they didn't see him." So, although Luke clearly knew that two disciples ran to the tomb, in verse 12 he chose to focus only on Peter. Wright comments: "Luke is quite capable of highlighting one person when he knows, and tells us later, that more than one was involved. . . . If Luke can say that there was one person, and then later that there was more than one, the numerical differences between the different accounts of the women and the angels cannot be regarded as serious historical problems."[34] This principle must also be remembered when comparing Luke's/Paul's three accounts of Paul's conversion in Acts (9:1–9; 22:6–16; 26:12–18).

The question of where Jesus met with His disciples is another issue to be wrestled with, but again the discrepancy may be more apparent than real. Mark 16:7 only refers to a proposed meeting of Jesus with His disciples in Galilee. Matthew recounts only a meeting with the men in Galilee (28:16–20), though Jesus appears to the women in Jerusalem (28:7–10). Luke only has meetings in Jerusalem, with no mention of Galilee (Luke 24:13–49). Finally, John has meetings with Jesus in Jerusalem (John 20:14–29) then Galilee (21:1–23). Looking more closely at Mark 16:7, we find an angel telling the women to take a message to the disciples "and Peter," instructing them to meet Him in Galilee, "just as he told [them]." This was to remind the disciples of the account in Mark 14:27–31. There Jesus predicted at the Last Supper that they would "fall away" when he, their "shepherd," was stricken. "But after I have risen," He said, "I will go ahead of you to Galilee." Then came Peter's foolish denial that he would fall—thus the angel's words, "and Peter." Neither Mark nor Matthew denies that Jesus met with the disciples as described in Luke and John. They do not even record the women's carrying the message. Most scholars consider that Mark ended his account with verse 8 of chapter 16: "They went out and ran from the tomb, because trembling and astonishment overwhelmed them. And they said nothing to anyone, since they were afraid." Nevertheless, we know from Luke and John that the women did eventually overcome their fear and report to the disciples, who refused to believe such "nonsense" (Luke 24:11)—until the accounts were confirmed by others and eventually by the appearance of Jesus himself.

The Last Supper

Are the Gospel Accounts Late Inventions?

Do the varying reports make it difficult for us to piece together a precise chronology of the events surrounding Jesus's resurrection appearances? Most definitely. Can the events described in the various Gospels be plausibly put together into a harmonious narrative? Yes. In his book *Easter Enigma,* New Testament scholar John Wenham does a credible job, though other scholars differ on the understanding of some details.[35] But one thing we cannot say is that the Gospel narratives are just late inventions or even reports that have been distorted and corrupted by multiple retellings. Even critic Gerd Lüdemann demonstrates that belief in Jesus's bodily resurrection arose within a year or two of His death,[36] Actually, evidence from the apostle Paul and others would shorten this to a few weeks. Yes, the Gospel accounts were written a few decades after Jesus's death, but the three primary reporters of the resurrection—Matthew, Luke, and John—can be demonstrated to be have cataloged "very early oral tradition, representing three different ways in which the original astonished participants told the stories."[37] By "oral tradition" I include the recorded reports of eyewitnesses and of those who consulted eyewitnesses. And according to Luke, Jesus's disciples were not only eyewitnesses, but teachers in the early church, "servants of the word," who "handed . . . down to us" the events they themselves had witnessed (Luke 1:1–2).[38] As New Testament scholar Richard Bauckham demonstrates, "The traditions were originated and formulated by named eyewitnesses, in whose name they were transmitted and who remained the living and active guarantors of the traditions."[39]

> Can the events described in the various Gospels be plausibly put together into a harmonious narrative? Yes.

> Gospel accounts were written a few decades after Jesus's death, but the three primary reporters of the resurrection—Matthew, Luke, and John—can be demonstrated to be have cataloged "very early oral tradition, representing three different ways in which the original astonished participants told the stories.

We also have no evidence for the common assumption that the Gospels were first circulated without their authors' names, which are given in all the earliest manuscripts.[40] Mark was probably written first, in the late 50s to mid-60s. But the evidence is strong (mainly from Papias, the early second-century bishop of Hierapolis[41]) that the author was John Mark, a Jewish Christian and relative of Barnabas, who was an eyewitness to some extent, though his primary eyewitness source was almost certainly Peter, supplemented by others, especially some women (the two Marys and Salome).[42] Matthew's origin is highly disputed, but at least by the second century the book was unanimously attributed to Matthew the tax collector who became an apostle and eyewitness. It is often dated between 70 and 100, but many argue for the likelihood of the 60s.[43] The same is the case with the two-volume work of Luke-Acts, which does not mention an event later than AD 62. It was written by a well-educated Gentile Christian who was a companion of Paul and other apostles and evidently interviewed many eyewitnesses.[44]

Although John was probably written after the other Gospels, evidence is strong that it was written by "one of his disciples," whom "Jesus loved" (John 13:23), a man who "testifies to these things and who wrote them down. We know that his testimony is true" (21:24). This disciple was an eyewitness to all that he describes and tells us about in his Gospel (see 19:35). He knew Jesus personally from the very "beginning" of His ministry (cp. 15:27) and even had a close relationship with Him. John was probably the anonymous companion of Andrew in 1:35–40.[45] Jesus loved him and talked with him and told him things He wanted John to tell others.[46]

Contrary to the once popular critical view that John's Gospel was written in the late second century, a discovered fragment of John 18 dates from about AD 130.[47] Although the Gospel could have originated as early as 65, many favor a date closer to 95, with several favoring a date in the mid-80s or early 90s.[48] And contrary to the claim often heard that John's Gospel is theology rather than history, Bauckham demonstrates that, like the other Gospels, John reflects the "vital importance" Greco-Roman historiography attached to "the firsthand testimony of eyewitness participants in the events."[49]

> *John reflects the "vital importance" Greco-Roman historiography attached to "the firsthand testimony of eyewitness participants in the events.*

Aroma of Authenticity

For anyone willing to look beyond the critics' sensationalist literature and examine the evidence, many books have been written demonstrating the historical reliability of the New Testament as a whole and of the Gospels in particular.[50] New Testament scholar Craig Blomberg's assessment is typical of these. He writes,

> No other examples from antiquity have been preserved of this abundance of information from multiple authors in writings so close to the people and events being described. To reject *a priori* the New Testament Gospels as potential sources of excellent historical information about Jesus of Nazareth is to impose a bias on the study of history, which, if consistently applied elsewhere, would leave us completely agnostic about anything or anyone in the ancient world![51]

Besides the variation found in the resurrection accounts, several facts point to their early origin and aroma of authenticity. N. T. Wright, for example, points out that the accounts contain no flourish of fulfilled prophecies, assurances of Christian hope based on the resurrection, and no sightings of Jesus "in blinding light or dazzling radiance, or wreathed in clouds, that one might expect to find in the Jewish apocalyptic tradition."[52] The stories are told with a surprisingly naïve simplicity. Wright's conclusion is, "Nobody inventing stories after twenty years, let alone thirty or forty, would have done it like that."[53]

> *The stories are told with a surprisingly naïve simplicity. Wright's conclusion is, "Nobody inventing stories after twenty years, let alone thirty or forty, would have done it like that."*

Another fact is their emphasis on the empty tomb. Paul, writing 20 years later to Christians in Greece does not make a point of it, but all the Gospel accounts do because it was a fact that stared in the face of anyone living in Jerusalem a few days after the crucifixion, and especially after Peter and the disciples began claiming Jesus was alive. His body, after all, had not been placed among the rocks on a Judean hillside but in the tomb of a wealthy man everyone knew—Joseph of Arimathea, a member of the Sanhedrin, mentioned in all four Gospels.[54] It was a fact to be reckoned with. Anyone who has seen the movie *The Santa Clause,* with Tim Allen, remembers the scene in which Scott Calvin is trying to wrap his brain around Santa Clause showing up and having a fatal accident at his front door. Scott keeps coming up with plausible explanations, but every time he is forced back to the undeniable fact of "reindeer on the roof." That's what he cannot get past. Jesus's empty tomb was that kind of undeniable fact. How many people must have beat a path to the tomb of Joseph of Arimathea to check out the stories of Jesus's resurrection and walked away scratching their heads repeating, "There's no body in the tomb"?

A fact that stared in the face of anyone living in Jerusalem a few days after the crucifixion, and especially after Peter and the disciples began claiming Jesus was alive.

How many people must have beat a path to the tomb of Joseph of Arimathea to check out the stories of Jesus's resurrection and walked away scratching their heads repeating, "There's no body in the tomb"?

Another fact pointing to the authenticity of the Gospel accounts, as many researchers have noted, is the essential part played by the women in each case. No one living at that time, wanting to convince people Jesus was alive again, would have made up a legend about an empty tomb discovered by women being the ones who find it. The point has been made many times, and the evidence for it is indisputable. Back then, "Women were simply not acceptable as legal witnesses." Wright adds Josephus's comment on the law of witnesses in Deuteronomy 19:15. He states, "From women let no evidence be accepted, because of the levity and temerity of their sex" (*Antiquities* 4.219).[55]

A tomb from the Second Temple Period in the area of Jerusalem. Slabs can be seen on either side of the tomb. Bodies of the deceased were laid on these slabs, prepared with spices and wraps, and allowed to decompose.

Wright also points out that in early Christian debates with unbelievers, the resurrection is scoffed at in part because of the reliance on the testimony of the women.[56] Yet every Gospel account of the resurrection includes it. The writers cannot get away from it because that is the way it happened.

CONCLUSION: THE UNAVOIDABILITY OF THE IMPROBABLE

Now to return to our initial question. Since Jesus's resurrection is essential to our safe experience of God's presence, how can we be confident that Jesus rose bodily from the dead? Is it just too hard to believe? Is it just too good to be true? Yes, resurrection is contrary to our experience and our understanding of how the world works, which would lead us to regard it as highly improbable. But there are some facts that might lead us to determine that the alternative is even more improbable. And to parody Sherlock Holmes, when you have eliminated the extremely improbable, the less improbable alternative, must be the truth.[57]

When you have eliminated the extremely improbable, the less improbable alternative, must be the truth.

I believe it was Presbyterian pastor Donald Grey Barnhouse that I was reading long ago when I ran across the statement that on the Friday when Jesus died on a Roman cross almost 2,000 years ago, there was not a living soul on earth, whether friend or foe, who believed he would ever be seen again, despite Jesus's own predictions to the contrary. When asked what things they had been talking about, the despair expressed by Cleopas and his friend was palpable: "The things concerning Jesus of Nazareth, who was a prophet powerful in action and speech before God and all the people, and how our chief priests and leaders handed him over to be sentenced to death, and they crucified him. But we were hoping that he was the one who was about to redeem Israel" (Luke 24:19–21). And this was in the face of fresh reports of "some women from [their] group" who had visited the empty tomb and had "a vision of angels who said he was alive" (24:22–23)! Yet within weeks of His death, thousands of people in Jerusalem within an easy walk of His tomb were convinced that Jesus had risen from the grave. How can that be explained?

On the Friday when Jesus died on a Roman cross almost 2,000 years ago, there was not a living soul on earth, whether friend or foe, who believed he would ever be seen again.

Another striking fact Craig Blomberg points to is the Jewish conviction based on Deuteronomy 21:23 that "anyone hung on a tree is under God's curse." The rabbis had already determined that Roman crucifixion qualified. As Blomberg puts it,

> No would-be Messiah could possibly be legitimate if crucified as a criminal by the Roman regime. How then did a group of all Jewish followers of Jesus come from earliest days onward to believe that Jesus was still the Messiah and a divine Messiah, no less? Only a supernatural return to life, like Christ's bodily resurrection, can explain that incongruity.[58]

"How then did a group of all Jewish followers of Jesus come from earliest days onward to believe that Jesus was still the Messiah and a divine Messiah, no less?"

In pondering the meaning of existence, we often hear the profound question, "Why is there something rather than nothing?" A similar question applies in our case. Why does the Christian movement, the Christian faith, the church, exist at all? Blomberg observes that the first

Why does the Christian movement, the Christian faith, the church, exist at all?

century saw many revolutionary "bandits, prophets and messiahs" whose movements were violently obliterated by Roman might. In a few cases, a survivor would recover the flag for a while and press on as the new messianic leader. However, he notes, "There is no evidence from any ancient source that one of Jesus's followers was ever treated as the new Messiah, and yet his movement was not squelched." Rather, it thrived in the shadow of and even under the banner of the cross. The movement was led not by new messiahs but by "slaves of Christ," who no longer hid behind locked doors but preached the resurrection of Christ and salvation in His name in the city streets, the Jerusalem temple, the synagogues, and the halls of political power. To those who had the power to take their lives, they declared, "Whether it's right in the sight of God for us to listen to you rather than to God, you decide; for we are unable to stop speaking about what we have seen and heard" (Acts 4:19–20). As Blomberg says, "Only a miracle as dramatic as a resurrection" could account for the continued existence and flourishing of the Christian faith for these 2,000 years.[59]

"Whether it's right in the sight of God for us to listen to you rather than to God, you decide; for we are unable to stop speaking about what we have seen and heard."

"Only a miracle as dramatic as a resurrection" could account for the continued existence and flourishing of the Christian faith for these 2,000 years."

Many other points could be made here and have been made by others. But an effective conclusion to our investigation of the foundation of our faith in the resurrection of Christ would be these words from N. T. Wright.

The empty tomb and the "meetings" with Jesus, when combined, present us with not only a *sufficient* condition for the rise of early Christian belief, but also, it seems, a *necessary* one. . . . The early Christians did not invent the empty tomb and the "meetings" or "sightings" of the risen Jesus in order to explain a faith they already had. They developed that faith because of the occurrence, and convergence, of these two phenomena. Nobody was expecting this kind of thing; no kind of conversion-experience would have generated such ideas; nobody would have invented it, no matter how guilty (or how forgiven) they felt, no matter

"The early Christians did not invent the empty tomb and the "meetings" or "sightings" of the risen Jesus in order to explain a faith they already had."

how many hours they pored over the scriptures. To suggest otherwise is to stop doing history and to enter into a fantasy world of our own. . . . In terms of the kind of proof which historians normally accept, the case we have presented that the tomb-plus-appearances combination is what generated early Christian belief, is as watertight as one is likely to find.[60]

NOTES

1. Among my favorites are Daniel P. Fuller, *Easter Faith and History* (Grand Rapids: Eerdmans, 1965); William L. Craig, *Knowing the Truth about the Resurrection: Our Response to the Empty Tomb* (Ann Arbor, MI: Servant, 1988); Stephen T. Davis, *Risen Indeed: Making Sense of the Resurrection* (Grand Rapids: Eerdmans, 1993); John Wenham, *Easter Enigma: Do the Resurrection Accounts Contradict One Another?* 2nd ed. (Grand Rapids: Baker, 1993); Paul Copan, ed., *Will the Real Jesus Please Stand Up? A Debate between William Lane Craig and John Dominic Crossan* (Grand Rapids: Baker, 1998); N. T. Wright, *The Resurrection of the Son of God* (Minneapolis: Fortress, 2003); Gary R. Habermas and Michael R. Licona, *The Case for the Resurrection of Jesus* (Grand Rapids: Kregel, 2004); Michael R. Licona, *The Resurrection of Jesus: A New Historiographical Approach* (Downers Grove, IL: InterVarsity Press, 2010); Craig A. Evans, *Jesus and the Remains of His Day: Studies in Jesus and the Evidence of Material Culture* (Peabody, MA: Hendrickson, 2015).

2. Lewis Carroll, *The Adventures of Alice in Wonderland,* chap. 1.

3. Lewis Carroll, *Through the Looking Glass,* chap 5.

4. Annie Dillard, *An American Childhood* (New York: HarperCollins, 1987), 169, 173.

5. Dillard, *An American Childhood,* 170.

6. Dillard, *An American Childhood,* 172.

7. Frances Young, "Two Roots or a Tangled Mass?" in *The Myth of God Incarnate,* ed. John Hick (Philadelphia: Westminster, 1977), 31.

8. J. Lust, E. Eynikel, and K. Hauspie with the collaboration of G. Chamberlain, *A Greek-English Lexicon of the Septuagint*, Second Edition (Stuttgart: Deutsche Bibelgesellschaft, 2003).

9. Joel B. Green, *The Gospel of Luke,* New International Commentary on the New Testament (Grand Rapids: Eerdmans, 1997), 63, 66.

10. See Paul R. Williamson, *Death and the Afterlife: Biblical Perspectives on Ultimate Questions,* New Studies in Biblical Theology (Downers Grove, IL: InterVarsity, 2018), 7–21.

11. Wright, *The Resurrection of the Son of God,* 551. The only exceptions were those forms of Christianity, especially at Nag Hammadi, that were heavily influenced by Gnosticism (see pp. 534–51).

12. See Davis, *Risen Indeed,* vi–xii.

13. See 1 Sam 10:9; 1 Kgs 18:37; 2 Chr 36:22/Ezra 1:1; Prov 21:1; Isa 29:18; 35:5; 42:6–7; Jer 32:40; Mal 4:6; Luke 24:45; Acts 16:14.

14. Davis, *Risen Indeed,* 10–12.

15. See Gerd Lüdemann, *The Resurrection of Jesus: History, Experience, Theology* (trans. John Bowden; London: SCM, 1994), 82–84, 95–100, 176–77.

16. Emphasis added. Reginald H. Fuller, *The Foundations of New Testament Christology* (New York: Scribner's, 1965), 142. Also see James D. G. Dunn, *The Evidence for Jesus* (Louisville: Westminster, 1985), 75.

17. John Dominic Crossan, *Jesus: A Revolutionary Biography* (San Francisco: HarperCollins, 1991), 145.

18. See Gary Habermas and Antony Flew, *Did Jesus Rise from the Dead?* Terry L. Miethe, ed. (San Francisco: Harper & Row, 1987), 142.

19. Gordon D. Kaufman, *Systematic Theology: A Historicist Perspective* (New York: Scribner's, 1968), 430.

[20] Paul Barnett, *Jesus and the Rise of Early Christianity: A History of New Testament Times* (Downers Grove, IL: InterVarsity, 1999), 181.

[21] On the date of 1 Corinthians, see Anthony C. Thiselton, *The First Epistle to the Corinthians,* New International Greek Testament Commentary (Grand Rapids: Eerdmans, 2000), 29–32.

[22] Ben Witherington III, *New Testament History: A Narrative Account* (Grand Rapids: Baker, 2001), 353–55 (esp. p. 355).

[23] See Barnett, *Jesus and the Rise of Early Christianity,* 182.

[24] See H. W. Hoehner and J. K. Brown, "Chronology," in *Dictionary of Jesus and the Gospels,* 2nd ed., ed. Joel B. Green, Jeannine K. Brown, and Nicholas Perrin (Downers Grove, IL: InterVarsity, 2013), 137–38.

[25] Craig L. Blomberg, *The Historical Reliability of the New Testament: Countering the Challenges to Evangelical Christian Beliefs* (Nashville: B&H, 2016), 698.

[26] On James, see Gary R. Habermas and Michael R. Licona, *The Case for the Resurrection of Jesus* (Grand Rapids: Kregel, 2004), 67–69.

[27] Wright, *The Resurrection of the Son of God,* 610.

[28] As Davis notes, secular historian Michael Grant (*Jesus: An Historian's Review of the Gospels* [New York: Scribner's, 1977], 176, 200) argues that "discrepancies in secondary details do not affect the historical core of a narrative" (*Risen Indeed,* 70).

[29] N. T. Wright, *Surprised by Hope: Rethinking Heaven, the Resurrection, and the Mission of the Church* (New York: HarperOne, 2008), 31–32.

[30] Wright, *Surprised by Hope,* 32–33.

[31] Wright, *The Resurrection of the Son of God,* 612.

[32] Davis, *Risen Indeed,* 69. Also see p. 53.

[33] Davis, *Risen Indeed,* 69. Emphasis original.

[34] Wright, *The Resurrection of the Son of God,* 613. He also cites Josephus's different accounts of events he was involved in.

[35] See the book's full citation in n. 1 of this chapter. Also, see Craig Blomberg's assessment in *The Historical Reliability of the New Testament,* 704–5.

[36] Gerd Lüdemann with Alf Özen, *What Really Happened to Jesus: A Historical Approach to the Resurrection* (Louisville: WJK, 1995), 9–16. He goes on to argue, however, that Jesus's appearances were only visionary (pp. 82–130).

[37] Wright, *The Resurrection of the Son of God,* 611.

[38] See Richard Bauckham, *Jesus and the Eyewitnesses: The Gospels as Eyewitness Testimony* 2nd ed. (Grand Rapids: Eerdmans, 2017), 12–38, esp. 37–38.

[39] Bauckham, *Jesus and the Eyewitnesses,* 290.

[40] See Bauckham, *Jesus and the Eyewitnesses,* 536–38.

[41] Hieropolis was a city near Laodicea and Colossae and an important crossroad connecting Palestine with the major Jewish and Christian settlements in Asia Minor. It was an ideal location to encounter early Christian leaders, including early students of the apostles. See Bauckham, *Jesus and the Eyewitnesses,* 12–21.

[42] See D. A. Carson, Douglas J. Moo, and Leon Morris, *An Introduction to the New Testament* (Grand Rapids: Zondervan, 1992), 99; Bauckham, *Jesus and the Eyewitnesses,* 124–27, 202–39, 520–24, 535, 538–42.

[43] See Carson, et al., *An Introduction to the New Testament,* 79.

[44] See Carson, et al., *An Introduction to the New Testament,* 113–18.

[45] See Richard Bauckham, *Gospel of Glory: Major Themes in Johannine Theology* (Grand Rapids: Baker, 2015), 151–52.

46 See E. Ray Clendenen, *Jesus's Opening Week: A Deep Exegesis of John 1:1–2:11* (Eugene, OR: Wipf & Stock, 2019), 8–10. See also Blomberg, *The Historical Reliability of the New Testament*, 153–60.

47 Carson, et al., *An Introduction to the New Testament*, 172.

48 See Andreas J. Köstenberger, *A Theology of John's Gospel and Letters* (Grand Rapids: Zondervan, 2009), 82; Carson, et al., *An Introduction to the New Testament*, 166–68.

49 Richard Bauckham, *The Testimony of the Beloved Disciple: Narrative, History, and Theology in the Gospel of John* (Grand Rapids: Baker, 2007), 105–6.

50 Craig L. Blomberg has devoted considerable expertise to this issue, writing *The Historical Reliability of the Gospels*, 2nd ed. (Downers Grove, IL: InterVarsity, 2007); *The Historical Reliability of John's Gospel: Issues and Commentary* (Downers Grove, IL: InterVarsity, 2001); and *The Historical Reliability of the New Testament*. See also Mark D. Roberts, *Can We Trust the Gospels: Investigating the Reliability of Matthew, Mark, Luke, and John* (Wheaton: Crossway, 2007); Paul R. Eddy and Greg A. Boyd, *The Jesus Legend: A Case for the Historical Reliability of the Synoptic Tradition* (Grand Rapids: Baker, 2007); James H. Charlesworth and Petr Pokorný, eds., *Jesus Research*, 2 vols. (Grand Rapids: Eerdmans, 2009–2014); Craig S. Keener, *Christobiography: Memory, History, and the Reliability of the Gospels* (Grand Rapids: Eerdmans, 2019).

51 Blomberg, *The Historical Reliability of the New Testament*, 18–19.

52 Wright, *The Resurrection of the Son of God*, 599–607 (esp. p. 604).

53 Wright, *The Resurrection of the Son of God*, 610.

54 See Robert H. Stein, "Was the Tomb Really Empty?" *Themelios* 5 (September, 1979), 11.

55 Wright, *The Resurrection of the Son of God*, 607.

56 Wright, *The Resurrection of the Son of God*, 608.

57 For the original, see Arthur Conan Doyle, *The Sign of the Four* (1890; repr., New York: Oxford University Press, 1993), 41.

58 Blomberg, *The Historical Reliability of the New Testament*, 707.

59 Blomberg, *The Historical Reliability of the New Testament*, 708.

60 Wright, *The Resurrection of the Son of God*, 706–7.

CHAPTER 9

WHO AM I?

We have identified our transportation to the afterlife—the only way, in fact, to get there. In the next chapter, we will deal with the question of whether our flight will be nonstop or will have a layover in what is often called "the intermediate state." But to decide that question, we must first have a clearer picture of who is going to be making the trip. "Have your driver's license or passport ready!"

Traveling is a hassle. The farther you go and the longer you plan to stay, the greater the hassle. So many things to think about and plan for. Transportation and accommodations are major hurdles. But whether reserving an airplane seat, a rental car, or a room in a hotel, vacation rental, or long-term accommodations, the people you deal with will need to know exactly who you are. You will need a credit card with a CVV code on the back for security, a government-issued picture ID, a driver's license, passport, and visa (granting you permission to enter, leave, or stay in a country for a specified period). Passports must contain your photo, name, date of birth, gender, and physical characteristics. You clearly must know who you are, and you need to prove it.

Thankfully, we do not need any of that to get into heaven. God's grace through Christ is enough. And he already knows who we are. But who is that, exactly? What is a human being or person? How does the Bible describe or speak of someone who is born, lives, dies, is raised from the dead, and is in relationship with other persons and with God? Who or what is the person who will spend eternity with God? Are we essentially spirit/soul, with an expendable body we can leave behind? Or is our body a necessary part of who we are? The answers to these questions will largely determine whether our flight to the afterlife will have a layover or be nonstop.

HOW THE BIBLE DESCRIBES US

The Bible says that I am 'adam ("human"), either "man" ('ish) or "woman" ('ishah), that is, "male" or "female" (Gen 1:26–27; 2:23). I am also "a living being" (nephesh chayyah, Gen 2:7), who is God's "image/likeness" (Gen 1:26–27; 9:6; 1 Cor 11:7).

Older, traditional thought confined the meaning of "image of God" to the inner, immaterial life of mind, emotions, and will. We now commonly understand "image" to refer to a person holistically as a psychosomatic unity intended to "mirror God and to represent God."[1] It describes not just what we are but what we do. The word "likeness" keeps us from thinking that we are *just like* God, however. We are a likeness-image. Apart from Jesus, God has no body but "is spirit" (John 4:24), without "flesh and bones" (Luke 24:39). Moses remind-

We now commonly understand "image" to refer to a person holistically as a psychosomatic unity intended to "mirror God and to represent God.

ed Israel that when they heard God's voice "out of the fire" at Horeb (Sinai), "[they] did not see any form" (Deut 4:15). As Old Testament scholar Gordon McConville explains, this was not because God was only in the heights of heaven and not actually present with them. The pervasive phrase "before the Lord" indicates otherwise (Gen 18:22 and about 200 times elsewhere in the Bible). The reason Israel saw no divine form at Sinai was not because He was not really there. God is "near" to us "whenever we call to him" (Deut 4:7), but He is invisible (Col 1:15; 1 Tim 1:17; 6:16); and "invisibility does not mean absence,"[2] as any observer of a hurricane or tornado can attest. As Christina Rossetti expressed it,

> Who has seen the wind?
> Neither you nor I:
> But when the trees bow down their heads,
> The wind is passing by.[3]

The nighttime "invisible" devastations of a tornado or hurricane are always seen the next morning.

Do our bodies, then, play no part in our being God's image? The many references in the Bible to God's face, eyes, ears, mouth, hands, and even nostrils (see, for example, Exod 15:8; 2 Sam 22:9, 16; Job 4:9), though apparently metaphorical, nevertheless show that a connection exists between our bodies and the nature of God. Our being God's image may not be confined to the inner self. Although God is spirit and not body, "our human structure faithfully and adequately shows" that God sees our needs, hears our cries, and can act mercifully on our behalf.[4] God's gift of our bodies enables us to encounter and deal with our world, as He can more perfectly do without one. So our physical characteristics do reflect God in certain ways. That concept prepares us for the idea that one's "real self" is an embodied self (see the section below, "Is Any Body There?").[5]

The Bible also designates or describes me in terms of physical organs that represent visible or invisible aspects of who I am. For instance, I am "flesh and bones" (soft + hard tissue = body; Job 2:5; Prov 14:30), and I am "flesh," like "wind that passes and does not return" (Ps 78:39), as well as "flesh and blood" (Matt 16:17; Heb 2:14). I am also "heart and flesh" (inner and outer being, together called "I") that "cry out for the living God" (Ps 84:2; see Pss 16:9; 73:26; Prov 14:30; Eccl 11:10; Ezek 44:7).

The terms for "soul" (Hb. *nephesh*; Gk. *psuchē*) and "spirit" (Hb. *ruach*; Gk. *pneuma*) will be examined later. But they often designate a non-physical and, therefore, invisible aspect of life distinguished from the outer, visible aspects. I can be described as having a "willing" spirit and "weak" flesh (Matt 26:41). I am "soul and body" (Matt 10:28); I am body and spirit (1 Cor 5:3; 7:34; Col 2:5; Jas 2:26); and I am "spirit, soul, and body" (1 Thess 5:23). The pairing of "heart and soul" in the Bible (as in the immensely popular 1938 Hoagy Carmichael/ Frank Loesser song) often represents my inner life of thoughts, emotions, and intentions (Deut 4:29; 6:5; 10:12; 11:13; 13:3; 26:16; 30:2, 6, 10; Josh 22:5; 23:14; 2 Chr 15:12; 34:31; Acts 4:32). The pairing of heart and spirit may also describe my inner life (Pss 51:10, 17; 77:6; 78:8; 143:4; Prov 15:13; 17:22; Eccl 7:9; Isa 57:15; 65:14; Ezek 18:31; 21:7; 36:26; Dan 5:20; 1 Pet 3:4), as well as the combination of soul, spirit, and heart (Heb 4:12) or heart, soul, and mind (Matt 22:37/Mark 12:30/Luke 10:27). The latter trio of passages, however, reflect God's command in Deuteronomy 6:5 to love him with "all [one's] heart, with all [one's] soul, and with all [one's] strength." As we will see, this probably involves more than just the inner self.

Another Hebrew term the Bible uses for the seat of human emotions is *kelayot*, always plural, meaning "kidneys." It is translated "inward parts" in Psalm 139:13. God is said to examine or test the "kidneys and heart" (Ps 26:2; Jer 11:20; 17:10; 20:12; CSB "heart and mind"). Hebrew "hearts and kidneys" is appropriately rendered "thoughts and emotions" in Psalm 7:9. The son whose heart is wise causes his father's heart to rejoice and his kidneys ("innermost being") to celebrate (Prov 23:15–16). Jeremiah accuses Israel of having God "ever on their lips, / but far from their kidneys [CSB, "conscience"]" in 12:2. In Psalm 16:7 my "thoughts" that trouble me at night are literally "my kidneys" (though this is not a reference to frequent urination). The man in Psalm 73 who is bitter because of the unpunished wicked describes himself as "wounded" in his kidneys (his "innermost being"). Job spoke of God as piercing his "kidneys without mercy" (16:13; also Lam 3:13), and yet "[Job's] kidneys ["heart"] long[ed] within [him]" for God (Job 19:27).

So, such terms as "kidneys" (KJV "reins") and even "liver" (CSB "heart"; Lam 2:11) often designated the seat of our emotions, attitudes, and desires. Since today's world does not think of kidneys and livers as radiating emotion, our modern Bibles usually follow custom and use "heart."

On the other hand, we do speak of butterflies in the stomach, of our stomachs being in knots, and of gut feelings. The Hebrew word *qereb* could refer to the intestines or insides/interior of a person or animal. Since strong or persistent emotions such as anxiety can even cause physical problems in our bowels, the use of *qereb* for human thoughts or emotions should not surprise us. Sarah, for example, is described as laughing inwardly or literally "in her insides" (Gen 18:12; CSB "to herself"). A liar "speaks peaceably with his friend, / but *inwardly* he sets up an ambush" (Jer 9:8, emphasis added). *Splanchnon,* a Greek word for the inner organs, is used in Acts 1:18 of Judas's "intestines" that "spilled out." Otherwise, the noun designates the seat of feelings of compassion or affection (CSB "heart" but KJV "bowels"; Phlm 7, 12, 20) or, more often, the emotion itself (Luke 1:78; Phil 2:1; Col 3:12; KJV "bowels"). The related verb (*splanchnizomai*), found only in the Gospels, usually describes Jesus being moved with compassion (Matt 9:36; 14:14; 15:32; 20:34; Luke 7:13). The exceptions are when it describes the compassion of the Samaritan for the beaten man (Luke 10:33) and the father for his repentant, returning son (15:20).

The Bible uses so many terms for the various aspects and dimensions of a person that we should be awed by humanity's complexity! Drawing clear distinctions between these terms and concepts is often impossible. A term for one part may be singled out that refers to the whole person (a figure called *synecdoche*), such as when David speaks of God creating his "kidneys" in Psalm 139:13 and his "bones" (or skeletal structure) in 139:15. And terms often overlap in meaning, as when emotions are connected to the heart, the spirit, the soul, and the kidneys or intestines. Nevertheless, one observation we can make about the various terms used for a person is that they often reflect the dual aspects of outer, visible life and inner, invisible life.

> *The Bible uses so many terms for the various aspects and dimensions of a person that we should be awed by humanity's complexity.*

Even though individual passages such as Genesis 2:7 or 1 Thessalonians 5:23 may sound like a recipe for the components of a human being (dust + God's breath = living being; or spirit + soul + body = person), the multiplication of terms elsewhere introduces hopeless confusion. The Bible is clearly not a textbook on physiology or psychology.[6] It is more like a doxological anthem on the greatness of God and his works. As David concludes when he honestly faces the complex and overpowering wonder that is God, we must also declare when faced with the complexity and wonder of his human creation, "This wondrous knowledge is beyond me. / It is lofty; I am unable to reach it" (Ps 139:6). As David further tries to imagine God's weaving of him (his "inward parts" or "kidneys") into an amazing human tapestry in his "mother's womb" (literally "belly"), he declares, "I will praise you / because I have been remarkably and wondrously made. / Your works are wondrous, / and I know this very well" (vv. 13–14).

The Bible is clearly not a textbook on physiology or psychology.

"I will praise you / because I have been remarkably and wondrously made. / Your works are wondrous, / and I know this very well."

Although the many biblical terms applied to persons in whole or in part are meaningful and useful in understanding our nature and identifying our many aspects, they do not clearly distinguish or define our individually separate and distinct *parts*. Theologian John Cooper, whose view of personhood may be called "dualistic holism," explains: "There are no texts in which soul or spirit or person must be interpreted as an immaterial substance which functions independent of the body. No uses of organic, bodily terminology suggest that bodily functions are purely biological, much less independent of soul functions."[7] And, as in the making of authentic Texas chili, with its blend of many different spices and flavors, the whole is greater than the sum of its parts.

NOT A SOUL

Merriam-Webster gives eight definitions of the English word *soul*: (1) "the immaterial essence, animating principle, or actuating cause of an individual life"; (2) "the spiritual principle embodied in human beings, all rational and spiritual beings, or the universe"; (3) "a person's total self"; (4) "an active or essential part"; (5) "the moral and emotional nature of human beings" or "the quality that arouses emotion and sentiment"; (6) "a person," as in "not a *soul* in sight"; (7) a "personification," as in "she is the *soul* of integrity"; (8) "a strong positive feeling (as of intense sensitivity and emotional fervor) conveyed especially by African American performers," as in "soul music," "soul food," or "soul sister/brother."[8] As in so many cases, answering a question such as "Does my dog Mayday have a soul?" requires a definition of terms. Of course, if our interest is in what the Bible says about the "soul," we need to deal with the Bible's own words, understanding that the Bible wasn't written in English.

Nephesh /Psuchē

The Hebrew term *nephesh*, found in the Old Testament 754 times, came to be commonly rendered "soul" in English because Jerome's Latin Vulgate used the term *anima*, "soul," for it in the fourth century, and the Greek Septuagint had already translated it with *psuchē* (compare English *psyche*) a few hundred years before that. As early as Homeric Greek (that is, the eighth century BC and the time of Isaiah), *psuchē* was the animating force that left someone at death to wander the underworld forever. In the sixth century BC (about the beginning of the Jewish exile), *psuchē* was understood as "the epitome of the individual" that was trapped in a body. Classical Greek, before the New Testament was written, identified *psuchē* with a person's intellectual and emotional life that survived bodily death, was not spatially limited, and was more valuable than the body as the butterfly is more valuable than the cocoon. Moral instruction essentially disregarded the body and was "a training of the soul for virtue."[9]

> *Classical Greek, before the New Testament was written, identified psuchē with a person's intellectual and emotional life that survived bodily death, was not spatially limited, and was more valuable than the body as the butterfly is more valuable than the cocoon.*

One's body, in fact, was often considered a hindrance to true life. The Greek apocryphal book known as the Wisdom of Solomon speaks of "a perishable body [that] weighs down the soul, and . . . burdens the thoughtful mind" (Wisdom 9:15, NRSV).[10] As N. T. Wright explains, this idea still reverberates in the modern world:

> We have been buying our mental furniture for so long in Plato's factory that we have come to take for granted a basic ontological contrast between "spirit" . . . and "matter." . . . We assume that to be bodily, to be physical, is to be impermanent, changeable, transitory, and that the only way to be permanent, unchanging, and immortal is to become non-physical.[11]

Contrary to Greek dualism with its temporary body and immortal soul, the Bible teaches that only God inherently possesses immortality and that every "living being" (Gen 2:7) derives life through his creative act. God, however, can bestow immortality on people as a result of the redemptive work of Christ (Rom 2:7; 1 Cor 15:53–54).[12]

> *Contrary to Greek dualism with its temporary body and immortal soul, the Bible teaches that only God inherently possesses immortality.*

Hebrew scholar Bruce Waltke defines the Hebrew word *nephesh*, though, as simply "passionate vitality." The Old Testament uses it for "passionate drives and appetites of *all* breathing creatures." The related verb meant "to breathe." It is a person's yearning or craving for God that distinguishes the human *nephesh* from that of animals.[13] The word's translation (hunger, self, life, etc.) depends on the context. The Good News Bible only uses the word "soul" 39 times, the CSB uses it 62 times, the NLT 72 times, and the NIV 95 times, whereas the KJV used it 498 times. Even the Hebrew dictionary that was widely used over a century ago gives the various meanings of *nephesh* in different contexts as "soul, living being, life, self, person, desire, appetite, emotion, and passion."[14] Earlier, the basic meaning of *nephesh* may have been "throat" or "neck" (Pss 69:1; 105:18; Isa 5:14; Jonah 2:5), which is related to "appetite/desire" (Num 11:6; Eccl 6:7; Hab 2:5) and then "life" or "self."

> *It is a person's yearning or craving for God that distinguishes the human nephesh from that of animals.*

When *nephesh* refers to the self, it has in view the entire person, not just the immaterial self.[15] The word *nephesh* could even be used of a dead body or corpse that was not to be touched (Lev 19:28; 21:1, 11; Num 5:2; 6:6, 11; 9:6–10; 19:11, 13; Hag 2:13), although that use may refer to the *person* who died (see Num 19:13) rather than to his or her corpse, since it is often modified by the adjective "dead." Pagan rituals involving cutting the flesh were also not to be done "on [the Israelites'] bodies [that is, their flesh] for the dead [*nephesh*]" (Lev 19:28; also see Jer 16:6). Here *nephesh* refers not to the body or to a bodiless "soul," but simply to the person who has died.[16] Old Testament scholar Hans Walter Wolff claims *nephesh* "is never given the meaning of an indestructible core of being."[17]

Many have turned to Genesis 2:7 to understand the nature of personhood and of the soul, since the KJV rendered it, "And the Lᴏʀᴅ God formed man of the dust of the ground, and breathed into his nostrils the breath of life; and man became a *living soul*" (emphasis added). The phrase "living soul" translates the Hebrew phrase *nephesh chayyah.* Many have understood this verse to mean that personhood consists of an immaterial essence, the *soul,* inhabiting flesh and blood, the *body,* which is infused with life by God's breath in one's *spirit.*

But modern translations render the verse something like, "and the man became a *living being.*" Hebrew *nephesh* occurs four times in Genesis before God makes a man. In chapter 1 it refers to "creatures" (1:20, 21, 24) or to "breath" (1:30). The phrase *nephesh chayyah* is first used in Genesis 1:20 of fish and is translated in KJV as "the creature that hath life." In 1:24 (also in 2:19; 9:12, 15–16) it is used of land animals called "living creatures," then in 1:30 of all animals having *nephesh chayyah,* that is, "living breath" (usually rendered "the breath of life"; KJV simply "life"). So, Genesis 2:7 offers us little regarding the nature of a person. The next use of Hebrew *nephesh* after Genesis chapter 2 is in 9:4, where it is equated with blood and is usually translated "life." The verse says literally, "However, flesh with its *nephesh* ["life"], its blood, you must not eat."

The meaning of *nephesh chayyah* in Genesis 2:7 or even of *nephesh* itself is irrelevant to the question of whether disembodied persons survive death[18] (that will be discussed in the next two chapters). But even the claim that *nephesh* never refers to a deceased person can be disputed. Some references to the *nephesh* being in Sheol may speak figuratively of a person escaping an almost fatal illness. Consider these examples:

> Lᴏʀᴅ, you brought [my *nephesh*] up from Sheol; / you spared me from among those going down to the Pit. (Ps 30:3)
> For your faithful love for me is great, / and you rescue my [*nephesh*] from the depths of Sheol. (Ps 86:13)

But other such references are not so easily dismissed.

> For you will not abandon [my *nephesh*] to Sheol; / you will not allow your faithful one to see decay. (Ps 16:10)
> But God will redeem [my *nephesh*] / from the power of Sheol, / for he will take me. (Ps 49:15)

Cooper suggests that such uses may imply the possibility of a disembodied person even if they do not designate it. He cites Hebrew scholar Otto Kaiser, who adds two other passages. Jacob's wife Rachel named her last son Ben-oni (Jacob called him) as she was dying in Genesis 35:18. The phrase "with her last breath" is literally "as her *nephesh* was going out." Elijah prayed over the dead body of the widow's son: "Lord my God, please let this boy's life come into him again!" (1 Kgs 17:21). The Hebrew reads more literally: "Let the *nephesh* of this boy return upon his body." According to Kaiser, "The Hebrew could indeed actually understand the 'soul' (*nephesh*) to mean the soul of the deceased, and at least later did understand it this way."[19]

> *"The Hebrew could indeed actually understand the 'soul' (nephesh) to mean the soul of the deceased, and at least later did understand it this way."*

In Matthew 10:28 Jesus says, "Don't fear those who kill the body but are not able to kill the soul [*psuchē*]; rather, fear him who is able to destroy both soul and body in hell [*Gehenna*]." As New Testament scholar R. T. France explains, here the term *psuchē* has to be translated with "a term that denotes the continuing life of the person after the life of the body has been terminated, and 'soul,' despite its Greek philosophical connotation, . . . is probably the best English word to denote that continuing life."[20]

Soul Versus Heart

The first use of "soul" in modern English Bibles is usually found in Deuteronomy, where it often occurs with "heart." The Hebrew term for "heart" (*leb*) often refers to the center of human thinking (mind), feeling (emotions), and deciding (will) and so could be used of one's inner being. Waltke calls *leb*, which is found 853 times, "the most important anthropological term in the Old Testament." It also controlled all the body's functions, including our facial expressions and tongues.[21] Along with "heart," *nephesh* refers to someone's whole being or self. So, seeking God with heart and soul (Deut 4:29) would mean to seek only him with all one's being. Loving God "with all your heart, with all your soul, and with all your strength" would mean to hang on to the Lord alone with everything you are and everything you have (the probable sense of "strength").[22]

> *The Hebrew term for "heart" (leb) often refers to the center of human thinking (mind), feeling (emotions), and deciding (will) and so could be used of one's inner being.*

> *Loving God "with all your heart, with all your soul, and with all your strength" would mean to hang on to the Lord alone with everything you are and everything you have.*

Ruach/Neshamah/Pneuma

Another essential element of one's inner being, or invisible self, is the "spirit," Hebrew *ruach* and Greek *pneuma* (compare the English words *pneumonia* and *pneumatic*). The Hebrew term, found 378 times, is also used for "wind" or "breath," and the meaning "spirit" can apply either to the human spirit or (more often) to the Spirit of God (as in Gen 1:2, where the meaning "wind" can also be in view).

The use of *ruach* for human breath deserves pondering. The earthy, earthly creature that God sculpted in Genesis 2:7 became a living, human being because God shared with him something of his own divine life by breathing "the breath of life into his nostrils." The term here for "breath" is not *ruach*, however, but a synonym: *neshamah* (or *nishmat*, "breath of"). The Hebrew phrase *nishmat chayyim*, which occurs only here, is synonymous with *ruach chayyim*, "breath/spirit of life" (Gen 6:17; 7:15). The two words for "breath" occur together in the phrase, "the breath of the spirit of life" in Genesis 7:22. Hebrew *neshamah*, "breath," is found in the Old Testament only 24 times, usually indicating that someone is "alive" (see

The earthy, earthly creature that God sculpted in Genesis 2:7 became a living, human being because God shared with him something of his own divine life by breathing "the breath of life into his nostrils.

Josh 11:11, 14). In Ezekiel's dry bones passage, however, it is the Lord's *ruach*, "breath/Spirit" that gives life (Ezek 37:5–6, 8–10, 14). Both terms are used synonymously in Job 34:14–15: "If [God] put his mind to it / and withdrew the spirit [*ruach*] and breath [*neshamah*] he gave, / every living thing would perish together / and mankind would return to the dust."

The fact that humans share the divine breath has several implications. One is our privileged and honored nature and position as divine image-bearers that distinguishes us from God's other creatures and gives us the ability and authority to subdue, rule, and name the other creatures and to care for them and their environment (however poorly we do).[23] The NIV rendering of Genesis 1:26 is defensible: "Let us make mankind in our image, in our likeness, *so that they may rule . . .*" (emphasis added). It is in the context of God's transcendent glory that the Davidic psalmist asks,

> What is a human being that you remember him,
> a son of man that you look after him?
> You made him little less than God
> and crowned him with glory and honor.
> You made him ruler over the works of your hands;
> you put everything under his feet. (Ps 8:4–6)

On the other hand, our privileged sharing in the divine breath does not alter the fact that we are *dependent* on it—on Him—for life (see Ps 104:29). In this context, David again asks,

> LORD, what is a human that you care for him,
> a son of man that you think of him?
> A human is like a breath;
> his days are like a passing shadow. (Ps 144:3-4)

Job, too, knew that he was alive only as long as "the breath [*ruach*] from God remain[ed] in [his] nostrils" (27:3; also Dan 5:23). Isaiah declared that a time is coming when "the pride of mankind will be brought low, / and human loftiness will be humbled; / the LORD alone will be exalted on that day" (Isa 2:17). The prophet then, in verse 22, urges the people, "Put no more trust in a mere human, / who has only the breath [*neshamah*] in his nostrils. / What is he really worth?" The KJV has a useful literal rendering of Isaiah's sentiment: "Cease ye from man ['*adam*], whose breath is in his nostrils." Humans are limited in every respect, as represented by the fact that each of us is always one breath away from death. Therefore, ultimately, in the long run, humans cannot be relied on. The prophet is not denying human worth. He is simply placing it in the context of divine worth. Every breath I take reminds me I am not in control, nor is any other human. God is.

Humans are limited in every respect, as represented by the fact that each of us is always one breath away from death.

Waltke suggests that as one's manner of breathing may show his or her frame of mind, mood, morale, or general disposition (for example, slow and deep, rapid and shallow, holding one's breath, snorting through the nose; see 1 Kgs 10:5; Prov 29:11; Isa 25:4), so the term "spirit" is often used to represent the psychical "locale" or seat of various emotions.[24] According to Proverbs 17:27, a wise person knows when to "restrain his words" and keep a "cool spirit" (CSB "cool head"; also, Prov 16:32). Caleb's faithful "spirit" was "different" from that of his fellow Israelites', who refused to trust God (see Num 14:24). King Ahab was "resentful [or "sullen, dejected"] and angry" at Naboth (1 Kgs 21:4), and Queen Jezebel asked him, "Why is your spirit [CSB "why are you"] so upset [or "resentful, sullen, dejected"] that you refuse to eat?" (21:5). The psalmist's troubles in Psalm 77 cause him to think of God and groan, "[M]y spirit becomes weak," that is, overwhelmed (vv. 2–3). In Isaiah 57:15 God promises to revive the spirit of those who are "low," that is, who are crushed by oppression, guilt, and shame (Matt 5:3, "poor in spirit"). Daniel awakes from a remarkable dream and admits, "My spirit was deeply distressed within me, and the visions in my mind terrified me" (Dan 7:15; also, Gen 41:8). Frequently in these descriptions of emotions, "spirit" and "heart" are closely associated so that they are essentially synonymous (see Exod 35:21; Deut 2:30; 28:65; Pss 51:17; 77:6; 78:8) and either together or separately represent the inner self. John Cooper concludes, "In sum, *ruach* is used in a wide variety of ways in the Old Testament, some of them coinciding with *nephesh*. But none of them clearly points to an immaterial subsistent self," that is, an independently existing "soul" as found in Platonic thought.[25]

According to a recent *Dictionary of New Testament Theology*, in extrabiblical Greek literature Greek *psuchē* ("soul") and *pneuma* ("spirit") were closely related, the former being "a purely functional" term and the latter[26] Greek *pneuma* is used over 300 times in the Septuagint, mostly to translate Hebrew *ruach*. It is found

Kylie Lawrence, Gallatin firefighter. As the oxygen tank sustains the life of a firefighter in duty, so too does the Holy Spirit's "breath" sustain the Christian in their line of duty.

about 380 times in the New Testament, mostly of the Holy Spirit (more than 250 times). About forty times it designates what might be called the human personality— "insofar as it belongs to, or interacts with, the spiritual realm." Thus, the same volume states, "The spirit is that aspect of our human nature through which God most immediately encounters us" (see Rom 8:16; Gal 6:18; Phil 4:23; 2 Tim 4:22; Phlm 25; Heb 4:12; Jas 4:5). It is "that dimension whereby we are most directly open and responsive to God" (see Matt 5:3; Luke 1:47; Rom 1:9; 1 Pet 3:4) and "that area of human awareness most sensitive to matters of the spiritual realm" (Mark 2:8; 8:12; John 11:33; 13:21; Acts 17:16; 2 Cor 2:13; 7:13).[27]

> *The spirit is that aspect of our human nature through which God most immediately encounters us.*

Passages that speak of the spirit's departure at death or return at being revived may be best understood in the context of *pneuma* as breath or the divinely controlled power that imparts life (Matt 27:50; Luke 8:55; 23:46; Acts 7:59). The returning *nephesh* ("life") of the widow's son in 1 Kings 17:21–22 may be considered a parallel, as is the raising of the Shunammite woman's son in 2 Kings 4:32–35.

IS ANY BODY THERE?

Although a duality of material and immaterial human nature seems to emerge from Scripture, it is not one of dispensable husk and enduring kernel. Rather, the Bible presents the body as an essential part of God's precious handiwork. As Old Testament scholar Gordon McConville points out, the terms "image" and "likeness" have physical implications.[28] Even though "God is spirit" according to John 4:34, the fact that humans mirror and represent Him must include our bodies. We may object to God's having begun his creative work on us with common "dust" (see Ps 103:14). But God is pictured in Genesis 2:7 as the ultimate master Sculptor, whose divine skill enables Him to create "beauty" out "of ash-

> *Although a duality of material and immaterial human nature seems to emerge from Scripture, it is not one of dispensable husk and enduring kernel.*

> *God is pictured in Genesis 2:7 as the ultimate master Sculptor, whose divine skill enables Him to create "beauty" out "of ashes.*

es" (Isa 61:3). Besides, "the dust from the ground" he started with is not just dirt. Rather, it constitutes the raw material that God himself created in order to form life (see Prov 8:26). Ethel Waters famously said, "I am somebody 'cause God don't make no junk." Not only does that include our bodies, but it includes the stuff out of which we are made. And even if "dust" is something considered common or profane, it ceased to be so when God's own "breath of life" filled us.

> *I am somebody 'cause God don't make no junk.*

Yes, because of Adam's sin, our origins also became our destiny; indeed, our bodies "return to dust" (Gen 3:19; Job 34:15; Eccl 3:20; 12:7).[29] Therefore, those whose worldly wisdom must be based only on what can be learned through observation "under the sun" (see Eccl 3:16–21) must conclude with the agnostic, Who knows what happens to a person (or an animal) at death? The one whose knee bows before the Creator God, however, has an additional source of knowledge in divine revelation, which tells us, "Many who sleep in the dust / of the earth will awake, / some to eternal life, / and some to disgrace and eternal contempt" (Dan 12:2). Job also affirms, "Even after my skin has been destroyed, / yet I will see God in my

Workers in Indonesia separating the kernels of rice of their husk

flesh" (Job 19:26). And through Isaiah God assures his people, "Your dead will live; their bodies will rise. / Awake and sing, you who dwell in the dust! / For you will be covered with the morning dew, / and the earth will bring out the departed spirits" (Isa 26:19).

The New Testament, of course, is even more informative. The Christian message is not about the immortality of the soul but about God's redemption of our whole selves, including our bodies, through the work of Christ (see Rom 8:23). As Paul makes clear in 1 Corinthians 15, this includes bodily resurrection. Christ's resurrection means that all in Christ will also be raised. There is, in fact, no life after death that does not include the resurrection of the body. Paul says that if believers are not raised from the dead, "those, then, who have fallen asleep in Christ [that is, those who died trusting in Christ] *have also perished*" (v. 18, emphasis added). Yet we have the divine promise that "everyone who believes in him *will not perish* but have eternal life" (John 3:16). Therefore, eternal life necessarily entails the resurrection of the body. So, "if the dead are not raised," it does not matter what we do with our lives (15:32) because we are condemned. The idea that "I will go to heaven when I die" is not the gospel. The good news we are urged to receive by faith that God has redeemed our whole selves in Christ and welcomed

> *"Your dead will live; their bodies will rise. / Awake and sing, you who dwell in the dust! / For you will be covered with the morning dew, / and the earth will bring out the departed spirits."*

> *The Christian message is not about the immortality of the soul but about God's redemption of our whole selves, including our bodies, through the work of Christ.*

> *Eternal life necessarily entails the resurrection of the body.*

us into eternal fellowship with him. Thus, after we die we will be raised to brand new, incorruptible, immortal life (1 Cor 15:50–57).

As Paul explains in 1 Thessalonians 4, Christians who are grieving the loss of their loved ones are not without hope. As we explained in the chapter, "But Is Heaven Our Forever Home?" this is not because we know our deceased loved ones are already comfortably enjoying Jesus, although we will discuss that exciting possibility in the next chapters. The reason Paul gives for our hope in the face of such loss is our knowledge of the resurrection. He says, "The dead in Christ will rise first," when the Lord returns (1 Thess 4:16). Combining this with what Paul says in 1 Corinthians, Christians can have hope (that is, assurance or confidence) when fellow believers die because we know that they have not "perished." But still the point is not just that they continue to live, but that they will be raised bodily from the dead when Christ returns.

The point of all this is that followers of Jesus who are preparing for relocation to "heaven" should not expect to spend the rest of eternity floating around as disembodied "souls," playing harps and guitars or discussing how many angels they can get into a Volkswagen Beetle. Wherever we will be, and whatever we will be doing, at least for the biggest part of eternity, we will have our glorified bodies with us. One implication of this is that we should not think of our bodies now as eventual discards or future landfill, like the paper wrapper from our burger. As Old Testament scholar Kenneth Mathews explains, "How the human body is cared for is important to God. Both libertine [give my body whatever it wants] and ascetic [deny my body anything it wants] views toward the body that demean it are destructive to the whole person."[30]

Followers of Jesus who are preparing for relocation to "heaven" should not expect to spend the rest of eternity floating around as disembodied "souls.

How the human body is cared for is important to God.

So, what's next—after death, that is. Is our trip to the new creation or "heaven" a non-stop flight, or is there a stopover in "the intermediate state"?

NOTES

1   See Bruce K. Waltke and Charles Yu, *An Old Testament Theology* (Grand Rapids: Zondervan, 2007), 216, quoting Anthony Hoekema, *Created in God's Image*, 67.

2   J. G. McConville, *Deuteronomy*, Apollos Old Testament Commentary (Downers Grove: InterVarsity, 2002), 106.

3   Christinia Rossetti, *Rossetti: Poems* (New York: Alfred A. Knopf, 1993), 128.

4   See Waltke, *Old Testament Theology*, 217.

5   John Goldingay writes, "A person does not *have* a body, but *is* a body. The body is the self; to put it less paradoxically, the body is the embodiment of the person" (*Biblical Theology: The God of the Christian Scriptures* [Downers Grove: IVP, 2016], 189.

6   See G. C. Berkouwer, *Man: The Image of God* (Grand Rapids: Eerdmans, 1962), 199.

7   John W. Cooper, *Body, Soul, and Life Everlasting* (Grand Rapids: Eerdmans, 2000), 43.

8   See "soul" at https://www.merriam-webster.com/.

9   See G. Kittel, G. Friedrich, and G. W. Bromiley, *Theological Dictionary of the New Testament Abridged in One Volume* (Grand Rapids: Eerdmans, 1985), 1342–43.

10 This extra-biblical book was first referred to in the second century AD but probably originated in Alexandria during the first century BC or first century AD. See Michael Kolarcik, "The Book of Wisdom," in *The New Interpreter's Bible Commentary* (Nashville: Abingdon, 2015), 6:428). Kolarcik, however, thinks the passage cited describes "human weakness and fragility" more than "the precise nuances of the Platonic distinction between the body and the soul" (6:489).

11 Wright, *Surprised by Hope*, 153.

12 Berkouwer, *Man: The Image of God*, 270, states, "Scripture never takes up a natural immortality of the soul because of its inherent nature, but always concerns itself with the relationship of the whole man to God." New Testament scholar Oscar Cullmann, (*Immortality of the Soul or Resurrection of the Dead? The Witness of the New Testament* [London: Epworth, 1964], 15) even declares that the idea of the immortality of the soul "is one of the greatest misunderstandings of Christianity."

13 Bruce K. Waltke and Charles Yu, *An Old Testament Theology* (Grand Rapids: Zondervan, 2007), 224.

14 This was written by Francis Brown, Samuel R. Driver, and Charles A. Briggs, *The Brown-Driver-Briggs Hebrew and English Lexicon* (Clarendon Press: Oxford, 1906). The dictionary, commonly known as BDB, has been republished by Hendrickson.

15 Cooper, *Body, Soul, and Life*, 39.

16 See B. K. Waltke, "*nephesh*," *Theological Wordbook of the Old Testament*, ed. R. L. Harris, G. L. Archer, Jr., B. K. Waltke (Chicago: Moody, 1980), 590.

17 Hans Walter Wolff, *Anthropology of the Old Testament* (Philadelphia: Fortress, 1974), 10.

18 This point is also made in James Barr, *The Garden of Eden and the Hope of Immortality* (London: SCM, 1992), 37. Barr correctly identifies as a fallacy the argument that because *nephesh chayyah* here refers to the whole person, then the term "soul," traditionally given to the word *nephesh*, also refers to the whole person.

19 Cooper, *Body, Soul, and Life*, 61, citing Otto Kaiser and Eduard Lohse, *Death and Life* (Nashville: Abingdon, 1981), 40.

20 R. T. France, *The Gospel of Matthew*, New International Commentary on the New Testament (Grand Rapids: Eerdmans, 2007), 399. According to Craig S. Keener, "Contrary to most commentators, most extant early Jewish writers also distinguished body and soul." See *The Gospel of Matthew: A Socio-Rhetorical Commentary* (Grand Rapids: Eerdmans, 2009), 326.

21 Waltke, *Old Testament Theology*, 225.

22 See Daniel I. Block, *Deuteronomy*, NIV Application Commentary (Grand Rapids: Zondervan, 2012), 182–84.

23 The Hebrew word ('*abad*) rendered "work" in Gen 2:15 has several meanings, also including "serve." NET renders the phrase here "to care for it and to maintain it."

24 Waltke, *Old Testament Theology*, 227.

25 Cooper, *Body, Soul, and Life Everlasting*, 40.

26 *New International Dictionary of New Testament Theology and Exegesis: Second Edition* (*NIDNTTE*), ed. Moisés Silva (Grand Rapids: Zondervan, 2014), 3:803.

27 *NIDNTTE*, 3:807.

28 J. Gordon McConville, *Being Human in God's World: An Old Testament Theology of Humanity* (Grand Rapids: Baker, 2016), 17.

29 Kenneth A. Mathews, *Genesis 1–11*, Christian Standard Commentary (Nashville: Holman, 2022), 141.

30 Mathews, *Genesis 1–11*, 141.

CHAPTER 10

IS THIS A DIRECT FLIGHT?: OLD TESTAMENT EVIDENCE

As indicated in the last chapter, the issue to be tackled here is whether our flight will be nonstop or will have a layover in "the intermediate state." The trip we are preparing for is not a vacation, but an immigration. So, there is more involved than looking for a hotel or a B&B. We have all known people, or been people, who take a new job in a new location or are transferred there. If they're moving from Biggsville, Illinois to Cape Town, South Africa, for example, the one with the new job may need to leave first with minimal belongings and find temporary accommodations. Then perhaps the rest of the family will come to help look for a permanent home. Many people understand from the Bible that a person moving to the new heavens and earth will find it a two-stage process. The initial stage, called *the intermediate state*, begins the instant we die and ends with our resurrection at Christ's return. We have already seen that despite what many Christian songs tell us, *heaven* is not what God ultimately has in store for us. As N. T. Wright says, alluding to a book on the subject, "Heaven is important but it's not the end of the world."[1] What lies ahead for us, rather, is a radically renovated earth, which has been infused with or "married" to heaven, which has been "brought down" to us by Christ (see Rev 21–22). So, the new creation will not begin until Christ's return and the resurrection of the dead.

> *Heaven is important but it's not the end of the world.*

So, what can we know about the state of those believers who die before Christ returns? (We will discuss what happens to nonbelievers in a later chapter.) That is what this chapter and the following one are about. We will look here at various proposals that have been made, then at many passages in the Old Testament relevant to the subject. In the next chapter, we will examine the New Testament evidence, then we will summarize the biblical teaching on what happens when we die.

VIEWS REGARDING THE INTERMEDIATE STATE

The question of life after death has two possible answers: either yes or no. If the answer is yes, we have three basic options: reincarnation, immortality of the soul, or resurrection of the body.[2] The first two views hold that the body can be peeled off the soul/spirit or immaterial essence of a person as one peels a banana. Reincarnation involves the continued existence of a person's essence in a succession of different bodies. The clearest biblical passage addressing this view is Hebrews 9:27: "It is appointed for people to die once—and after this, judgment." New Testament scholar Tom Schreiner explains: "Human life is not repeated over and over again. There is a finality and distinctiveness about human existence. Certainly what is said here rules out any notion of reincarnation."[3]

> *"Human life is not repeated over and over again."*

The option of the immortality of the soul means that after its peeling is gone, the banana itself lives on forever in an immaterial world (a view known as *radical dualism*). Some Christians have held to the soul's inherent indestructibility, by which rebellious unbelievers will survive in hell, while believers will enjoy heavenly bliss as spirits. Many theologians, however, have shown that the Bible never speaks of the "immortality of the soul." Theologian Anthony Hoekema, for example, notes that "the word *immortality* is applied to God [Rom. 1:23; 1 Tim. 1:17; 6:16], to man's total existence at the time of the resurrection [1 Cor. 15:52–54], and to such things as the imperishable crown [1 Cor.9:25] or incorruptible seed of the Word [1 Pet. 1:23]," but never to the human soul.[4] To some, however, the idea of the soul's immortality is taken to mean more loosely that a person's (especially a believer's) immaterial essence survives death, awaiting the resurrection, when the soul/spirit will be reunited with a glorified body.[5] According to theologian Millard Erickson, this combination of the soul's immortality and bodily resurrection primarily constituted orthodoxy prior to the twentieth century. Twentieth-century liberalism then denied bodily resurrection and held only to the immortality of the soul. Next came the neoorthodoxy of Emil Brunner and others who advocated resurrection but affirmed the monistic view that the soul cannot exist without the body.[6]

Those who recognize the biblical stress on the resurrection of the body typically understand the state of believers between death and the resurrection as either conscious or unconscious. A conscious existence in temporary accommodations in God's presence would be either in an immaterial, bodiless state (as "spirit/soul") or in an intermediate body of some sort. The latter would be exchanged at Christ's return for a resurrected, glorified body like Christ's.

> *A conscious existence in temporary accommodations in God's presence would be either in an immaterial, bodiless state (as "spirit/soul") or in an intermediate body of some sort.*

Those advocating an unconscious state after death could be holistic dualists who believe the spirit of a person sleeps somewhere until being reunited with the body at Christ's return. This view could be appropriately called "soul sleep." Monists such as Seventh Day Adventists describe the believer's state as "sleep," since the Bible often uses that term. But they do not believe in soul sleep, since they define "soul," based on Genesis 2:7, as the whole person. Rejecting any kind of dualism, Adventist theologian Norman Gulley states, "Wholistic anthropology is biblical." Therefore, "there is no such thing as a surviving soul," for "nowhere in Scripture are there disembodied souls."[7] Adventists summarize their doctrines in 28 Fundamental Beliefs. According to the official Adventist website explaining them, number 26 on "Death and Resurrection" affirms that "a soul is the combination of a body plus the breath of life. The soul cannot exist without the body or the breath."

It also declares, however, "Death is like a deep sleep. Your *body and spirit rest* as the breath of life—which makes *body and soul* one, and alive—has returned to God until the resurrection."[8] This explanation is quite confusing. First, the term "spirit" is introduced without explanation, and then the phrases "body and spirit" and "body and soul" seem to be equated.[9] Adding to the confusion, the term "soul" is used suddenly as if it were an element of the person rather than the whole, as previously declared. The term "sleep" is also confusing, since it raises more questions. What exactly is sleeping, and where is this "rest" taking place? If "the breath of life" has returned to God, and "the soul cannot exist without the body or the breath," nothing is left of the person but a dead, decaying body, at best. It may very well have been reduced to random molecules. Rest or sleep demands a center of consciousness, yet nothing is left but the breath of life, which is with God. If the breath of life were said to carry the invisible essence of the person, how is that different from the traditional soul/spirit is with God after death (though unconscious)?

The website goes on to deny this possibility by saying that a loved one who has passed away is "*resting peacefully in the grave*. They are not in pain. They are not somewhere else being tormented. They are simply *waiting in the grave* until Jesus comes back."[10] But how is this possible, especially if there is no "grave" and

no body? The verbs to "rest" and to "wait" may sound comforting to surviving loved ones, but do they actually mean anything? According to Gulley, a person who dies ceases to exist. He compares a person to a box made of wood and nails. If the nails, representing God's breath, were removed, "there is no box—just two piles, of wood and nails, once more. So at death the total person ceases to exist."[11] The Adventist website illustrates with an electric light that requires a light bulb, representing the body, and electricity, representing God's breath. If either one is missing, there is no light. But although we might personify the light bulb and say that it is "resting" or "waiting" for the restoration of electricity, such personification would be meaningless if the bulb is destroyed.

The bottom line is that anti-dualistic arguments for death as sleep awaiting the resurrection seem to be only a euphemistic way of advocating death as non-existence followed by re-creation.[12] Whether re-creation is a valid type of resurrection is questionable because it carries with it the problem of identity. But how can *I* be raised from the dead if *I* have ceased to exist? Christian philosophers Steven Cowan and James Spiegel point to the example of the manuscript in the ancient monastery that is admired by a visitor. The monks tell him it is the very one created by Saint Augustine, even though the Arians had burned down the monastery and its manuscripts sometime later. When the visitor then asks how the manuscript could be the one Augustine created, he is told that God miraculously re-created it. But this visitor points out that if it is true, the manuscript he is looking at is not the one Augustine made. It is a duplicate, however perfectly God may have re-created it. "Its earliest moment of existence would have been after Augustine's death; it would never have known the impress of his hand; it would not have been a part of the furniture of the world when he was alive."[13]

Anti-dualistic arguments for death as sleep awaiting the resurrection seem to be only a euphemistic way of advocating death as non-existence followed by re-creation.

So far, then, those who affirm the bodily resurrection of believers after death may understand their situation between death and resurrection in one of three ways. First, they may expect a conscious enjoyment of God's presence in some kind of body. A second option would be soul sleep in God's presence, that is, a bodiless existence (though this seems to contradict 2 Cor 5; see our chap. 5). The third option we have discussed is the monistic non-existence view, which has problems with issues of identity.

Before examining some of the relevant Bible passages to help us consider what we are to believe about these issues, we might consider one more uncommon view that may have possibilities. This view eliminates the need for temporary accommodations by relying on a belief in God's sovereignty over time. The question of God's relationship to time has been controversial since before the Christian era.[14] But there is good reason to believe that God is transcendent and above time, yet he also interacts with humans authentically in the world of temporal succession. It seems reasonable to suggest, then, that God, who created time at creation and is sovereign over it, might eliminate the time interval between the death of believers and their resurrection. As in the views of human unconsciousness

God, who created time at creation and is sovereign over it, might eliminate the time interval between the death of believers and their resurrection.

Intricately-designed, astronomical clock in Prague.

between death and resurrection, all the believers of all the ages thus would encounter God's presence together simultaneously, at the same "time." This view might be compared to the idea of time travel. At death each person might be said to enter a "portal" and be transported in time to the event of Christ's return and our bodily resurrection.[15] This view will be considered more closely in the next chapter.

DUALISM AND THE INTERMEDIATE STATE

Our previous chapter on the nature of our identity as *persons* considered the predominant biblical perspective to be that a person is a unity of outer, visible, material life on the one hand (body/flesh and bone), and inner, invisible, immaterial life (soul/spirit) on the other. Their relationship, however, is not one of disposable body and enduring spirit/soul. The Bible presents the body as an essential part of God's complex and precious handiwork.

But does this mean that the immaterial *cannot exist* apart from the material? The *monist* says yes, both aspects are necessary for human existence. The *dualist* says no, immaterial human life can exist, either permanently or temporarily, without material life. What John Cooper describes as dualistic or functional (as opposed to ontological) holism or holistic dualism, "does not necessarily imply that if the whole is broken up, all parts disintegrate into chaos or nothingness." He illustrates by noting, "Hydrogen and oxygen atoms can survive separation from water molecules even though the breakup alters them."[16] Surely the soul/spirit can exist, at least for a time, without the body.

Immaterial human life can exist, either permanently or temporarily, without material life.

Some form of dualism allows for the possibility of an intermediate state, a layover in heaven. Monism does not. So, which theory is true? Approaching the question from the other end, however, if the Bible teaches a temporary dwelling of believers with God apart from their resurrected bodies, then some form of dualism must be true. This, then, will be our main concern as we consider the biblical evidence.

Some form of dualism allows for the possibility of an intermediate state, a layover in heaven.

The Old and New Testaments take different approaches to the issue, however. While both reliably declare truth, they furnish each other with a wider context that lets us see truth with greater depth than if we only had one. The Bible is not a monolith, with only one uniform perspective on the truth, though its perspectives are compatible. The relationship of Old to New Testament may be understood as problem/solution, promise/fulfillment, prequel/sequel, preparation/celebration, outline/painting, and so forth. Although the New Testament does not give us a complete picture of the afterlife, it gives us much more than the Old Testament, which is more focused on this life.

The Bible is not a monolith, with only one uniform perspective on the truth, though its perspectives are compatible.

Largely because of the extensive use of figurative language in the Old Testament, it gives us a greater depth of feeling about the truth. Nevertheless, the New Testament gives us more detail. One final note is that the Old Testament was written over the course of at least a thousand years, which helps us appreciate its greater complexity.

AFTERLIFE IN THE OLD TESTAMENT
Enoch and Elijah

The apparent physical disappearances of Enoch and Elijah mentioned in the Bible are exceptional, but they still open the possibility of a continued afterlife existence for Old Testament believers.

Kenneth Mathews, an Old Testament scholar, observes the contrast between the moral character of the descendants of Cain in Genesis 4:17–24 and that of Seth's descendants in 4:25–5:32. Whereas Cain's descendants are "typified by the polygamous and murderous Lamech," who concludes Cain's genealogy in 4:23–24, Seth's descendants are typified by Enoch, who (we are told twice) "walked with God."[17] This phrase indicates that Enoch "had a lifestyle characterized for his devotion to God" (see 6:9).[18] Enoch's place in Seth's genealogy stands out for several reasons. Contrary to all the others, who clearly "died," Enoch, we are told, "was not there because *God took him*" (5:24, emphasis added). A second difference is that only Enoch is said to have "walked with God." Though the others listed may have also been men of faith, only Enoch's grandson Lamech testified to it when Noah was born (5:29). Also unique in the genealogy is Enoch's relative youth when he died. The others died at 930, 912, 905, 910, 895, 962, 969, and 777, whereas Enoch left the earth at the early age of only 365! We must not miss the fact that though Enoch is singled out for both faithfulness and divine blessing, he is the one taken "prematurely." Contrary to the view of some, "premature death" is not a sign of God's disfavor.

Contrary to the view of some, "premature death" is not a sign of God's disfavor.

Enoch's skipping of death, it should be noted, is not explicit in this passage. The verb for "took" (*laqach*) means simply that. In fact, it can even refer to death, as when Elijah complains of people looking to "take" his life (1 Kgs 19:10, 14; also Jonah 4:3) or God taking Ezekiel's spouse (Ezek 24:16). On the other hand, the psalmist expects that whereas death will shepherd the "arrogant," who "will waste away in Sheol" (Ps 49:13–14), "God will redeem [him] from the power of Sheol, for *he will take [him]*" (v. 15; emphasis added). Old Testament scholar Allen Ross explains that this psalm is one of many expressing "the confidence of believers in the continual, uninterrupted communion with God, i.e., the strong belief in eternal life with God."[19]

Another such psalm is Psalm 73, where the writer meditates his way from bitterness against the prosperous wicked to faith in God's constant and eternal presence (73:23–26).

> Yet I am always with you;
> you hold my right hand.
> You guide me with your counsel,
> and afterward you *will take me up in glory*.
> Who do I have in heaven but you?
> And I desire nothing on earth but you.
> My flesh and my heart may fail,
> but God is the strength of my heart,
> my portion forever.

According to Dutch Old Testament scholar Klaas Spronk, the psalmist's "tension between his absolute trust in his God and the negative experiences of life" is resolved by his conviction that the Lord has power over life and death. Therefore, death is not the end of the believer's communion with him. "The communion of the faithful with God shall last forever."[20]

Death is not the end of the believer's communion with him. "The communion of the faithful with God shall last forever."

It seems reasonable to reckon from the omission of "and he died" and from the connection between Enoch walking with God and God "taking" him that Enoch did not experience death. This is the interpretation of the author of Heb 11:5: "By faith Enoch was taken away, and so he did not experience death. . . . For before he was taken away, he was approved as one who pleased God." The avoidance of death would suggest that God took Enoch's body as well, and that, like the psalmist, Enoch was taken "up in glory" to remain with God (see Ps 73:24).

Enoch was taken "up in glory" to remain with God (see Ps 73:24).

The same verb for "took" is used of God taking Elijah "up to heaven in a whirlwind," as his disciple watched (2 Kgs 2:1, 11–12). His body clearly went with him. Although we do not hear from Enoch again (except in apocryphal literature), Elijah's continued conscious life is verified by his appearance on the mountain with Jesus and Moses (Matt 17:1–8). Now, unlike Enoch and Elijah, Moses's death is recounted in the Old Testament, as well as his burial (see Deut 34:5–7). Yet, since Jesus's disciples saw both Elijah and Moses talking with Jesus, we may affirm that both their conscious lives have continued. Since they were

Elijah Ascends to Heaven by Gustave Doré

seen and then disappeared, we might also guess that they have glorified bodies ("changed," as in 1 Cor 15:51), like that of Jesus after his resurrection, and that they dwell in God's presence. The nature of their physical existence, however, must be speculative. The case of Enoch, Moses, and Elijah must be acknowledged, however, as evidence that the earthly life of a believer may continue uninterrupted after death.

But what about the location? Although some scholars have claimed that the Old Testament portrays all deceased persons as "descending" to Sheol, this has been credibly disputed, as we will see. Elijah, at least, offers a counter example. Although he did not die, God took him, not to Sheol, but to heaven, God's dwelling place.

Death as Unconsciousness in the Old Testament

Several verses are commonly cited by Adventists as teaching there is no intermediate state between death and resurrection because death is an unconscious state in which "the dead know nothing." Norman Gulley quotes without further comment two passages from Ecclesiastes (9:5–6; 12:7), three from Psalms (6:5; 88:10–12; 146:4), one from Isaiah (38:18), and one from Job (34:14–15). These, he says, "provide evidence that the soul is not immortal," that "there is no such thing as a surviving soul," and that "there is no life after death." Immortality is available, however, "through supernatural means in the future," being "conferred at the second coming."[21] Gulley fails to explain how immortality can be conferred on something that no longer exists.

The Old Testament verses Gulley cites to demonstrate the Adventist view of death are given only as prooftexts, with no biblical context or exegetical explanation of how they fit his argument. For example, the reader of Psalm 146:3–4 can see that the psalmist's point is that we should trust in the God of Jacob, who "remains faithful forever" (vv. 5–6), not in a person who may promise to help but in the end "cannot save" from the grave.

> Do not trust in nobles,
> in a son of man, who cannot save.
> When his breath leaves him,
> he returns to the ground;
> on that day his plans die.

This is irrelevant to the question of life after death. Also irrelevant to the issue is Job 34:14–15.

> If [God] put his mind to it
> and withdrew the spirit and breath he gave,
> every living thing would perish together
> and mankind would return to the dust.

The point is simply that God is sovereign over life, and all creatures depend on him for breath (echoing Gen 2:7). It is concerned only with the earthly life of God's creatures. The word for "perish" means to stop breathing and die (Gen 25:8).

Psalm 6:4–5 (and similarly Ps 115:17) is David's prayer for deliverance with his implied promise of subsequent public testimony and worship, which he couldn't do if he were dead. The passage says,

> Turn, LORD! Rescue me;
> save me because of your faithful love.

For there is no remembrance of you in death;
who can thank you in Sheol?

The word for "remembrance" is used 23 times, always of public renown, fame, or reputation (Pss 102:12; 135:13; 145:7; Isa 26:8). So, the point is not that the deceased have no memory, nor even that they do not remember God. The word is explained by its parallel, to "thank." Indeed, the deceased person does not "thank" God and declare his praise on the earth (similar Ps 115:17).[22] We no longer have the dead among us, testifying to God's great works and worshiping with us in God's house.

We will examine the word *Sheol* later, but it is not portrayed in the Old Testament as a place of nonexistence or unconsciousness. It is often described as a place of inactivity, but Isaiah 14:9-10 and Ezekiel 32:21 both picture its inhabitants speaking.

Old Testament scholar Philip Johnston calls Psalm 88 the song of "utmost despair."[23] It is full of nothing but emotional anguish without a response from God. But this is because the psalmist is letting us see him in the *middle* of the dark tunnel (although he opens with "LORD, God of my salvation" in v. 1); he comes to us as he is. The psalm cannot be adequately understood on its own, then; it must be set in the context of at least the rest of the Psalms. As one commentator explains, "This is the language of emotional questions, not of divine answers."[24] The psalmist is describing not the state of the dead but *This is the language of emotional questions, not of divine answers.* how he feels in his situation of apparent abandonment. On the other hand, verses 10–12 clearly show that death does not glorify God but is the great enemy to be defeated by Jesus. Johnston lists nine commentators on the Psalms who agree with him that references to being in the underworld in Psalm 88 are rhetorical, which is clearly in keeping with the literary character of the psalms.

Finally, using verses from Ecclesiastes to settle a doctrinal issue is problematic because of the challenges in interpreting this book. It has been described as "perhaps the most enigmatic book in the Old Testament."[25] In the first place, it is a book of Wisdom and cannot be treated as if it were written by a prophet like Moses or Isaiah. As Jeremiah 18:18 testifies, God reveals truth differently through the instruction from the priest, the word from the prophet, and the counsel from the wise. We encounter Old Testament truth most directly and literally in the Torah, less directly and more poetically in the Prophets, and most artfully and poetically in the Writings—especially in the Psalms and in the books of Wisdom such as Ecclesiastes and Job. In the ancient world "wisdom literature" had a unique character and style. Adventist scholar Gerald Klingbeil discusses the many similarities between Ecclesiastes and the wisdom literature of ancient Mesopotamia, Syria, and Egypt, especially regarding its "pessimistic outlook," its iconoclastic style, and the themes of the limitations of human wisdom and of *carpe diem* ("seize the day").[26]

Arising out of the wisdom character of the book is the second reason it is difficult to derive a doctrine of death from Ecclesiastes. I refer to the book's autobiographical nature. Rather than simply declaring what God says, the author describes his own search for truth, limiting himself to what may be perceived through the senses and achieved through human reason. As he says in 1:13, "[He] applied [his] mind to examine and explore through wisdom all that is done under heaven." That means the author limited himself to what the secular man may discover in this world "under heaven" and in this life "under the sun" (see Eccl 1:14; 2:11; 3:16; 4:7; 6:1, 12; 8:15, 17; 9:11, 13; 10:5). Thus, as far as knowledge is concerned, the repeated answer is, Who knows?"(2:19; 3:21; 6:12; 7:24; 8:1, 7; 10:14). Life on such terms appears to be without meaning or purpose, and as far as we can tell, one fate awaits everyone, whether good or bad. This leads the writer of Ecclesiastes to say things like this:

> [T]he living know that they will die, but the dead don't know anything. There is no longer a reward for them because the memory of them is forgotten. Their love, their hate, and their envy have already disappeared, and there is no longer a portion for them in all that is done under the sun. (Eccl 9:5–6)

The Teacher/Investigator's words about death in chapter 9 must be understood in terms of the parameters he set. The same is true of the Teacher/Investigator's final words on death and contentment in 11:7–12:7 that conclude with "and the dust returns to the earth as it once was," and (we assume) "the spirit returns to God who gave it." As we look on the dead, death does appear to have the final word.

We should notice one further problem with interpreting the Ecclesiastes verses as if they were the didactic words of a prophet. They say too much. Gulley would have us accept the words of 9:5–6 as prophetic words regarding the nature of death. But if the dead (quoting the NKJV as he does) "have no more reward, for the memory of them is forgotten," and even their love has "perished" (CSB "disappeared"; NIV "vanished"), and "nevermore will they have a share in anything done under the sun," then that is the end of hope and there is nothing else to be said.

There is another word in the book, however, coming from another voice besides that of the Teacher/Investigator. The one who introduces the book and "the Teacher" in the third person in 1:1–11 returns at the end of the book in 12:9–14 to help the reader interpret and to put the book in its broader context. He does not answer the Teacher/Investigator's questions or resolve his dilemmas. He has nothing to add regarding death. What he leaves us with instead is that amid life's apparent futility and absurdity and our confusion, we are to hang onto God and his instructions to us, trusting that He is going to sort everything out, "bring every act to judgment," and reveal the true nature of things, "whether good or evil" (12:14). Old Testament scholar Barry Webb may be right in understanding the final clause of 12:13 to mean, "For this is the whole of what it means to be human."[27] By God's grace and mercy, however, revelation proceeds after Ecclesiastes, and we have Isaiah and the other prophets to tell us what lay in store when the Messiah should come to swallow up death in victory. So, Gulley's use of Ecclesiastes to describe the nature of death involves taking the verses out of context, almost as badly as extracting from Psalm 14:1 the statement of the fool, who "says in his heart, 'There's no God.'

> *Amid life's apparent futility and absurdity and our confusion, we are to hang onto God and his instructions to us, trusting that he is going to sort everything out.*

So, like the other Old Testament verses Gulley quotes to demonstrate that "there is no life after death," these verses from Ecclesiastes fail to make his point. As dependent as we are on God for wisdom as well as for life, we should know that we are going no further in our understanding than he is prepared to take us. And in Old Testament times, he had very little to say about what happens after death, especially for the believer. In fact, even in the New Testament his revelation on what happens between death and resurrection is relatively sparse (see the next chapter).

> *As dependent as we are on God for wisdom as well as for life, we should know that we are going no further in our understanding than he is prepared to take us.*

Necromancy and Veneration of the Dead

The ancients outside Israel almost universally believed in an underworld/netherworld, ruled by one or more gods, where the dead were thought to dwell. In Mesopotamia what survived death was "some form of intangible, but visible and audible" ghost called the *etemmu*,[28] which would reside among the other dead ancestors in the "land of No Return," the "Wasteland," or the "dark house."[29] It was described as a dark, dusty place full of frightening creatures where the inhabitants ate dust and wore feathers like birds. Samuel Kramer, an expert in ancient Sumer, explains that when someone died, "his emasculated spirit descended to the dark, dreary nether world where life was but a dismal and wretched reflection of its earthly counterpart."[30] The underworld city was surrounded by walls entered through seven gates. These protected the world of the living from the departed spirits, who were also kept at bay by offerings of food and drink through mortuary cults. Literature mentions clay tubes through which liquids were poured for the dead.[31]

On the other hand, benefits could be gained from departed ancestors through necromancy, the attempt to gain information from the dead, especially regarding

the future (a form of divination). This, however, was strictly forbidden by God in the Old Testament. Leviticus 19:31 declares, "Do not turn to mediums or consult spiritists, or you will be defiled by them." The meaning of

Do not turn to mediums or consult spiritists, or you will be defiled by them.

the term translated "medium" is uncertain, hence the CSB's note, "or *spirits of the dead.*" Another proposal is that it refers to a pit the necromancer dug from which to call up the spirits (see 1 Sam 28:13).[32] Regardless, Deuteronomy 26:14 makes clear that God had prohibited offerings to be made "for the dead."

Jewish scholar Jacob Milgrom points out, "Both archaeology and written records supply unambiguous evidence for the prevalence of ancestor worship in the ancient Near East. . . . Their worship included the consumption of ritual foods, rites in which the names of the dead were recited, offerings of animal and vegetable sacrifices, and the worship of small cultic images of royal ancestors." The purpose of this ancestor cult, he explains, was "to secure favors from the deceased" and "to prevent the malevolent behavior of the dead spirits."[33] The purpose of this ancestor cult, he explains, was "to secure favors from the deceased" and "to prevent the malevolent behavior of the dead spirits."

A fifteenth-century BC ritual text found at Ugarit in northern Syria called the "Document of the Feast of the Protective Ancestral Spirits" describes a Canaanite feast for the dead called a *marzih.* The deceased, whose spirits were summoned for help and protection, were called *rp'um* (or *Rapiuma*), a term apparently related to Hebrew *repa'im* (or *rephaim*), "departed spirits" (see Job 26:5; Ps 88:10; Prov 2:18; 9:18; 21:16; Isa 14:9; 26:14,19). The head of the *rp'um* was the god *Rapiu*, thought to be identified with the gods Resheph, Baal, and Molek (spelled Molech in the Bible), to whom child sacrifices were made (Lev 18:21; 20:2–5; 2 Kgs 23:10; Jer 32:35).

Although before 1970, Milgrom says, many scholars denied the cult's practice in Israel, "Necromancy was as pervasive in Israel as in the ancient Near East.

Because it was associated with ancestor worship, it was deemed a form of idolatry."[34] Old Testament scholar Daniel Block, however, explains that the concept of "malevolent spirits remains remarkably undeveloped in the Old Testament." Contrary to the views of the surrounding peoples, then, "[In Israel] Yahweh . . . assumed all power over life and death, health and illness, fortune and misfortune."[35] Despite Yahweh's condemnation, though, the people refused to abandon their fearful practices. Block notes that "scholars are uncovering more and more evidence that mortuary cult activities persisted throughout the nation's history." This evidence is coming from both archaeology and the Bible.[36] Johnston's conclusion, on the other hand, is that "the Hebrew Bible does not substantiate the scholarly view that veneration of the ancestors was widespread in Israel and that evidence of it was later suppressed." He thinks that instead, "While it may have occurred, it was of marginal importance. . . . Israelites seem to have been more concerned with the living than the dead."[37]

> *[In Israel] Yahweh . . . assumed all power over life and death, health and illness, fortune and misfortune.*

Old Testament scholar Stephen Cook points out "specific biblical texts" that "unambiguously attest that Israelites had an idea of an underworld and a concrete belief in the continuation of the human personality after death." Yet he points out the lack of current scholarly consensus over the degree to which ancient Israelites believed in and had dealings with spirits of the dead.[38] Philip Johnston agrees with J. B. Burns that "the Old Testament . . . contains no evidence of a highly developed demonology. Nor is it suggested anywhere that the spirits of the dead have power to harm the living."[39]

Jewish scholar Matthew Suriano has collected impressive evidence for the veneration of the dead in ancient Israel, which, he says, is different from worship of the dead and, unlike necromancy, was not condemned.[40] A Judahite tomb, he explains, "typically had three benches carved out of the side walls opposite the entrance. It also included a separate area for the secondary disposal of the dead, called the repository, which was either a pit, a unit carved under a bench like a crawl space, or a specific place on the floor."[41] Burial in ancient Judah was done in two phases. The first phase, the primary burial, involved carrying the body to the tomb and laying it on one of the benches for final preparation. This included provisioning the body "with food, drink, and other supplies such as lamps."[42] A few tombs, after all, have been found with the skeleton still on its back on the bench, with various items placed around it. Although some tombs had niches with soot marks above where a lamp had burned, "the placement of lamps next to the head of the corpse indicates a symbolic function that was directed specifically at the dead individual."[43] Other items placed by the body were jugs, juglets, and cooking pots. The remains expressed a "need to provide sustenance for the dead while they lay inside the tomb, . . . particularly related to the existence of the interred individual, recumbent upon the bench."[44]

The second phase of burial was when the bench was needed for another body. The bones would be gathered, along with the grave goods, and placed with the bones of earlier ancestors in the repository.[45] Suriano explains, "Scholars have noted that the presence of grave goods indicates a belief in the continued existence of the dead inside the tomb."[46]

Model burial of the Late Predynastic period. The body, which is not mummified but desiccated by the dry, hot sand that covered it, is placed on its left side in a contracted position.

Another feature often found inside or outside the tombs is an inscription. Some of these included a divine blessing, showing that "Yahweh was not separated from the dead and that his protection extended to the tomb."[47] Also found in repositories are engraved silver amulets with blessings like the one in Numbers 6:23–27. These were rolled tightly and would have been worn to protect from evil. They indicate that the person was buried with it to continue protecting him.[48] To whatever extent Suriano's interpretations are correct, it seems undeniable that the population of ancient Judah generally believed in the continued existence of the dead and that Yahweh cared about them individually.

Saul and the Medium at En-dor

The most obvious Old Testament evidence of the continuation of the human personality after death is the account of King Saul and the medium at En-dor recorded in 1 Samuel 28. Jewish scholar Jon Levenson calls this "the most developed and extensive account of necromancy in the Hebrew Bible," which offers "further evidence that in ancient Israel the dead were not always thought to have passed into oblivion."[49] Although clearly a unique event in the Bible and not recommended for either the faint or strong of heart (Saul was dead less than twenty-four hours later), I see no way to deny it happened without cashing in all my biblical chips. Old Testament scholar Joyce Baldwin cautions, "The incident does not tell us anything about the veracity of claims to consult the dead on the part of mediums, because the indications are

The most obvious Old Testament evidence of the continuation of the human personality after death is the account of King Saul and the medium at En-dor recorded in 1 Samuel 28.

that this was an extraordinary event for [the medium]."[50] Maybe it only happened once, but the medium at En-dor and others like her acquired a reputation somehow (v. 7). While her scream in verse 12 is often taken to suggest surprise, shock, and fear—as if she is a charlatan who has never before succeeded in raising a spirit, her immediate question to Saul indicates that it was not the spirit but the visitor whom she feared. Saul the king had outlawed all mediums and spiritists (vv. 3, 21), and he was not the only leader to think his laws applied to everyone but himself. "Why did you deceive me? You are Saul" (v.12)! Williamson suggests, "The text does not imply that there was anything atypical about the success of this séance."[51]

If it happened as described here, however, then Samuel is another person (like Enoch, Moses, and Elijah) who was still around somewhere after he died. But was it really Samuel? Could it have been "an evil spirit impersonating Samuel," as some ancient church fathers and modern Adventists claim?[52] The inspired author tells us in verse 12, "When the woman saw *Samuel*, she screamed." (Emphasis added.) Nothing in the passage itself indicates this was not Samuel himself or his spirit, at least as understood by the medium, Saul, and the biblical writer.

Yet when Saul, who could not see anything (though he later heard Samuel's voice), asked the woman what she saw, she used a striking Hebrew word. According to the CSB, she said, "I see *a spirit form* coming up out of the earth" (28:13, emphasis added). The NIV similarly calls the object "a ghostly figure," the NKJV uses "a spirit," and the NJB "a ghost." Several translations, however, have "a god/a divine being" (ESV, NASB, NET, NLT, NRSV). The Hebrew word is *'elohim,* the usual word for "God," although it is grammatically plural. When used with a singular verb, it refers to the one God, but with a plural verb, as here ("coming up"), it often refers to pagan "gods" (the KJV rendering here). Could the Roman emperor Vespasian have been right, then, when he said, just before he died, "I think I am becoming a god"? If so, he needed more than this verse to go on.[53]

Levenson compares the word *'elohim*'s breadth of meaning to the English word "spirit," which "can denote anything from God to an angel, a demon, a ghost, a tone of an organization, or an alcoholic beverage." Calling the dead *'elohim, then,* did "not in the least imply that they were divine."[54] Philip Johnston takes the medium's answer to be "I see spirits coming up out of the earth," which is a conjuring formula meaning that she's been successful.[55] Saul, assuming she has raised Samuel, asks what he looks like. Then the woman describes what she saw as "an old man . . . wearing a robe." This was enough to assure Saul that this spirit was really Samuel. Then, as if to verify for us that Saul was not wrong, the biblical writer says, "Samuel said to Saul," and he quotes the spirit ("Why have you disturbed me by bringing me up?").

What the medium saw had the appearance of physical form—an old man in a robe. Could this have been either a glorified, resurrection body, or a temporary body? Perhaps. Williamson doubts this, since Saul did not see anything. Therefore, he says, it was likely "Samuel in his disembodied state."[56] Yet with Enoch and Elijah walking away with their bodies and Moses appearing with one centuries after his own death, who is to say?

Joyce Baldwin believes that Samuel's words "suggest that Saul has interrupted a life of restfulness which Samuel had been enjoying and had been reluctant to leave."[57] The account, she says, shows ...

> how pervasive and entrenched were Canaanite practices, even among the Israelites. Though violation of the law carried the death penalty, and necromancers were officially banished from the land, they were still to be found, ready to operate if given an assurance of protection. People evidently wanted their services and were ready to pay for the privilege. Whether they were deceived, or whether they genuinely saw and heard the ghosts of the dead, the biblical writers do not say. . . . [Yet] even after his death, the prophet Samuel speaks.[58]

The spirits of the dead continue to exist, albeit in some somnolent form, between death and resurrection.

Johnston concludes that though necromancy could be effective, it benefitted no one.[59] Williamson agrees that "the spirits of the dead continue to exist, albeit in some somnolent form, between death and resurrection," though little is known of the nature of that existence.

It seems possible to speak even from an exclusively Old Testament perspective of an 'intermediate state.'

"Saul and the Witch of Endor" by Benjamin West

Nevertheless, "it seems possible to speak even from an exclusively Old Testament perspective of an 'intermediate state.'"[60] Cooper agrees that "Old Testament people believed that the dead continue to exist in a ghostly form in an underworld location called Sheol."[61]

Old Testament people believed that the dead continue to exist in a ghostly form in an underworld location called Sheol.

Idioms for Death

In situations of relational or chronological distance, we might ask if someone is dead or when they died. (Is Queen Elizabeth II dead? Yes, she died in 2022.) But in closer relational situations, especially those calling for sympathy and tact, we commonly use euphemisms. I might ask, "When did she pass away?" Or, "When did you lose your mother?" In 2021 I heard someone report, "Argentinian evangelist Luis Palau was called home." This invites us to ask what idioms for death are used in the Old Testament.

Genesis 25:8 says, Abraham "*took his last breath* and died at a good old age, old and contented, and he was *gathered to his people*" (emphasis added). The same phrases are used of Ishmael (Gen 25:17). Isaac, too, "took his last breath and died, and was *gathered to his people*, old and full of days" (Gen 35:29). Coming after the notice that they "died," we might think the phrase "gathered to his people" referred to burial. But Jacob instructed his sons by saying, "I am about to be *gathered to my people*. Bury me with my ancestors in the cave in the field of Ephron the Hethite" (Gen 49:29). Then he "drew his feet into the bed," and—as expected—"took his last breath, and was *gathered to his people*" (Gen 49:33), even though he was not buried until much later (Gen 50:13).[62] Centuries after that, God told Moses this: "You will die on the mountain that you go up, and you will be *gathered to your people*, just as your brother Aaron died on Mount Hor and was *gathered to his*" (Deut 32:50). This particular idiom may derive from the practice of burying bodies in family tombs, as Block and others suggest, but Moses and Aaron were both buried alone, and Abraham was only buried "with his wife Sarah" (Gen 25:10). So the sense appears to be that the spirits of these men would "join the spirits of kinsfolk in Sheol" (the place of the dead).[63] Since they were brothers, "your people" and "his people" were evidently the same people.

That the spirits of these men would "join the spirits of kinsfolk in Sheol" (the place of the dead).

Similarly, Joshua's "whole generation was also *gathered to their ancestors*" (Judg 2:10). And later the Lord said to King Josiah, "[B]ecause your heart was tender and you humbled yourself before [me], . . . I will indeed *gather you to your ancestors*, and you will be *gathered* to your grave in peace. Your eyes will not see all the disaster that I am bringing on this place" (2 Kgs 22:19–20).

Another expression referring explicitly to peaceful, natural death was to sleep/rest with one's ancestors. Jacob had told his son Joseph, "When I *rest with my ancestors*, carry me away from Egypt and bury me in their burial place" (Gen 47:30, emphasis added). God had told Moses, "You are about to *rest with your ancestors*" (Deut 31:16). God had similarly told Abraham that his descendants would live in Egypt for 400 years, but that Abraham would "*go to [his] ancestors* in peace and be buried at a good old age" (Gen 15:15). Otherwise, the expression was used over 30 times of Israel's kings who died peacefully (see 2 Sam 7:12;

Remnants of the Monolith of Silwan, a First Temple period tomb.

1 Kgs 11:43; 14:20, 31; 15:8, etc.).[64] David also "rested with his ancestors and was buried in the city of David" (1 Kgs 2:10), although his ancestors were not buried there. The expression came to signify peaceful death, yet it had its origin in the concept of joining one's ancestors in the afterlife.

Sheol, the Pit, and Abaddon

We have seen that the Old Testament speaks of a place where the dead reside in an underworld called *Sheol*, which may often be a figurative way of speaking of the grave in terms of a "metaphorical and transcendent realm." Because of this, Old Testament scholar Bruce Waltke cautions against building from it a doctrine of the intermediate state.[65] It is also sometimes called "the Pit" (usually *shachat* [Job 33:18] or *bor* [Ps 28:1]) or "Abaddon," which is Hebrew for "place of destruction" (Prov 15:11). "Sheol" and "the Pit" often occur together, suggesting they are synonyms (Ps 30:3; Prov 1:12). "Abaddon" is related to the Hebrew word for "perish," and Waltke explains its sense as a rhetorical intensification of "the grave as a place of destruction."[66] It also occurs synonymously with Sheol (Prov 15:11; 27:20) as well as "grave" (Ps 88:11) and is personified along with Death in Job 28:22. Abaddon and Death know nothing of true wisdom. In Revelation 9:11 it appears as "the angel of the abyss." A postbiblical Christian work (perhaps second century AD) called the Ascension of Isaiah places Abaddon below Sheol (10:8) and equates it with Gehenna, where the wicked dead are and where Satan and his angels (now in the heavenly realm) will be thrown (4:14).[67] But this understanding of Abaddon has no biblical support.

Philip Johnston observes that the Hebrew name *Sheol* is unique to the Hebrews, which should caution us from reading into it the underworld trappings from the surrounding pagan nations.[68] Although always depicted as the opposite of heaven, and so down in the depths of the earth, if it is a literal place, it is surely, like heaven, in a different dimension of reality. As Levenson says, "Literalistic efforts to locate the abode of the dead in space are misconceived." Various metaphors for it "communicate a mode of existence."[69]

Literalistic efforts to locate the abode of the dead in space are misconceived.

The term *Sheol* is found 65 times in the Hebrew Bible, most commonly in the poetic books of Psalms (16), Isaiah (9), Proverbs (9), and Job (8). Johnston points out that considering how often death is mentioned in the Old Testament (at least a thousand times), this is a remarkably small number. Thus, the underworld was only "a minor Old Testament theme." He claims it was "a place of little interest to the Hebrew writers. They praised and feared Yahweh in this life and this world alone and had little interest in the world below."[70] Death is often viewed in the Old Testament as the removal of

Death is often viewed in the Old Testament as the removal of a person from the assembly of the still living, worshiping saints.

a person from the assembly of the still living, worshiping saints, who testify to God's faithfulness. This is the force of many passages often claimed to describe what is or is not happening in the afterlife (see, for example, Isa 38:18–20).

The nature of *Sheol* is hotly disputed. Is it simply the place of the dead, inhabited by all departed spirits, perhaps divided into at least two compartments—one for the wicked and one for the righteous? Or is it only for the wicked, perhaps serving as a place of punishment? Do the inhabitants there have physical forms? On the other hand, could *Sheol* simply be figurative for "the grave" (the usual NIV rendering)? Some consider its semantics to be contextual, meaning "the grave" when referring to godly people, but "the underworld" when referring to the wicked. The common appearance of the term *Sheol* in poetic literature, "a medium in which imagination normally triumphs over realism," according to commentator Jack Sasson,[71] may suggest it is merely an implied comparison to a fictional or imagined place, as we might speak of having been in Heartbreak Hotel, Lonesome Town, Camelot, Wonderland, or Narnia. There seems to be more to it than that, however.

Arguments can be found for and against each of these views, and many Scriptures are cited that are claimed to support these arguments. Even the relative absence of passages refuting them is sometimes claimed to support certain arguments. What seems crystal clear from a certain passage to one person, however, may not appear that way to someone else. We tend to interpret passages to fit whatever view we hold to, sometimes (unfortunately) even ridiculing someone else's understanding as absurd.[72] Most people who have devoted their lives to the study of God's Word, though, know very well that many passages can be reasonably interpreted in more than one way. For instance, some verses that speak of God's deliverance from death or Sheol may concern either His faithfully protecting someone from going there or His retrieving them from the pit once they are there. Moreover, our determination of whether the writer is speaking literally or figuratively may be a tangled process. Bible scholars try to follow the data of Scripture until it forms a coherent picture that seems to arise from that data and that connects the most dots of Scripture in the most reasonable way. The picture must fit not only the Bible's content and overall context, but also what we know of its historical and cultural background. Interpretation is not an easy task, especially when dealing with topics such as the afterlife which, frankly, is not what the Bible is mainly about: Who God is, who we are, what obstacles our sin has thrown in our way, what God is doing for us, and how He wants us to respond is the Bible's main focus. There are certainly whispers in the Bible about many other things, but we dare not let them divert too much of our attention from the main thing.

Johnston notes that taking *Sheol* as simply a reference to the grave would not account for the prophets' describing its inhabitants as speaking (Isa 14:9–17;

Most people who have devoted their lives to the study of God's Word, though, know very well that many passages can be reasonably interpreted in more than one way.

Interpretation is not an easy task, especially when dealing with topics such as the afterlife which, frankly, is not what the Bible is mainly about: Who God is, who we are, what obstacles our sin has thrown in our way, what God is doing for us, and how he wants us to respond is the Bible's main focus.

Ezek 32:21, 31),[73] although such description may be more rhetorical than literal.[74] A better argument is David's statement in Psalm 139:8: "If I go up to heaven, you are there; / if I make my bed in Sheol, you are there." As Old Testament scholar John Walton explains, "One could hardly contend that God is in the grave, while his access to the netherworld is of appropriate significance" (also see Prov 15:11; Amos 9:2).[75] Writers could surely speak of *Sheol* figuratively as a situation or state of mind, "from the depths" of which they could be delivered (see Pss 18:4–5; 30:3; 86:13; 88:6; Jonah 2:2–6), as someone might say to a friend, "I was in hell till you got here." But Sheol is so often treated as a place that the ball seems to be in the court of those denying its existence. Another reason for thinking Sheol was regarded as a real place is the use of the term *rephaim*, "departed spirits," for its inhabitants (see below).

There is no doubt that believers and unbelievers all were thought to go to Sheol when they died.

Regarding the question of who inhabits Sheol in the Old Testament, not everyone agrees with John Cooper:

> Although the Old Testament has a few hints that even in death the Lord spares and communes with his righteous ones, ... there is no doubt that believers and unbelievers all were thought to go to Sheol when they died. Job asserts repeatedly that this is where he is headed. So some form of existence in Sheol is the common lot of humanity in the Old Testament, with the notable exceptions of Elijah and Enoch, who were taken by God.[76]

Some scholars understand that Sheol had various compartments separating the wicked and the righteous.[77] The wicked may have been segregated into Abaddon and the Pit. But Old Testament scholar Desmond Alexander and others argue that this view is found only in intertestamental Jewish literature (specifically, the apocryphal 1 Enoch, which has four compartments in Sheol). The Old Testament suggests no such internal borders.[78]

Another view is that Sheol is a place only for the wicked to exist in separation from God. According to this view, when the righteous die, their spirits ascend to heaven, while the wicked go to Sheol. Indeed, the psalmist prays, "Let the wicked be disgraced; / let them be quiet in Sheol" (Ps 31:17).

Another view is that Sheol is a place only for the wicked to exist in separation from God.

When Korah the Levite led a rebellion against God's chosen servant Moses, "The earth opened its mouth and swallowed them and their households, all Korah's people, and all their possessions. They went down alive into Sheol [NIV, "the realm of the dead"] with all that belonged to them. The earth closed over them, and they vanished from the assembly" (Num 16:32–33).

The Bible's perspective is that death itself is not natural but punitive and therefore to be feared. Like sin, it is a source of defilement.[79] It can only become a positive experience as a result of God's supernatural act of forgiveness and redemption (see Ps 49:5–15). Therefore, Alexander argues that "apart from a few references that are indecisive" (for example, Eccl 9:10; Song 8:6), "Sheol always conveys negative overtones" and is usually "linked

"Apart from a few references that are indecisive."

Punishment of the Sons of Korah. Fresco by Sandro Botticelli in the Sistine Chapel, 1480–82.

unquestionably with evil-doers." Therefore, "it does indeed denote the ultimate abode of the wicked alone."[80] Johnston agrees: "Sheol cannot be identified simply as the Hebrew term for the underworld which awaits all. It is almost exclusively reserved for those under divine judgment.... Thus Sheol is not used indiscriminately to describe human destiny at death."[81]

> "Sheol always conveys negative overtones."

> "Sheol cannot be identified simply as the Hebrew term for the underworld which awaits all. It is almost exclusively reserved for those under divine judgment."

Indeed, some passages that seem to suggest the righteous also end up in Sheol can be understood otherwise. When Jacob's sons presented him with evidence that Joseph had been killed, he "tore his clothes, put sackcloth around his waist, and mourned for his son many days. All his sons and daughters tried to comfort him, but he refused to be comforted. 'No,' he said. 'I will go down to Sheol to my son, mourning'" (Gen 37:34-35). In passages like this, however, Sheol may be used only as a figurative reference to death.[82] Or, as Alexander suggests, "Jacob's unwillingness to be comforted ... could suggest that he considers Joseph to have been divinely punished, and hence with the wicked in the nether world."[83]

Another righteous person who speaks of going to Sheol is King Hezekiah. When he becomes ill and seems likely to die, God informs him through Isaiah the prophet—in response to Hezekiah's prayer—that 15 years have been added to his life. The king later wrote a poem recounting his prayer. The poem begins this way:

> I said: In the prime of my life
> I must go to the gates of Sheol [NIV, "through the gates of death"];
> I am deprived of the rest of my years. (Isa 38:10)

Did Hezekiah expect his spirit to descend to Sheol at death, or was he speaking figuratively? He expresses his gratitude for God's love delivering him (that is, his *nephesh*, NIV "life") "from the pit of destruction" and throwing "all [Hezekiah's] sins behind [his] back" (38:17). Then he declares that his life will be a testimony to the Lord's faithfulness:

> For Sheol cannot thank you [God];
> Death cannot praise you.
> Those who go down to the Pit
> cannot hope for your faithfulness.
> The living, only the living can thank you,
> as I do today;
> a father will make your faithfulness known to children. (Isa 38:18–19)

Did Hezekiah contemplate going to the Pit where there was no hope for God's faithfulness? Again, Alexander suggests that considering God's initial indictment in verse 1 and his own sense of guilt in verse 17, "Hezekiah may have had every reason to believe that he was doomed to join the wicked in the nether world. It is thus possible that both Hezekiah and Jacob understood *Sheol* to denote the final abode of the wicked."[84]

Alexander Heidel was an Assyriologist at the Oriental Institute of the University of Chicago. In his work on the Babylonian Gilgamesh Epic, he published a study on "Death and the Afterlife," comparing the Bible to the Babylonian myth. In it he discusses the uses of *Sheol* in the Bible. He writes,

> Since there is no conclusive evidence that the souls of pious persons, among whom Hezekiah must be numbered, were believed to descend to *She'ol* in the sense of the subterranean spirit world, [and] there are passages which state clearly that the souls of the righteous ascended to heaven, ... it is reasonable to assume that Hezekiah uses *She'ol* in the sense of "the grave."[85]

> *"There are passages which state clearly that the souls of the righteous ascended to heaven."*

Against this view, Bible scholar Justin Bass argues that "besides Enoch and Elijah [Heidel] cannot produce one example of someone specifically said to have been taken to heaven."[86] How many examples, though, would it take? Could we not conclude from these two cases, with Alexander, that "God has the power to take to himself those who enjoy an intimate relationship with him" (see Ps 73:24)?[87] N. T. Wright sees in Psalm 73:24–26 "a tantalizing glimpse of a life beyond the grave."[88]

> *"God has the power to take to himself those who enjoy an intimate relationship with him."*

For his view that everyone went to Sheol, Bass presents as "the strongest evidence ... that the real spirit of righteous Samuel came from Sheol, not heaven."[89]

But the account in 1 Samuel 28 never mentions Sheol. As we saw earlier, the medium's statement, "I see spirits coming up out of the earth," may be just a conjuring formula meaning that she's been successful in summoning the dead. According to Johnson, although the word for "earth" here (*'erets*), which occurs about 2,500 times in the Old Testament, can, in a few passages, refer to the underworld, nowhere is this meaning demanded. The medium may have just been describing something coming up from beneath her. "It is wiser to conclude that *'erets* is not a Hebrew term for the underworld."[90] Perhaps that's where Samuel's spirit was, but we cannot be sure.

The Old Testament does not describe Sheol as a place of torment, so the KJV rendering "hell" is probably not appropriate.[91] Nevertheless, Levenson agrees with its portrayal by earlier scholars as an experience of "slackness, sorrow, exhaustion, curses." In short, it is "wholly undesirable," epitomizing "the struggle against the powerful and malignant forces that negate life and deprive it of meaning" and "very often has to do with punishment."[92] It is anything but the kind of family reunion depicted in the phrases "gathered to . . ." or "rested with one's people/ancestors." The afterlife in Sheol is the opposite: "Those who go down to it are said to feel isolated and abandoned, and the absence of kin in the descriptions of the group imprisoned there is striking."

The Old Testament does not describe Sheol as a place of torment, so the KJV rendering "hell" is probably not appropriate.

"Those who go down to it are said to feel isolated and abandoned, and the absence of kin in the descriptions of the group imprisoned there is striking."

There are "no grounds whatsoever for assuming that one who 'slept/lay with his [ancestors]' did so in Sheol."[93] Although a few passages do sound as if all end up in Sheol (see Ps 49:8), these are probably best understood rhetorically. References to Sheol in the book of Job will be discussed later, but what was said about the difficulty of interpreting Ecclesiastes also applies to Job. The important thing here is that it gives us strong evidence for the existence of spirits after death.

Although a few passages do sound as if all end up in Sheol (see Ps 89:48), these are probably best understood rhetorically.

But there is more.

Departed Spirits

We saw earlier that in ancient religious texts from fifteenth-century BC Ugarit, those in the underworld could be called *Rapiuma,* a word generally thought to have some connection to Hebrew *rephaim.* The Hebrew word occurs 27 times, but only 8 times in reference to the dead. Otherwise, it's used of an ancient ethnic group of Canaanites in the region east of the Jordan River (see Gen 14:5; 15:20). They and the Anakim were noted for their height (Num 13:33; Deut 2:11, 20; 3:11, 13; Josh 12:4). Also, a valley near Jerusalem was called "Rephaim Valley" (Josh 15:8), which may have a connection to a possible group of Philistines by that name (1 Chr 20:4).[94]

The eight references to the dead as *rephaim* (Job 26:5; Ps 88:10–12; Prov 2:18; 9:18; 21:16; Isa 14:9; 26:14, 19) occur mostly in connection to Sheol and death. Bible versions often render the Hebrew word with "the dead," but the CSB and NASB use "departed spirits," the JPS and REB use "the shades" (a disembodied spirit or ghost), and the NJB uses "the Shadows." The problem with translating *rephaim* as "the dead" is that there was a more common Hebrew word for "the dead," using a form of the verb meaning "to die." This word, which just indicates someone who has died, is sometimes used parallel to *rephaim* (Ps 88:10; Isa 26:14, 19). To distinguish the two terms in these passages, other versions must translate *rephaim* as "the departed" (ESV), "departed spirits" (NET), "their spirits" (NIV), or "shades" (NRSV). In other words, *rephaim* seems to be something that remains after death. According to German Old Testament scholar R. Litwak, whatever the Rapiuma in Ugaritic texts were, "the OT admits no doubt that the Rephaim inhabit the realm of the dead."[95] Johnston distinguishes the *rephaim* from the Ugaritic *Rapiuma* in that the *rephaim* are "lifeless and need rousing, they tremble before God, they are not limited to heroes or kings, they are never individually named, they do not travel, participate at banquets or play any role . . . as protectors or patrons" of the living.[96]

Seems to be something that remains after death.

Several early twentieth-century Old Testament scholars have been cited as declaring that "Old Testament souls do not dwell in bodies," and that the words for "soul" and "spirit" do not refer to the essence of a person that survives death.[97] Even if there is some truth in this, Cooper explains, "[I]n reality the Israelites did affirm the existence of the departed. . . . They simply had another term for them—*rephaim.*"[98] He also quotes H. Wheeler Robinson, the most prominent British Old Testament scholar of his day: "The dead are thus supposed to go on existing in some sense or other, even by the early thought of Israel. But it is an existence which has no attraction for the Israelite. . . . It is not his soul that survives at all; the dead are called 'shades' (*rephaim*), not 'souls' in the Old Testament. The subterranean place of their abiding is called Sheol."[99] The clearest evidence for this is the passages where *rephaim* parallels the words for "the dead" and "death."

"[I]n reality the Israelites did affirm the existence of the departed. . . . They simply had another term for them—rephaim."

Do you work wonders for *the dead?*
Do *departed spirits* rise up to praise you? Selah
Will your faithful love be declared in the grave,

your faithfulness in *Abaddon*?
Will your wonders be known in the darkness
or your righteousness in the *land of oblivion*? (Ps 88:10-12)
The dead do not live;
departed spirits do not rise up.
Indeed, you have punished and destroyed them;
you have wiped out all memory of them. . . .
Your dead will live; their bodies will rise.
Awake and sing, you who dwell in the dust!
For you will be covered with the morning dew,
and the earth will bring out the *departed spirits*. (Isa 26:14, 19)
for her [that is, the wayward woman's] house sinks down to death
and her ways to the land of the *departed spirits*. (Prov 2:18)

These verses depict the departed spirits in "Abaddon" or "the grave," in "darkness,"
and "the land of oblivion" (or "forgetfulness"). Isaiah 14 places the departed spirits of Israel's oppressors, "the kings of the nations," in "Sheol below" (v. 9), among
the maggots and worms (v. 11), and in "the deepest regions of the Pit" (v. 15).

The *departed spirits* tremble
beneath the waters and all that inhabit them.
Sheol is naked before God,
and *Abaddon* has no covering. (Job 26:5-6)

But [the inexperienced man] doesn't know that the *departed spirits* are there
[with the rowdy woman],
that her guests are in the *depths of Sheol* (Prov 9:18)

> The person who strays from the way of prudence
> will come to rest in the *assembly of the departed spirits*. (Prov 21:16)

Evidence that the Israelites believed in the continuation of human personality after death and that the Old Testament itself teaches the same thing is difficult to deny. We have the evidence of Enoch, Elijah, Moses, and Samuel. The archaeological evidence of venerating the dead and the biblical repudiation of mortuary practices is sufficient to demonstrate the people's chronic commitment to it. Disagreement over the nature of the realm of the dead and the departed spirits who inhabited it does not alter the biblical evidence of their existence. Many psalms also confirm that followers of Yahweh were convinced that death was not the end of the believer's communion with God, much less of their conscious existence.[100] From the beginning of Israel's history, worshipers of the Lord believed that death involved not just a departure from surviving family but a joining in the fellowship of their ancestors.

Though containing "no detailed account of the fate of the righteous immediately after death," the Old Testament affirms the bodily resurrection of departed believers (see esp. Dan 12:2), whose spirits have remained in an intermediate state.[101] Moreover, nothing in the Old Testament denies that the spirits of believers may be enjoying, to some degree, fellowship with God between death and resurrection. After Abraham's death, God said to his son Isaac, "I am the God of your father Abraham" (Gen 26:24). Long after the patriarchs had died, God said to Moses, "I am the God of your father, the God of Abraham, the God of Isaac, and the God of Jacob" (Exod 3:6). While we may think God was only speaking historically, Jesus saw something more in these statements. In response to the question of whether the dead are raised (see Mark 12:26), Jesus quoted God's words to Moses, then said, "He is not the God of the dead, but of the living" (Matt 22:32).

NOTES

1 N. T. Wright, *Surprised by Hope: Rethinking Heaven, the Resurrection, and the Mission of the Church* (New York: HarperOne, 2008), 41.

2 Stephen T. Davis, *After We Die: Theology, Philosophy, and the Question of Life after Death* (Waco, TX: Baylor University Press, 2015), 27.

3 Thomas R. Schreiner, *Commentary on Hebrews*, Biblical Theology for Christian Proclamation (Nashville: Holman, 2015), 286.

4 Anthony A. Hoekema, *The Bible and the Future* (Grand Rapids: Eerdmans, 1979), 89–90.

5 The second-century apologist Tatian argued, "The soul is not in itself immortal, O Greeks, but mortal." He was followed in this by Tertullian. Early Christian writers, then, saw the views of the soul's immortality and bodily resurrection as being opposed to each other. According to historian Jaroslav Pelikan, however, later Christian thinkers began to combine the soul's supposed immortality with the resurrection of the body. Ambrose in the fourth century, for example, took "the standard view" in arguing that "resurrection meant the conferral upon the body of that deathless life which the soul already possessed." See Jaroslav Pelikan, *The Emergence of the Catholic Tradition (100–600)*, volume 1 of *The Christian Tradition: A History of the Development of Doctrine* (Chicago: University of

Chicago Press, 1971), 51–52. Also see Jon D. Levenson, *Resurrection and the Restoration of Israel: The Ultimate Victory of the God of Life* (New Haven: Yale University Press, 2006), 106.

6   See Millard J. Erickson, *Christian Theology* (Grand Rapids: Baker, 1985), 1175–76.

7   Norman R. Gulley, *Systematic Theology: Creation, Christ, Salvation* (Berrien Springs, MI: Andrews University Press, 2012), 114, 116, 122.

8   Emphasis added. See "Death, the State of the Dead, and the Resurrection," Seventh Day Adventist, accessed March 7, 2023, https://www.adventist.org/death-and-resurrection/.

9   Emphasis added. See "What Adventists Believe about the Nature of Humanity," Seventh Day Adventist, accessed March 7, 2023, https://www.adventist.org/nature-of-humanity/. Under Belief 7, "Nature of Humanity," it is said that each "created free being" is "an indivisible unity of body, mind, and spirit, dependent upon God for life and breath and all else." No clarification is offered on how mind and spirit relate to the body or the breath of life.

10   Emphasis added. See "Death, the State of the Dead, and the Resurrection." According to an earlier Adventist source, "All men, good and evil alike, remain in the grave from death to the resurrection." See *Seventh-day Adventists Answer Questions on Doctrine* (Washington: Review and Herald, 1957), 13.

11   Gulley, *Systematic Theology: Creation, Christ, Salvation*, 119.

12   Anthony Hoekema describes this as the view also of Dutch philosopher G. Van der Leeuw (1890–1950) and Jehovah's Witnesses (*The Bible and the Future*, 93).

13   Steven B. Cowan and James S. Spiegel, *The Love of Wisdom: A Christian Introduction to Philosophy* (Nashville: B&H, 2009), 223.

14   For a brief survey of this topic, see J. P. Moreland and William Lane Craig, *Philosophical Foundations for a Christian Worldview* (Downers Grove, IL: IVP, 2003), 511–15.

15   See Paul R. Williamson, *Death and the Afterlife: Biblical Perspectives on Ultimate Questions*, New Studies in Biblical Theology (Downers Grove, IL: InterVarsity, 2018), 33.

16   John W. Cooper, *Body, Soul & Life Everlasting: Biblical Anthropology and the Monism-Dualism Debate* (Grand Rapids: Eerdmans, 1989), 45–46.

17   Kenneth A. Mathews, *Genesis 1–11*, Christian Standard Commentary (Nashville: Holman, 2022), 255–56.

18   Mathews, *Genesis 1–11*, 272.

19   Allen P. Ross, *A Commentary on the Psalms: Volume 2 (42–89)* (Grand Rapids: Kregel, 2013), 151.

20   Klaas Spronk, *Beatific Afterlife in Ancient Israel and in the Ancient Near East* (Kevelaer: Butzon & Bercker, 1986), 326, 345. He translates Ps 73:24, "and afterwards there is glory: Thou wilt take me" (p. 319).

21   Gulley, *Systematic Theology: Creation, Christ, Salvation*, 114.

22   See, for example, Allen P. Ross, *A Commentary on the Psalms*, Volume 1 (1–41) (Grand Rapids: Kregel, 2011), 266. Ross understands the point of Ps 115:16–18 being that unbelievers "had no relation with the living God; they will go down to the land of silence, still excluded from the covenant people of God and from God himself. But the righteous will not be silent; they will bless the LORD from now throughout eternity" (*A Commentary on the Psalms*, Volume 3 [90–150] [Grand Rapids: Kregel, 2016], 419).

23   Philip S. Johnston, *Shades of Sheol: Death and Afterlife in the Old Testament* (Downers Grove, IL: InterVarsity, 2002), 96.

24   Geoffrey W. Grogan, *Psalms,* The Two Horizons Old Testament Commentary (Grand Rapids: Eerdmans, 2008), 154.

25   Barry G. Webb, *Five Festal Garments: Christian Reflections on the Song of Songs, Ruth, Lamentations, Ecclesiastes and Esther,* New Studies in Biblical Theology (Downers Grove,

IL: InterVarsity, 2000), 83. Webb says further, "Like the desert Sphinx, it teases us with questions, yields its secrets only grudgingly, and will not allow us the luxury of easy answers. In other words, it is thoroughly irritating, but at the same time almost mesmeric in its appeal. It draws us towards it by mirroring the perplexity we all feel as we grapple with life."

26 G. A. Klingbeil, "Ecclesiastes 2: Ancient Near Eastern Background," *Dictionary of the Old Testament: Wisdom, Poetry and Writings,* ed. Tremper Longman III and Peter Enns (Downers Grove, IL: InterVarsity, 2008), 132–40.

27 Webb, *Five Festal Garments,* 102.

28 See John H. Walton, *Ancient Near Eastern Thought and the Old Testament* 2nd ed.; (Grand Rapids: Baker, 2018), 298.

29 This paragraph relies on E. R. Clendenen, "Religious Background of the Old Testament," in *Foundations for Biblical Interpretation,* ed. D. S. Dockery, K. A. Mathews, and R. B. Sloan (Nashville: B&H, 1994), 281.

30 S. N. Kramer, *The Sumerians* (Chicago/London: University of Chicago, 1963), 123.

31 Jacob Milgrom, *Leviticus 17–22,* The Anchor Bible (New York: Doubleday, 2000), 1772.

32 Harry A. Hoffner, "'obh," *Theological Dictionary of the Old Testament* (Grand Rapids: Eerdmans, 1974), 1:133. Also Milgrom, *Leviticus 17–22,* 1768.

33 Milgrom, *Leviticus 17–22,* 1772.

34 Milgrom, *Leviticus 17–22,* 1700. He describes it as "consulting ghosts and wizard-spirits."

35 Daniel I. Block, "Beyond the Grave: Ezekiel's Vision of Death and Afterlife," *Bulletin for Biblical Research* 2 (1992): 117–18. However the "evil spirit" in Judg 9:23; 1 Sam 16:14 is understood, it is clearly not a demon from the underworld but a spirit totally under Yahweh's control.

36 Block, "Beyond the Grave," 129.

37 Johnston, *Shades of Sheol,* 195.

38 Stephen L. Cook, "Funerary Practices and Afterlife Expectations in Ancient Israel," *Religion Compass* 1/6 (2007): 661.

39 Johnston, *Shades of Sheol,* 166.

40 Matthew J. Suriano, *A History of Death in the Hebrew Bible* (Oxford: Oxford University Press, 2018), 32–33.

41 Suriano, *A History of Death in the Hebrew Bible,* 40.

42 Suriano, *A History of Death in the Hebrew Bible,* 47.

43 Suriano, *A History of Death in the Hebrew Bible,* 48.

44 Suriano, *A History of Death in the Hebrew Bible,* 48.

45 Suriano, *A History of Death in the Hebrew Bible,* 46–48.

46 Suriano, *A History of Death in the Hebrew Bible,* 51.

47 Suriano, *A History of Death in the Hebrew Bible,* 116.

48 Suriano, *A History of Death in the Hebrew Bible,* 124.

49 Levenson, *Resurrection and the Restoration of Israel,* 52–53.

50 Joyce G. Baldwin, *1 & 2 Samuel,* Tyndale Old Testament Commentaries (Leicester/Downers Grove, IL: Inter-Varsity, 1988), 159.

51 Williamson, *Death and the Afterlife,* 43.

52 See Williamson, *Death and the Afterlife,* 43. Jack J. Blanco, *The Clear Word: An Expanded Paraphrase to Build Strong Faith and Nurture Spiritual Growth* (Hagerstown, MD: Review and Herald, 2003), 345, has this rendering of 1 Sam 28:15.

53 Robert D. Bergen believes the medium accepted a pagan idea that Samuel had become a god, that is, "a spirit-being possessing capabilities beyond those of mortals." See *1,2*

Samuel, The New American Commentary (Nashville: B&H, 1996), 268. Robert P. Gordon thinks *'elohim* refers here to "the spirit of a deceased person," and he notes that "the earth" may refer to the underworld. See *1&2 Samuel: A Commentary,* Library of Biblical Interpretation (Grand Rapids: Zondervan, 1986), 195–96. Ronald Youngblood agrees that "in ancient times the deceased could be referred to as 'gods' in that they lived in the realm of the preternatural," and that *ha'ares* may refer to "netherworld" ("1, 2 Samuel" in *Expositor's Bible Commentary* [Grand Rapids: Zondervan, 1990], comment on 2 Sam 28:7–14. Baldwin notes that the term "used with plurals" can mean "judges" or authority figures. (*1 & 2 Samuel,* 159).

54 Levenson, *Resurrection and the Restoration of Israel,* 57.

55 Philip S. Johnston, *Shades of Sheol: Death and Afterlife in the Old Testament* (Downers Grove, IL: IVP, 2002), 146. He argues that the term *'elohim* in Isa 8:19 also refers to the spirits of the dead (pp. 146–47). Some want to seek guidance from the spirits: "Inquire of the mediums and the spiritists who chirp and mutter." The issue is where the response starts (Hebrew does not use quotation marks). Some translations begin it immediately with the question in v. 19 (CSB: "Shouldn't a people inquire of *their God*? Should they inquire of the dead on behalf of the living?"; similarly ESV, NASB, NKJV, NIV). In this case, *'elohim* refers to "God." Two problems with this are (1) Hebrew marks only one question, and (2) after the first question is literally, "on behalf of the living to the dead." So other translations begin the response in v. 20 ("Go to God's instruction and testimony! If they do not speak according to this word, there will be no dawn for them"). In this case, the people urge in v. 19, "Should people not seek oracles from *their gods,* by asking the dead about the destiny of the living?" (NET, emphasis added; similarly NRSV, JPS, NJB, REB). Johnston argues that *'elohim* is clarified by "the dead" and so refers to "their spirits [of the dead]" (*Shades of Sheol,* 146–47).

56 Williamson, *Death and the Afterlife,* 44.

57 Baldwin, *1 & 2 Samuel,* 160.

58 Baldwin, *1 & 2 Samuel,* 163–64.

59 Johnston, *Shades of Sheol,* 158.

60 Williamson, *Death and the Afterlife,* 44.

61 Cooper, *Body, Soul & Life Everlasting,* 59.

62 Emphasis added. Johnston, *Shades of Sheol,* 34.

63 Block, *Deuteronomy,* 778. Johnston reaches the same conclusion.

64 See Johnston, *Shades of Sheol,* 34–35.

65 Bruce K. Waltke, *The Book of Proverbs Chapters 1–15,* New International Commentary on the Old Testament (Grand Rapids: Eerdmans, 2004), 116.

66 Waltke, *The Book of Proverbs,* 622–23.

67 Richard Bauckham, *The Fate of the Dead: Studies on the Jewish and Christian Apocalypses* (Atlanta: Society of Biblical Literature, 1998), 77.

68 Johnston, *Shades of Sheol,* 79.

69 Levenson, *Resurrection and the Restoration of Israel,* 45.

70 Johnston, *Shades of Sheol,* 72–73, 124.

71 Jack M. Sasson, *Jonah,* Anchor Bible (New York: Doubleday, 1990), 171.

72 According to Levenson, the field of biblical studies is "renowned for its deficit of basic agreement and the depth of its controversies" (*Resurrection and the Restoration of Israel,* 35).

73 Johnston, *Shades of Sheol,* 74.

74 See Williamson, *Death and the Afterlife*, 41.

75 Walton, *Ancient Near Eastern Thought and the Old Testament*, 302. *Sheol* also never occurs with the Hebrew article, which suggests it is a place name rather than "the grave." See T. Desmond Alexander, "The Old Testament View of Life after Death," *Themelios* 11.2 (1986): 43.

76 Cooper, *Body, Soul & Life Everlasting*, 55. Also Justin W. Bass, *The Battle for the Keys: Revelation 1:18 and Christ's Descent into the Underworld*, Paternoster Biblical Monographs (Milton Keynes, Bucks, UK: Paternoster, 2014), 44–47.

77 For an argument for compartments in Sheol see Bass, *The Battle for the Keys*, 78–101. The compartments are paradise or Abraham's bosom; the abyss or Tartarus; and Gehenna or the lake of fire.

78 Alexander, "The Old Testament View of Life after Death," 43.

79 Alexander, "The Old Testament View of Life after Death," 42.

80 Alexander, "The Old Testament View of Life after Death," 44.

81 Johnston, *Shades of Sheol*, 83.

82 Heidel, *The Gilgamesh Epic and Old Testament Parallels*, 186–87.

83 Alexander, "The Old Testament View of Life after Death," 44.

84 Alexander, "The Old Testament View of Life after Death," 44.

85 See Alexander Heidel, *The Gilgamesh Epic and Old Testament Parallels* (Chicago: University of Chicago Press, 1949), 180.

86 Bass, *The Battle for the Keys*, 45.

87 Alexander, "The Old Testament View of Life after Death," 44.

88 N. T. Wright, *The Resurrection of the Son of God* (Minneapolis: Fortress, 2003), 106.

89 Bass, *The Battle for the Keys*, 46.

90 Johnston, *Shades of Sheol*, 109, 114.

91 See Johnston, *Shades of Sheol*, 73.

92 Levenson, *Resurrection and the Restoration of Israel*, 35, 72–73. He cites Johannes Pedersen and John Gray.

93 Levenson, *Resurrection and the Restoration of Israel*, 74.

94 See Johnston, *Shades of Sheol*, 130–34.

95 See the *Theological Dictionary of the Old Testament*, ed. G. J. Botterweck, H. Ringgren, and H.-J. Fabry (Grand Rapids: Eerdmans, 2004), 13:610.

96 Johnston, *Shades of Sheol*, 142.

97 See Gulley, *Systematic Theology: Creation, Christ, Salvation*, 110. He quotes George A. F. Knight (*A Biblical Approach to the Doctrine of the Trinity* [Edinburgh: Oliver and Boyd, 1957], 10), who cites Otto Eissfeldt, Johns Pederson, and H. Wheeler Robinson.

98 Cooper, *Body, Soul & Life Everlasting*, 54.

99 H. Wheeler Robinson, *The Christian Doctrine of Man* (Edinburgh: Clark, 1911), 92, as quoted in Cooper, *Body, Soul & Life Everlasting*, 52–53.

100 According to R. E. Friedman and S. D. Overton, "We *know* that there was belief in an afterlife in Israel. The combination of the archaeological record and the references that we do have in the text leave little room for doubt." ("Death and Afterlife: The Biblical Silence," in *Judaism in Late Antiquity*, vol. 4: *Death, Life-After-Death, Resurrection and the World-to-Come in the Judaisms of Late Antiquity*, ed. A. J. Avery-Peck and J. Neusner (Leiden: Brill, 2000), 35–36.

101 Alexander, "The Old Testament View of Life after Death," 44–45. Levenson affirms that "the Hebrew Bible is strikingly silent" on the immediate fate of the righteous," which "forces us into conjecture" (*Resurrection and the Restoration of Israel*, 75).

CHAPTER 11

IS THIS A DIRECT FLIGHT?: NEW TESTAMENT EVIDENCE

Determining whether our trip to the new heavens and new earth will have a layover in an intermediate state between death and resurrection has turned out to be like solving a mystery. Rather than just looking at our tickets, or turning to a Bible verse, we have found it necessary to assemble bits and pieces of information from the Bible. Those from the Old Testament have led us to expect that death is not the end—even temporarily. Long movies like *Lawrence of Arabia, Gone with the Wind,* and *Ben-Hur* used to have intermission, that is, for refreshment and replenishment. Could human lives be like that? Now we need to assemble bits and pieces from the New Testament to add to our picture of life during the intermission between the end of earthly life as we know it and the beginning of life in the new creation. Since Hebrews 11 is still about Old Testament believers, we will start there.

THE CEMETERY OF FAITH: HEBREWS 11

Hebrews 11 is like a cemetery we visit to meditate on the world of memories that testify to us of an unseen world that is only now beginning to materialize in our sight. We pass by memorials to Abel, Enoch, Noah, Abraham, Sarah, Isaac, Jacob, Joseph, Moses, Joshua (unnamed but implied in v. 30), Rahab, Gideon, Barak, Samson, Jephthah, David, Samuel, "the prophets," Daniel (unnamed but implied in v. 33), and countless others of whom "the world was not worthy" (v. 38). As we listen, we hear their *testimonies of faith* by which they pleased God and gained his approval as "righteous" (vv. 6–7).

Yet their faith went at least relatively unrewarded in this life (for some blessings they received, see 11:11, 29–30, 33–35). Nevertheless, they believed that God exists and that "he rewards those who seek him" (v. 6). They believed he would give them "an inheritance" (v. 8), "the city ... whose architect and builder is God" (v. 10), "a homeland" (v. 14), "a better place" (v. 16). And yet during their lifetimes they remained "foreigners and temporary residents on the earth" (v. 13). They all died believing, but not receiving the things God had promised them (v. 13). So, could they have received them right after death? Verse 16 says that the "better place" they desired was "a heavenly one." Is that where they are now, then, enjoying the heavenly city God had promised them?

They all died believing, but not receiving the things God had promised them (v. 13). So, could they have received them right after death.

The answer must be no, for several reasons. First, verse16 says, "But they *now* desire a better place." The verse begins with the Greek word *nun*, "now," and the verb (*oregō*), a present tense, means to "reach out for, aspire to, be eager for, long for, have a craving for."[1] Their earthly lives have ended, but they still have not received what they were promised and *are still looking for it.* If they are "now" looking for a better place, could they be in heaven in an "intermediate state"? Surely Enoch, whom God "took away" (v. 5), is there with God. Even the Adventists say God "took him to heaven without seeing death" (*Clear Word* paraphrase of Heb. 11:5). And yet Enoch is included in the list of those who "had not received the things that were promised" (v. 13), but who "now desire a better place—a heavenly one" (v. 16).

The second reason we know that Old Testament believers did not receive their reward in heaven is verses 39–40, which say "they did not receive what was promised, since God had provided [or "planned"] something better for us, so that they would not be made perfect without us." Verse 39 does not say "they did not receive what was promised *before they died.*" The point of verse 40, according to New Testament scholar David Peterson, is that "their enjoyment of perfection through Jesus Christ would only be together with us."[2] We are all to cross the finish line together.[3] Peterson explains that Hebrews uses here "the language of perfection previously employed to highlight the *total benefits* of Christ's saving work for those who believe (cp. 12:2). . . . Those who were called to trust God in the Old Testament era receive the promised eternal inheritance when they are resurrected," while "those who approach God now on the basis of his Son's perfect work become citizens by faith of the heavenly Jerusalem, with their names already 'written in heaven' (12:23)."[4] What was not received by the Old Testament believers during their lives was also not received by them after their death. In fact, even though Jesus the Messiah has now come and brought us life and light, making us citizens of God's heavenly kingdom, the object of the promises made to the Old Testament believers has still not been fully bestowed.

> *"Their enjoyment of perfection through Jesus Christ would only be together with us."*

> *"Those who were called to trust God in the Old Testament era receive the promised eternal inheritance when they are resurrected."*

The "heavenly city" that all God's children, living and dead, "now desire," therefore, is not something we will experience *in heaven.* The "enduring city" we seek is "the one to come" (13:14). However, it will come to a recycled earth *from heaven* to be received and experienced in the new heavens and earth, as we saw in chapter six.

> *The "heavenly city" that all God's children, living and dead, "now desire," therefore, is not something we will experience in heaven.*

The word in Hebrews 11:16 that is translated "heavenly," *epouranios*, can mean not only "in heaven," but also "proceeding from heaven."[5] This is its meaning in 1 Corinthians 15:48–49, where Christ, the last Adam, the one "of heaven" (i.e., heavenly) is clearly the one "from heaven" (*ex ouranou*) according to verse 47. The city anticipated by the Old Testament believers in Hebrews 11 and by Christians now is the one described in Revelation 3:12 as "the new Jerusalem, which comes down out of heaven from . . . God." According to Hebrews 11:13, the things God has promised to Old Testament believers (and to us) "they saw . . . from a distance" and "greeted" or "welcomed" them (NIV). This is not because we are going to heaven but because heaven is coming to us. And, like grandparents who see our grandchildren coming to see us, we believers, living and dead, are reaching out to our inheritance with open arms. You and I too are "foreigners and temporary residents on the earth," not because we are to be taken from the earth, but because what was our homeland (a sinless planet) has been taken from us as a result of the fall and is occupied by the forces of darkness (see John 12:31). Like the French patriots welcoming the Allies after D-Day, we welcome our Liberator into our lives today, knowing that ultimately he will restore to us a rebuilt homeland with the New Jerusalem at its center.

> *Like grandparents who see our grandchildren coming to see us, we believers, living and dead, are reaching out to our inheritance with open arms.*

> *Like the French patriots welcoming the Allies after D-Day, we welcome our Liberator into our lives today, knowing that ultimately he will restore to us a rebuilt homeland with the New Jerusalem at its center.*

INTERTESTAMENTAL JUDAISM

I have often been asked what Baptists believe about something and have had to explain that we are like a bag of trail mix and are always changing. Similarly, the Jews living between the Old and New Testament eras (from roughly 400 BC to AD 100) held dozens of opinions on the afterlife, which may be boiled down to three. N. T. Wright, one of the most prominent New Testament scholars and the author of over seventy books, explains that by the time of Jesus, "most Jews either believed in some form of resurrection or at least knew that it was standard teaching."[6] We find this view among the Pharisees (see Acts 23:7–9), several apocryphal works (see 2 Macc 7:9), Josephus's writings, and in rabbinic Judaism.[7]

> *By the time of Jesus, "most Jews either believed in some form of resurrection or at least knew that it was standard teaching."*

A few, like the Sadducees (the conservatives of Jesus's day, who were no longer around after AD 70) and the author of Ecclesiasticus (also called Sirach), denied an afterlife. The latter writes, "From the dead, as from one who does not exist, thanksgiving has ceased. . . . human beings are not immortal" (Sir 17:28, 30).

Wright points out that others, following Platonic dualism, affirmed that "a blessed, albeit disembodied, immortality awaited the righteous after their death." But those who believed in resurrection "believed also that the dead, who would be raised in the future but had not been yet, were alive somewhere, somehow, in an interim state." Resurrection meant "life *after* 'life after death': a two-stage future hope, as opposed to the single-stage expectation of those who believed in a non-bodily future life."[8]

> *Those who believed in resurrection "believed also that the dead, who would be raised in the future but had not been yet, were alive somewhere, somehow, in an interim state."*

Wright summarizes the understanding of mainstream Judaism between the Testaments and later regarding the state of the dead like this:

> Who or what are they? They are, at present, souls, spirits or angel-like beings [though not angels], held in that state of being not because they were naturally immortal but by the creative power of YHWH [the LORD

The Triumph of Judas Maccabeus, Rubens. During the time between the Old and New Testaments, Judas Maccabeus defended his country against Antiochus IV Epiphanes and preserved the Jewish religion.

God, Yahweh]. Where are they? They are in the hand of the creator god; or in paradise; or in some kind of Sheol, understood now not as a final but as a temporary resting-place. What's wrong? They are not yet re-embodied, not least because their God has not completed his purposes for the world and Israel. What's the solution? Ultimate re-embodiment, which will be caused by YHWH's power and spirit. What time is it? It is still "the present age"; the "age to come" has not yet begun.[9]

LAZARUS AND THE RICH MAN
Luke 16:19–31

This parable is an obvious place to turn for New Testament insight on the whereabouts of the dead, since it is about two men who die and end up in another place—or places.

One day, a poor man named Lazarus dies and is "carried away by the angels to Abraham's side." About the same time, an unnamed man (tradition calls him "Dives," but that's just Latin for "rich") who ignored Lazarus's destitute condition dies too and finds himself tormented "in Hades" (Luke 16:22–23). As New Testament scholar James Edwards points out, Luke 16, which follows the three parables in chapter 15 about the lost sheep, the lost coin, and the lost son, is first about the handling of wealth. Chapter 16 begins with the parable of the dishonest manager (16:1–13), which teaches that "wealth can be used for one's welfare," and it ends with this parable (16:19–31) about a hard-hearted rich man, which teaches that "wealth can pave the way for disaster."[10] Both parables begin with "there was a rich man." While the primary audience of the first parable is Jesus's "disciples" (16:1), the Pharisees are the main ones addressed in the second parable (16:14). They were "lovers of money" and had been "scoffing" (the word means "to wrinkle the nose" and suggests a sneer) as Jesus told the first parable, because it condemned their focus on money. These two parables and the five short sayings in between (16:14–18) teach that "wealth and possessions, like allegiances to masters, spouses, and Torah, are given their rightful place in life and fulfill their purpose when they are made subservient to the sovereignty and service of God."[11] Against that background, Jesus does not condemn the rich man in verse 19 for being rich but for *misusing* his riches (v. 30, after all, seems to imply the man's need for repentance).[12] And Lazarus does not serve as an example of godliness but only as a recipient of God's mercy.

Beyond that, anyone who has squabbled over the meaning of a story knows it can be challenging, and, like most parables, this one is a story. A lot has been written about how to interpret Jesus's parables, and several principles are generally accepted.[13] Here are some useful principles expressed as questions to ask of any parable:

1. How is it structured?
2. How does it fit a first-century Palestinian context? (Parallels from ancient Egyptian or late rabbinic parables are of little help.)
3. Who is the audience?
4. What clues are found in the parable's introduction and conclusion? Interpretations should not be based on what is left *unstated* in the parable.

Lazarus at the Rich Man's House by Gustave Doré.

5. Why is a parable placed where it is within a book?
6. How does it fit Jesus's other teachings?
7. What comparisons, contrasts, and correspondences are found in the parable?
8. Which elements are essential, and which are incidental (such as the number of the rich man's brothers)?
9. Does the parable have just one message or more than one?

Now, what can we learn from this parable of Jesus, especially about the afterlife?

Regarding the parable's structure, we have a two-part story of reversal (vv. 19–21, 22–23) followed by a three-part dialogue between the (formerly) rich man and Abraham (vv. 24–26, 27–29, 30–31). The reversal story takes a rich man from the experience of luxury in life to torment in Hades, and it takes poor Lazarus from the experience of suffering in life to blessing at Abraham's side. New Testament scholar Klyne Snodgrass suggests that just as a "chasm" is to separate the two men in the afterlife in verse 26, so in life they were separated by the rich man's "gate" in verse 20.[14] New Testament scholar Darrell Bock points out that the Greek word for "gate" (*pulon*) is usually used of entrances to cities, temples, or palaces and thus shows the house was like a mansion.[15] New Testament scholar Arland Hultgren observes that the rich man's gate shows he "lives in a mansion surrounded by a wall designed to keep the 'have nots' at a distance. The wall and the gate make a statement. Although he may well be aware that poverty surrounds him, the rich man does not want to see it or do anything to alleviate it."[16]

Whereas the rich man's burial is probably with an ostentatious ceremony (although Jesus ignores it with "the rich man also died and was buried"), Lazarus's death would hardly have been noticed on earth. Jewish observers thus would have assumed the rich man to be divinely blessed and the poor man to be cursed. Yet even while the rich man's corpse was being ceremonially carried to his carefully prepared tomb, God's "angels" were escorting Lazarus to "Abraham's side" (v. 22). The Greek word *kolpos,* translated "side," can refer to one's bosom, chest, or lap and occurs 41 times in the Greek Old Testament (Septuagint), often speaking of embracing a spouse or child.[17] It also suggests the intimate association of dining close beside a friend. John 1:18 describes "the one and only Son, who is himself God and is at the Father's side." The word portrays not only closeness but affection, intimacy, and protection. It is also found in John 13:23 describing the beloved disciple's position at the Last Supper, "reclining close beside Jesus," which would have been the place of honor (see John 21:20). Being at Abraham's bosom or side in the afterlife thus would have been understood as an unexcelled privilege and blessing. Lazarus, being next to Abraham, had the best seat in the house at a heavenly feast better than the rich man ever had (see Luke 13:28–29).[18] The rich man who trusted in wealth and boasted of "abundant riches" (Ps 49:6) was now in a situation of torment in Hades (Luke 16:23). As the psalmist wrote,

One can see that the wise men die;
the foolish and stupid also pass away.
Then they leave their wealth to others.
Their graves are their permanent homes,
their dwellings from generation to generation,
though they have named estates after themselves. . . .
Do not be afraid when a person gets rich,
when the wealth of his house increases.
For when he dies, he will take nothing at all;
his wealth will not follow him down. (Ps 49:10–11, 16–17)

Icon of Jesus's second coming. The bottom left portion depicts the "bosom of Abraham."

Lazarus, however, was redeemed "from the power of Sheol" (49:15). And as that same verse from Psalms indicates, that happened because God took him.

In ancient Greek literature, *Hades*—the place to which the rich man relocated—is simply the place of the dead. In the Septuagint the word almost always renders *Sheol.* The New Testament portrays it generally as a place where the wicked are held in humiliation and abandonment prior to the resurrection (see Matt 11:23/Luke 10:15; Acts 2:27, 31; Rev 1:18; 6:8; 20:13–14), though in this parable torment is also involved. Some suggest that both the rich man and Lazarus are in different parts of Hades, the realm of the dead. Indeed, the understanding of Sheol as an intermediate state with different locations for the righteous and the wicked awaiting final glory or condemnation was the dominant view in postexilic Judaism, with the righteous and the wicked already experiencing preliminary delight or suffering (*1 En* 22:3–13; *2 Esd* 7:36; Josephus, *Ant.* 18:1, 3).[19] However, according to Jesus only the rich man ended up in Hades. The opinions of extrabiblical literature often differ from those of the Bible.

If Jesus had ended his parable here, it would have been clear that the message was just a warning against the neglect of the poor. Yet of the 13 verses comprising the parable, all but the first three take place *in the afterlife*. And even more takes place than the rich man's suffering and Lazarus's blessing. For instance, at least a second point must be recognized—it seems there will be no opportunity for repentance after death. Unlike the ancient Egyptian and late rabbinic parable tellers, Jesus does not make moral differences an issue in his parable.[20] "What is wrong with the situation in this world, according to the parable," Bauckham says, "is the stark inequality in the living conditions of the two men. . . . What is not stated is not relevant" (see point 4 above).[21] Snodgrass points out that a common awareness of stories of "descent to the underworld, reversal of circumstances, and denunciation of the rich for their neglect of the poor" would not be surprising, but to propose Jesus's dependence on one or more of these stories, few of which can be dated to first-century Palestine, is "neither convincing, helpful, nor necessary."[22]

In the parable, dialogue begins when the rich man "looked up and saw Abraham a long way off, with Lazarus at his side" (Luke 16:23). Each of the exchanges between Abraham and the man in Hades begins with the man pleading for Lazarus to be sent to serve him. Even in Hades, then, he believes—at least at first—he is entitled to be served (vv. 24, 27).[23] First, he wants Lazarus to alleviate his agony. His odd request for Lazarus only to "dip the tip of his finger in water and cool [his] tongue" is like a homeless person's sign that says, "Anything will help" (v. 24). It is probably intended to correspond to the scraps that Lazarus had longed for. Next, the man wants Lazarus "to warn" his brothers, a request he repeats in the last exchange (v. 28, 30). Although this man believed the borders between earth and heaven and between Hades and Abraham's side were traversable, Abraham says they are not.

> *Each of the exchanges between Abraham and the man in Hades begins with the man pleading for Lazarus to be sent to serve him.*

Abraham, who we are to assume speaks for God, makes two points in the first exchange. First, being satisfied with "good things" in this life at the expense of other people will lead to a deprived, unpleasant afterlife (v. 25; see Deut 15:7–11).[24] Second, the afterlife situation is irreversible because a great untraversable "chasm" stands between the faithful and the unfaithful there (Luke 16:26). The existence of such a chasm may not be literal. Nevertheless, the parable is a picture or vision of truth. It is, at least, *as if* a great chasm existed.

> *Being satisfied with "good things" in this life at the expense of other people will lead to a deprived, unpleasant afterlife.*

> *A great untraversable "chasm" stands between the faithful and the unfaithful there.*

Grand Staircase-Escalante National Monument

Abraham's brief response to the rich man's plea that Lazarus be sent to warn his brothers simply asserts that "Moses and the prophets," that is, the Old Testament, are sufficient warning to render them without excuse (vv. 27–29). Since the rich man had the same warning, of course, he too is without excuse. The man is suffering in Hades because he refused to "listen to Moses and the prophets." The rich man's final plea emphatically and presumptuously repeats the address. He cries, "Father Abraham," as if to say, "Please! You have to do this because I'm your child!" (v. 30). Yet this plea that just repeats the second one impertinently begins with an emphatic "No," as if to say that Abraham/God is wrong. Moses and the prophets are *not* enough. Their warning is *insufficient* to make a clear and persuasive case for obedience to God. This implies that *God* is at fault for this man's tormented situation.[25] What Abraham/God must do is to provide a messenger from the dead (that is, Lazarus) to go and warn his brothers.

The man is suffering in Hades because he refused to "listen to Moses and the prophets.

The man was likely thinking of Lazarus's spirit rising like Samuel (1 Sam 28).[26] But even a resurrection cannot trump a refusal to accept the clear testimony of Scripture. As Williamson concludes, "That is surely the main point of the parable."[27] Point four listed above suggests that serious consideration be given to how a parable ends. This parable reinforces what is taught by Jesus elsewhere about the enduring power of God's Word (see Luke 16:16–17; 24:27, 44–45). As Darrell Bock declares, "If God's Word is believed, a resurrection is not necessary to engender faith; it only bolsters it."[28]

Even a resurrection cannot trump a refusal to accept the clear testimony of Scripture.

"If God's Word is believed, a resurrection is not necessary to engender faith; it only bolsters it."

The use of the Greek word *anistēmi*, "rises," by Abraham/Jesus in verse 31 foreshadows the response of unbelief to Jesus's resurrection on the part of those whose hearts were hardened, since the term is used in that way in Luke 18:33; 24:7, 46, and elsewhere. However, the audience would not have comprehended this meaning.[29] Nor would they have thought of the people Jesus raised from the dead. Although these miracles testified to Jesus's messianic identity (Matt 11:4–6), none of those raised are said to have brought a message from the dead. The raising of a different Lazarus (since the brother of Mary and Martha was still alive when this parable was told) convinced only those whose hearts were not hardened; it led the others to plot Jesus's death (John 11:41–53).

The raising of a different Lazarus (since the brother of Mary and Martha was still alive when this parable was told) convinced only those whose hearts were not hardened; it led the others to plot Jesus's death (John 11:41–53).

Abraham's final statement in the parable should be heeded by those who give greater weight to their own experience or that of someone else than to the testimony of Scripture. He says, "If they don't listen to Moses and the prophets, they will not be persuaded if someone rises from the dead" (Luke 16:31). An implication of this is that there is no higher authority or more powerful testimony than God's Word breathed out by the Spirit in the Scriptures.

There is no higher authority or more powerful testimony than God's Word breathed out by the Spirit in the Scriptures.

Blomberg argues that three lessons may be derived from this parable. (Their order below is from my own sense of their importance).

1. "Through Abraham, Moses and the prophets (and now through Jesus), God reveals himself and his will so that none who neglect it can legitimately protest their subsequent fate."
2. "Like the rich man, the unrepentant, disclosed especially by their miserliness, will experience irreversible punishment."
3. "Like Lazarus, those whom God helps will be borne after their death into God's presence."[30]

Surely Jesus would agree that part of his message is that someone "like Lazarus," who unlike the rich man has listened to and been persuaded by the Scriptures to love God and follow his commandments, God will help and bless—if not in this world, then in the next. According to Snodgrass, "In most scholarly treatments we find the caution that the parable is not intended to give a description of life after death." While he agrees with this in some sense, he also says, "It would be as foolish to ignore the parable's relevance for future eschatology as it would be to think it presented a picture of the actual state of affairs."[31]

It is possible that all we can say for sure about the afterlife from this parable is that although covenant breakers will be punished after death, the faithful will be with the Lord. But Dutch theologian Herman Ridderbos follows his countryman G. C. Berkouwer on the question of what the intermediate state is like: other than being with Christ, the Bible gives us no information. He comments, "The soul is nowhere spoken of in this context as the subject of continued existence after death, however frequently 2 Corinthians 5 and Philippians 1 have been interpreted in this way." Paul says of living believers in Colossians 3:3 that their lives are "hidden with Christ in God," and Ridderbos questions whether we can say more than that about the deceased. They are "no longer in the earthly body and therefore freed from all imperfection, sin, and affliction in this body." It is better than the trials of this life. But, he also points, out, "[I]t is not yet to be in the glorified body and thus for us an inconceivable mode of human existence." From Romans 8 we can only describe it as being loved by Christ and inseparable from him.[32]

I believe, however, that such a way of understanding these and other texts leaves too much biblical revelation on the table. It would be like paraphrasing John 3:16 to say, "God loves us." After scooping out the sections of a sweetened grapefruit half with my spoon, I always squeeze the juice out to drink before I am finished. While we are not to add to the biblical text what we want to be there or think might be there, but at the same time we are to squeeze out of it everything that is actually there (of course, my illustration fails because I add sugar). The minimalist view of Berkouwer and Ridderbos seems to leave the text unsqueezed. After all, much of the parable's view of the afterlife correlates with the common view in postbiblical Judaism (for example, see the late second-century AD book 4 Ezra 7:75–101).[33] If Jesus rejected such ideas, then why did he include them? Just as conservative biblical scholars rejected liberal attempts to disregard much of what Jesus said on the grounds that he was just accommodating himself to the perspective of his audience, we should reject the idea that Jesus was just going along with the crowd regarding the afterlife. Hoekema concludes that "the parable would be utterly pointless if there is not in actual fact a difference between the lot of the godly and that of the ungodly after death."[34] Paul Williamson also wisely states,

> Even if the main point of the parable is ethical, it may still affirm common eschatological ideas; it is certainly difficult to dismiss all the details of the story as mere dramatic setting, especially in view of its correlation with what seem to be mainstream or popular Jewish eschatological beliefs of the time. In other words, to use such suggestive imagery, without intending to endorse the eschatological premise contained therein, would surely constitute gross naïveté or an error of judgment on the part of Jesus. . . . [W]hile we must be suitably cautious about pressing all the details of the parable literally, we should equally beware of dismissing the entire scenario as devoid of eschatological significance.[35]

He adds that since the rich man's brothers are still living, the parable portrays a situation prior to the final resurrection. In using "the premise of an intermediate state" to make his point, "Jesus is giving at least tacit approval to the concept of an intermediate state."[36]

In using "the premise of an intermediate state" to make his point, "Jesus is giving at least tacit approval to the concept of an intermediate state."

How many of the parable's details picture "the actual state of affairs," however, is uncertain. Are the faithful carried away by angels after death? Is there a literal chasm, across which the departed can see and communicate? Will the afterlife of the unrepentant involve literal flames? Such questions may be impossible to answer with confidence.

PARADISE TODAY
Luke 23:43

Jesus, as we know, was not crucified alone. The Romans, priding themselves on efficiency as well as brutality, had two other "criminals" to deal with. Perhaps because the sign on Jesus's cross said he was "King of the Jews," he was placed in the middle. Regardless, whereas at least one of the criminals parroted the Jewish leaders and soldiers in mocking him (Luke 23:39; but see Matt 27:44), the other, for reasons of his own, decided to join company with Pilate and Herod (Luke 23:4, 14–15) in judging Jesus to be innocent. Of him, he said, "This man has done nothing wrong" (23:41). He even surpassed the pair and concluded that Jesus really was the Messiah, who despite being crucified, was somehow at some point going to bring in God's kingdom. And even beyond that, remarkably, he believed that Jesus might be mercifully forgiving at that time and allow *even him* to have a part with the righteous! He said, "Jesus, remember me when you come into your kingdom" (23:42). Judging from common Jewish belief of that day, the man was hoping for mercy at the end of time when the Messiah came to deliver his people. According to Daniel 12:2, a time is coming when . . .

> *Judging from common Jewish belief of that day, the man was hoping for mercy at the end of time when the Messiah came to deliver his people.*

> Many who sleep in the dust
> of the earth will awake,
> some to eternal life,
> and some to disgrace and eternal contempt.

This condemned criminal, then, hoped against hope to be one of those who will wake to eternal life. The response he received from his dying Messiah was not only a promise but a solemn oath. It's one of only six "truly" sayings of Jesus in Luke.[37] Jesus said, "Truly I tell you, today you will be with me in paradise" (Luke 23:43). That word "today" may have shocked his aching heart even more than the word "paradise."

> *That word "today" may have shocked his aching heart even more than the word "paradise."*

The Greek word for "today" is found 39 times in the New Testament, 11 of which are in Luke, with 9 more in Acts. Luke seemed to like the word. English translations often place it first in a sentence and sometimes last. But the Greek word mostly occurs in the middle of a clause and only six times at the end. Only twice besides here (Matt 16:3; Luke 19:5) is it found at the beginning of a Greek clause (except in Hebrews when quoting the Gk. translation of Ps 95:7).[38] A word out of its normal order in any language is often intended to be emphasized, sometimes in contrast to another word. For instance, contrasting how unpleasant the weather will be for the rest of the week, a meteorologist might say, "Today, we'll have blue skies and moderate temperatures" (cp. Jesus's words in Matt 16:3: "Today will be stormy"). I might seek sympathy from my Facebook friends by posting, "Yesterday I was napping at the beach. Today I am staring at a computer screen." When I was growing up, I longed for the day I could drive myself around in a car. Then one day, I awoke with the excited thought: *Today I'm getting my driver's license!* With the expectation of igniting a similar excitement, Jesus looks up into a sycamore tree and declares to Zacchaeus, "Today I must stay at your house" (Luke 19:5, NASB).[39] Then after Zacchaeus comes down Jesus says to him, "Today salvation has come to this house" (19:9). As a tax collector, hated by the Jews, that word "today" must have shocked Zacchaeus all on its own. The same sense is found when Jesus declared in the Nazareth synagogue, to people presumably longing for the Messiah, "Today as you listen, this Scripture [Isa 61:1–2] has been fulfilled" (Luke 4:21).

Since we have seen the New Testament's emphasis on the resurrection of believers at Jesus's return, however, some may be surprised to find Jesus assuring this man that paradise would be his "today." Seventh Day Adventists, believing deceased Christians "sleep" until the second coming, point out that the resurrected Jesus tells Mary in John 20:17, "I have not yet ascended to the Father." This means, they say, that Jesus spent the three days after his crucifixion asleep in the tomb.[40] If so, he could not have been "with" this new convert in "paradise" on the day of his crucifixion because *he never left the tomb.* But that is not what John 20:17 says. Christ's *ascension* was a highly significant event in his redemptive work, marking his physical departure from the earth to remain with the Father until the second advent. It was surely this event Jesus was referring to. His point, then, may have been that Mary did not need to hang onto him as if He was about to ascend in the next moment.[41] He had things to do first. And things for her to do.

Gulley and other Adventists argue that since Jesus never left the tomb, the traditional understanding of Luke 23:43 must be wrong. Since Greek manuscripts had no commas, they explain, we can and should read the verse, "Truly I tell you today, you will be with me in paradise."[42] This interpretation, however, has many fatal flaws, which is why all the major editions of the Greek New Testament—the seventeenth-century *Textus Receptus* of Erasmus, Tischendorf's edition in the mid-eighteenth century, that of Westcott and Hort in the late eighteenth century, and all the modern editions by Nestle and Aland and the United Bible Society— place the comma before "today" (*sēmeron*). The same is true of over 30 English translations I have checked, as well as several translations in French, German, Italian, Korean, Romanian, and Spanish. The same is true of at least a dozen of the most highly regarded commentaries on Luke in English. No non-Adventist translation or commentary I have found—regardless of religious affiliation—interprets the syntax of this verse the way Gulley and the Adventists do. That suggests denominational doctrine is driving interpretation instead of the other way around.

One Adventist scholar, Wilson Paroschi, however, makes the surprising claim that the traditional punctuation of this verse is based on theological bias![43] The most obvious reason scholars have treated "today" as part of the following clause in Luke 23:43 is that in the 75 occurrences of Jesus's words, "truly [truly] I say to you," the content of what he says *always immediately follows these words*. Finally, a prefatory "I say to you today" would seem pointless and meaningless. Based on Daniel 12:2 many Jews had come to believe in a resurrection at the end of time. All the man would have been hoping for from Jesus was a chance to be included with those receiving life then. Thus, as almost all scholars recognize, Jesus's emphasis was on the "today" of fulfillment, which was Friday.

> *Thus, as almost all scholars recognize, Jesus's emphasis was on the "today" of fulfillment, which was Friday.*

This is the reason most interpreters of Jesus's promise on the cross understand him to be saying in effect, "This very day, not at the end of time, you and I will be alive together in the place of the righteous." Just as Jesus had been "with" his disciples at the Passover table (Luke 22:11, 15), and even as his betrayer Judas had been "with" him there (22:21), this executed criminal would be, that very day, at table *with Jesus*, thanking God and singing with "joy and gladness" in "the garden of the LORD" (Isa 51:3).

> *"This very day, not at the end of time, you and I will be alive together in the place of the righteous."*

The term "paradise" (Gk. *paradeisos*) was borrowed perhaps in the fifth century BC from the Medo-Persians of ancient Iran and originally meant "enclosure." It came to be used for various kinds of vineyards, orchards, gardens, or wooded parks, often containing streams or springs. The Greek term was often used of royal parks that were luxuriously maintained, sometimes with pavilions and walking paths. In the Hellenistic world of Egypt during the last three centuries BC, when the Greek translation of the Old Testament (the Septuagint) was done, *paradeisos* symbolized a leisurely life of luxury and wealth.[44] This was the word the Greek translators chose for the garden of Eden (Gen 2:8–10, 15–16; 3:1–3), where God walked with Adam and Eve "at the time of the evening breeze" (3:8, 10).

New Testament scholar Howard Marshall explains that in Jewish writings from the New Testament era, the term "paradise," reflecting the garden of Eden, had come to refer to "the intermediate resting place for the souls of the righteous dead." In this passage, he says, "it represents the state of bliss which Jesus promises to the criminal directly after death," so that the day of Jesus's crucifixion was "the day of entry into paradise."[45] N. T. Wright presents evidence that many Jews at this time also held the form of dualism that allowed the soul to be "a guest in the house of life" to experience "a joyful rest in anticipation of final glory."[46] Those like the Pharisees who

> *In Jewish writings from the New Testament era, the term "paradise," reflecting the garden of Eden, had come to refer to "the intermediate resting place for the souls of the righteous dead."*

believed in resurrection believed not just in life after death but in "life after life after death, the second of two stages in the post-mortem programme." They believed that "the *present* state of those who had died would be replaced by a *future* state in which they would be alive once more."[47]

Those like the Pharisees who believed in resurrection believed not just in life after death but in "life after life after death, the second of two stages in the post-mortem programme."

But in both cases, they would be *with* Jesus, and Jesus would be *with* them. Jesus could have qualified his promise to his newly converted follower with the explanation that the man would be in a state of sleep while they were together. It would still be true that he would be "with" Jesus. How likely is it, however, that this is what Jesus meant? Luke's Gospel refers to being "with" someone almost 50 times, usually walking or eating together. What would Jesus have expected the man to think He meant? And why would Jesus add "in paradise" if the man were to be asleep with no awareness of where he was and no ability to enjoy the situation? How would my son respond if he claimed never to Jesus been to Disney World and I pointed out to him that he was there when he was a baby? "That does not count!"

Before leaving Luke 23:43, we should notice one other point of emphasis in what Jesus says. In every single case of the 75 occurrences of Jesus's "Truly [truly] I say to you [sing. or pl.]" in the Gospels, the dative pronoun "to you" *always follows the verb* "I say"—*except* in Luke 23:43. Thus, I can imagine that with great pain Jesus turned his head toward the converted sinner on the cross at his side, looked him in the eyes, and said, "Truly, *to you*, I say, *today* you will be with me in paradise." This verse does not settle the issue, however, of whether "paradise" is the final destination for resurrected believers or just a stop along the way.

Our next visit will be with the apostle Paul, who used the phrase "be with Christ" in Philippians 1:23.

BEING WITH CHRIST:
Philippians 1:23–24

Here Paul speaks of death as "gain" and as being "with Christ," which he thinks is "far better" than living "on in the flesh" (physically alive) doing "fruitful work." To be exact, he says, "For me, to live is Christ and to die is gain. Now if I live on in the flesh, this means fruitful work for me; and I don't know which one I should choose. I am torn between the two. I long to depart and be with Christ—which is far better" (Phil 1:21–23). Paul seems to understand that like the believing criminal next to Jesus on the cross, every believer will be "with Christ" immediately after death. Does this describe an "intermediate state" in heaven (see also our look at Phil 3:20–21 in chap. 5)? The concept of being *with Christ* has a long and exciting history beginning with God's being *with Israel*. First, then, we must understand what Paul and Jesus are saying within that context.

In the Old Testament God assured his chosen servants like Jacob and Moses that he would be *with* them, making their way successful in achieving his ends.[48] He also lived or made his presence known among his people for a time in a sanctuary (Exod 25:8), and he would be *with* a redeemed and restored people under a new covenant (Isa 43:2; Jer 30:11; 46:28; Ezek 37:27). God accomplished this by sending Jesus the Messiah to be "God *with* us" (Matt 1:23, emphasis added) and

to live among his people in the temple of his body (John 1:14). For a time, Christ was *with* them bodily, walking and talking beside them daily. Who today is not envious of those disciples? But his enemies crucified him, destroying the temple of his body. Nevertheless, God raised him from the dead (John 2:19–22). After 40 days of appearing on earth in his glorified body (Acts 1:3), Jesus ascended, returning to "heaven" (Luke 24:50–51; Acts 1:9–11), and is, in Jesus's words of anticipation, "no longer in the world" (John 17:11) but is *bodily* at the Father's right hand.[49]

Nevertheless, while He is absent from the world in the bodily sense, we are assured that He remains here in a powerful sense, as He promised before His departure: "And remember, I am *with* you always, to the end of the age" (Matt 28:20, emphasis added). Even in the upper room, according to John 14:23, Jesus had told His disciples, "If anyone loves me, he will keep my word. My Father will love him, and we will come to him and make our home *with* him." In the context of Jesus's upcoming departure, which is his topic of discussion in John 14–17, He promised that He and the Father would permanently move in with each of His children (defined as those who love Jesus). This applies to us now.

Colonel Robert L. Scott was a WWII fighter pilot who wrote his autobiography titled *God Is My Copilot.* His point was that he was never alone in combat. But he was wrong. It is better than that. God is the pilot. He just lets us hold the stick. Anyone who receives Jesus by believing in His name is reborn as God's child (see John 1:12–13) and gains the Creator and Redeemer as not just his permanent house guest but as the Master of the house. This, in fact, is a serious condition of God being *with* us.

But if God the Father and Jesus the Son are in heaven, how is this possible? Jesus had already said to His disciples a few verses before in John 14:16–17: "I will ask the Father, and he will give you another Counselor [or "Comforter" or "Encourager" or "Advocate"] to be *with* you forever. He is the Spirit of truth. . . . he remains *with* you and will be *in* you" (emphasis added). In 14:26 Jesus confirms that He is talking about the Holy Spirit: "the Counselor, the Holy Spirit, whom the

Father will send in [his] name." The Holy Spirit is the one we know to be the "third person" of the one Trinitarian God, comprising Father, Son, and Spirit. In the next chapter, Jesus, still teaching his disciples, refers again to "the one [he would] send to [them] from the Father—the Spirit of truth who proceeds from the Father" (15:26). In John 16 Jesus even tells them, "It is for your *benefit* that I go away, because if I don't go away the Counselor will not come to you. If I go, I will send him to you" (16:7, emphasis added). This, in fact, may be one reason the resurrected Jesus told Mary to stop holding on to Him. She would be better off after He ascended to heaven and sent the Holy Spirit (see John 20:17).[50] Don't miss that: we who have the Spirit are better off than the first disciples! And according to Jesus, those first disciples would be *better off* with the Holy Spirit's presence after His death, resurrection, and ascension than they had been with Jesus's bodily presence before.

The world of narrative fiction and even of history is full of episodes in which a group of people, such as the defenders of the Alamo, are in a dire situation they cannot handle on their own. It calls for someone from their group to "go for help." The result is different in the various stories. Sometimes, as at the Alamo, the help arrives too late. Sometimes the one who goes for help does not make it. But sometimes he does, and in the old western movies at the sound of the trumpet, someone yells, "Here comes the cavalry!" (or is it the calvary?). Trying to draw a parallel between these stories and the mission of Jesus is paper thin and perhaps even blasphemous. He was not just a messenger sent for help. He was and is the help we needed. Calvary is the cavalry. The point of the analogy is simply that Jesus's departure was necessary

Calvary is the cavalry. ▎

and for the benefit of those who looked to him in faith. According to Jesus, they were *better off* with the Holy Spirit's presence after his death, resurrection, and ascension than they had been with Jesus's bodily presence before.

This divine, special-delivery gift of the Spirit, which Jesus had referred to, arrived on the day of Pentecost, as Peter explained in his sermon that day: "[S]ince [Jesus] has been exalted to the right hand of God and has received from the Father the promised Holy Spirit, he has poured out what you both see and hear" (Acts 2:33).[51] And it is in and through the Holy Spirit that God now mediates to us His presence and makes His home *with* us.[52] But we must understand the Spirit is no mere representative of the Godhead. He is all the greatness of the power and wisdom and love and presence of God making Himself at home within us (see Ps 139:7; Matt 28:19).[53]

In 1 Corinthians 3:16 Paul says we are God's temple because "the Spirit of God lives in [us]." When Ananias lied "to the Holy Spirit," he lied "to God" (Acts 5:3–4). In Romans 8 Paul refers to the Spirit of God and the Spirit of Christ as the same person, and he declares that Christ lives in us because the Spirit does.[54] He says,

> You . . . are not in the flesh, but in the Spirit, if indeed the Spirit of God lives in you. If anyone does not have the Spirit of Christ, he does not belong to him. Now if Christ is in you, the body is dead because of sin, but the Spirit gives life because of righteousness. And if the Spirit of him who raised Jesus from the dead lives in you, then he who raised Christ from the dead will also bring your mortal bodies to life through his Spirit who lives in you. (Rom 8:9–11)

Jesus, who had promised the Holy Spirit would be "*in*" his disciples (John 14:17), refers to them in His prayer to the Father in John 17:23: "I am in them and you are in me." When we look up at night and see a full moon, we do not say, "There's half of the moon," just because we know we are only looking at the side of the moon facing us. We say, "There's the moon." This is why Paul can say in Galatians 2:20, "Christ lives in me" (also Rom 8:10), even though it is through the Spirit that this is true, and he can say in Colossians 1:27 that the "glorious wealth" of the gospel, which is our hope, is "Christ in [us]," even though Christ is bodily in heaven.

But we find something new and even more exciting in Philippians, reminiscent of Luke 23:43. It is something "far better" than even all the wonderful descriptions we've seen of the believer's experience in this age. It is far better than "God *with* us"—far better than Jesus being *with* us "to the end of the age"—even far better than the Father and Son making their home *with* us. It's even far better than the "benefit" of Jesus's ascension so that the Holy Spirit and the Godhead would come to live *in* us. So, what could possibly be better than such immeasurable blessings? Paul says in Philippians 1:23–24 that his longing was "to depart and be with Christ," that is, to die, because doing so would be "far better" for him personally than to continue his physical life, even though he was engaging in "fruitful [gospel] work" (v. 21).

Paul says in Philippians 1:23–24 that his longing was "to depart and be with Christ," that is, to die, because doing so would be "far better" for him personally than to continue his physical life, even though he was engaging in "fruitful [gospel] work" (v. 21).

As Paul says in Romans 8:31, "What then are we to say about these things?"

> In all these things we are more than conquerors through him who loved us. For I am persuaded that *neither death nor life*, nor angels nor rulers, nor things present nor *things to come*, nor powers, nor height nor depth, nor any other created thing will be able to separate us from the love of God that is in Christ Jesus our Lord. (8:37–39, emphasis added)

Paul says that when he—and every believer—departs from this earthly life in death, "even better" than God being with [and even in] us, we will be *with God.*

Writing from prison, perhaps in Rome, Paul bares his soul in Philippians 1:12–26, revealing his feelings of uncertainty and indecision. He knows he can be executed at any time, but he has no doubt that his circumstances have "actually advanced the gospel" (v. 12) and are therefore a cause for him to "rejoice" (v. 18). He also is rejoicing because he has no doubt that by God's grace his circumstances have him on a road that will lead him to ultimate and eternal "salvation through [their] prayers and help from the Spirit of Jesus Christ" (vv. 18–19).[55]

In verse 20 Paul assures us the certainty of his final destination and vindication is not lessened by its being an "eager expectation and hope." These words only mark the event as something Paul was excitedly anticipating in the future "the intense expectation of something that is sure to happen."[56] His only uncertainty is expressed in the phrase "whether by life or by death" (cp. Rom 8:38, "neither death nor life"). Although Paul does not know what lies in the immediate future, he expects to face it with courage so that "Christ will be highly honored in [his] body."

Paul returns to certainty in verse 21 when he explains that regardless of his circumstances, even if they lead to physical death, "to live is Christ." In other words, death cannot end his life because he is in Christ, and that is where life resides. His life is forever consumed with, resting on, fueled by, and enveloped in Christ. More than water means life to a fish, or air means life to an eagle, life for Paul consists in Christ (see Gal 2:20; Phil 3:8; Col 3:4). The reason he can rejoice in unpleasant circumstances is because he knows they "advance the gospel" (Phil 1:12).

And death for one who is in Christ, Paul says, is "gain," using a word referring to "profit." We think of death as loss; Paul thinks of it as profit. Having once tallied his profits in terms of human privileges and achievements, he had turned his balance sheet on its head when he came to Christ (Phil 3:7). He had come to know that *death* belongs not in the "loss" column of the ledger but is the ultimate "profit." It only means for Paul that "the goal of 'living' has been reached,"[57] which is the presence of Christ in a way he had *never before experienced it* (even when briefly "caught up into paradise" in 2 Cor 12:2–4). Paul would be *at home in Christ's physical presence.* He "long[ed] to depart and be *with* Christ" because it would be "far better" than any experience of Jesus's presence he'd ever known (Phil 1:23).

We cannot bypass this point in our guidebook without an excursion into the subject of death itself. As if Paul knew we would be using this guidebook approach to consider "heaven and hell," he chose to speak of death here, as well as in

Paul says that when he— and every believer— departs from this earthly life in death, "even better" than God being with [and even in] us, we will be with God.

Although Paul does not know what lies in the immediate future, he expects to face it with courage so that "Christ will be highly honored in [his] body."

Death cannot end his life because he is in Christ, and that is where life resides.

More than water means life to a fish, or air means life for Paul consists in Christ.

Having once tallied his profits in terms of human privileges and achievements, he had turned his balance sheet on its head when he came to Christ.

2 Timothy 4:6, in terms of departure.[58] Outside the Bible, Paul's word for "depart" (*analuo*) was used of a ship weighing anchor and sailing away, as in *The Lord of the Rings,* when Bilbo and Frodo Baggins and company sail away. Bilbo's last words before this are appropriately, "I think I'm ready for another adventure." This word for "depart" is also used of soldiers packing up the tents and marching on.[59] It was familiar outside the Bible too as a metaphor for death. Furthermore, Paul uses a Greek construction here that binds together *departing* and *being with Christ* as if they are simply two sides of the same proverbial coin.[60] Death as departure for the believer entails the inevitable consequence of being with Christ, even more than a trip to Yellowstone National Park with my wife made inevitable a happy memory. Departing this life for the believer means taking up residence in the Lord's presence.[61] What child of God would not be eager for such an experience?

> *Death as departure for the believer entails the inevitable consequence of being with Christ.*

And yet remaining alive would allow Paul to continue his fruitful and satisfying life of serving Christ and his people "for [their] progress and joy in the faith" (Phil 1:25). He knows the choice is ultimately God's to make; but if it were up to him, he would sacrifice his own personal preference for execution ("far better," as strange as that sounds) in order to remain and continue serving God's people. He strongly believes, in fact, that this is what will happen (vv. 25–26). Moses could have continued experiencing the wealth of the treasures of Egypt but chose rather to depart in order to "suffer with the people of God" (Heb 11:24–26). Inversely, Paul might have been allowed to depart and experience right away the treasures of paradise with Jesus but chose rather to remain in order to suffer with the people of God. In both cases, like Christ (Phil 2:5–11), God's servant chose to put "the interests of others" over "his own interests" (see Phil 2:4, 20–21), and so they should be examples to the rest of God's people.[62]

Paul illustrates death as merely one who puts out to sea and "departs" on a journey.

Paul's perspective on death being "gain" runs in the opposite direction from that of our own culture and for the most part our own hearts. We speak of an ultimately crucial issue as "a matter of life or death" and want to live and avoid death at all costs. That perspective is wrong because it is blind to spiritual reality (see 2 Cor 4:18) and exalts the value of earthly life in "this present evil age" (Gal 1:4) over true life "in the age to come" (Mark 10:30; 1 Tim 6:19).

Paul's perspective on death being "gain" runs in the opposite direction from that of our own culture and for the most part our own hearts.

So, what happens to the believer who dies? The view that existence ends at death is ruled out by Paul. Dying is not loss; rather, to die is gain. It is merely a departure to be with Christ. Could we end up asleep or unconsciousness awaiting Christ's return and our resurrection? Probably not.[63] As in the case of Luke 23:43, such does not seem the most likely interpretation of Paul's meaning. It would be a possible way of understanding "to die is gain," since the believer's next waking moment would be to see Christ. However, the concept of being "with Christ" seems to mean far more than that. Paul not only joins death (which he refers to as departure) to being "with Christ" (the experience we discussed from Luke 23:43), but he speaks of it as being "far better." The Greek phrase, in fact, could be rendered "more better," to the dismay of English teachers. One who sees soul sleep as being "far better" can't be focusing on the actual situation of the unconscious believer. He or she must be thinking of the conscious experience of going to "sleep in Jesus" (1 Thess 4:14, KJV) and waking to the resurrection and the new creation. It is difficult to imagine, though, that Paul would consider being asleep to be better than actively serving Jesus.

Perhaps our next passage, also by Paul, will reveal something else to help in our investigation.

THE NAKED AND THE DEAD
2 Corinthians 5:1–8

Whereas Norman Mailer's great debut novel, *The Naked and the Dead* (1948), points to the meaninglessness of war, Paul's words to the Corinthians here are about the meaning of the believer's death. We began our look at 2 Corinthians 5 in our chapter 5, "But Is Heaven Our Forever Home?," but there we only considered our final destiny. The first verse has special value to our topic here. It says, "For we know that if our earthly tent we live in is destroyed [that is, "dismantled"], *we have* a building from God, an *eternal* dwelling in the heavens, not made with hands" (emphasis added). By Paul's conditional "if" here he limits from consideration those believers

Our eternal dwelling will be much better than any earthly tent.

who "are still alive at the Lord's coming" (1 Thess 4:15; nonbelievers will be considered in a later chapter). They, according to 1 Corinthians 15:51–52, will also receive new bodies.

We saw earlier the significance of *when* Paul says our earthly body/tent will be replaced. Its dismantling will naturally occur at death. But its replacement will not occur until the resurrection. Nevertheless, David Garland points out that the present tense "we have" in 5:1 seems to indicate that its replacement will occur immediately following death. Paul does not say that "we *will* have a building from God." He seems to conceive of no "homeless interlude . . . between the destruction of the earthly tent house and receiving the building from God."[64] This "building" is further qualified as "eternal," which appears to rule out a temporary body. It will be the real thing. The fact that it is "not made with hands" highlights God as the "builder."

Paul further says in verses 3–4 that at no time will the believer be found "naked," that is, bodiless, but rather will be "clothed" in immortality. Garland therefore rejects the idea that we will become "disembodied ghosts or ethereal spirits." He also cautions that we should not "read into [Paul's] imagery an interim period or an interim state."[65] Philo, the first-century Jewish philosopher, described Moses's death as his shell-like body "being stripped away and the soul laid bare."[66] This is something Paul says the believer will never experience: "We will not be found naked" (5:3).

> *Paul further says in verses 3–4 that at no time will the believer be found "naked," that is, bodiless, but rather will be "clothed" in immortality.*

Paul seems to emphasize this by mixing his initial metaphor of dismantling a tent in verse 1 with *putting on* our dwelling that will come from heaven. The Greek lexicon gives the verb's meaning as "to put a garment on over an existing garment."[67] This seems to rule out our ever being bodiless. Garland favors the argument of New Testament scholar Murray Harris that "we have" in 5:1 points to "an immediate succession between two forms of embodiment without implying a longstanding or even momentary coexistence of two bodies." Harris paraphrases, "As soon as our earthly tent-dwelling is taken down, we are the recipients of a building from God."[68]

Therefore, although our experience of being "at home in the body" before death involves being "away from the Lord" in some sense (see our discussion of Phil 1:23–24 in this chapter), we know that when we die and are "away from [this earthly] body" we will be "at home with the Lord" (2 Cor 5:6–8). This echoes Jesus's promise to the crucified convert: "Today, you will be *with me* in paradise" (Luke 23:43, emphasis added). It also echoes Paul's eager expectation that at the resurrection when Christ returns, "we will always be *with the Lord*" (1 Thess 4:17).

> *We know that when we die and are "away from [this earthly] body" we will be "at home with the Lord."*

As the influential twentieth-century biblical scholar F. F. Bruce says, a disembodied presence with the Lord is ruled out by Paul's assurance that "we will not be found naked," which would mean "to be without a body of any kind." So "physical death will mean no hiatus of disembodiment but the immediate enjoyment of being 'at home with the Lord.'"[69]

This leaves us, though, with the conundrum of how we can receive our new resurrection bodies immediately following death and avoid a "homeless interlude." Bruce suggests that the immediacy of receiving our resurrection bodies at death "might be relieved today if it were suggested that in the consciousness of the departed believer there is no interval between dissolution and investiture, however long an interval might be measured by the calendar of earth-bound human history."[70] My Adventist brothers and sisters would favor this solution. But the problem with this is that Paul seems to speak not of "consciousness" but of reality. As soon as we die, "*we have* a building from God" (2 Cor 5:1, emphasis).

Furthermore, as Bruce himself says, physical death means "the *immediate enjoyment* of being 'at home with the Lord.'" Only in this light can we understand that Paul "would prefer" death (5:8) to his continuing life as minister of the "new covenant" of reconciliation

Physical death means "the immediate enjoyment of being 'at home with the Lord.'"

(3:6; 5:18–19) and "ambassador for Christ" (5:20). This life, Paul elaborates, involves "being transformed" into the Lord's glory (3:18), "proclaiming . . . Jesus Christ as Lord" (4:5), walking by faith to please the Lord (5:7, 9), and living "for the one who died . . . and was raised" (5:15). Paul could not prefer unconscious existence to such a life, however painful it could be.

But how would it be possible for a believer's death to bring immediate conscious enjoyment of Jesus's presence in a new resurrection body if the resurrection comes at Jesus's return? Garland appears to favor the possible explanation of God's timelessness mentioned in chapter 10. He suggests this:

> Our difficulties with this issue are compounded by the enormous difficulty in trying to grasp what happens in conditions of time and space so different from our own. . . . Confined by our perceptions of time and matter, we cannot comprehend God's time sequence. . . . Whatever God's timetable for the resurrection, Paul believes that resurrection—not waiting—is the next thing the dead in Christ experience.[71]

Whether this possible understanding of death is credible or satisfying cannot be determined here. Appeals to divine timelessness are not silver bullets. Christian philosopher William Lane Craig proposes that "apart from the idea of God, I know of no concept so profound and so baffling as that of time."[72] His tongue-in-cheek definition of time as "what keeps everything from happening at once" might be worth some speculation. Indeed, what if all death and resurrection happened at once, but we have to experience and talk about it as being separated by chunks of time?

To parody the apostle Paul, all things are possible, but not all things are supportable by Scripture. We can easily support that God is eternal. For instance, the psalmist writes, "Before the mountains were born, / before you gave birth to the earth and the world, /

from eternity to eternity, you are God" (Ps 90:2). Or the prophet Isaiah writes, "Who has performed and done this, calling the generations from the beginning? I am the LORD, the first and with the last—I am he" (Isa 41:4). Isaiah 57:15 seems to stress God's sovereign rulership over everything (ESV): "Thus says the One who is high and lifted up, who inhabits eternity, whose name is Holy: 'I dwell in the high and holy place.'" Paul wrote "in the hope of eternal life that God, who cannot lie, promised before time began. In his own time he has revealed his word" (Titus 1:2). Finally, Jude entrusts his readers "to the only God our Savior, through Jesus Christ our Lord, be glory, majesty, power, and authority before all time, now and forever" (Jude 25).

God is certainly not timeless in that he cannot understand and experience time as we do. It is widely understood, however, that time as we know it began at creation, so God existed before time.[73] After considering these issues in some detail, Craig's conclusion is that since creation God speaks of what will be, causes things to come into being, and speaks of what has been. He is "temporal since creation." Creation, Craig continues, involved "a decision on God's part to abandon timelessness and to take on a temporal mode of existence." He did this that we might "come to share the joy and blessedness of the inner life of God. He stooped to take on a mode of existence inessential to His being or happiness in order that we might have being and find supreme happiness in Him."[74]

Does this mean that God could not overrule time to cause the death and resurrection of all believers to occur at the same "time" at Christ's return, which from our present perspective in time is still future? Yes, I think he could. By this view we receive a *resurrection body at death.* But there are at least two other credible interpretations of the relevant biblical texts.[75]

The more common alternative is that each believer will be given an actual *resurrection body at Christ's return.* Paul's statement in 2 Corinthians 5:1, "*We have* a building from God," could be a special use of the present tense that Greek students call a futuristic present (emphasis added). It is sometimes used to emphasize the certainty of a coming event (it is used especially with verbs of coming and going and for dramatic effect). For instance, you might use it to assure your mother, "*I am coming* to see you on Saturday," as Jesus says, "Yes, I am coming soon" (Rev 22:20). In these cases, adding "on Saturday" or "soon" makes it clear the present tense does not refer to something happening *now.* Nothing in our verse, however, indicates a future "having." Paul could have made it clear by saying, "If our earthly tent . . . is destroyed, *we know that we will have* a building from God." If we are convinced for other reasons (as we very well may be) of a temporal gap between death and resurrection, this may be how we understand Paul's statement. This is all that justifies the expanded NLT translation: "When this earthly tent we live in is taken down (that is, when we die and leave this earthly body), we *will have* a house in heaven" (2 Cor 5:1, emphasis added).

Harris cites another difficulty with this view of a temporal gap between death and acquiring a new and permanent body. How much consolation would it have been to Paul to know that his sorrowful and painful death would be followed by a new body coming over 2,000 years in the future, a gift all believers are already promised whether they die or not? (See 1 Cor 15:51.) Some may find that to be a problem.[76]

A third possibility is that the believer receives the *resurrection body at death as an ideal possession to be realized at Christ's return*. Perhaps the illustration might help of our receiving a check that only later results in money deposited in our account. Some may feel this view is an attempt to have your cake and eat it too. After all Harris, who favors this view now, considers the possibility that "a distinction between ideal and real possession" might not have made sense to Paul. Nevertheless, in its defense, he points out that in John's Gospel and in Paul's writings eternal life is in some sense both a future blessing and a present possession. In other words, he points to the principle we find in New Testament theology of "already but not yet."[77]

However we choose to understand the details, we should be clear on at least two points. First, as Garland explains, "death does not shatter the Christian's intimate union with Christ in this life, even for a moment"; rather, it "perfects that union." Second, immortality comes from God's transforming work in raising us from the dead.[78]

> *"Death does not shatter the Christian's intimate union with Christ in this life, even for a moment"; rather, it "perfects that union."*

One more passage that seems to suggest a layover in heaven in an intermediate state is Revelation 6:9–11. The apostle John writes,

> I saw under the altar the souls of those who had been slaughtered because of the word of God and the testimony they had given. They cried out with a loud voice, "Lord, the one who is holy and true, how long until you judge those who live on the earth and avenge our blood?" So they were each given a white robe, and they were told to rest a little while longer until the number would be completed of their fellow servants and their brothers and sisters, who were going to be killed just as they had been.

At times in this book I have cautioned against confusing literal and figurative speech in the Bible. The issue is especially relevant in certain types of literature, such as wisdom, poetry, and prophecy. We also quoted earlier (in chap. 6, "New Creation") N. T. Wright's caution regarding the Bible's portraits of the future, which he labels "signposts into the mist," observing that they seldom include a photo of what the end of the road looks like. All those cautions must especially come into play when engaging the Old Testament books of Ezekiel and Daniel—but even more so when reading the apostle John's book of Revelation. John labeled his book "the revelation [or apocalypse] of Jesus Christ that God gave him to show his servants what must soon take place" (1:1). The novice reader may respond to that verse with the excitement that Adam felt when he first saw Eve: "At last!" (Gen 2:23). After all, we all think we want to know the future. But the careful reader soon discovers that John's book contains a series of visions from God that are full of mysterious symbolic objects, persons, and events. As one of my seminary professors would say, "God didn't put the cookies on the lower shelf." That seems true, but he did put the meat and vegetables and fruit on the lower shelf. He's not in the business of satisfying our curiosity, but what we really need to know, he says, "is very near [us] . . . so that you may follow it" (Deut 30:14).

"The Four Horsemen" by Albrecht Dürer (ca 1496-1498).

John's concluding book is clear that although the forces of the evil one were crippled and doomed at the cross, God in his mysterious wisdom is using them even now to inflict trials—and sometimes even physical death—on humanity. But Christ's death and resurrection "made the world forces of evil his agents to execute his purposes of sanctification and judgment for the furtherance of his kingdom."[79] And while those trials will increase as we get closer to Christ's victorious return to end them once and for all, God—just as he limited the effects of the Egyptian plagues for the sake of his people (Exod 7–12; cp. 8:22–23; 9:4, 26; 10:23; 12:13)—still seals his children (Rev 7:2–8; 9:4), those who have "his name and his Father's name written on their foreheads" (14:1), the "redeemed from the earth" (14:3), to protect us—not necessarily from pain or death—but from destruction and from trials that are more than we can bear (see 1 Cor 10:13).[80] "What must soon take place," then, is the aftermath and death throes of the one whom Christ defeated at the cross (Rev 1:1). God's people are urged to hold fast to "the word of God and to the testimony of Jesus" until Christ returns to finish him off (Rev 1:2).

Revelation 6 begins with the Lamb's breaking the first four seals, an act which releases the infamous four horsemen of the Apocalypse and climaxes with Death and Hades in 6:8. The group "lends itself to being interpreted as a relay team of menacing figures presaging unparalleled destruction."[81] That there are four horsemen shows the universal extent of the tribulation throughout the earth: it will impact north, south, east, and west. They also correspond to Daniel's four kingdoms that were given temporary dominion to devour, crush, and trample (see Dan 7:7). Suffering will continue until Christ's return, but "authority over" Death and Hades is in God's hands (Rev 6:8). Commentator Greg Beale points out that the cross became "the basis of judgment for those rejecting its saving significance."[82]

Only here in 6:9–11 and again in 20:4 is *psuchē* used in Revelation for deceased believers. In the latter John sees "the souls of those who had been beheaded because of their testimony about Jesus and because of the word of God, who had not worshiped the beast or his image, and who had not accepted the mark on their foreheads or their hands. They came to life and reigned with Christ for a thousand years. . . ." Whether this scene in 20:4 unfolds on earth or in heaven is debated, as is the identity of those "given authority to judge."

New Testament scholar David deSilva argues that all references to "temple precincts and paraphernalia in Revelation have in view the heavenly temple, the place of God's dwelling in heaven."[83] Certainly the altar mentioned in 6:9 is in heaven since persecution is continuing (6:10–11). Only one altar is mentioned in Revelation, apparently the golden altar of incense, from which "incense symbolic of the church's prayers rises."[84] Although the "souls" under the altar reference believers who have died, the white robes suggest perhaps that they had glorified but pre-resurrection bodies as implied in 2 Corinthians 5. The robes with which they are awarded and comforted acknowledge and symbolize their faithfulness and innocence. They are praying, not for personal vengeance, but for justice and public vindication—declaring that they were in the right and their persecutors were in the wrong. They are told this will not happen, however, until the time of testifying and persecution is ended.

Meanwhile, these individuals are sheltered by God, as symbolized by their position under the altar, which in Revelation and in Jewish writings is virtually equated with "the throne of God, whose sovereign purposes ultimately protect the saints."[85] In addition to white robes, they are also given "rest." The term for rest (Gk. *anapausis*) is used of Sabbath rest (Exod 16:23; Deut 5:14), but it also connotes security and protection from enemies (1 Kgs 5:4; 1 Chr 22:9, 18; Esth 9:22), freedom from pain and anxiety (Ps 23:2; Isa 14:3; Matt 11:28–29), and compassionate provision of needs with a sense of being "at home" (Ruth 1:9; Dan 12:13). As Beale suggests, resting for them also means to "be patient in their desire for God to answer their request."[86]

All this is intended to encourage those still living to endure in keeping "God's commands and their faith in Jesus" because "blessed are the dead who die in the Lord from now on. 'Yes,' says the Spirit, 'so they will rest [*anapauō*] from their labors, since their works follow them'" (Rev 14:12–13). That is, like the men and women of enduring faith in Hebrews 11, their works continue testifying to God's righteousness and loving mercy even after their deaths. When these "souls" are mentioned again in 20:4, by the way, they are receiving the answer to their prayer, vindication at the judgment of Satan and his kingdom. And, unlike the beast's followers, who will be tormented forever and will find "no rest day or night" (Rev 14:11; cp. Matt 12:43), the believer's rest will be eternal.

NOTES

1   F. W. Danker, *The Concise Greek-English Lexicon of the New Testament* (Chicago: University of Chicago, 2009), 254.

2   David G. Peterson, *Hebrews,* Tyndale New Testament Commentaries (Downers Grove, IL: InterVarsity, 2020), 278.

3   David deSilva, *Perseverance in Gratitude: A Socio-Rhetorical Commentary on the Epistle "To the Hebrews"* (Grand Rapids: Eerdmans, 2000), comment on 11:40. (Kindle). Our being made perfect, he says, will occur at the time of our "actual entrance into the unshakable kingdom."

4   Peterson, *Hebrews,* 280; citing William L. Lane *Hebrews,* Word Biblical Commentary (Dallas: Word, 1991), 2:393.

5   H. Balz and G. Schneider, eds., *Exegetical Dictionary of the New Testament* (Grand Rapids: Eerdmans, 1991), 47.

6   N. T. Wright, *The Resurrection of the Son of God* (Minneapolis: Fortress, 2003), 129.

7   See Wright, *Resurrection of the Son of God,* 146–206.

8   Wright, *Resurrection of the Son of God,* 129–30. Also see p. 174, 203.

9   Wright, *Resurrection of the Son of God,* 203.

10 James R. Edwards, *The Gospel According to Luke,* Pillar New Testament Commentary (Grand Rapids: Eerdmans, 2015), 449

11 Edwards, *The Gospel According to Luke,* 449.

12 Christopher Wright explains that "giving to the needy is not only a sacred duty to God, but it also is the defining point for any claim to have kept the law. *The law is kept only if the poor are cared for.*" Deuteronomy, New International Biblical Commentary (Peabody, MA: Hendrickson, 1996), 271.

13 See Garwood P. Anderson, "Parables," in *Dictionary of Jesus and the Gospels, Second Edition,* ed. J. P. Green, J. K. Brown, N. Perrin (Downers Grove, IL: InterVarsity, 2013), 657–60; Craig L. Blomberg, *Interpreting the Parables, Second Edition* (Downers Grove, IL: InterVarsity, 2012), 33–67; Klyne Snodgrass, "Modern Approaches to the Parables," in *The Face of New Testament Studies: A Survey of Recent Research,* ed. S. McKnight and G. R. Osborne (Grand

Rapids: Baker, 2004), 177–90; Snodgrass, *Stories with Intent: A Comprehensive Guide to the Parables of Jesus*, Second Edition (Grand Rapids: Eerdmans, 2016), 24–31; David Wenham, *The Parables of Jesus* (Downers Grove, IL: InterVarsity, 1989), 14–19.

14   Snodgrass, *Stories with Intent*, 423.

15   Darrell L. Bock, *Luke*, Baker Exegetical Commentary on the New Testament (Grand Rapids: Baker, 1996), 1366.

16   Arland J. Hultgren, *The Parables of Jesus: A Commentary* (Grand Rapids: Eerdmans, 2000), 112. See Prov 18:11: "The wealth of the rich is his fortified city; / in his imagination it is like a high wall." Also see Bock, *Luke*, 1372.

17   See Gen 16:5; Num 11:12; Deut 13:6; 28:54, 56; Ruth 4:16; 2 Sam 12:3, 8; Isa 49:22; Lam 2:12; Sir 9:1.

18   See I. H. Marshall, *Commentary on Luke*, New International Greek Testament Commentary (Grand Rapids: Eerdmans, 1978), 636; Joel B. Green, *The Gospel of Luke*, New International Commentary on the New Testament (Grand Rapids: Eerdmans, 1997), 607. Ronald F. Hock, "Lazarus and Micyllus: Greco-Roman Backgrounds to Luke 16:19–31," *Journal of Biblical Literature* 106 (1987): 456, argues on the basis of Greek sepulchral epigrams that the emphasis is "less on the honor that Lazarus supposedly now enjoys than on the protection and care he at last possesses."

19   See Richard Bauckham, "Life, Death, and the Afterlife in Second Temple Judaism," in *Life in the Face of Death: The Resurrection Message of the New Testament*, ed. R. N. Longenecker (Grand Rapids: Eerdmans, 1998), 89; Joseph A. Fitzmyer, *The Gospel According to Luke 10–24*, Anchor Bible (New York: Doubleday, 1985), 855.

20   Bauckham, "The Rich Man and Lazarus," 97–100, 104–6.

21   Bauckham, "The Rich Man and Lazarus," 104.

22   Snodgrass, *Stories with Intent*, 426. This would include the view of Kim Papaioannou ("The Parable of the Rich Man and Lazarus and Tales of Revelations from the Afterlife," *Ministry* [July, 2016]: 17) that Jesus was alluding to and debunking or deconstructing "stories of reversal of fortune at death, as in the parable, as well as revelations from afterlife, as requested in the parable."

23   See Blomberg, *Interpreting the Parables*, 258.

24   Also, Lev 25:35; Prov 3:27–28; 14:21, 31; 21:13; Isa 58:6–7; Jer 22:16; Ezek 16:49; 18:7. See the study of material possessions in the Old Testament in Craig L. Blomberg, *Neither Poverty nor Riches: A Biblical Theology of Possessions*, New Studies in Biblical Theology (Downers Grove, IL: InterVarsity, 1999), 33–85.

25   Marshall, *Commentary on Luke*, 638.

26   Bauckham ("The Rich Man and Lazarus," 108–16) and others claim that Jesus's audience *could* have been aware of stories either about living persons visiting the realm of the dead and bringing back a message to repent or about people dying temporarily and then returning to describe the experience. Some of these stories are about "mistaken identities" in which bungling death "angels" take the wrong person and have to return him to this world. They sound strangely like plots from several modern movies (*Angels in the Outfield*, 1951; *Heaven Can Wait*, 1978). If such stories were familiar to them, they only add that, contrary to stories they had heard, if anyone did rise from the dead with a warning testimony, his testimony would be rejected by anyone who had not already accepted the testimony of the Scriptures. Most such stories, though, were later than the time of Jesus.

27   Williamson, *Death and the Afterlife*, 54.

28   Bock, *Luke*, 1376.

29   Blomberg, *Interpreting the Parables*, 261.

30 Blomberg, *Interpreting the Parables,* 259. Snodgrass considers "judgment for the use of wealth and the sufficiency of the Scriptures" to be "equally important" (*Stories with Intent,* 428).

31 Snodgrass, *Stories with Intent, 334.*

32 Herman Ridderbos, *Paul: An Outline of His Theology* (Grand Rapids: Eerdmans, 1975), 507–8.

33 See Emil Schürer, *The Literature of the Jewish People in the Time of Jesus* (New York: Schocken, 1972), 93–114; James H. Charlesworth, ed., *The Old Testament Pseudepigrapha* (Peabody, MA: Hendrickson, 1983), 1:517–59.

34 Hoekema, *The Bible and the Future,* 101.

35 Williamson, *Death and the Afterlife,* 52–53.

36 Williamson, *Death and the Afterlife,* 54.

37 See Luke 4:24; 12:37; 18:17, 29; 21:32. The God's Word Translation (Baker, 2010) renders the phrase *amēn legō* as "I can guarantee this truth."

38 See Heb 3:7, 15; 4:7. In a few other passages the word *sēmeron* is preceded by only one word such as "that" (Luke 19:9) or emphatic "you (yourself)" (Mark 14:30).

39 English translations often put "today" at the end, but Greek has it at the beginning of the clause.

40 Gulley, *Systematic Theology,* 115.

41 D. A. Carson, *The Gospel according to John,* Pillar New Testament Commentary (Grand Rapids: Eerdmans, 1991), 644.

42 The Adventist paraphrase has the verse saying almost the opposite of what is in the Greek: "I promise you today, when I return with the glory of my Father, I will take you home with me to paradise" (Blanco, *The Clear Word*).

43 Wilson Paroschi, "The Significance of a Comma: An Analysis of Luke 23:43," *Ministry* (June, 2013): 6. Several medieval Greek manuscripts insert *hoti,* "that" before "today," ruling out the Adventist view. Paroschi strangely takes this as evidence for his claim of theological bias. However, the most likely reason for its addition is the occurrence of *hoti* after "truly I say to you" in thirty other passages in the Gospels. Paroschi also claims that the fourth-century manuscript Vaticanus "has a point on the line right after, not before, the adverb *sēmeron,*" a possible scribal indication of a "short pause." This manuscript is available online through the Center for the Study of New Testament Manuscripts (http://www.csntm.org/Manuscript/View/GA_03), and it shows no point on the line. Evidently those digitizing the manuscript considered whatever mark Dr. Paroschi found to be one of the "sparse accidental dots or inkblots" he mentions.

44 On the term *paradeisos,* "paradise," see Jan N. Bremmer, *The Rise and Fall of the Afterlife* (New York: Routledge, 2002), 109–27. The translators of *A New English Translation of The Septuagint,* ed. Albert Pietersma and Benjamin G. Wright (Oxford: Oxford University Press, 2007), rendered the term "orchard."

45 Marshall, *Commentary on Luke,* 873. Also see Wright, *Surprised by Hope,* 41.

46 N. T. Wright, *The Resurrection of the Son of God* (Minneapolis: Fortress, 2003), 142. See also pp. 168–69, 189–90, 198–99, 203, 438 n. 114.

47 Wright, *The Resurrection of the Son of God,* 201. James Edwards offers no reason for disagreeing that "paradise" referred to a "temporary eschatological state" prior to Jesus's return. He claims that it "appears to signify the full presence of God, the highest heaven" (*The Gospel according to Luke,* 692).

48 See Gen 26:3; 31:3; Exod 3:12; Josh 1:5; Judg 6:16; Jer 1:8.

49 See Luke 22:69; Acts 2:33–34; 3:21; 5:31; 7:55–56; Rom 8:34; Eph 1:20; Col 3:1; Heb 1:3; 4:14; 7:26; 8:1; 9:24; 10:12; 12:2; 1 Pet 3:22. See Peter C. Orr, *Exalted above the Heavens: The Risen and*

Ascended Christ, New Studies in Biblical Theology (Downers Grove, IL: InterVarsity, 2018), 77. On the verses in Hebrews, see Orr, pp. 94–98.

[50] See Carson's discussion of the verse in *The Gospel according to John*, 641–45.

[51] Also see Acts 10:45; Rom 5:5; Titus 3:6.

[52] See Orr, *Exalted above the Heavens*, 78, who explains that Christ's "absence is a function of his ongoing humanity and possession of a discrete, localizable body. . . . Christ *is* present to believers in a real way. But it is never an unqualified presence—that remains for the future" (see also p. 94).

[53] As Paul says in Eph 3:19, "to know Christ's love that surpasses knowledge" is to "be filled with all the fullness of God." And in Col 1:19 he tells us that "God was pleased to have all his fullness dwell in [Christ]." Paul even repeats himself for emphasis and elaboration in 2:9: "The entire fullness of God's nature dwells bodily in Christ." The same thing is found in Heb. 1:3: "The Son is the radiance of God's glory and the exact expression of his nature." These verses don't just mean that Jesus is God. They mean that the Godhead resides by nature in Jesus, so that Jesus can say, "The one who has seen me has seen the Father" because "I am in the Father and the Father is in me" (John 14:9–10). He even said, "I and the Father are one" (John 10:30). The same is true of the person of the Holy Spirit. The fullness of the divine nature dwells in him (not it).

[54] Theologians call this interfacing of divine persons in the one trinitarian God "mutual indwelling" (they also use the Gk. word *perichoresis* and the Lat. *circumcession*). Although God exists in three distinct persons whose roles are not identical (the Father plans, the Son executes, the Spirit applies; see 1 Pet 1:1–2), it is also true that "all three persons are involved in all the works of God in and for creation." See John M. Frame, *The Doctrine of God* (Phillipsburg, NJ: P&R, 2002), 693–96. See also John C. Clark and Marcus Peter Johnson, *The Incarnation of God: The Mystery of the Gospel as the Foundation of Evangelical Theology* (Wheaton, IL: Crossway, 2015), 66–67.

[55] Although rendered in some versions as "deliverance" (Phil 1:19) and sometimes interpreted to refer to release from prison, the word clearly refers to final "salvation" in v. 28 and would happen, Paul says in v. 20, whether he lives or dies.

[56] Frank Thielman, *Philippians,* NIV Application Commentary (Grand Rapids: Zondervan, 1995), 77.

[57] Gordon D. Fee, *Paul's Letter to the Philippians,* New International Commentary on the New Testament (Grand Rapids: Eerdmans, 1995), 141.

[58] An excellent Japanese film called *Departures* was released in 2008. It's about a Japanese cellist forced to take a job as a funeral professional to "prepare the deceased for burial and entrance into the next life." It won the academy award for best foreign language film and was recognized by Roger Ebert as having "tremendous emotional impact."

[59] Paul uses the tent imagery of death in 2 Cor 5:1 without the same word.

[60] The construction involves binding two nouns together with only one article.

[61] See Peter T. O'Brien, *The Epistle to the Philippians,* New International Greek Testament Commentary (Grand Rapids: Eerdmans, 1991), 130.

[62] See Thielman, *Philippians,* 79. Paul's attitude, he says, "can only strike us as strange in the modern church if we have allowed the comforts of our present physical existence to usurp the place of Christ in our lives as our chief priority. If we are to let this passage speak to us on its own terms, we will need to stare Paul's astonishing indifference toward death squarely in the face and ask ourselves whether our attitude toward death imitates his" (p. 83).

[63] Fee thinks it "very likely" that Paul was thinking of consciously being with Christ, "although in this case such a conclusion goes beyond the certain evidence we possess from Paul himself" (*Philippians*, 149).

[64] Garland, *2 Corinthians*, 278.

[65] Garland, *2 Corinthians*, 286. Scott Hafemann (*2 Corinthians*, The NIV Application Commentary [Grand Rapids: Zondervan, 2000], 208–13) adopts C. Marvin Pate's view that being naked/unclothed here alludes to Adam's state of condemnation and shame at the final judgment, devoid of God's glory. Our spiritual resurrection in Christ clothes us in Christ's spiritual body, assuring that we will not be found "naked." It also anticipates our physical resurrection at Christ's return, when we receive our "building from God." Garland points out significant problems with this view. He says, "Paul simply says that the dead rise with a body" (*2 Corinthians*, 286–87).

[66] Garland, *2 Corinthians*, 287, n. 700.

[67] BDAG, s.v. "σκῆνος," 929.

[68] Murray J. Harris, *The Second Epistle to the Corinthians: A Commentary on the Greek Text*, The New International Greek Testament Commentary (Grand Rapids: Eerdmans, 2005), 377. This is the view Harris took in "2 Corinthians 5:1–10: A Watershed in Paul's Theology?" *Tyndale Bulletin* 22 (1971):43; quoted in Garland, *2 Corinthians*, 278.

[69] F. F. Bruce, *Paul: Apostle of the Heart Set Free* (Grand Rapids: Eerdmans, 1977), 311.

[70] Bruce, *Paul: Apostle of the Heart Set Free*, 312, n. 40.

[71] Garland, *2 Corinthians*, 279.

[72] William Lane Craig, *Time and Eternity: Exploring God's Relationship to Time* (Wheaton: Crossway, 2001), 11.

[73] Craig, *Time and Eternity*, 14–20.

[74] Craig, *Time and Eternity*, 241.

[75] Harris, *The Second Epistle to the Corinthians*, 374–80, discusses five views. The three mentioned here are those he considers the most common and those with the fewest difficulties. While he defended the first view in 1971, he favors the third view in his 2005 commentary.

[76] Harris, *The Second Epistle to the Corinthians*, 380.

[77] Harris, *The Second Epistle to the Corinthians*, 379.

[78] Garland, *2 Corinthians*, 283,

[79] G. K. Beale, The Book of Revelation, The New International Greek Testament Commentary (Grand Rapids: Eerdmans, 1999), 385.

[80] See David A. deSilva, *Discovering Revelation: Content, Interpretation, Reception* (Grand Rapids: Eerdmans, 2021), 112. I share his view that the 144,000 servants of God in Rev 7 are probably symbolic of the entire bride of Christ, the new Israel. See DeSilva, 113; Beale, *The Book of Revelation*, 425–26.

[81] deSilva, *Discovering Revelation*, 108.

[82] Beale, *The Book of Revelation*, 385.

[83] See 6:9–11; 7:15; 8:2–5; 11:1–2, 19; 13:6; 14:15, 17; 15:5–8; 16:1, 7, 17. deSilva, *Discovering Revelation*, 115.

[84] Dennis E. Johnson, *Triumph of the Lamb: A Commentary on Revelation* (Phillipsburg, NJ: P&R, 2001), 125. He suggests that "the altar" for John "serves the purposes of both altars." Cf. Beale, *The Book of Revelation*, 391.

[85] Beale, *The Book of Revelation*, 391.

[86] Beale, *The Book of Revelation*, 394.

CHAPTER 12

THE OTHER PLACE: HADES AND ITS VISITORS

We have talked about Sheol and Hades in the last two chapters. Now it's time for us to take a tram-ride to those less pleasant regions of the afterlife. They are often collectively described as "hell," but that English word—though it's used in the title of this book—presents a problem. Why? Well, we use the word to designate negative aspects of the place of the dead, often generically called the underworld or netherworld, due to the common conception of its location somewhere below the earth's surface (or "under the earth"). The word "hell" is used to designate a place of torment, either literally of the dead, or figuratively of the living. And then there is its use for a severe scolding or as an interjection. Since the Bible was written in Hebrew, Aramaic, and Greek, however, the answer to the question, "What does the Bible teach about hell?" must be, technically, "Nothing." The word "hell" does occur in English Bibles but is only a translation. The KJV uses it 31 times in the Old Testament to translate *Sheol* and 23 times in the New Testament for either *Gehenna, Hades,* or *Tartarus*. That highlights the additional complication of whether different words are used for the different afterlife destinations of the wicked, whether human or demonic, and whether before judgment or after.

This is why we usually speak more broadly of the *afterlife*, which the

Cumaean Sibyl by Andrea del Castagno. In Virgil's Aeneid, the Cumaean Sibyl was a guide to people who wished to visit Hades.

Bible portrays differently, depending on who goes there. It is common to designate the various aspects of the afterlife as Sheol/Hades, paradise/Abraham's bosom, the Pit, the abyss, Tartarus, Gehenna, and the lake of fire. Besides the "underworld," some refer to the place of the dead generally as Sheol or Hades, within which we find the righteous dead in Abraham's bosom or paradise. The abyss or Tartarus is identified as the place of evil powers: disobedient angels, demons, Satan, and the antichrist. But we will see in the next chapter that "the abyss" is used more broadly than that. Gehenna or the lake of fire are not considered chambers in Hades/Sheol but are terms for the final destiny of those evil powers and also of wicked persons.[1]

It is common to designate the various aspects of the afterlife as Sheol/Hades, paradise/Abraham's bosom, the Pit, the abyss, Tartarus, Gehenna, and the lake of fire.

In this and the other chapters ahead, we will evaluate these common designations as we look more closely at the Hebrew and Greek words behind the terms and the Scriptures that use them. But an expectation that these are used throughout the Bible in a uniform, distinct, and technical way with narrow definitions will prove overly optimistic.

HADES

We examined the Hebrew word *Sheol* in chapter 10 ("Is This a Direct Flight?"). Now it is time to consider the Greek word *Hades*. It is almost always used to translate the term *Sheol* in the Old Testament and is found 10 times in the New Testament (in Matthew, Luke, Acts and Revelation). A relatively recent dictionary of New Testament Greek words and theology explains that in the time of Homer, many centuries before Jesus arrived, the word Hades was used of the Greek god of the world of the dead and also of his realm. The dead were thought to have a "shadowy existence" there, but only gradually did the Greeks attach to it the idea of reward for the good and punishment for the godless and wicked.[2]

In the time of Homer, many centuries before Jesus arrived, the word Hades was used of the Greek god of the world of the dead and also of his realm.

In the opinion of New Testament scholar Joachim Jeremias, in Judaism and the New Testament the dead are conscious. The New Testament seems sometimes to place all the dead in Hades (Acts 2:27), although elsewhere believers are in paradise (Luke 16:9, 19–31), or "at home with the Lord" (2 Cor 5:8), or "under the altar" (Rev 6:9). If these locations are separate from Hades, then it is considered only the abode of the wicked (Luke 16:23; Rev 20:13-14).[3] Contrary to Jeremias, New Testament scholar Jonathan Lunde argues that the New Testament does not maintain a strict distinction between Hades and Gehenna, which we will consider in the next chapter.[4] D. A. Carson points out that although some consider Hades to have been the place of the dead "in the intermediate state" and Gehenna was the eternal hell for the wicked, "more commonly the two terms are synonymous and mean 'hell.'"[5] Other scholars, though not all, agree: "The lines of definition" between Hades and the abyss "are just as fluid as is the case with [Gehenna]."[6]

"The lines of definition" between Hades and the abyss "are just as fluid as is the case with [Gehenna]."

Many passages in the Old Testament and in Jewish and pagan literature mention the gates of Sheol/Hades, of death, or of the underworld (see esp. Job 17:16; 38:17;

Pss 9:13; 107:18; Isa 38:10; Jonah 2:6). In the New Testament the phrase "gates of Hades" occurs in Matthew 16:18, in which Jesus promises that "the gates of Hades will not overpower" his church. The major Greek lexicon of the New Testament explains the meaning of the verb as "to have the capability to defeat, *win a victory over*."[7] According to D. A. Carson, the phrase seems to refer to "death and dying," reflected in the RSV rendering, "The powers of death shall not prevail against" the church. Carson comments that "because the church is the assembly of people Jesus Messiah is building, it cannot die."[8] In this case, the gates are simply what shuts "behind" the spirits of the dead (see Jonah 2:6).

This is the meaning in Job 17:15–16, where Job asks, "Where then is my hope? / Who can see any hope for me? / Will it go down to the gates of Sheol, / or will we descend together to the dust?" The gates are even called "the gates of death" and "the gates of deep darkness [KJV, "shadow of death"]" (Job 38:17; Pss 9:13; 107:18).

> *"Because the church is the assembly of people Jesus Messiah is building, it cannot die."*

As we will see in the next section, however, pagan literature refers to gates that protect the world of the living from the spirits of the dead, as well as protecting the underworld from unwanted guests from among the living trying to interfere with its affairs. When we look at Ephesians 4:7–10 later in this chapter, we will find that Asia Minor had a goddess of witchcraft and sorcery believed to wield "the keys of Hades." According to New Testament scholar Clinton Arnold, this meant she could unlock the gates of Hades and unleash "the demonic souls" from there. In their commentary on Matthew, Davies and Allison caution against reading the Old Testament usage into Matthew, for "conceptions about Hades and Sheol changed over time." They explain that by the first century Hades tended to be considered the place of the *ungodly* dead, as well as demons and evil spirits. They favor understanding Jesus's promise as his assurance that "when the powers of the underworld will be unleashed from below, from the abyss, and rage against the saints . . . even the full fury of the underworld's demonic forces will not overcome the church."[9]

Before we move in for a closer look at the world(s) of the dead, however, let's pause to listen to various ancient stories of "descents" and "tours of hell" and consider how they compare to the Bible.

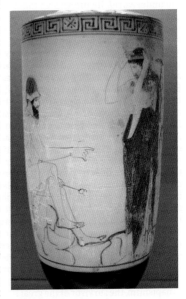

Greek god Hermes preparing to lead a dead soul to the Hades.

TOURS OF HELL

Some more imaginative and adventurous explorers than I have attempted to escort travelers into the depths of the underworld in much the same way novelist Jules Verne took us a *Journey to the Center of the Earth in 1864*. But no tour I lead will be nearly so ambitious or scary.

I've read that in 2022 average life expectancy in the U.S. is about 76 years. We wish it were higher. But in ancient Greece and Rome, which we imagine were advanced civilizations for their time, average life expectancy was about 20 to 25 years. Only 40 percent of people reached that age, and only 50 percent of children made it to their tenth birthdays.[10] Therefore, we should not be surprised that the ancients thought and wrote a great deal about what takes place after death. The Greek playwright Euripedes (writing ca. 400 BC) put little confidence in these descriptions, however. He said, "The life of man is all suffering, and there is no rest from pain and trouble. There may be something better than this life; but whatever it be, it is hidden in mists of darkness."[11]

In ancient Greece and Rome . . . average life expectancy was about 20 to 25 years.

Paul Williamson, Richard Bauckham, and others have surveyed ancient accounts of the afterlife.[12] Bauckham pays special attention to stories about the underworld. He informs us that in the early Christian centuries many pagans, Jews, and Christians located the realm of the wicked dead in the lower heavens rather than under the earth.[13] Even Jesus's parable in Luke 16 simply says the rich man ended up in "Hades," but he does not tell us where that is. Nevertheless, most of the ancient stories of what are known as "tours of hell" involve descents to the underworld.[14] These come from many cultures of the ancient world including Mesopotamia (Sumerian, Babylonian, and Assyrian), Egypt, Syria and Palestine, Iran, Greece and Rome, and early post-biblical Jewish and Christian literature. Some of the descent stories involve an attempted rescue of someone who died. Some of them are associated with the seasons, with a divine or semi-divine being representing fertility spending part of each year in the underworld, as in the Greek myth of Persephone, who spent part of each year with her mother on Olympus and part with her husband Hades as queen of the underworld (this is similar to the myth of Adonis). In ancient Egyptian mythology the sun god descended in the west each night, traveled under the earth, and rose again in the east each morning. Many of the descent stories involve trances, visions, and dreams that were recalled as experiences of the soul temporarily leaving the body. However, some employ entrances by means of springs, rivers, lakes, caves, chasms, or—as in the case of Jules Verne's story—volcanoes. In the Babylonian Gilgamesh epic, the hero goes on a long and arduous journey to the western mountains and then across the sea and the waters of death to find Utnapishtim, the survivor of the great flood, in the underworld.[15] The accounts often have the character of literary devices to describe the underworld to prepare the living for their journeys and to warn them of retribution for their current behavior in this life.

In the early Christian centuries many pagans, Jews, and Christians located the realm of the wicked dead in the lower heavens rather than under the earth.

Bauckham's survey of the stories, as he points out, shows "how remarkably lacking they are in the biblical literature itself."[16] He notes, "There is no Old Testament instance of a true descent to and return from the underworld by a living human," although the language of going down and returning is used of God's deliverance of individuals who barely escaped death (see 1 Sam 2:6; Pss 9:13; 30:3; 86:13; 88:6; 107:18).[17] Certain items from the stories, however, do show up in various Scriptures. Gates, for example, are often mentioned: they serve to keep the

> *"There is no Old Testament instance of a true descent to and return from the underworld by a living human."*

living out and the dead in (see Job 17:16; 38:17; Isa 38:10; Jonah 2:6). The Greeks also had a multi-headed dog, Cerberus, guarding the gate. Virgil (in a first-century BC update of eighth-century Homer) had it guarded by the river Styx, over which the boatman Charon would only carry the dead. In both Mesopotamia and Israel, the message is clear that those who go down do not come back (see Job 7:9; 2 Sam 12:23). Greek and Latin accounts exist, however, of journeys to Hades and back, to rescue (in the case of Heracles) or to consult (in Odysseus's case) someone there. Others describe a disembodied, near-death experience. Passing through the various obstacles represented the process of death, and the journey from life to death is sometimes said to take three days (cp. Jonah 1:17). A few stories tell about someone taken to the underworld too soon by mistake who must be sent back. These clearly inspired Hollywood movies such as *Here Comes Mr. Jordan* (1941) with Robert Montgomery; in 1978, it was remade as *Heaven Can Wait* with Warren Beatty and Julie Christie.

Richard Bauckham informs us that Homer's description of Hades in the *Odyssey* (a major source of knowledge among the Greeks) shows all the undifferentiated dead in "joyless gloom," "neither happy nor suffering punishment." Three exceptional cases included Sisyphus incessantly rolling a huge stone up a hill, only to have it roll back again and again, and

Persephone supervising Sisyphus in the Underworld.

Tantalus, eternally "tantalized" by unreachable food and drink.[18] The common view up to Virgil's time, however, was of a "sunlit paradise" for the blessed, either in the sky (Plato) or more often with the wicked in Hades. But when Odysseus meets the great Achilles in Hades, he is told, "Never try to reconcile me to death, glorious Odysseus. I should choose, so I might live on earth, to serve as the hireling of another, some landless man with hardly enough to live on, rather than to be lord over all the dead."[19] N. T. Wright tells us that for most of the dead in Homer's day and later—shades, ghosts, and phantoms, "in no

> *"Never try to reconcile me to death, glorious Odysseus."*

way fully human beings, though they may look like them"—even for "those who have been great and good in their former life, Hades holds no comforts, no prospects, but only a profound sense of loss," gloom, and sometimes terror. No idea of an immortal soul, one's *"Hades holds no comforts, no prospects, but only a profound sense of loss," gloom, and sometimes terror.*
"true self," enjoying life away from the body was held before Plato in about 400 BC. In fact, Homer's hero Achilles sent "many valiant souls of warriors" down to Hades "to be the spoil for dogs and birds of every kind." And that Homeric tradition "remained powerful well into the early Christian period."[20]

In N. T. Wright's masterful study of *The Resurrection of the Son of God,* he concludes his introductory study of "Life beyond Death in Ancient Paganism" like this:

> The road to the underworld ran only one way. Throughout the ancient world, from its "Bible" of Homer and Plato, through its practices (funerals, memorial feasts), its stories (plays, novels, legends), its symbols (graves, amulets, grave-goods) and its grand theories, we can trace a good deal of variety about the road to Hades, and about what one might find upon arrival. As with all one-way streets, there is bound to be someone who attempts to drive in the opposite direction.... But the road was well policed. Would-be violators ... were turned back or punished. And even they only occurred in what everybody knew to be myth.[21]

"We can trace a good deal of variety about the road to Hades."

The Greek and Latin sources sometimes employ a guide to Hades, such as Virgil's prophetess the Sibyl, who guided Aeneas. In extra-biblical Jewish sources such as the third- or second-century BC book of 1 Enoch, the guides are Uriel and other angelic messengers. These take Enoch to the place of the sinking sun on the western horizon. There he sees four categories of the deceased kept until the time of final judgment.[22] He also sees "a deep pit with heavenly fire on its pillars," which is "a desolate and terrible place, ... the prison house for the stars and the powers of heaven." The mentioned stars are the ones transgressing God's commands "because they did not arrive punctually." Also imprisoned are "the spirits of the angels which have united themselves with women" and led the people to offer sacrifices to demons (1 Enoch 18:11–19:1). The stars would be punished for ten million years, but the angels would be imprisoned there forever (21:6–10).

Before the first two Christian centuries, the Jews thought the punishment of the wicked would not begin at death but at the judgment. Then under the influence of the Greeks, who rejected future judgment, many began to believe that eternal punishment commenced immediately in Hades, where only the wicked were found. The later view allowed for tours of hell where the wicked could be seen in torment. The oldest of these tours appears in the first-century Latin Apocalypse of Elijah, which describes, as would later works, how "sinners are hung up by the part of the body with which they had sinned."[23] The "main concern" of many later

Before the first two Christian centuries, the Jews thought the punishment of the wicked would not begin at death but at the judgment.

tours of hell is to show how "a wide range of particular sins is specifically punished by appropriate forms of judgment."[24] Many of these were "extremely popular in the medieval period" and formed "a literary tradition whose greatest product was Dante's *Divine Comedy*" (see our chapter 3: "Heaven the Celestial Fire").[25]

Since I am neither a prophet nor an angel and have never traveled disembodied or in any other way to heaven, much less to hell, I and everyone else I know must confine ourselves to the Bible for knowledge of these places. That is why I say our trip to them must be on the order of a tram-ride. We can only look down on what God has shown us in his Word, and that revelation is tantalizingly meager. Evidently God's interest is primarily on our following him now as he leads us and trusting him for what comes later.

After our brief survey of tours of hell and stories of individuals who descended into it, we will examine in the next chapter claims that one individual in the Bible did descend to and return from hell/Hades.

NOTES

1 See Justin Bass, *The Battle for the Keys: Revelation 1:18 and Christ's Descent into the Underworld*, Paternoster Biblical Monographs (Milton Keynes: Paternoster, 2014), 78 (Kindle).

2 *New International Dictionary of New Testament Theology and Exegesis: Second Edition*, ed. Moisés Silva (Grand Rapids: Zondervan, 2014), 1:152–53.

3 Joachim Jeremias, "Hades," in *Theological Dictionary of the New Testament: Abridged in One Volume*, ed. G. Kittel, G. Friedrich, and G. W. Bromiley (Grand Rapids: Eerdmans, 1985), 22.

4 Jonathan Lunde, "Heaven and Hell," in *Dictionary of Jesus and the Gospels*, ed. J. B. Green, S. McKnight, and I. H. Marshall (Downers Grove, IL: InterVarsity, 1992), 311.

5 D. A. Carson, "Matthew," in *Expositor's Bible Commentary*, ed. F. E. Gaebelein (Grand Rapids: Zondervan, 1990), Accordance Version 2.9, comments on Matt 5:22–23.

6 Otto Bösher, "Hades," in *Exegetical Dictionary of the New Testament, Volume 1*, ed. H. Balz and G. Schneider (Grand Rapids: Eerdmans, 1990), 30.

7 *A Greek-English Lexicon of the New Testament and Early Christian Literature, Third Edition*, ed. F. W. Danker (Chicago: University of Chicago Press, 2000), 534.

8 Carson, "Matthew," comments on Matt 16:18. See also Grant R. Osborne, *Matthew*, Zondervan Exegetical Commentary on the New Testament (Grand Rapids: Zondervan, 2010), 628; R. T. France, *The Gospel of Matthew*, New International Commentary on the New Testament (Grand Rapids: Eerdmans, 2007), 624, who declares that "gates of Hades is a metaphor for death."

9 W. D. Davies and D. C. Allison, *Matthew 8–18*, International Critical Commentary (London: T&T Clark, 2004), 633.

10 Peter G. Bolt, "Life, Death, and the Afterlife in the Greco-Roman World," in *Life in the Face of Death: The Resurrection Message of the New Testament*, ed. R. N. Longenecker (Grand Rapids: Eerdmans, 1998), 52.

11 Bolt, "Life, Death, and the Afterlife," 64.

12 Williamson, *Death and the Afterlife*, 7–21; Richard Bauckham, *The Fate of the Dead: Studies on the Jewish and Christian Apocalypses* (Atlanta: Society of Biblical Literature, 1998), 9–48.

13 Bolt tells us that "throughout these periods of development regarding an afterlife, it is possible to detect a growing shift toward the idea of an astral immortality; whereas the

dead once resided in the underworld, as time went by, they were understood to be located in the astral regions" ("Life, Death, and the Afterlife," 66).

[14] The following discussion depends heavily on Bauckham, "Descents to the Underworld," in *The Fate of the Dead*, 9–48.

[15] See Alexander Heidel, *The Gilgamesh Epic and Old Testament Parallels* (Chicago: University of Chicago Press, 1949), 8–9.

[16] Bauckham, *The Fate of the Dead*, 10.

[17] Bauckham, *The Fate of the Dead*, 16.

[18] Bauckham, *The Fate of the Dead*, 29.

[19] Wright, *The Resurrection of the Son of God*, 42.

[20] Wright, *The Resurrection of the Son of God*, 43–44.

[21] Wright, *The Resurrection of the Son of God*, 81–82.

[22] Bauckham, *The Fate of the Dead*, 33.

[23] Bauckham, *The Fate of the Dead*, 35.

[24] Bauckham, *The Fate of the Dead*, 35.

[25] Bauckham, *The Fate of the Dead*, 35.

CHAPTER 13

CHRIST'S DESCENT TO HADES

Christ's Descent into Hell by an anonymous follower of Hieronymus Bosch.

The sixteenth-century painting by an anonymous follower of Hieronymus Bosch is called *Christ's Descent into Hell*. It portrays a desolate landscape with a burning city on the right and the river Styx to the left. It includes Adam and Eve kneeling on top of a tower and Old Testament figures ascending stairs from the depths of hell. These include Abraham and Isaac with the sacrificial ram, and Noah with a model of the ark.

Although the final form of the so-called Apostles' Creed dates from the eighth century AD, the phrase "He descended into hell" that's included within it may come from as early as the end of the second century. Justin Martyr (who died ca. AD 165) declared, "The Lord God remembered his dead people of Israel who lay in their graves, and he descended to preach to them his own salvation" (*Dial. 72.4*).[1] Our first sure evidence of it, though, is from the fourth century, where it is worded, Christ "... was crucified and died and descended into the underworld." By this time the function of Christ's descent was thought to be a declaration of his triumph over the devil and his evil forces.[2] The wording most familiar is that of the Apostles' Creed, which states, "I believe ... in Jesus Christ, ... who was ... crucified, dead and buried, descended into hell, on the third day rose again from the dead. ..." The reason earlier versions of the creed did not include "and descended into the underworld/hell," according to Justin Bass, is that it was assumed to be included in "he was buried," as found, for example, in the AD 381 restatement of the Nicene Creed. In fact, Justin Bass argues, "It is clear from the Fathers' writings, beginning with Ignatius, that they all believed that Christ descended into the underworld between his death and resurrection."[3]

Many Christian theologians understand the church's statement of Christ's descent to mean no more than that he was buried. Others believe the church was simply wrong and that "descended into hell" should be removed from our creeds.[4] The issue, as always, is whether or not Christ's descent to hell, Hades, or "the place of the dead" is taught in Scripture. So, we will have to look briefly at the passages presented by recent scholars in defense of the teaching.

> *"It is clear from the Fathers' writings, beginning with Ignatius, that they all believed that Christ descended into the underworld between his death and resurrection."*

MATTHEW 12:40 AND JONAH 2

In response to the Jews' demand for a sign from Jesus, he says this: "An evil and adulterous generation demands a sign, but no sign will be given to it except the sign of the prophet Jonah. For as Jonah was in the belly of the huge fish three days and three nights, so the Son of Man will be in the heart of the earth three days and three nights" (Matt 12:39–40).

The prophet Jonah, then, was to be the crowd's only sign. Of course, at least Jesus's disciples and later readers of the Gospels would know that Jesus had performed many signs that should have been sufficient proof of his divine authority. As R. T. France explains, here "Jesus dismisses the present request because of the attitude of those who have made it."[5] Yet Jesus nevertheless points to a future parallel between himself and Jonah that could be a sign to anyone with an open mind. Jonah was "in the belly of the fish three days and three nights" (Jonah 1:17) and then was miraculously delivered by God (2:10).

> *"Jesus nevertheless points to a future parallel between himself and Jonah that could be a sign to anyone with an open mind."*

Likewise, Jesus would be "in the heart of the earth three days and three nights," and then would be miraculously delivered by God. But what does Jesus mean by "in the heart of the earth"?

Jonah spoke of his experience *as if* he had died, though he made it clear that his was a virtual death. He describes the belly of the fish, where he prayed, as literally "the belly of Sheol" (Jonah 2:2). But the great fish had already saved him from "the depths," that is, "the heart of the seas" (2:3), where he had been "banished" (2:4) in "the watery depths" (Hb. *tehom,* "the abyss" in the Septuagint; 2:5). Although he had literally felt the bars of the earth were "behind [him] forever,"[6] the Lord had raised his life "from the Pit" (2:6), just as he felt his "life was fading away" (2:7). So, what seemed the belly of Sheol turned out to be what God used to deliver Jonah "onto dry land" (2:10). It was *as if* Jonah had been to Sheol, the place of the dead.

Unlike Jonah, however, Jesus ("the Son of Man") really died on a cross, was buried, and rose again on the third day ("three days and three nights" is a Semitic idiom that can represent any portion of three twenty-four-hour days[7]). His death and resurrection are what the Jonah parallel typologically points to.[8] But does Jesus imply that he would literally go to Sheol, where he would remain for three days? Perhaps. But this passage does not prove it. The phrase "the heart of the earth" is not used to refer to Sheol in biblical or pre-Christian Jewish literature but is probably used here as parallel to "the heart of the seas" in Jonah 2:3.[9] Jesus could be referring to the tomb, which is how D. A. Carson understands it.[10]

ACTS 2:24–28 AND PSALM 16

In Peter's Pentecost sermon, he announces Christ's resurrection in Acts 2:24. He says, "God raised him up, ending [or "having freed him from"] the [labor] pains of death, because it was not possible for him to be held by death." Now, some might wonder if "ending the pains of death" could mean that Jesus was in pain until the resurrection. But Peter does not say that resurrection ended Jesus's pain; he only says that resurrection followed Jesus's painful death. John 19:28–30 is an important passage to consider regarding this question as well as the issue of Jesus's descent.

John 19:28–30 (an aside)

> After this, when Jesus knew that *everything was now finished* [teleo] that the Scripture might be *fulfilled* [teleo], he said, "I'm thirsty." A jar full of sour wine was sitting there; so they fixed a sponge full of sour wine on a hyssop branch and held it up to his mouth. When Jesus had received the sour wine, he said, "It is *finished* [teleo]." Then bowing his head, he gave up his spirit. (John 19:28–30)

The verb *teleo,* meaning "to complete, accomplish, or fulfill," occurs three times in this passage. After providing for his mother (19:25–27), Jesus had *completed* everything the Father had sent him to do (see John 4:34; 5:36; 17:4), with the exception of making the following statement (it's only one word in Greek): "I'm thirsty." This *fulfills* the prophecy in Psalm 69:21.[11] Even the verb translated "fulfilled" is not the usual Greek word for fulfillment (*plēroō,* used eight times in John in this sense) but again the word for completion (*teleō*). Commentator Edward Klink points out that the three uses of *teleō* "in such close proximity" amount to "an emphatic three-fold declaration that the work assigned to Jesus by the Father is *completed* on the cross."[12] The last item on Jesus's redemptive agenda of obedient actions was crossed off.

The last item on Jesus's redemptive agenda of obedient actions was crossed off.

Considering that fact in light of John's final verse boggles the mind. Imagine how extensive that agenda had been! He writes, "[T]here are also many other things that Jesus did, which, if every one of them were written down, I suppose not even the world itself could contain the books that would be written" (John 21:25). Everything after this which served to accomplish our atonement was done *to* Jesus rather than *by* him. The third time *teleō* occurs is on Jesus's lips in John 19:30, the participle *tetelestai:* "It is finished." The verb's perfect tense carries the sense of something that has occurred in the past resulting in a state of being in the present. The mission assigned to Jesus by the Father has been accomplished. As Klink declares, "In this moment of suffering and despair, God in the person of Jesus Christ declares victory over the forces of sin and death—a victory secured not in spite of but by means of the cross."[13] So, did Jesus have further pain to experience, leading up to the moment of his resurrection? I don't think so.[14]

Now back to Peter's sermon in Acts. To substantiate his claim that "it was not possible for [Jesus] to be held by death," Peter quotes from Psalm 16:8–11, which

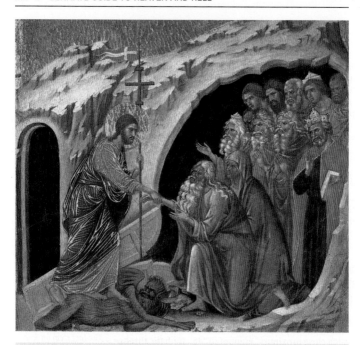

Christ's Descent Into Hell by fourteenth-century Italian painter Duccio di Buoninsegna.

he introduces with the statement, "For David says of him" (Acts 2:25). Peter interprets the verses as David's messianic descendant speaking in the past through David. The critical part of Peter's citation is in verse 27, though it begins at the end of verse 26:

> **Moreover, my flesh will rest in hope,**
> **because you will not abandon me** ["my *psuche/nephesh*"] **in Hades**
> **or allow** [give] **your holy one to see decay** ["the pit"].

Matthew Emerson and other defenders of the descent of Christ into Hades understand Psalm 16 as "a prophecy that speaks of the Messiah's soul in Hades and his body in the grave." Then "the Messiah's human body will be raised and rejoined with his human soul, previously in Hades."[15] The psalmist's "you will not abandon me to Sheol/Hades," then, is understood to say that the Messiah's human soul will not *remain* in Hades. Justin Bass claims that the descent of Christ to Hades "finds its clearest justification in the NT when Peter says twice of Christ [Acts 2:27, 31] 'You will not abandon my soul to Hades.'"[16]

A problem here is the second half of verse 27, which balances the first. "Abandon" is balanced by "allow," in Hebrew and Greek the more active word for "give." The idea of "allow/give" suggests not a passive *abandoning* but an active *sending*. "Hades" is balanced by "decay," which can mean "the pit," often used as a synonym for Sheol, a fitting word to balance "Hades."[17] That leaves "my *psuche/ nephesh*" balanced by "your holy one," which may suggest the common use of "*psuche/nephesh*" as "person." The argument from this verse (with its synonymous parallelism) for the Messiah having been split into soul and body seems far from conclusive. Peter's point could well be that the Davidic Messiah, the holy one, would not go to Hades when he died. This possibility is not overturned by Peter's paraphrase of the second half of verse 27 in verse 31 ("his flesh did not experience ["see"] decay ["the pit"]"), which uses "his flesh" rather than "your holy one." According to New Testament scholar Ben Witherington, "It was an early Jewish belief that the spirit of a person stayed with the body for three days and on the fourth day departed, at which point corruption of the flesh well and truly set in" (see John 11:17, 39).[18] If so, Jesus did not go to Hades when he died.

Peter's point could well be that the Davidic Messiah, the holy one, would not go to Hades when he died.

The spirit of a person stayed with the body for three days and on the fourth day departed.

We already looked at these passages in our chapter on Jesus's resurrection (chap. 7, "Jesus: The Solar Express"). There I argued that Peter's quotation of David in Acts 2:27 explains why Jesus could confidently say on the cross that his death would take him not to Hades, "the place where the dead are gathered for judgment," but to "paradise" that very day (Luke 23:43).[19]

ROMANS 10:6-8 AND DEUTERONOMY 30:11-14

Now for another pair of passages pertinent to our subject. Let's begin with a look at Romans 10:6-8:

> [T]he righteousness that comes from faith speaks like this: **Do not say in your heart, "Who will go up to heaven?"** that is, to bring Christ down or, **"Who will go down into *the abyss*?"** that is, to bring Christ up from *the dead*. On the contrary, what does it say? The message is near you, in your mouth and in your heart. This is the message of faith that we proclaim.

In the above, to stress the availability of the gospel of righteousness by faith to Jew and Gentile, the apostle Paul draws from Deuteronomy 30:11-14. There Moses says,

> This command that I give you today is certainly not too difficult or beyond your reach. It is not in heaven so that you have to ask, "Who will go up to heaven, get it for us, and proclaim it to us so that we may follow it?" And it is not across the sea so that you have to ask, "Who will cross the sea, get it for us, and proclaim it to us so that we may follow it?" But the message is very near you, in your mouth and in your heart, so that you may follow it.

We have many texts from the ancient Near East that lament people's ignorance of the will of the gods. As Moses in Deuteronomy represents any conceivable destination by the opposites of "heaven" and "across the sea," the ancient texts often represent it with heaven and the underworld. Daniel Block elaborates on this. One asks, "Who is so tall as to ascend to the heavens? Who is so broad as to compass the underworld?" Another asks, "Who knows the will of the gods in heaven? Who understands the plans of the underworld gods?"[20] By contrast, Moses declares here that "the demands of covenant relationship are not unknowable, unreasonable, incomprehensible, or impossible."[21]

The life God provides does not require climbing to a Himalayan mountaintop for insight or going on an impossible quest to prove one's worth. God's "command" (v. 11) and God's "message" (v. 14) were as near as the words in their mouths and the thoughts and desires in their hearts.

The life God provides does not require climbing to a Himalayan mountaintop for insight or going on an impossible quest to prove one's worth.

Yet Israel would abandon the covenant and be driven by God into exile (Deut 29:25–28). So, as Christopher Wright says, this first section of Deuteronomy 30 "comes like an oxygen mask to revive hope."[22] When Israel's hearts turned back to the Lord (as they would), he would turn back to them in delight, have compassion on them, and bring them back (vv. 1–10).

Verse six, however, in the center of these ten verses, complicates the relationship between Israel's repentance and the Lord's restoration. Moses explains, "The Lord your God will circumcise your heart and the hearts of your descendants, and you will love him with all your heart and all your soul so that you will live." Apparently, what makes the Lord's "command" (to love and follow Him) "not too difficult or beyond your reach" is His circumcision of their hearts. Israel's persistent failures could not stand against God's eternal purposes. Daniel Block explains that the spiritual operation of heart circumcision "is equivalent to implanting the Torah in peoples' hearts" (see Jer 31:33–34). As a result, "Yahweh's people will exhibit a new orientation, a new receptiveness, and a new obedience in compliance with Moses' teaching. Moses' optimism regarding Israel as a nation presupposes a divine act of heart circumcision. He expresses no confidence in the human will to maintain the course."[23] Old Testament scholar Gordon McConville declares that "ultimately the realization of an obedient people will depend on Yahweh's new act in compassion."[24] And as Wright says, "The fundamental demand of the law (to love God with all one's heart and soul) is presented as the ultimate fruit of God's grace in the human heart."[25]

"The fundamental demand of the law (to love God with all one's heart and soul) is presented as the ultimate fruit of God's grace in the human heart."

The apostle Paul was in full agreement with Moses, who wrote against "righteousness that is from the law," as Lev 18:5 was often understood (see Rom 10:4–5), but Moses declared the "righteousness that comes from faith" in Deuteronomy 30:11–14 (see Rom 10:6–8). Indeed, the coming of Christ and the gospel should put an "end" to any wrong use of the law to achieve our own righteousness (Rom 10:4). Paul definitely saw Moses's words in Deuteronomy in the light of the new covenant. The phrase rendered "that is" or "this is" three times in verses 6–8 shows

Angel with the Key to the Bottomless Pit, from the Apocalypse series (1497–98) by Albrecht Dürer.

Paul's identification of God's "command" (Deut 30:11) and God's "message" (30:14; Hb. *dabar*, Gk. *rhema*) with Christ. The message of grace that is so near us, of God's compassionate restoration and blessing when we turn to Him in faith and love, is the message of Christ and His righteousness that comes from faith. Or as Paul says in Romans 10:9, it is "If you confess with your mouth, 'Jesus is Lord,' and believe in your heart that God raised him from the dead, you will be saved." A heart confession of the risen Christ is what it means now to obey God's command to "love him with all [one's] heart and all . . . soul so that [he or she] will live" (Deut 30:6; also v. 16). Anyone trusting in Christ, whether Jew or Gentile, is fulfilling the law's demand and receiving the life God promised (see Deut 30:15–20).[26]

A heart confession of the risen Christ is what it means now to obey God's command to "love him with all [one's] heart and all . . . soul so that [he or she] will live."

Now, what about Paul's reference to "the abyss" in Romans 10:7? Where Moses had used crossing "the sea" in Deuteronomy 30:13 as the opposite of going up to "heaven" in 30:12, Paul changed it to going down "into the abyss," which he then identified with "the dead." The Greek wording for "from the dead" (*ek nekrōn*) is plural, suggesting that Christ was raised from among the dead,

Anyone trusting in Christ, whether Jew or Gentile, is fulfilling the law's demand and receiving the life God promised.

rather than from being dead. This plural term is found 45 times in the Septuagint, and in 16 of these passages it refers to the place of the dead.[27] As to why Paul might have changed "cross the sea" to "go down into the abyss," we might recall from our earlier tours of hell that in the apocryphal 1 Enoch the angels take Enoch to an entry into the underworld in the place of the sinking sun on the western horizon. The Babylonian Gilgamesh also had to cross the sea and the waters of death to find the flood survivor Utnapishtim in the underworld. As we will see in the next chapter, the Greek term for "the abyss" is the usual Septuagint translation for Hebrew *tehom*, the "watery depths," where Jonah felt he was in Sheol (Jonah 2:3). Thus, Paul may have simply changed the allusion to one that his readers would more readily recognize. Douglas Moo explains in his commentary on Romans that "the 'sea' and the 'abyss' were somewhat interchangeable concepts in the Old Testament and in Judaism." He also notes that "some Aramaic paraphrases of the Deuteronomy 30:13 used the language of the abyss."[28]

"The 'sea' and the 'abyss' were somewhat interchangeable concepts in the Old Testament and in Judaism."

As God brought the law to Israel with no effort on their part (quoting Deut 30:12–13), he brought us Christ, with no help from us either to bring Christ down from heaven at the incarnation or up from "the abyss," that is, "from the dead" at the resurrection.

EPHESIANS 4:7–10 AND PSALM 68:18

Another pair of passages sheds light on what is meant by Christ's descent. The first of these was penned by Paul, who incorporates the second. He writes,

Now grace was given to each one of us according to the measure of Christ's gift. For it says:

**When he ascended on high,
he took the captives captive;
he gave gifts to people.**
But what does "he ascended" mean except that he also descended to the lower parts of the earth? The one who descended is also the one who ascended far above all the heavens, to fill all things. (Eph 4:7–10)

According to New Testament scholar Clinton Arnold, the burden of the above selection is to explain how God's people can live the kind of life He wants for us. It comprises only two sentences in Greek, the first of which spans all three of the verses. The point of verses 7–10 is that God "has sovereignly endowed" every member of his Christian family with a grace-gift or special ability "to minister to all the other members." The verses begin with a statement of that fact in verse 7, which Paul supports by quoting Psalm 68:18 in verse 8, then explains in verses 9–10.[29] According to Arnold, Paul found in the prayer of Psalm 68 the exact point he wanted to impress on his readers: "The incomparably great power of God, who strengthens his people to stand against their enemies."[30] Although the enemies in David's psalm were "flesh and blood," the enemies Paul and all Christian believers "stand against" are (ultimately) the devil, the rulers, the authorities, "the cosmic powers of this darkness," and "evil, spiritual forces in the heavens" (Eph 6:11–12).

Although the enemies in David's psalm were "flesh and blood," the enemies Paul and all Christian believers "stand against" are (ultimately) the devil, the rulers, the authorities, "the cosmic powers of this darkness," and "evil, spiritual forces in the heavens."

The New Testament writers typically avoided proof-texting from the Old Testament, that is, using a verse without giving attention to its context.[31] The former master of Old Testament commentators, Cambridge scholar Derek Kidner (1913–2008), called Psalm 68 a "rushing cataract of a psalm—one of the most boisterous and exhilarating in the Psalter." He and others suggest that David may have written it for the procession of the ark into Jerusalem (2 Sam 6:12–15; see Ps 68:24–27).[32] Regardless, it figuratively portrays God as Warrior, who displayed his invincible power over His enemies and those of His people on many occasions in Israel's life, especially in His defeat of the Egyptians. As Arnold suggests, Psalm 68 is a "celebration of God's power to save his people from the clear and present threat of their enemies," in which Paul sees "Christ's power to save his people from the ultimate enemies" of sin, death, and "the principalities, powers, and authorities."[33] Verse one echoes Moses's words whenever the ark would set out in the wilderness: "Arise, LORD! / Let your enemies be scattered, / and those who hate you flee from your presence" (Num 10:35). The Canaanite storm god Baal was known as "rider of the clouds," but David's verse 4 of Psalm 68 ("Exalt him who rides on the clouds—/ his name is the LORD—and celebrate before him") declares that only Yahweh deserved that title.[34]

It's easy to imagine the apostle Paul having been studying, meditating on, and praying through Psalm 68 the morning before he composed his letter to the Ephesians, with its many echoes of the psalm, which concludes in verses 34–35 by praising the God of power, who "gives power and strength to his people" (see Eph 1:19–20; 3:7, 16, 20; 6:10).[35] Part of this divine power comes through the exercise of the grace-gifts that enable us to minister to each other (see Eph 4:7). Kidner notices that the psalm testifies with "almost uncontainable enthusiasm" to the union of God's "immense power and intense care."[36] The redemptive nature of God's victory comes out in his being "a father of the fatherless / and a champion of widows." He also "provides

It's easy to imagine the apostle Paul having been studying, meditating on, and praying through Psalm 68 before he composed his letter to the Ephesians.

homes for" the "deserted," sets "prisoners" free to prosper, and provides "for the poor" out of his "goodness" (68:5–6, 10).

In the ancient cultures surrounding Israel, the gods were thought to live on high mountains where they established their thrones, often after a great victory over their enemies.[37] The mountains of Bashan (v. 15) were impressive, but the smaller Mount Zion was the one "God desired for his abode" to "dwell there forever" (v. 16).[38] After scattering "his enemies" (v. 1) and causing "the kings of the armies" to flee (v. 12), God is addressed by David in Psalm 68:18:

> You ascended to the heights, taking away captives;
> You received gifts from people,
> even from the rebellious,
> so that the LORD God might dwell there.

Here and elsewhere in the psalm, David creates a visual message of God's invincible power over all evil and wickedness as well as of the passion with which he delivers and cares for his people. An actual procession led by the ark of the covenant, symbolizing God's throne (see Ps 99:1), ascending Mount Zion into the sanctuary may have represented the Lord's victories.[39] The captives that are taken are the rebellious enemies God has subjugated, who "bring" him "tribute" (68:29). John Hilber calls attention to abundant palace art from the ancient Near East that was "decorated with portraits of subdued people being led captive and bringing their gifts of tribute."[40] Thus, anyone visiting these residences of ancient potentates was given a visual lesson that they were not to be messed with.

As in Paul's aforementioned quotation of Deuteronomy 30:13 in Romans 10:7, he changes some wording in his citation of Psalm 68:18. Besides the minor change of the second person "you" in David's prayer to the third person "he" in applying

Assyrian King Sennacherib seated on his throne of judgment. Peoples subject to him were to offer tribute.

the psalm to the work of Christ, Paul changes "received gifts from [or "among"] people" to "gave gifts to [his] people." But this change may not be as great as it sounds. When God led Israel victoriously out of Egypt, the Egyptian people were not sorry to see them go. We are told this in Exodus 12:35–36:

> The Israelites acted on Moses's word and asked the Egyptians for silver and gold items and for clothing. And the LORD gave the people such favor with the Egyptians that they gave them what they requested. In this way they plundered the Egyptians.

So, the receiving of gifts from the conquered people benefited the children of the Lord. Maybe this is why the Aramaic and Syriac translations of Psalm 68:18 have the conquering king *distributing* the gifts he had received, as in Paul's citation of the psalm.[41] This also fits the context of the psalm, which ends in verse 35 with the God of Israel giving "power and strength to his people." So, Paul paraphrases Psalm 68:18 to focus on the effects of Christ's redemptive victory for his people.

Paul saw in God's victory over his enemies in Psalm 68 the greater victory of Christ over more powerful spiritual enemies. In God's ascending to the heights on Mount Zion in that chapter, Paul saw Christ's greater ascension "far above all the heavens" (Eph 4:10), even to the "right hand" of the Father (Eph 1:20). And in the

Paul saw in God's victory over his enemies in Psalm 68 the greater victory of Christ over more powerful spiritual enemies.

spoils of God's triumph over rebellious kings opposed to Israel in Psalm 68, Paul saw the spoils of Christ's triumph over "every ruler and authority, power and dominion" (Eph 1:20–22) as they were bestowed as gifts on all the members of God's spiritual household, the church. The victory of Christ's death and resurrection conquered sin, death, and the spiritual enemies that wielded them. So, Christ's work is the fulfillment of the message of this psalm, which fits Paul's purpose (according to Arnold) of showing us how it is "possible to live the kind of life that God calls his people to live."[42] The "power and strength" that God gives his people includes the gifts to every Christian, a grace-gift or special ability "to minister to all the other members." As Greek scholar and theologian S. M. Baugh explains, Ephesians 4:8 is "a free paraphrase" of Psalm 68:18 with Paul "incorporating elements of the whole psalm in light of its fulfillment in Christ's ascent and gifting."[43]

Ephesians 4:8 is "a free paraphrase" of Psalm 68:18 with Paul "incorporating elements of the whole psalm in light of its fulfillment in Christ's ascent and gifting."

But now we must ask and try to answer two questions. First, how does Paul's attention to Jesus's descent "to the lower parts of the earth" in Ephesians 4:9–10 fit his purpose? Second, what does the descent mean? The early church fathers and many later interpreters understood "the lower parts of the earth" to refer to the underworld or Hades, to which Christ, like all who died, descended when he died on the cross.[44] Jesus's victory over the underworld forces of evil enabled Jesus to ascend "far above all the heavens, to fill all things" (v. 10). Understanding "the lower parts" mentioned in Ephesians as the underworld is supported by the use of "the depths [literally "lower parts"] of the earth" in Psalm 63:9 as the destiny of "those who intend to destroy [David's] life" (although some think David was referring only to death or the grave; the phrase is also in Pss 71:20; 95:4; 139:15; Isa 44:23). This is a possible understanding of Paul's verses.

Several scholars, both modern and ancient, though, have proposed that Jesus's "descent" only involved his incarnation, so his descent was to "the lower parts, that is, the earth."[45] Another way of viewing the phrase is as the equivalent of "the earth down there" suggested by New Testament scholar Markus Barth, who lists several problems with the "descent to Hades" view. One problem is that the "ascent" Paul talks about is earth to heaven, which would seem to need a parallel descent from heaven to earth (see the parallel in John 3:13), not earth to under-world. A second problem is that the evil forces in Ephesians are said to be "in the heavens" (6:12; 2:2), not under the earth. A third problem is that Christ's victory over them is won by the cross, resurrection, and ascension—not a descent to Hades (see Eph 1:20–21; 4:8; Col 2:14–15). Barth thinks Paul had in mind Christ's "incarnation and, most likely, his crucifixion."[46] Other scholars have considered that Jesus's descent included the incarnation and death, by which he "won the victory over Satan and sin." To them, the "lower parts" refers to the grave. Commentator Harold Hoehner thinks this view has "the least problems."[47]

A third option is that Paul was thinking of Jesus's ascent to the Father followed by his descent in the person of the Holy Spirit at Pentecost. This is possible, since the translation "*had* descended" in several versions is not indicated in the Greek, and the supplying of "first" in many Greek manuscripts is surely just an early interpretation (reflected in the Vulgate and KJV). However, Psalm 68 climaxes in God's ascent and implies his prior descent to defeat, scatter, and destroy the wicked. Also, as commentator Andrew Lincoln points out, referring to the *Spirit's* descent as *Christ's* descent is "unusual" though not impossible.[48]

Psalm 68 climaxes in God's ascent and implies his prior descent to defeat, scatter, and destroy the wicked.

Arnold, however, thinks that Paul's phrase "makes the most sense" if it refers to the underworld or Hades.[49] The reason Paul makes a point of Christ's descent to Hades, Arnold says, is "to underline the cosmic supremacy of Christ" as he does in Ephesians 1:21. This would have been important to his readers, since first-century Asia Minor (the location of Ephesus) was a hotbed of belief in underworld deities, the most prominent of whom was Hekate, goddess of witchcraft and sorcery. She was believed to wield "the keys of Hades," which meant she could unlock the gates of Hades and unleash "the demonic souls" there. Hekate's priest-ess at her cult center, in fact, was called "the key bearer." In our study of necromancy in chapter 10 ("Is This a Direct Flight?") we saw that the ancients spoke of the underworld as "the Land of No Return," often viewed as a city with many gates. These supposedly protected the world from the departed spirits, and also offered them some protection from mortuary cults such as Hekate's. Paul's emphasis would be that Christ not only died as others do, "descending" to the realm of the dead, but he returned and "ascended far above all the heavens," demonstrating his supremacy by his victory over death and over all the rebellious powers of darkness. Arnold points out that this understanding of Christ's work fits with the apostle John's book written to the churches in Asia Minor, where Jesus declares, "Don't be afraid. I am the First and the Last, and the Living One. I was dead, but look—I am alive forever and ever, and I hold the keys of death and Hades" (Rev 1:17–18).[50]

Finally, we should notice that in Ephesians 4:10 Paul traces Christ's ascension to "far above all the heavens." The plural "heavens" fits the Hebrew, where the word for "heaven" or "sky" (*shamayim*) is always plural. But as Arnold points out, the Bible seems to portray heaven conceptually as having several levels (for instance, see "third heaven" in 2 Cor 12:2). If that is in view here, we notice that the ascended Christ is seated at the Father's "right hand in the heavens" (Eph 1:20), God's wisdom is "made known . . . to the rulers and authorities in the heavens" (3:10), Christ "ascended far above all the heavens" (4:10), and Christians struggle against "evil, spiritual forces in the heavens" (6:12). So, although these forces are "in the heavens," where God is, God is somehow "far above all the heavens." That is, Christ is "over all things, including the hostile principalities and powers" and will someday "fill all things" when there will no longer be "evil, spiritual forces" for us to struggle against.[51]

> Although these forces are "in the heavens," where God is, God is somehow "far above all the heavens."

Back to our question about why Paul brought up the issue of Christ's descent. It seems that the best answer is that of Baugh. Christ's "gifts" mentioned in Ephesians 4:8 are not the main issue in verses 7–10. Rather, Paul's main concern can be paraphrased from verse 10: "That one who descended is the very same person who also ascended." That is, Psalm 68, which talks of Yahweh's victorious ascent implies that he must have first descended. And the one who descended is Christ. That is, the God of "immense power and intense care" in Psalm 68 foreshadowed Jesus Christ, who "came down and went back up to be exalted" and to "distribute gifts to the church." As Jesus himself declares in John 3:13, "No one has ascended into heaven except the one who descended from heaven—the Son of Man."

So, as always, scholars disagree, partly because certain bits of evidence seem more important to one than to another as they work to assemble a coherent picture. But if Christ did go to Hades when he died, as many believe, did he actually *do* anything there, as many in the church have claimed? And if so, what did he do? Remember that in our glance at John 19:28–30 (in our study of Acts 2:24–28), the emphasis was on Christ's redemptive mission from the Father having been *completed* at the cross.

Hekate, whom many in Asia Minor believed to be the goddess of boundaries, crossroads, witchcraft, the Moon, necromancy, and ghosts.

> That one who descended is the very same person who also ascended.

> The God of "immense power and intense care" in Psalm 68 foreshadowed Jesus Christ, who "came down and went back up to be exalted" and to "distribute gifts to the church."

John testifies in the first chapter of Revelation that he saw "one like the Son of Man" (1:13). In verses 17 and 18 of that chapter, he elaborates on the encounter, saying, "When I saw him, I fell at his feet like a dead man. He laid his right hand on me and said, 'Don't be afraid. I am the First and the Last, and the Living One. I was dead, but look—I am alive forever and ever, and I hold the keys of death and Hades.'"

I already called attention to Jesus's statement in Revelation 1:18 that he holds "the keys of death and Hades." The verse, in fact, is considered by some to provide an answer to our question of why Jesus might have gone to Hades. According to Justin Bass, "Revelation 1:18 illuminates . . . the purpose for which Christ descended into the underworld, namely to conquer Death and Hades."[52] The main issue here is whether the keys referred to are keys to the *realms* of death and Hades or keys that once *belonged to* a personified Death and Hades. As commentator David Aune expressed it, "If the keys formerly belonged to the personified Death and Hades, they must have been forcibly taken from them" (although he does not think Christ's descent is the background for Rev 1:18).[53] As Emerson puts it, "There was a battle between them in the underworld in which Christ was victorious."[54]

But why was that battle fought? Bass explains one reason: "Everyone before Christ (except for Enoch and Elijah), the righteous and the wicked, descended into Hades at death. . . . If Abraham and all the rest of the OT worthies are in the underworld . . . then the descent of Christ to liberate them from the "gates of Hades" . . . fulfills the hope of the OT saints to be rescued from Sheol/Hades."[55] But future believers also benefit from Christ's victorious battle with death and Hades. Bass quotes William Hendrickson's commentary: "Does not the Son of man reveal that He has the keys of death whenever He welcomes the soul of a believer into heaven? And does He not prove that He has the keys of Hades when at His second coming He reunites the soul and body of the believer, a body now gloriously transformed?"[56]

One basis for seeing the aftermath of a battle in Revelation 1:18 is that elsewhere Death and Hades are sometimes personified. In Revelation 6:8, for instance, John tells us he saw a "pale green horse," whose "rider was named Death, and Hades was following after him." These "were given authority over a fourth of the earth" to kill. Then at the "great white throne" in 20:13–14 John sees them again. He writes, "Then the sea gave up the dead that were in it, and death and Hades gave up the dead that were in them; each one was judged according to their works. Death and Hades were thrown into the lake of fire. This is the second death, the lake of fire." In verse 13 they both seem to be locations, but they are personified again in verse 14. The terms only occur together in these passages in Revelation, but death is said to "reign" in Romans 5:14 and 17. Then in Romans 6:9 Paul says, "Christ, having been raised from the dead, will not die again. Death no longer rules over him." According to 1 Corinthians 15:26, "The last enemy to be abolished is death." Then in verses 55–56 Paul cites Isaiah 25:8 and Hosea 13:14: "Death has been swallowed up in victory. / Where, death, is your victory? / Where, death, is your sting?" Another reason for seeing personification in Revelation 1:18 is the presence of deified key holders such as Hekate (also known as Persephone,

Artemis, and Diana) in pagan underworld myths. Bass cites Aune as asserting, "Jesus holding the keys to Death and Hades is a polemic against the Hellenistic conceptions of the goddess Hekate."[57]

But granting the personification of Death and Hades in these verses does not lead to the further supposition of a battle between a literal Christ and a personified entity. If we allow Revelation 1:18 a degree of literalness, it seems reasonable to suggest that Christ may have gone to the realm of the dead and forced the keys from the hands of its previous ruler sometime between his death on the cross and his resurrection. But how much literalness is to be given to this passage in John's apocalyptic book? I am in sympathy with Bauckham's view:

> Revelation 1:18 . . . presupposes that the gates of Hades, which release no one who has entered them, have been for the first time opened for a man to leave. The divine prerogative of releasing from the realm of death . . . now belongs to Christ. That in his death and resurrection he has gained power over death and Hades is implied, but not the later notion of a victory won in Hades.[58]

One more set of passages must be considered.

1 PETER 3:18–22; 4:5–6

> Christ also suffered for sins once for all, the righteous for the unrighteous, that he might bring you to God. He was put to death in the flesh but made alive by the Spirit, in which [or "by whom"] he also went and made proclamation to the spirits in prison who in the past were disobedient, when God patiently waited in the days of Noah while the ark was being prepared. In it a few—that is, eight people—were saved through water. Baptism, which corresponds to this, now saves you (not as the removal of dirt from the body, but the pledge of a good conscience toward God) through the resurrection of Jesus Christ, who has gone into heaven and is at the right hand of God with angels, authorities, and powers subject to him. (1 Pet 3:18–22)

> They will give an account to the one who stands ready to judge the living and the dead. For this reason the gospel was also preached to those who are now dead, so that, although they might be judged in the flesh according to human standards, they might live in the spirit according to God's standards. (1 Pet 4:5–6)

Most would acknowledge that these are two of the most difficult passages in the New Testament, and I will not attempt to answer all the questions they inspire. As a friend says, "I don't want to stir up more snakes than I can kill." So, it is a good thing that "support for Christ's descent to the place of the dead does not hinge on 1 Peter 3:18–22." But, as Emerson also observes, "most doctrines do not rise or fall with one text."[59] Although true, this observation must be qualified. The doctrine of the Trinity, for example, is built from clear passages that assert God's oneness combined with other clear passages that assert his threeness; that is, the reality of the distinct divine Persons of Father, Son, and Spirit. It is not built from several *dubious* passages that *might* teach the Trinity.

As theologian and New Testament scholar Thomas Schreiner explains, 1 Peter 3:18–19 has two main points. First, "Christ suffered for the unrighteous to bring believers to God," and second, "By the power of the Spirit, he was raised from the dead and [he] proclaimed victory over demonic spirits." The other main point in this paragraph he finds in verse 22: Christ "is now exalted on high as the resurrected and ascended Lord, subjecting all demonic powers to himself." As a result, believers have no reason to fear evil.[60]

> *"By the power of the Spirit, he was raised from the dead and [he] proclaimed victory over demonic spirits."*

> *Christ "is now exalted on high as the resurrected and ascended Lord, subjecting all demonic powers to himself."*

Regarding the details of the text, the first important one is the statement in verse 18 that Jesus was "put to death in the flesh but made alive by the Spirit." The last phrase can also mean "in the spirit," that is, in the spiritual realm (ESV, NASB). But the main contrast here is not between flesh and spirit but between death and resurrection. Being "made alive" is often used of Christ's resurrection (see John 5:21; Rom 4:17; 8:11; 1 Cor 15:22, 36, 45). "We can be confident, therefore, that Peter does not envision Jesus merely living in the interval between his death and resurrection in terms of his human spirit," Schreiner says.[61]

> *"Peter does not envision Jesus merely living in the interval between his death and resurrection in terms of his human spirit."*

The next detail to concern us is Christ's "proclamation to the spirits in prison" in 1 Peter 3:19. Several interpretations have been offered over the years: (1) Augustine believed that Christ preached through Noah to the "disobedient" living at the time (v. 20).[62] (2) The "vast majority of the church fathers believed that Christ proclaimed release to Old Testament believers in Hades between his death and resurrection and took them with him to paradise when he ascended."[63]

(3) Clement of Alexandria and Origen believed that Christ preached in Hades to those "disobedient" who had perished in Noah's flood (4:6), "offering them the opportunity to repent and be saved." This would suggest that the gospel may be offered in hell to those who previously rejected it or never heard it.[64] But commentator J. H. Elliott observes that "any notion of a possibility of conversion or salvation after death would seriously undermine the letter's consistent stress on the necessity of righteous behavior here and now."[65] Schreiner also points to Peter's stress on perseverance in suffering, saying, "All motivation to endure would vanish if Peter now offers a second opportunity after death. The benefit of braving suffering is difficult to grasp if another opportunity to respond will be offered [then]."[66] Even Emerson agrees that "there is nothing in 1 Peter 3:18–20 or in the rest of the canon

> *"Any notion of a possibility of conversion or salvation after death would seriously undermine the letter's consistent stress on the necessity of righteous behavior here and now."*

of Scripture that demands or even implies that this preaching is a postmortem gospel proclamation that can be responded to in faith, resulting in the salvation of those who believe."[67]

(4) The most common interpretation today, because it best fits the evidence, is that Christ has pronounced doom to evil spirits as a result of his victory at the cross and resurrection.[68] Although the verb for "made proc-lamation" (*kerussō*), found 61 times in the New Testament, usually involved preaching the good news of the kingdom, it also is used with a neutral sense (see Luke 12:3; Rev 5:2). As Bass concludes, "The proc-lamation of Christ could not be an offer of redemption or salvation to them (see Heb 2:16), but must be one of condemnation and triumph."[69] The evil spirits would especially be those angels ("sons of God") who had sexual relations with women in Genesis 6:1–4, but they probably also included the "angels, authorities, and powers" mentioned in 1 Peter 3:22. Understanding Genesis 6 in this way was common among Jewish interpreters at the time and is notable in 1 Enoch, which was familiar to Jude (vv. 14–15) as well as Peter (2 Pet 2:4).[70] But scholars disagree (What?!) on the time and place of Christ's preaching.

Christ has pronounced doom to evil spirits as a result of his victory at the cross and resurrection.

Scholars disagree on the time and place of Christ's preaching, too. Some see his preaching of doom to the evil spirits as taking place in Hades between his death and resurrection. Others think it occurred in heaven after his resurrection. This seems to me what Peter probably had in mind, as Schreiner convincingly argues. The 11 uses in the New Testament of the verb for "made alive" (1 Pet 3:18), almost always involve resurrection. So, it was the resurrected Christ who, also by the Spirit's power (taking "in which" as "by whom"), "went" and proclaimed doom to "the spirits in prison" (v. 19). Nowhere else are we told that Christ "went" to the underworld, but verse 22 tells us he "has gone" (the same verb) "into heav-en and is at the right hand of God with angels, authorities, and powers subject to him." Bass points out that the plural "spirits" (v. 19) "almost without exception in the New Testament refers to angels." Only once are people called "spirits" (Heb 12:23, where they are called "righteous").[71] In Revelation 20:7, Satan is said to be in prison for a thousand years, and Schreiner lists many Jewish texts from first and second Enoch and Jubilees that speak of evil angels imprisoned.[72]

So, if Christ's proclaiming victory over evil angels took place after his resur-rection, it did not take place in Hades, and the "prison" was not there but in the heavens.[73] Calling the location "Tartarus" in 2 Peter 2:4 (CSB "hell") does not import its underworld location from Greek mythology. As Schreiner suggests, the lan-guage is likely symbolic of divine restraint.[74] First Peter 3:22 seems to suggest that Christ's proclamation announcing his victory and the subjecting of all demonic forces to him occurred during the ascension.

As Bauckham concludes, in the New Testament "Christ's descent to and sojourn in the realm of the dead seems to have no independent interest or significance beside his death and resurrection." Most scholars, he says, recognize that "in [1 Peter] 3:19 the proclamation to the spirits follows the resurrection, . . . while 'the spirits in prison' are most probably angels." He acknowledges that the sec-ond-century idea that Christ preached salvation after his death to Old Testament saints could more likely be the sense of 4:6. However, the statement that "the

Christ Preaching, called La Petite Tombe ca. 1657 by Rembrandt.

gospel was preached even to the dead" (RSV's more literal rendering) may refer to "those who heard the Gospel while alive, but subsequently died."[75] This is the interpretation followed by the CSB, NIV, NET, and NLT, who all have "those who are now dead." Kelly argues that to assume 3:19 and 4:6 are dealing with the same thing "is entirely arbitrary," since the proclaiming (*kerussō*) in 3:19 is to "spirits," that is, angels, and the gospel preaching (*euangelizō*) in 4:6 is to "dead persons," that is, people who believed the gospel of Christ preached to them (not by Christ) and subsequently died.[76]

CONCLUSION

As Bauckham explains, "The idea of Christ's defeat of the powers of Hades is sufficiently explained from the Jewish apocalyptic expectation that at the last day God would 'reprove the angel of death,' . . . command Sheol to release the souls of the dead, . . . abolish death," and seal up Sheol. The understanding was that death as a realm and power "had to be broken up by God," and these ideas "were transferred to the context of Christ's descent to Hades because of the early Christian belief that Christ's death and resurrection were the eschatological triumph of God over death." The details and "much of the phraseology and imagery," he says, came from Christ-focused study of the Old Testament. Christ's descent provided the early church with an answer to the question of what happened to Old Testament believers and also provided them a picture of the "definitive defeat of death." Christ's rescue of Old Testament believers and taking them to heaven was a sign of what he would do for them.[77] Finally, Bauckham finds it "striking" that in Matthew 27:52–53, where tombs were opened following Christ's death, "the interest is exclusively in the significance of the death of Christ, not in any activity of Christ in Hades."[78]

Although the passages we have examined may not demand the literal reality of a descent by Christ to the realm of the dead to storm the gates of Hades, capture the keys of death, and free the captives, the imagery of the story presents in broad strokes a powerful picture of Christ's victory over death.

> *Christ's descent provided the early church with an answer to the question of what happened to Old Testament believers and also provided them a picture of the "definitive defeat of death."*

NOTES

1. See Jaroslav Pelikan, *The Christian Tradition. Volume One: The Emergence of the Catholic Tradition (100–600)* (Chicago: University of Chicago Press, 1971), 150.

2. Pelikan, *The Christian Tradition*, 151.

3. Justin Bass, *The Battle for the Keys: Revelation 1:18 and Christ's Descent into the Underworld* (Eugene, OR: Wipf and Stock, 2014), 21–23. Likewise, Matthew Y. Emerson argues that "belief in Christ's descent . . . was ubiquitous throughout the patristic and medieval periods." See *"He Descended to the Dead": An Evangelical Theology of Holy Saturday* (Downers Grove, IL: InterVarsity, 2019), 67.

4. See the survey of opinions in Emerson, *"He Descended to the Dead,"* 4.

5. R. T. France, *The Gospel of Matthew,* New International Commentary on the New Testament (Grand Rapids: Eerdmans, 2007), 489.

6. Jack M. Sasson notes that one of the possible meanings of *'erets,* "earth," is "netherworld." See *Jonah,* Anchor Bible (New York: Doubleday, 1990), 188. The CSB "gates" in 2:6, however, is better rendered "bars," since the word refers not to gates but to the bars used to lock doors and gates. Although "gates" is commonly associated with Hades, the term for "bars" is not.

7. See France, *The Gospel of Matthew,* 491.

8. Typology is an interpretive practice with a long and complex history in biblical studies. I use the term of God's historical and biblical design by which certain persons, things, or events in the Old Testament revelation foreshadow and prepare for corresponding persons, things, or events in New Testament revelation. It generally is a kind of messianic prophecy. See Seth D. Postell, "Typology in the Old Testament," in *The Moody Handbook of Messianic Prophecy,* eds. M. Rydelnik and E. A. Blum (Chicago: Moody, 2019), 161–75.

9. France, *The Gospel of Matthew,* 491, citing G. M. Landes in *The Word of the Lord Shall Go Forth,* ed. C. L. Meyers and M. O'Connor (Winona Lake, IN: Eisenbrauns, 1983), 666–67.

10. D. A. Carson says the phrase is "a reference to Jesus' burial, not his descent into Hades." See "Matthew," comment on Matt 12:40. Robert H. Gundry declares that "'the heart of the earth' does not refer simply to a grave, but means the realm of the dead." This may be. But his citation of Sir 51:5 does not support his point, since the phrase there is "the depths of the belly of Hades." And the phrase in Eph 4:9, his other citation, is "the lower [parts] of the earth." See *Matthew,* Second edition (Grand Rapids: Eerdmans, 1994), 244.

11. Edward W. Klink III, *John,* Zondervan Exegetical Commentary on the New Testament (Grand Rapids: Zondervan, 2016), 809, argues that the "fulfillment formula" in v. 28 "is

grammatically (and arguably equally) connected both to what it concludes *and* what it prefaces." Klink also shows that "this one Greek word [*dipso*, "I thirst"] is the final statement of God, declaring that everything he wanted to accomplish has been completed to perfection in the person and work of his Son, Jesus Christ" (p. 811).

[12] Klink, *John*, 809.

[13] Klink, *John*, 811.

[14] That Jesus "gave up his spirit" contributes little to the issue of his descent to Hades. There is no explicit possessive "his," but identifying the object as the Holy Spirit makes no sense. Using the verb for "gave up" (which often means "deliver over") may allude to its use in Isa 53:12, "he willingly submitted to death." As Craig S. Keener says, "The departure of the spirit was a common enough Jewish expression for death," but Jesus's *surrender* of his spirit "probably underlines the point that Jesus died voluntarily." See *The Gospel of John: A Commentary* (Grand Rapids: Baker, 2003), 1149.

[15] Emerson, *"He Descended to the Dead,"* 34.

[16] Bass, *The Battle for the Keys*, 109.

[17] The word rendered "decay" (*diaphthora*) in Acts 2:27, 31 is often used in the LXX to translate Hebrew *shachat* with the meaning "pit" or "trap."

[18] Ben Witherington, *The Acts of the Apostles: A Socio-Rhetorical Commentary* (Grand Rapids: Eerdmans, 1998), 145.

[19] Darrell L. Bock, *Acts*, Baker Exegetical Commentary on the New Testament (Grand Rapids: Baker, 2007), 124–25. Justin Bass explains Jesus being in both Hades and paradise (or Abraham's bosom) on Good Friday by his claim that paradise was simply a compartment in Hades. The dilemma is that Paul calls "the third heaven" paradise (2 Cor 12:2, 4), and in Revelation it is identified with the New Jerusalem (Rev 2:7; 21:2). Bass calls paradise a "transferrable locale," whose location moves with Christ. See Bass, *The Battle for the Keys*, 86–87.

[20] See Daniel I. Block, *Deuteronomy*, NIV Application Commentary (Grand Rapids: Zondervan, 2012), 708.

[21] Block, *Deuteronomy*, 706.

[22] Christopher Wright, *Deuteronomy*, New International Biblical Commentary (Peabody, MA: Hendrickson, 1996), 289.

[23] Block, *Deuteronomy*, 698.

[24] J. G. McConville, *Deuteronomy*, Apollos Old Testament Commentary (Leicester, England: Apollos/InterVarsity, 2002), 429.

[25] Wright, *Deuteronomy*, 289–90.

[26] See N. T. Wright, "Romans," in *The New Interpreter's Bible, Volume 10* (Nashville: Abingdon, 2002), 660.

[27] See Deut 18:11; 2 Macc. 12:44; Pss 88:4, 10; 106:28; 115:17; 143:3; Eccl 9:3, 5; Isa 8:19; 26:14, 19; Baruch 3:11; Lam 3:6; Letter to Jeremiah 27; Ezek 32:18. The majority of these passages use the article with *nekroi*, specifying "the dead," but not all of them do. Few of the about 50 uses of "from the dead" in the New Testament have the article.

[28] Douglas Moo, *The Epistle to the Romans*, The New International Commentary on the New Testament (Grand Rapids: Eerdmans, 1996), 655.

[29] Clinton E. Arnold, *Ephesians*, Zondervan Exegetical Commentary on the New Testament (Grand Rapids: Zondervan, 2010), 241–42. There seems to be a problem with saying that the Old Testament quotation *supports* Paul's statement, since the quotation is introduced in v. 8 with Greek *dio legei*, "*Therefore* it says."

30 Arnold, *Ephesians,* 247.

31 See Jonathan M. Lunde and John Anthony Dunne, "Paul's Creative and Contextual Use of Ps 68 in Ephesians 4:8," *Westminster Theological Journal* 74 (2012): 106–17.

32 Derek Kidner, *Psalms 1–72,* Tyndale Old Testament Commentaries (London: Inter-Varsity, 1973), 238.

33 Arnold, *Ephesians,* 248. Paul may also have been thinking of the Roman triumphal processions in his day, an image he turns to in 2 Cor 2:14. See the thorough discussion of Paul's imagery in David E. Garland, *2 Corinthians,* Christian Standard Commentary (Nashville: Holman, 2021), 144–54.

34 See Geoffrey W. Grogan, *Psalms,* Two Horizons Old Testament Commentary (Grand Rapids: Eerdmans, 2008), 125.

35 See Arnold, *Ephesians,* 248.

36 Kidner, *Psalms 1–72,* 245.

37 See John W. Hilber, "Psalms," in *Zondervan Illustrated Bible Backgrounds Commentary, Volume 5,* ed. J. H. Walton (Grand Rapids: Zondervan, 2009), 362–64.

38 See Allen P. Ross, *A Commentary on the Psalms, Volume 2 (42–89)* (Grand Rapids: Kregel, 2013), 474–75.

39 See Craig C. Broyles, "The Psalms and Cult Symbolism: The Case of the Cherubim-Ark," in *Interpreting the Psalms: Issues and Approaches,* ed. D. Firth and P. S. Johnston (Downers Grove, IL: IVP, 2005), 148–50.

40 John Wilber, "Psalms," in *Psalms, Proverbs, Ecclesiastes, and Song of Songs,* ed. John H. Walton (Grand Rapids: Zondervan Academic, 2016), Psalm 68, EPUB edition.

41 Ross, *A Commentary on the Psalms,* 476. See Richard A. Taylor, "The Use of Psalm 68:18 in Ephesians 4:8 in Light of the Ancient Versions," *Bibliotheca Sacra* 148 (1991): 319–36.

42 Arnold, *Ephesians,* 241.

43 See S. M. Baugh, *Ephesians,* Evangelical Exegetical Commentary (Bellingham, WA: Lexham, 2016), 331. He also says Ps 68 is a "preliminary announcement of the gospel," which, "as redemptive history unfolded . . . came into focus as pointing ahead to the incarnation, death, and triumphant ascension of Christ, and to the distribution of the spoils of his victory to his compatriots" (p. 326).

44 Arnold, *Ephesians,* 253.

45 Peter T. O'Brien, *The Letter to the Ephesians,* Pillar New Testament Commentary (Grand Rapids: Eerdmans, 1999), 294–97.

46 See Markus Barth, *Ephesians 4–6,* Anchor Bible (New York: Doubleday, 1974), 433–34.

47 See Harold W. Hoehner, *Ephesians: An Exegetical Commentary* (Grand Rapids: Baker, 2002), 533–36. Bauckham, *The Fate of the Dead,* 35

48 Andrew T. Lincoln, *Ephesians,* Word Biblical Commentary (Dallas: Word, 1990), 247. He considers the first interpretation the least likely and the third one the most.

49 Arnold, *Ephesians,* 253–54.

50 Arnold, *Ephesians,* 254.

51 See Arnold, *Ephesians,* 255.

52 Bass, *The Battle for the Keys,* 157.

53 David F. Aune, *Revelation 1–5,* Word Biblical Commentary (Dallas: Word, 1997), 104.

54 Emerson, *"He Descended to the Dead,"* 51. Bass: "If they are possessive, as many commentators quoted above have suggested, then this implies a previous battle between Christ and Death/Hades in the underworld" (*The Battle for the Keys,* 160).

55 Bass, *The Battle for the Keys,* 104–5.

56 William Hendricksen, *More Than Conquerors: An Interpretation of the Book of Revelation* (Grand Rapids: Baker Academic, 1967): 57, quoted in Bass, *The Battle for the Keys*, 155.

57 Bass, *The Battle for the Keys*, 60. Also see p. 160.

58 Bauckham, *The Fate of the Dead*, 39.

59 Emerson, "*He Descended to the Dead*," 59. See also Bass, *The Battle for the Keys*, 119.

60 Thomas R. Schreiner, *1 & 2 Peter and Jude,* Christian Standard Commentary (Nashville: Holman, 2020), 204.

61 Schreiner, *1 & 2 Peter and Jude,* 209. He notes that 1 Tim 3:16 contains a similar parallel between flesh and Spirit.

62 Also see John Feinberg, "1 Peter 3:18–20, Ancient Mythology, and the Intermediate State," *Westminster Theological Journal* 48 (1986): 303–36. But Schreiner points out that the verb "went" in v. 19 does not fit this view, especially since "has gone [into heaven]" in v. 22 uses the same verb (Schreiner, *1 & 2 Peter and Jude,* 211–12).

63 Bass, *The Battle for the Keys*, 120.

64 Schreiner, *1 & 2 Peter and Jude,* 210, identifies some who have held this.

65 J. H. Elliott, *1 Peter,* Anchor Bible (New York: Doubleday, 2000), 662.

66 Schreiner, *1 & 2 Peter and Jude,* 213.

67 Emerson, "*He Descended to the Dead*," 62.

68 See J. N. D. Kelly, *A Commentary on the Epistles of Peter and of Jude,* Black's New Testament Commentaries (London: Adam & Charles Black, 1969), 156.

69 Bass, *The Battle for the Keys*, 125.

70 See Schreiner, *1 & 2 Peter and Jude,* 214.

71 Bass, *The Battle for the Keys*, 123, lists the places where "disobedient angels" are called "spirits" (LXX 1 Kgs 22:21; Luke 10:20; Acts 23:8–9; Heb 1:14; Tob 6:6; 2 Macc 3:24; Jub 15:31; 1 En 60.11; T. Dan 1.7; 5.5; 1QS 3.17; 1QM 12.8; 13:10).

72 Schreiner, *1 & 2 Peter and Jude,* 212–13. Also, Kelly, *Epistles of Peter and of Jude,* 155–56.

73 Bass, who places the prison in the underworld, nevertheless lists Jewish sources that locate it in the heavens (2 En 7:1-5; 18:3-6; T. Lev. 3:2; Odes Sol. 22:1. Cp. T. Naph. 3.5; T. Reub. 5.6; 2 Bar. 56:13). See Bass, *The Battle for the Keys*, 124.

74 See Schreiner, *1 & 2 Peter and Jude,* 403.

75 Bauckham, *The Fate of the Dead*, 39.

76 Kelly, *Epistles of Peter and of Jude,* 174; Schreiner, *1 & 2 Peter and Jude,* 237.

77 Bauckham, *The Fate of the Dead*, 43–44.

78 Bauckham, *The Fate of the Dead*, 39.

CHAPTER 14

YOU DON'T WANT TO GO THERE!

"The Vision of Death" by Gustave Doré.

As I mentioned at the beginning of this book, I asked Jesus to come into my heart, own it, and renovate it my last year in high school. Of course, given my limited understanding at the time, I probably just asked Him to forgive my sins. While I barely knew what I was doing, He accepted me as His own. I gradually became a reasonably zealous Christian in college and helped start a chapter of InterVarsity Christian Fellowship on our campus in Houston. I think it was my junior year that I teamed up with a new roommate. At times I found him *infuriating,* and I suspect his experience of me was mutual.

It pains me to admit it, but one day in college I went berserk and yelled this at my roommate: "Go to hell!" Then I slammed the door and stormed off. It did not take long before I came to my senses and felt ashamed of myself. There I was, a Christian leader wanting to see people come to know Jesus, and I just told a Christian friend to take the next jet to the Land of No Return. I went to see my prayer partner and confessed to him what I had just done. Then I went back to my room and apologized to my roommate for being such a jerk. I assured him I did not really want him to go there, and the more I've come to understand about the location we call hell, the more I wish that incident had never happened.

In this chapter, we'll look at the biblical terms for the various places that represent God's final judgment on those who refuse to trust and follow him and so enjoy his eternal presence. (This includes the fate of both human beings and supernatural creatures: Satan and the demonic forces.) The term we most commonly associate with final punishment is "hell." That word, however, is found in the CSB only 11 times—and all of them appear in the New Testament. In all but one case, "hell" is used to translate the Greek word *Gehenna* (in Matthew, Mark, Luke, and James). The other use is in 2 Peter 2:4, which we will look at later.

GEHENNA

Hinnom Valley and Isaiah 66:24

The Greek word *geenna,* found in the New Testament 12 times, is usually taken as the name Gehenna, a place of punishment in the afterlife. Justin Bass considers it a synonym that Jesus used for the "the lake of fire" in Revelation 19:20; 20:10, 14. Rather than seeing it as a compartment in the underworld, he calls it "the future, eternal destiny of the wicked (men and angels)." He also observes that the term only occurs in the New Testament and Old Testament Apocrypha (4 Ezra 2:29).[1] Most translations, however, render the word "hell" (an exception being the NAB, which uses "Gehenna," following Jerome's Latin Vulgate). Its history began as the name of the (Ben) Hinnom Valley (Hb. *gey (ben-) hinnom*), which was southwest of ancient Jerusalem's Temple Mount and outside the walls of the City of David. (It's first mentioned in Josh 15:8). But how did a valley outside Jerusalem get to be associated with a place of punishment in the afterlife? Several connections can be made.

Prior to King Josiah's reform described in 2 Kings 23, the valley was used for child sacrifice to Canaanite gods in a specific place called Topheth (see v. 10).[2] That was practiced at least by Kings Ahaz (2 Kgs 16:2–3) and Manasseh (21:1–6) in violation of God's instruction (see Lev 18:21; 20:2–5; Deut 12:31; 18:10). It was known as causing one's sons and daughters to "pass through the fire" (see 2 Kgs 16:3;

17:17; 21:6; 2 Chr 33:6; Ezek 20:31, NRSV), that is, to be burned as offerings, thus filling the valley with "the blood of the innocent" (Jer 19:4). King Josiah ended the valley's use for that purpose (2 Kgs 23:10), but we are not told how.[3] After Josiah's death in 609 BC, three of his sons and a grandson successively ruled, and—tragically—his son Jehoiakim oversaw the restoration of child sacrifice in Hinnom Valley (see Jer 7:31). This made necessary God's verdict to abandon that generation that had turned their backs on him and defiled his house and to bring disaster, destruction, and desolation on Judah and Jerusalem. Babylonians would come and burn the City of David where his people had angered their God by burning offerings for other gods, for as he said, "[T]his city has caused my wrath and fury from the day it was built until now. I will therefore remove it from my presence" (Jer 32:31–34). The Valley of Ben Hinnom would become known as the "Valley of Slaughter/Murder," for there they had murdered their children and would be slaughtered by the Babylonians. The place would be full of human corpses torn apart by scavenging birds and beasts and then fit for nothing but a burial spot, a "desolate waste" (see Jer 7:27–34; 19:1–9).

The prophet Joel does not mention Hinnom Valley but predicts a place of judgment on all the nations in the last days in what is called symbolically "the Valley of Jehoshaphat" (Joel 3:1–16). The apocryphal book of 1 Enoch (written in second century BC–first century AD) mentions an "accursed valley" near Jerusalem, where "all (those) accursed ones" will gather, "who speak with their mouth unbecoming words against the Lord and utter hard words concerning his glory" (27:2).

Although Isaiah does not mention Hinnom Valley, the last chapter of his book describes the final judgment against all who rebel against God and the vindication and joyous blessing on all who humble themselves before him—Jews and Gentiles. The judgment is expressed in terms of God's "wrath against his enemies," of his coming "with fire," of his executing "his anger with fury," and "his rebuke with flames of fire. / For the LORD will execute judgment / on all humanity with his fiery sword, / and many will be slain" (Isa 66:14–16). Old Testament scholar John Oswalt explains:

> To those who have been made holy by [God's] grace, the fire of his character poses no horrors, but those who are depending on their own efforts to stand in his presence will find him a roaring blast furnace. . . . Human rebellion can no more stand up to the terrible presence of God than a field of wheat can stand up to a tornado. If we survive in his presence, it can only be because he has done something to make that survival possible, and we have entrusted ourselves to him to do it.[4]

Oswalt also provides an additional caveat on our perception of God's judgment. He writes,

"To those who have been made holy by [God's] grace, the fire of his character poses no horrors, but those who are depending on their own efforts to stand in his presence will find him a roaring blast furnace. . . . Human rebellion can no more stand up to the terrible presence of God than a field of wheat can stand up to a tornado. If we survive in his presence, it can only be because he has done something to make that survival possible, and we have entrusted ourselves to him to do it."

[T]he *slain* here are those who fall as a result of the final effects of the world's choice of sin over righteousness. Corpses fill the streets of the city not because God in some arbitrary and tyrannical fashion decides to obliterate his enemies, but because to live in defiance of God's creation ordinances is to fill the world with cruelty and violence. God's work is to remove the restraining forces and let the evil that the world has chosen run its terrible course.[5]

God tells us through Isaiah that at the end of the age he will gather "all nations and languages" to see his "glory" (66:18). God will tear down all ethnic and religious barriers separating people, and "all humanity [that is, "all flesh"] will come to worship [him]" (66:23). This will include all the redeemed in the new creation. As Oswalt declares, "Now [they] can revel in the sight of his face, a face with no trace of a frown but wreathed only in smiles of joy, a face that once even to glance on was certain death but that is now the source of life itself."[6]

The reader of Isaiah, however, may be confused or even shocked to see that the book ends with a scene of judgment.[7] In 66:24 it says this: "As [the worshipers] leave, they will see the dead bodies of those who have rebelled against [God]; for their worm will never die, their fire will never go out, and they will be a horror to all humanity ["all flesh"]." It is not accidental that Isaiah's book ends as it begins, with an overture that speaks of "rebels and sinners" who "will be broken" and says that "those who abandon the LORD will perish" (1:28). A few verses later, in fact, one of these rebels, a "strong one," is described as burning, "with no one to extinguish the flames" (1:31).

Part of the Ben Hinnom Valley, which is on the southern end of the city of Jerusalem. The valley was the site where people gave their children as burnt offerings to the Canaanite god Molech (2Ch 28:3; 33:6).

Isaiah's last two verses show a striking contrast between "all humanity" that is, Jews and Gentiles from all over the world, worshiping the Lord, and, on the other, the smoldering corpses of those seen outside the place of worship who refused to do so. France says the figurative character of Isaiah 66:24 may be suggested, first, by the fact that Hinnom Valley would not have been visible to worshipers leaving the temple in Jerusalem and, second, by the questionable combination of worms and fire.[8] Nevertheless, the same ones who worship Yahweh will be horrified by the sight of those who did not. We must acknowledge with Childs that, "[i]n spite of God's new heavens and earth, the exaltation of Zion, and the entrance of the nations to the worship of God, there remain those outside the realm of God's salvation."[9] The word for "dead bodies," often rendered "corpses," is found in 21 Old Testament passages, almost all portraying a grisly battlefield or a scene of divine judgment. After the Lord's angel struck dead 185,000 Assyrians whose massive army had assembled outside Jerusalem to destroy it after "mock[ing] the living God" (Isa 37:4–6), when the people of Jerusalem "got up the next morning—there were all the dead bodies!" (37:36). Only once does the term refer to the carcass of an animal (Gen 15:11).

> *"In spite of God's new heavens and earth, the exaltation of Zion, and the entrance of the nations to the worship of God, there remain those outside the realm of God's salvation."*

The tone of Isaiah 66:24 is not one of gloating and pride (see Obad 12), or even pity, but rather "horror" or abhorrence (Hb. *dera'on*). I remember being horrified by the attitude of a fellow student in college toward a religion professor who was critical of the Bible. My friend, who claimed to be a Christian, declared that he would *laugh* at the sight of Dr. So-in-so burning in hell. Now, that might have been how the writer of the apocryphal folktale Judith felt in 16:17; it alludes to Isaiah 66:24: "Woe to the nations that rise up against my people! / The Lord Almighty will take vengeance on them in the day of judgment; / he will send fire and worms into their flesh; / they shall weep in pain forever." But the apocryphal Jewish author Sirach took a different stance: "Humble yourself to the utmost, / for the punishment of the ungodly is fire and worms" (7:17).

The word translated "horror" in Isaiah 66:24 occurs elsewhere only in Daniel 12:2, where it is rendered "contempt" ("Many who sleep in the dust / of the earth will awake, / some to eternal life, / and some to disgrace [or "reproaches"] and eternal contempt"). "Disgrace" in the Daniel passage appears to point to the emotional experience of the wicked, who may—according to Block—experience "taunts and reviling of all who pass by."[10] "Contempt" would be the emotional response of others to the wicked themselves. Stephen Miller, commenting on the Daniel passage, suggests this: "So shocking will be the fate of the lost that onlookers must turn their faces away in horror (or disgust)."[11] That the contempt will be "eternal" may be because "the grave is not the end for anyone—righteous or wicked," Block notes.[12] Abhorrence suggests a feeling of repulsion, disgust, or loathing. An Arabic word related to *dera'on*, "horror," means "to repel, ward off danger."[13] Block says it describes "the disposition one has toward the putrid and malodorous carcass of a dead animal infested with maggots and in an advanced stage of decay."[14] But we can only guess the onlookers' thoughts and the exact cause of their emotional response. It could be intense hatred or revulsion for anyone disputing the infinite worth of our great God or for those trying to destroy his children. It could also be a sense of the deep tragedy of meeting such an end contrasted with the eternal bliss that could have been found in submission to our gracious and merciful Lord. Or perhaps they were "recalling the fate that would have been [their own]—but for the grace of God."[15]

Another possibility is suggested by Psalm 52, which is about an Edomite thug named Doeg in the employ of King Saul (1 Sam 21:7). He catches sight of Saul's enemy David being aided by the priest at Nob, and he rushes that juicy bit of information to his boss. Saul practically turns purple with rage and orders Doeg to execute the priests. Without hesitation Doeg murders 85 of them at Nob and wipes out the town—"both men and women, infants and nursing babies, oxen, donkeys, and sheep" (1 Sam 22:19). The psalmist sarcastically calls Doeg a "hero" or mighty man (Hb. *gibbor*) who "boast[s] about evil" (Ps 52:1, 6). He's like "a sharpened razor," his "tongue devis[ing] destruction, working treachery" (v. 2). The man loves evil, lying, and "any words that destroy" (vv. 3–4). So, when God rips him out of his tent and destroys him, "the righteous will *see and fear,* / and they will derisively say about that 'hero,' / 'Here is the man / who would not make God his refuge, / but trusted in the abundance of his riches, / taking refuge in his destructive behavior" (vv. 5–7, emphasis added). Perhaps like these righteous ones, the worshipers pictured in Isaiah 66 will also see and fear, as will all who are "humble, submissive in spirit," and "tremble at" God's Word (v. 2). New Testament scholar Doug Moo quotes the nineteenth-century Roman Catholic theologian Cardinal Newman as saying, "Our great security against sin lies in being shocked at it." Indeed, as Moo says, "The sight of sin and the ravages it creates should shock us into avoiding it at all costs"[16] (cp. our upcoming study of Mark 9:43–48).

One explanation for the connection between Hinnom Valley and an underworld place of torment is that it goes back to Rabbi David Kimhi's commentary on Psalm 27 (written around AD 1200). He says, "Gehenna is a repugnant place, into which filth and cadavers are thrown, and in which fires perpetually burn in order to consume the filth and bones; on which account, by analogy, the judgement of the wicked is called 'Gehenna.'"[17] In other words, the wicked would be punished in a place like the garbage dump to be found in Hinnom Valley. While this theory is often heard, biblical scholar Lloyd Bailey counters that "Kimhi's otherwise plausible suggestion ... finds no support in literary sources or archaeological data from the intertestamental or rabbinic periods. There is no evidence that the valley was, in fact, a garbage dump, and thus his explanation is insufficient."[18] Peter Head, a New Testament scholar at Oxford University, echoes this view, declaring that there is "no convincing evidence in the primary sources for the existence of a fiery rubbish dump in [the Hinnom Valley] location." Nevertheless, many scholars use the garbage dump connection to emphasize the *destructive* elements of the judgment.[19] This is especially true of Edward W. Fudge, Church of Christ minister and lawyer, in his 1982 book *The Fire that Consumes.*[20]

> *"There is no evidence that the valley was, in fact, a garbage dump, and thus his explanation is insufficient."*

> *There is "no convincing evidence in the primary sources for the existence of a fiery rubbish dump in [the Hinnom Valley] location."*

Further information comes from Jeremiah. Chapters 30–33 of the biblical book titled with his name, which are on the new covenant and the final restoration of Israel in the last days, contain a prophecy of God's reconsecration of his city of Jerusalem. In 31:38–40, God promises this: "The whole valley—the corpses, the ashes, and all the fields as far as the Kidron Valley [or "brook"] to the corner of the Horse Gate to the east—will be holy to the LORD. It will never be uprooted or demolished again (v. 40)." The Hinnom Valley joins the Kidron Valley south of the City of David. "The whole valley," defiled by corpses and sacrificial ashes in the days of Jeremiah, refers to both. Jack Lundbom notes they and the "fields" (or "terraces" with NIV) above them on the city slopes, both of which were outside the city walls and needing to be consecrated, will be holy to the Lord, like the city itself (31:23).[21] As we saw earlier, Hinnom Valley was defiled by child sacrifices made to Canaanite gods in the Lord's land by people defying the God who had loved them. Consequently, it was further desecrated by piles of corpses left by Judah's Babylonian invaders to be "food for the birds and the wild animals" (Jer 7:32–34). The same Old Testament scholar believes these are the rotting corpses of Isaiah 66:24. Because of all this, he thinks, Hinnom Valley suffered the "perpetual disgrace" of giving its name to hell, that is, Gehenna in the New Testament.[22]

Old Testament scholar Daniel Block agrees with Lundbom that the scene greeting the departing worshipers in Isaiah 66 is not of the underworld or "hell" but a battlefield, although it came to be associated with hell by intertestamental Jews. So, while not a picture of hell, we could call it a "reflection."[23]

> *The scene greeting the departing worshipers in Isaiah 66 is not of the underworld or "hell" but of a battlefield.*

According to Lundbom, it was the valley of the Kidron, which was nearer the Temple Mount, that had been "a dumping area for fat-soaked Temple ashes." (Leviticus 1:16 refers to "the east side of the altar at the place for ashes," and 4:12 to "the ash heap" where "the rest of the bull" was to be burned.) It was also a cemetery for common people. Ancient burial sites have been found in both valleys, as are modern cemeteries.[24] So, although the term *Gehenna* can be traced to Hinnom Valley, evidence for our picture of a place of punishment derived from an ever-burning waste dump there is lacking.

Also fanciful, Peter Head notes, is the idea of worshipers in the new heavens and earth departing from glorious celebrations of God's infinite grace and mercy in somber silence as they must pass by piles of smelly, smoldering human carcasses being continuously eaten by worms.[25] The prophets painted vivid word pictures that conveyed messages calling for action motivated by God's nature as wildly compassionate, gracious, patient, and forgiving, yet consistently guarding the righteous character of his moral universe against unrighteousness. This means that while he has provided a way for his unrighteous creatures to become righteous, God executes appropriate punishment on those rebellious creatures who refuse to follow it. The obstinately and inexorably defiant and rebellious against God have horrible prospects after death.

> *The obstinately and inexorably defiant and rebellious against God have horrible prospects after death.*

The punishment in Isaiah 66:24 is at least horrible death. Does the never-ending activity of "their worm" and "their fire" imply continual torment? Commentator

Jan Koole suggests we can at least suppose the continuing existence of the carcasses.[26] But now let's see what Jesus had to say about Isaiah 66:24.

Gehenna in the New Testament

All but one of the uses of *geenna*, "hell," in the New Testament come from the lips of Jesus. Seven are in Matthew (5:22, 29–30; 10:28; 18:9; 23:15, 33), three are in Mark (9:43–47), one is in Luke (12:5, parallel to Matt 10:28), and one is in James 3:6.

All but one of the uses of geenna, "hell," in the New Testament come from the lips of Jesus.

Gehenna in Mark

The uses in Mark are all in one passage about temptation (9:42–50; parallel in Matt 18:6–9), which also mentions "unquenchable fire" (Mark 9:43) and quotes Isaiah 66:24 (9:48). Mark 9:48 accurately quotes the Hebrew and Greek of the Isaiah passage as saying that "their fire will not be quenched." Yet in verse 44 Jesus (or Mark?) turns the verb into the adjective *asbestos,* "unquenchable" (Matt 18:8 has the common word "eternal"; in English, we use *asbestos* to refer to a fireproof mineral). The rarity of this adjective, occurring only here in the New Testament and nowhere in the Greek Old Testament, makes it stick out. That and the two references to the fire's unquenchability in Mark 9 suggest that Jesus was emphasizing it. The mineral asbestos has been known since prehistoric times, and the Greek adjective, Liddell and Scott note, could mean "endless, ceaseless."[27] So it would be unwise to overlook the word's significance.

Jesus's warnings in Mark 9:42–50 are about the dangers of either causing a fellow disciple ("one of these little ones who believe") to "fall away" or to "fall away" ourselves (see the parallel in Matt 18:6–9, referring to "hellfire," literally "the Gehenna of fire," also representing divine judgment in Matt 5:22). The Greek verb for "fall away" is *skandalizō*, meaning literally "to stumble," from which English gets "scandal." Its first use in Mark is of the seed that falls on rocky ground, representing people who give up their faith and cease being disciples "when distress or persecution come" (Mark 4:17). Its application to the 12 disciples in Mark 14:27–29, however, tells us it could be only a temporary surrender of faith. It could also mean simply "cause to sin," as in Matthew 5:29, where Jesus applies it specifically to sexual sin.

Jesus's warning in Mark 9:42 is against intentionally luring someone away from their faith in him. The penalty is not specified, but France insists the offense is so serious that "a quick drowning would be preferable to the fate it deserves."[28] It is commonly recognized that the point of a biblical prohibition is often, at least secondarily, to exhort the opposite behavior. For instance, Matthew 6:7, "Don't babble like the Gentiles," surely calls for "simplicity, directness, and sincerity in talking to God," as Blomberg notes. [29] If luring someone from the faith carries such a horrible penalty, God's delight would be comparably great in the person who strengthens and guards the faith of spiritual siblings against "savage wolves" that "distort the truth to lure . . . disciples into following them [instead]" (Acts 20:28–31).

A parallel to the warning in Mark 9:42 is found in Jesus's sermon of woes against the scribes and Pharisees in Matthew 23. In their efforts to lure a convert away from Jesus, they "make him twice as much a child of hell [Gehenna] as [they] are!" (23:15). In the conclusion to his sermon, Jesus calls them "Snakes! Brood of vipers!" and asks, "How can you escape being condemned to hell [Gehenna]?" (23:33). Grant Osborne explains that "the Pharisees have virtually completed storing up wrath, and there will now be no escape" from the eternal lake of fire.[30]

Now, back to Mark. Jesus specifies the penalty he is warning about in the case of our negligently allowing our own sinful desires (whether indulged by the use of the hand, foot, or eye) to entice us into turning away from following him. He says,

> [I]f your hand causes you to fall away, cut it off. It is better for you to enter life maimed than to have two hands and go to hell, the unquenchable fire. And if your foot causes you to fall away, cut it off. It is better for you to enter life lame than to have two feet and be thrown into hell. And if your eye causes you to fall away, gouge it out. It is better for you to enter the kingdom of God with one eye than to have two eyes and be thrown into hell, where **their worm does not die, and the fire is not quenched**. (Mark 9:43–48)

On one side, Craig Evans says, the penalty includes our failure to "enter life," that is, the life to come, life in "the kingdom of God" (9:43, 45, 47), where resurrection would entail full restoration, with no maimed or lame or blind.[31] On the other side, it includes our departing this life ("go" in v. 43 is literally "depart") for Gehenna, "the unquenchable fire" (Matt 18:8 has "eternal fire"), where the flames cannot be put out. In verses 45 and 47 the penalty is being "thrown into" Gehenna.

New Testament scholar Robert Yarbrough explains that Jesus uses the term Gehenna, "a despicable, disgusting, and harrowing geographical reference familiar to him and his listeners, to warn of an eschatological destiny that his listeners should seek to avoid at all costs."[32]

The various body parts Jesus focuses on are almost personified as enemies, as in Job 31:1–8 and Proverbs 6:16–19. In Job, for instance, his eyes could "look [lustfully] at a young woman" (31:1), his foot could rush "to deceit" (31:5), and his hands could be "stained" with "impurity" (31:7). Among the seven things that the Lord "hates" and are "detestable" to him in Proverbs 6 are "arrogant eyes," "hands that shed innocent blood," and "feet eager to run to evil" (6:17–18). Commentator Bruce Waltke concludes that someone possessing these characteristics "will be removed from [God's] benevolent presence and consigned to perdition."[33] Arrogant eyes, he explains, show "a denial of the Lord's authority . . . and a disregard for human rights." Shedding innocent blood involves murder out of "covetous greed." "Where the godly use property to help others," the greedy use people to get property. The feet, like those of Doeg in Psalm 52, are full of "zeal and zest to follow the inner evil compulsion as soon as possible."[34]

The various body parts Jesus focuses on are almost personified as enemies.

Whether or not Jesus was alluding to Job 31 or Proverbs 6, he used the human hand, foot, and eye to represent our spiritually dangerous tendencies, which need careful oversight. Jesus might have expected his audience to think of the accounts in 2 Maccabees 6–7 of Jews enduring the tortures of Antiochus IV rather than denying the laws of God. In that passage, the priest Eleazar declares, "Even if for the present I would avoid the punishment of mortals, yet whether I live or die I will not escape the hands of the Almighty" (6:26). And a Jewish woman must watch her seven sons accept the loss of tongue, scalp, hands, and feet rather than to "transgress the laws of [their] ancestors" (7:2). When the fourth son is "near death," he declares, "One cannot but choose to die at the hands of mortals and to cherish the hope God gives of being raised again by him" (7:14). Nevertheless, almost all scholars agree with Craig Evans that " [Jesus's] grotesque recommendations are not to be taken literally," especially since self-mutilation was forbidden in the Old Testament (see Deut 14:1; 1 Kgs 18:28; Zech 13:6).[35] No amount of self-mutilation will protect a person from sin of any kind, so Jesus's point is surely to underscore the infinite worth of the life that He came to provide and to warn of what an infinite tragedy it would be to miss it. Or, as Peter Head puts it, hell "should be treated with such extreme seriousness that any steps should be taken in this life to avoid it because what you do [now] determines your future destiny."[36]

Jesus used the human hand, foot, and eye to represent our spiritually dangerous tendencies, which need careful oversight.

"Jesus's grotesque recommendations are not to be taken literally," especially since self-mutilation was forbidden in the Old Testament.

Jesus's point is surely to underscore the infinite worth of the life that He came to provide and to warn of what an infinite tragedy it would be to miss it.

Jesus does not elaborate here on what His audience was to understand about the punishment of being thrown into the unquenchable fire of Gehenna. Did it involve eternal, conscious torment, since the worm could not be killed, and the fire could not be put out? Robert Yarbrough claims, "It requires a studied effort not to see eternal conscious punishment implied" in the words "unquenchable fire."[37] Some, like Fudge, who oppose the interpretation of eternal punishment see here a "devouring worm aided by unquenchable fire" that "continues to destroy *until nothing remains*."[38] But if that is what Isaiah and Jesus had in mind, it is not what they said. When the food and fuel was gone, the worm would die, and the fire would go out. That fire, then, would not be "unquenchable." In Matthew 18:8, in fact, Jesus calls it "eternal fire." It is true that the *results* of the destruction would be eternal, but that is not what Isaiah and Jesus said.

"It requires a studied effort not to see eternal conscious punishment implied" in the words "unquenchable fire."

Gehenna in Matthew

Jesus first mentions Gehenna in his Sermon on the Mount (5:22) as a symbol of divine condemnation on someone who commits murder in his or her heart. The phrase he uses is "hellfire," literally "the Gehenna of fire," also found in 18:9. He uses Gehenna in the same way for the sin of adultery in the heart in 5:29–30, a passage parallel to Mark 9:43–48. We will look at Matthew 10:28 below, but let us first consider what Jesus teaches in 25:41 and 46. The emphasis here is my own:

> "Then he will also say to those on the left, 'Depart from me, you who are cursed, into *the eternal fire* prepared for the devil and his angels! . . .

> "And they will go away into *eternal punishment*, but the righteous into *eternal life*."

Although Gehenna is not mentioned here, perhaps the clearest teaching on eternal punishment is in Jesus's description of a separation between sheep (true believers) and goats (unbelievers), "when the Son of Man comes in his glory" (Matt 25:31). The gathered nations of the world will be separated based on whether each individual displayed a transformed heart through acts of mercy toward Jesus's followers, his "brothers and sisters," as Matthew often calls them.[39] Those who showed mercy, the "sheep" on Jesus's right, would enter the kingdom because their actions reflected their faith in him. But those who did not, the "goats" on his left, would be told, "Depart from me, you who are cursed, into the eternal fire prepared for the devil and his angels!" (25:41). Craig Blomberg appropriately calls our attention to the ones for whom God prepared "the eternal fire." He writes,

God originally made no provision for lost people or hell in his creative purposes, but once humans and angels freely chose to rebel, then a place of punishment was prepared. No Scripture ever indicates that the fallen angels had any subsequent chance to repent. But people do. So no one need join the demons in this fire. Still, some will opt for hell by rejecting Christ. When they do, they have no one but themselves to blame.[40]

"God originally made no provision for lost people or hell in his creative purposes, but once humans and angels freely chose to rebel, then a place of punishment was prepared."

As a result of their actions of the heart, guilty persons "will go away into *eternal punishment*, but the righteous into eternal life" (25:46). So *eternal fire* in verse 41 and *eternal punishment* in verse 46 are equated, and their exact opposite is *eternal life*. For obvious doctrinal reasons, the Adventist paraphrase renders verse 41, "You will perish in the same fire which will destroy the devil and his angels." And verse 46 is rendered, "I have no choice but to end your lives, because in my kingdom everyone cares about everyone else."[41] But since in the biblical text the same adjective "eternal" (Gk. *aiōnios*) is used of both the punishment of the cursed and the life of the righteous, it is "difficult to see in the former any kind of annihilationism, even if the word 'eternal' can refer to a qualitative rather than quantitative attribute of life and [as] attractive as doctrines of conditional immortality ought to be to anyone with a sensitive heart."[42]

> *The same adjective "eternal" (Gk. aiōnios) is used of both the punishment of the cursed and the life of the righteous.*

In the above sentence Blomberg is alluding to the meaning of *aiōnios*, especially in John, as life that "belongs to the age to come," which John views as having invaded the present age at Christ's resurrection and that's now possessed by believers through faith in him.[43] Despite its qualitative sense, however, theologian J. I. Packer points out that in contrast to the present age, the age to come will not end. He explains that "eternal punishment means a divine penal infliction that is ultimate in the same sense in which eternal life is," in other words, "everlasting and unending."[44] The *Exegetical Dictionary of the New Testament* points out that *aiōnios* can be rendered by *eternal* "throughout the New Testament." When speaking of "*eternal* fire and judgment, . . . the meaning *unceasing, everlasting* comes through even more strongly than is true" in cases where *aiōnios* has a positive stress."[45] As biblical scholar Thomas Schreiner explains, the eternal life that believers possess now is "not the consummation of God's purposes" but "the guarantee that believers will experience physical resurrection." Similarly, "unbelievers already stand under judgment . . . (John 3:18) and God's wrath abides on them now (John 3:36), and yet there will also be final judgment on the day when unbelievers are resurrected."[46]

> *Eternal punishment means a divine penal infliction that is ultimate in the same sense in which eternal life is," in other words, "everlasting and unending."*

If eternal, conscious torment is taught by Jesus, was it physical, spiritual, or both? Well, in one of Matthew's parallels to Mark 9, Jesus speaks of "[one's] whole body" being thrown into hell (5:29–30), and in Matthew 10:28 he urges, "Don't fear those who kill the body but are not able to kill the soul; rather, fear him who is able to destroy both soul and body in hell." It is not uncommon for people to donate their organs or their bodies after they die, with the understanding that after death they will not need them. But based on what Jesus says, it may be that "hell" happens to more than just a person's spirit. R. T. France argues that these references to the body in hell belong to "the pictorial imagery" and should not be "the basis for a doctrinal debate over either the nature of human existence after death or the physicality of hell. Nor should [Matt 5:29–30] be used to suggest that amputees will be raised in an imperfect body." He has a good point that we must be careful not to take literally what Jesus intends figuratively.

> *Jesus speaks of "[one's] whole body" being thrown into hell.*

Jesus is speaking of a conscious existence in an unpleasant place after death, which could have been avoided. France proposes that the theme here is "impediments to ultimate salvation, and the importance of eliminating them at all costs."[47]

Jesus is speaking of a conscious existence in an unpleasant place after death, which could have been avoided.

Yet Jesus's urging not to fear persecution in Matthew 10:28 (quoted above) is not part of a word picture. God, he says, "is able to destroy both soul and body in hell."[48] Shockingly, Jesus really is referring to the whole person. D. A. Carson points out, "In this context . . . the thought that hell is a place of torment for the whole person" is "unavoidable. . . . There will be a resurrection of the unjust as well as of the just."[49] If the experience of the unrighteous in the afterlife is purely spiritual, then why will they be

The thought that hell is a place of torment for the whole person" is "unavoidable."

resurrected, as Paul affirms in Acts 24:15? There he says, "I have a hope in God, which these men themselves also accept, that there will be a resurrection, both of the righteous and the unrighteous." (See also, Dan 12:2; John 5:29.)

The use of the word "destroy" in Matthew 10:28 and elsewhere is often pointed to as evidence against eternal *punishment*. But as New Testament scholar Craig Keener informs us, "Although some Jewish teachers spoke of the instantaneous *annihilation* of the wicked at the judgment, 'destroy' presumably refers to the same picture of judgment" that we find elsewhere in the Gospels: "Jesus will burn the wicked with 'unquenchable,' that is, eternal fire."[50] On the question of whether the unbeliever's death and destructive judgment involved the cessation of existence, Peter Head calls attention to what Jesus said about towns that refused to embrace the gospel he and his disciples were preaching in word

Figurines from traditional site of Sodom.

and action. Although Sodom and Gomorrah had been reduced to ashes and condemned to extinction (2 Pet 2:6; see Gen 13:10; 19:13–14, 29), Jesus warned, "It will be more tolerable on the day of judgment for the land of Sodom and Gomorrah than for that town" (Matt 10:15; 11:22–24).

"The language of extinction and destruction can be used to refer to a judgment through which existence continues."

Jesus's words demonstrate his "assumption of a continued existence for the inhabitants of Sodom and Gomorrah" after their "destruction." This, according to Head, shows that "the language of extinction and destruction can be used to refer to a judgment through which existence continues."[51]

Although we cannot base our Christian beliefs on the vicissitudes of church history, a historical note on this topic is of interest here. One study on the nature of hell has pointed out that "the first explicit defense of the annihilation of ungodly souls in hell" dates no earlier than the early Christian apologist Arnobius, who died in AD 330. He was noted, however, more for zeal than for Christian orthodoxy or knowledge of Scripture. His views were "deemed heretical by the Second Council of Constantinople in 553 and again by the Lateran Council in 1513."[52]

THE LAKE OF FIRE

This phrase is only mentioned in Revelation 19–20. In John's vision, he sees the beast and the false prophet, who had waged war against the rider and his army, "thrown alive into the lake of fire that burns with sulfur" (19:19–20). The next chapter deals with the evil one of many names: the dragon, the ancient serpent, the devil, or Satan (20:2). After being thrown into the abyss for a thousand years, he is "released for a short time" (20:3). John reports that after Satan's deceiving of the nations and gathering another vast army against "the saints, the beloved city," fire from heaven consume the army (20:7–9). Then the devil is "thrown into the lake of fire and sulfur where the beast and the false prophet are, and they will be tormented day and night forever and ever" (20:10). Finally, Death and Hades are thrown into this burning lake, followed by "anyone whose name was not found written in the book of life" (20:14–15).

Jesus's references to Gehenna and its "unquenchable" or "eternal fire" as the destiny of the wicked appears to match what Revelation says about the lake of fire. Matthew 25:41, in particular, refers to "the eternal fire prepared for the devil and his angels," which parallels Revelation 20:14–15. Jesus also speaks of "the eternal fire" in Matthew 18:8 and in the next verse calls it "hellfire" (the Gehenna of fire).

TARTARUS AND THE ABYSS
Tartarus in 2 Peter 2:4

As already mentioned, "hell" is found in the CSB 11 times, all but once translating *Gehenna*. The other case is in 2 Peter 2:4, where the phrase "cast . . . into hell" renders a verb related to Greek *Tartaros*, better known by the Latin name Tartarus. The classical Greek lexicon defines Tartarus as "a dark abyss, as deep below Hades as earth is below heaven, the prison of the Titans."[53] The Titans were pre-Olympian gods who rebelled against their father Uranus but were defeated and imprisoned by the younger god Zeus. The reference in 2 Peter, however, is to the place where God cast "the angels who sinned" and "delivered them in chains of utter darkness to be kept for judgment."

Peter uses three historical examples in 2 Peter 2:4–6 to show that God's future judgment is certain: (1) the sinning angels of Genesis 6:1–4 are being held in "chains of utter darkness" as they await it (2) judgment of "the world of the ungodly" by the flood has happened, and (3) extinction of Sodom and Gomorrah through fire has too. The latter serve to foreshadow what's to come. He also gives two examples of God rescuing and protecting the godly: (1) Noah (v. 5), and (2) Lot (vv. 7–8).[54]

Peter does not specify the reason for God's judgment of angels but apparently assumes his readers know the account from Genesis and from Jewish tradition (esp. 1 Enoch). The parallel passage in Jude 6 identifies "the angels who did not keep their own position but abandoned their proper dwelling." As a result, "Jesus" (the antecedent from v. 5) "has kept [them] in eternal chains in deep darkness for the judgment on the great day." By the word "likewise," beginning his comments in Jude 7 about Sodom and Gomorrah, we know Jude understood the angels' sin to be their sexual intercourse with the daughters of men. But this resulted from their not keeping "their own position" but abandoning "their proper dwelling." Schreiner explains that this means they left "the domain … or sphere of influence" assigned to them by God and assumed male bodies on their own authority.[55]

> They left "the domain … or sphere of influence" assigned to them by God and assumed male bodies on their own authority.

The objection often raised to this interpretation of Genesis 6 is a statement by Jesus that some take to mean angels are asexual (Matt 22:30). What Jesus said, however, is that angels in heaven "neither marry nor are given in marriage." And Schreiner points out that angels can assume physical bodies when they enter the human sphere. For instance, the three angels who visited Abraham ate his food (Gen 18:8; 19:1), "showing that their bodies were real." So, we may assume that the human form of angels "is genuine, not a charade, so that the sexuality of angels when they appear on earth is genuine."[56]

Regardless, the immediate consequence of the angels' sin was that they were "kept in eternal chains in deep darkness for the judgment" yet to come (Jude 6). Peter calls the place of chains not *Gehenna*, "hell," but "Tartarus" (see the n. in CSB), where they were incarcerated in "utter darkness" (2 Pet 2:4). For his original audience, the term probably called to mind familiar stories of the dark abyss below Hades where the Titans had been imprisoned. As Schreiner says, "Peter [thus] communicates with his readers in terms of their own idiom," even though neither he nor his readers were necessarily familiar with classical literature.[57] The term Tartarus even occurs in the Septuagint translation of Job 40:20 ("[Behemoth] went up on a steep mountain, it brought gladness to the quadrupeds in Tartarus") and 41:23–24 ("[Leviathan] makes the deep boil like a caldron and regards the sea as a pot of ointment and Tartarus of the deep as a captive").

> "Peter [thus] communicates with his readers in terms of their own idiom."

According to Doug Moo, the angels' chains may be figurative, representing divine restraints on their "sphere of activity."[58] Biblical scholar Norman Hillyer says,

Qumran fragment of book of Enoch.

We are not intended to imagine a literal dungeon in which fallen angels are fettered. Rather, Jude was vividly depicting the misery of their conditions. Free spirits and celestial powers, as once they were, are now shackled and impotent. Shining ones, once enjoying the marvelous light of God's glorious presence, are now plunged in profound darkness.[59]

The Abyss

Although Tartarus is not found in most English Bibles, the term translated "the abyss" (Gk. *abussos*) is used nine times in the New Testament, mainly in Revelation, as its apparent equivalent. The word may have been derived from a Sumerian word that meant "bottomless, unfathomable,"[60] and that is its meaning prior to its use as a noun in the Greek Old Testament (Septuagint). There it is almost always the exclusive translation of Hebrew *tehom, which* is rendered "watery depths" in the CSB. First, it designates the primordial waters covered by both darkness and God's Spirit in Genesis 1:2. After that, it became "the water under the expanse," then the "watery depths" that flooded the earth (Gen 1:7; 7:11; 8:2). It was also the underground waters that nourished the earth (see Gen 8:7; Deut 33:13).

The Hebrew poets sometimes allude to the abysmal flood waters of judgment ("the deep/depths") on God's enemies (Ezek 26:19; 31:15) or to represent their own experience of God's trials (see Ps 42:7; 71:20; Jonah 2:5). They also sometimes allude to the underground springs of blessing (see Ps 78:15; Prov 3:20; Ezek 31:4). The author of Psalm 71 laments his weakness in old age, as his enemies plot to disgrace him. In verse 20 he expresses his feeling of being in "the depths [*tehom/abussos*] of the earth." According to Old Testament scholar Allen Ross, this "may refer to *she'ol*, or more specifically the masses of water stored in the earth and so the subterranean abysses where *she'ol* was to be located." It is "figurative," he says, with the psalmist expressing his deliverance as if he were "being rescued from the underworld."[61] The psalmist is confident that the Lord, his "rock of refuge" will revive him, bring him back up, and restore his honor and comfort. This chapter contains the only use of "the depths [*tehom/abussos*] of the earth" in the Old Testament, although the English phrase occurs with other terms rendered "depths" in Psalms 63:9; 95:4;

> *The only use of "the depths [tehom/abussos] of the earth" in the Old Testament.*

139:15; and Isaiah 44:23. The same phrase as in Psalm 71:20 occurs in the second-century BC Jewish book of Jubilees, which is an imaginative retelling and expansion of Genesis. It recounts the angels who had corrupted the earth (Gen 6) being bound "in the depths of the earth forever, until the day of great judgment" (5:6, 10).[62] Here we notice the similarity to 2 Peter 2:4 and Jude 6. The abyss could also be used of "the depths of the oceans" (Job 38:16), the home of Leviathan (Job 41:31–32), and the deepest recesses of the earth ruled by our sovereign God (Isa 24:27; 51:10; 63:13; Hab 3:10; Sir 24:5, 29; 42:18; 43:23).

The book of Revelation refers to the abyss seven times. Greg Beale, New Testament scholar and expert on that book, explains that the abyss became symbolic of the forces of evil. Its first mention in Revelation 9:1–2 affirms it to be "a place of punishment where evil spirits are confined under God's sovereignty." Beginning in this chapter, is "an ever-expanding definition of the extent of God and the Lamb's sovereignty. God and the Lamb are in ultimate control of Satan's realm."[63] Verse 11 identifies "the angel of the abyss," who is king over the demons, as Abaddon/Apollyon, meaning "destruction." Beale identifies him as either the devil himself or his evil representative.[64] The fact that "the key for the shaft to the abyss *was given* to him" in 9:1 (emphasis added) means that God has ultimate control, and the destruction and torment that spewed forth was divinely limited (vv. 4–5). Revelation 11:7 speaks for the first time of "the beast that comes up out of the abyss" to make war on the two witnesses (11:1–6), "conquer them, and kill them." Schreiner suggests this beast merges the four beasts of Daniel 7 and is "beastly" in that it is like a "carnivorous animal, rapacious and cruel, ripping open and consuming those who opposed it."[65] In Revelation 13:1 another beast comes "up out of the sea," which Beale says equals the abyss, "the spiritual storehouse of evil" appearing in 9:1–2.[66] In 16:13 this beast from the sea is called "the false prophet." The origin of the beast and false prophet shows their demonic nature and power. The beast especially echoes Daniel's prophecy of a beast who was "extremely terrifying, with iron teeth and bronze claws, devouring, crushing, and trampling." It had a horn that "waged war against the holy ones" (the community of the faithful, that is, the two witnesses of Rev 11 according to Beale)[67] and was prevailing over them until "the Ancient of Days arrived" and "the holy ones took possession of the kingdom" (Dan 7:19–22).

The beast appears again in Revelation 17:8, as the one who "was, and is not, and is about to come up from the abyss and go to destruction." This parodies and counterfeits "the Lamb who was slaughtered / to receive power and riches / and wisdom and strength / and honor and glory and blessing" (5:12). The Lamb is the one "who is, who was, and who is to come" (1:4), the "Lord God, the Almighty" (4:8). Beale explains that applying the "threefold formula for divine eternity to the beast is intended to ridicule the beast's vain efforts to defeat the *true* eternal being and his forces."[68] Although evil will appear to rise again and even grow stronger in the end, "the Lamb will conquer them because he is Lord of lords and King of kings" (Rev 17:14). He was dead but is "alive forever" and holds "the keys of death and Hades" (1:18), which means He owns the key to the abyss.

The final reference to the abyss is in Revelation 20:1–3. The first six verses of this chapter are the most controversial in this challenging book by John, and a millennial excursion into the adventure of investigating them must be kept for another day.[69] What I must emphasize here is confirmation of God's ultimate control. His invincible angel holds not only "the key to the abyss" but also "a great chain"; both are symbolic of God's confinement of "the dragon, that ancient serpent who is the devil and Satan" in the absolutely inescapable, spiritual Alcatraz, God's maximum-security facility, the abyss. Only God could release him after what is perhaps a symbolic thousand years, and then only so that he could lead the malevolent, delusional nations in a futile battle against the King of kings and his heavenly armies. The result will be that the beast, the false prophet, and the devil will be "thrown into the lake of fire and sulfur" to be "tormented day and night forever" (19:11–21; 20:7–10). Death and Hades, that is, the abyss itself and all the dead "whose [names were] not found written in the book of life" will also be "thrown into the lake of fire" (20:11–15).

> God's people will experience persecution and will struggle against him until Christ returns and destroys the forces of evil completely.

John's revelation is about the church undergoing persecution by the evil one, even though he was defeated at the cross and resurrection of Christ. God's people will experience persecution and will struggle against him until Christ returns and destroys the forces of evil completely. Meanwhile, we have God's "full armor" with which to "stand against the schemes of" Satan (see Eph 6:11–18).

THE LOVE OF GOD

I need to acknowledge here the difficulty people have in reconciling our understanding of God's love and what the Bible says about His eternal punishment of those who reject it. Many believers and nonbelievers alike, in fact, find the two concepts irreconcilable. Anyone whose sinful heart has been softened by the gracious love of God in Christ and filled with His Spirit will naturally wrestle with this issue. And no one I know—least of all me—has a theological wand to wave and make this problem go away. Suggestions that the fires of hell are just figurative and that we should not speak of it as "torture" may help us feel better, but they do not solve our dilemma. So, it is important that we try to understand the nature of God's love and see what help that offers us.

Discussions of this issue often include this quotation from John's first letter. He writes, "Dear friends, let us love one another, because love is from God, and everyone who loves has been born of God and knows God. The one who does not love does not know God, because God is love. God's love was revealed among us in this way: God sent his one

> "God is love."

and only Son into the world so that we might live through him" (1 John 4:7–9). Love, especially for one's fellow believers, is an essential characteristic of a child of God. But to look out on the mass of humanity that is running from God, or even fighting against God, or looking into the face of one of them without a feeling of compassion and broken-heartedness over the blindness of his or her heart may also be a sign that we are not as close to God as we thought. He, after all, does not want "any to perish but all to come to repentance" (2 Pet 3:9). I think, in fact, that's the reason John moves in verse 8 beyond love for one another to the more absolute description of "the one who does not love." That person "does not know God." Why? "Because God is love." Unfortunately, many take that statement in directions not intended by John. I have heard many interpret it to mean that everything God does is an expression of his love. That may be so, but it is not what John is saying. Rather, he clearly explains what he means by "God is love" in verse 9: "God's love was revealed among us in this way: God sent his one and only Son into the world so that we might live through him." Jesus said the same thing in John 3:16: "For God loved the world in this way: He gave his one and only Son, so that everyone who believes in him will not perish but have eternal life." The sense in which "God is love" is that he provided his "one and only Son" to die that we might have life everlasting.

> *"God's love was revealed among us in this way: God sent his one and only Son into the world so that we might live through him."*

Perhaps the most we can say in our confusion over God's love versus eternal punishment is that we must acknowledge that God's mind and purposes are ultimately way beyond our finite capability of comprehending. After all, Augustine, bishop of Hippo in fourth-century north Africa, once said that anyone claiming to comprehend God is obviously comprehending something other than God.[70] Dutch theologian Herman Bavinck began his fine work on *The Doctrine of God* with a chapter on "God's Incomprehensibility," in which he states that, according to Scripture, "God is incomprehensible yet knowable, absolute yet personal."[71] The prophet Isaiah describes God's "thoughts" and "ways" as high as the heavens (Isa 55:8–9). And the psalmist says this:

> *Anyone claiming to comprehend God is obviously comprehending something other than God.*

> I will shout for joy
> because of the works of your hands.
> How magnificent are your works, LORD,
> how profound your thoughts!
> A stupid person does not know,
> a fool does not understand this:
> though the wicked sprout like grass
> and all evildoers flourish,
> they will be eternally destroyed. (Ps 92:4–7)

The word translated "profound" in verse 5 is literally "deep." The NET renders it "intricate" and explains that the "thoughts" here, as in Isaiah 55:8–9, refers specifically to his plans and purposes. What is profound, deep, intricate, or complex

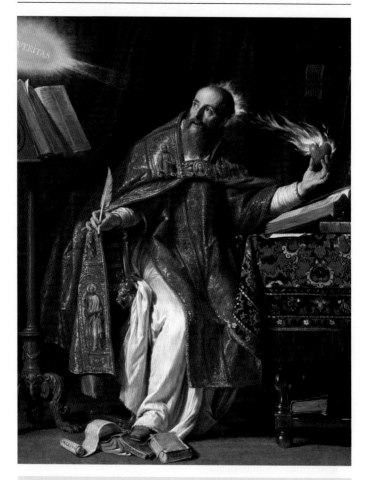

Saint Augustine by Philippe de Champaigne.

is God's "moral design of the world" (see n. b. in NET). Even Job's "friend" Zophar understood that we cannot "fathom the depths of God" or "discover the limits of the Almighty" (Job 11:7). He facetiously says that "a stupid person will gain understanding / as soon as a wild donkey is born a human!" (11:12). Even the most intelligent among us, however, is stupid compared to God. Perhaps the psalmist David was never as wise as when he wrote this in Psalm 131:1–3:

> LORD, my heart is not proud;
> my eyes are not haughty.
> *I do not get involved with things*
> *too great or too wondrous for me.*
> Instead, I have calmed and quieted my soul
> like a weaned child with its mother;
> my soul is like a weaned child.
> Israel, put your hope in the LORD,
> both now and forever (emphasis added).

In the face of theological conundrums, I choose to accept my best understanding of the Bible's teaching and let Him resolve the difficulties when and if He wishes. I will bury my face in His chest and be content simply to be with Him, "like a weaned child with [his] mother."

CRIME IN THE AFTERLIFE

As we approach the end of our guidebook to the afterlife, it is natural for someone contemplating moving there to ask things like this: Is there much crime in the land beyond death? Is it safe? What if I make it to heaven but just can't hack it? What if I flunk out? I remember hearing a Christian speaker say that if any one of us went to heaven as we are, we would wreck the place. As Paul says in 1 Corinthians, though we are "sown in corruption, [we'll be] raised in incorruption; sown in dishonor, raised in glory; sown in weakness, raised in power.... [Mere f]lesh and blood cannot inherit the kingdom of God.... [but] the trumpet will sound, and the dead [in Christ] will be raised incorruptible, and we will be changed" (1 Cor 15:42–43, 50, 52). Everyone who goes to dwell with Jesus in the afterlife will be a fully converted and sanctified child of the King, body and soul. And while we do not yet understand the bodily forms we'll inhabit between our last breaths and Christ's return, we can rest in what Paul tells us in 2 Corinthians: "We all, with unveiled faces, are looking as in a mirror at the glory of the Lord and *are being transformed into the same image from glory to glory;* this is from the Lord who is the Spirit" (2 Cor 3:18, emphasis added). This statement by Paul means that right now we are being prepared for the trip ahead! To this thought John added, "Dear friends, we are God's children now, what we will be has not yet been revealed. We know that when he appears, *we will be like him* because we will see him as he is" (1 John 3:2, emphasis added; cf. Rev 22:4).

If any one of us went to heaven as we are, we would wreck the place.

Perhaps, though, you still worry that the forces of evil will somehow manage to obstruct your path and keep you from even getting to the gates of heaven or from enjoying life on the new earth. The rest of Peter's words in 2 Peter 2 are helpful here. He tells us how "distressed" Lot was "by the depraved behavior of the immoral.... his righteous soul was tormented by the lawless deeds he saw and heard" (2 Pet 2:7–8). Therefore God, just as he had "protected Noah" when the flood destroyed "the ungodly" (2:5), also "rescued righteous Lot" (2:7). Peter's concluding encouragement is that "the Lord knows how to rescue the godly ... and to keep the unrighteous under punishment for the day of judgment" (2:9; cf. John 17:15; 2 Cor 1:22; Eph 1:13; 4:30; Jude 24; Rev 9:4). One who repents and

"Jesus Heals a Demon-Possessed Man" by Gustave Doré.

personally trusts in what Jesus accomplished at the cross and tomb on his or her behalf has no need to fear missing out on the afterlife blessings promised throughout Scripture.

Something that must not be missed as we consider what Scripture teaches about the forces of evil, darkness, and death is that they are powerless before our sovereign God. When we as believers experience periods of darkness and despair, we can know that, as John said of "the Word," that is, Jesus, "In him was [and is] life, and that life was [and is] the light of men. That light shines in the darkness [still], and yet the darkness did not [and will never] overcome it" (John 1:4–5). As Jesus assures us in Matthew 16:18, "[He] will build [his] church, and the gates of Hades will not overpower it" (See more on "Hades" in our chap. 12: "The Other Place."). Luke recounts for us Jesus's confrontation and defeat of a large army of demons in a possessed man among "the Gerasenes" (Luke 8:26–39). The demon gave his name as "Legion," which was the largest unit in a Roman army. They begged Jesus not to "banish them to the abyss" but to permit them to enter a large herd of pigs (vv. 31–32), which Mark 5:13 numbers at about two thousand. Jesus complied.

As New Testament scholar Darrell Bock assures us in his introduction to Luke 8:26–39, "All forces—nature, demons, disease, and death—that could be regarded as stronger than humanity and that stand opposed to God as rivals to his power are rendered impotent in this section. Relationship to Jesus brings security."[72] Only Luke among the Gospels mentions the abyss; Matthew's parallel

"Relationship to Jesus brings security."

question by the demons was, "Have you come here to torment us before the time?" (Matt 8:29). This assumes an understanding, even on the part of the demons, that their time of operation is rigidly bound by God's plans and purposes, and they have expectations of torment in their future.

Doug Moo calls our attention to how comforting this should be to us, and he also cautions us against imbalance when it comes to our attitude toward Satan and demonic influence in the world. The Bible is clear that they exist. But "they have been judged and 'put on a chain' by God himself." God's child has no reason to fear them. Moo quotes J. I. Packer, who pointed out that the early church and Middle Ages took Satan "too seriously," resulting in "morbid fears and fancies." We should avoid a negative view of the Christian life "as primarily a course of devil-dodging exercises and anti-Satanic manoeuvres" [sic].[73]

NOTES

[1]   Justin Bass, *The Battle for the Keys: Revelation 1:18 and Christ's Descent into the Underworld* (Eugene, OR: Wipf and Stock, 2014), 21, 78, 90. The rabbis, Bass says, departed from the New Testament in speaking of Gehenna as a place of temporary punishment.

[2]   This may have referred to "the stand over the fire upon which the child was placed." See Mordechai Cogan and Hayim Tadmor, *II Kings*, Anchor Bible (New York: Doubleday, 1988), 287.

[3]   The Tophet may have been some kind of altar that Josiah "dismantled" (Jack R. Lundbom, *Jeremiah 1–20*, Anchor Bible [New York: Doubleday, 1999], 495). In his comments on Matt 5:22–23, D. A. Carson claims that Josiah defiled the valley "by making it a dumping ground for filth and the corpses of criminals," but he mentions no evidence for this. See "Matthew," in *Expositor's Bible Commentary*, ed. F. E. Gaebelein (Grand Rapids: Zondervan, 1990), Accordance Version 2.9.

[4]   John N. Oswalt, *The Book of Isaiah Chapters 40–66*, The New International Commentary on the Old Testament (Grand Rapids: Eerdmans, 1998), 684–85.

[5]   Oswalt, *The Book of Isaiah Chapters 40–66*, 685.

[6]   Oswalt, *The Book of Isaiah Chapters 40–66*, 692.

[7]   Many scholars, reckoning themselves smarter than the biblical writers, consider v. 24 to be a late addition to the book. Even the Jewish translation (JPS) repeats v. 23 at the end of v. 24 to end the book on a positive note.

[8] R. T. France understands the language as "evocative" and "better appreciated in its awful deterrence than analysed [sic] as to precisely how the two methods of destruction relate to each other, or just what is the function of the worm" (*The Gospel of Mark,* The New International Greek Testament Commentary [Grand Rapids: Eerdmans, 2002], 382.

[9] Brevard S. Childs, *Isaiah,* The Old Testament Library (Louisville, KY: WJKP, 2001), 542.

[10] Daniel I. Block, "The Old Testament on Hell," in *Hell under Fire,* ed. C. W. Morgan and R. A. Peterson (Grand Rapids: Zondervan, 2004), 63–64.

[11] Stephen R. Miller, *Daniel,* New American Commentary (Nashville: B&H, 1994), 317.

[12] Block, "The Old Testament on Hell," 64.

[13] See Joe Sprinkle, *Daniel,* Evangelical Biblical Theology Commentary (Bellingham, WA: Lexham, 2020), 330.

[14] Block, "The Old Testament on Hell," 64.

[15] Block, "The Old Testament on Hell," 60.

[16] Douglas J. Moo, *2 Peter, Jude,* NIV Application Commentary (Grand Rapids: Zondervan, 1996), 118.

[17] Lloyd R. Bailey, "Gehenna: The Topography of Hell," *Biblical Archaeologist* (Sept. 1986): 188.

[18] Bailey, "Gehenna: The Topography of Hell," 189.

[19] Peter Head, "The Duration of Divine Judgment in the New Testament," in *Eschatology in Bible and Theology,* ed. K. E. Brower and M. W. Elliott (Downers Grove, IL: InterVarsity, 1997), 223.

[20] Edward W. Fudge, *The Fire that Consumes: A Biblical and Historical Handbook of the Doctrine of the Final Punishment,* rev. ed. (Carlisle: Paternoster, 1994).

[21] Jack R. Lundbom, *Jeremiah 21–36,* The Anchor Bible (New York: Doubleday, 2004), 492.

[22] Lundbom, *Jeremiah 1–20,* 498.

[23] Block, "The Old Testament on Hell," 61.

[24] Lundbom, *Jeremiah 21–36,* 492.

[25] Peter Head points out that most commentaries on Isaiah consider the reference to monthly and weekly worship to be a remnant of Old Testament language for what will be enduring, everlasting worship ("The Duration of Divine Judgment," 223).

[26] Jan L. Koole, *Isaiah III: Volume 3/Isaiah 56–66,* Historical Commentary on the Old Testament (Leuven: Peeters, 2001), 530.

[27] Henry George Liddell and Robert Scott, *Liddell and Scott's Greek-English Lexicon* (Simon Wallenberg Press, 2007).

[28] France, *The Gospel of Mark,* 380.

[29] Craig L. Blomberg, *Matthew,* New American Commentary (Nashville: Broadman, 1992), 118.

[30] Grant R. Osborne, *Matthew,* Zondervan Exegetical Commentary on the New Testament (Grand Rapids: Zondervan, 2010), 855.

[31] See Craig A. Evans, *Mark 8:27–16:20,* Word Biblical Commentary (Nashville: Nelson, 2000), 71.

[32] Robert W. Yarbrough, "Jesus on Hell," in *Hell under Fire,* ed. C. W. Morgan and R. A. Peterson (Grand Rapids: Zondervan, 2004), 79.

[33] Bruce K. Waltke, *The Book of Proverbs Chapters 1–15,* New Testament International Commentary on the Old Testament (Grand Rapids: Eerdmans, 2004).

[34] Waltke, *The Book of Proverbs,* 346–47.

[35] Evans, *Mark 8:27–16:20,* 71. A remarkable exception is Robert H. Gundry, *Mark: A Commentary on His Apology for the Cross* (Grand Rapids: Eerdmans, 1993), 514. He even considers it possible that believers may literally enter the kingdom with maimed bodies,

just as the resurrected Jesus still had the scars of crucifixion. Going through eternity missing a hand or foot or eye, however, would not be the same as forever having a scar.

36 Head, "The Duration of Divine Judgment," 222.

37 Yarbrough, "Jesus on Hell," 74.

38 This is Edward W. Fudge's view in Fudge and Robert A. Peterson, *Two Views of Hell* (Downers Grove, IL: InterVarsity, 2000), 44. Emphasis added.

39 See Blomberg, *Matthew,* 377–78. As D. A. Carson says, "The reason for admission to the kingdom in this parable is more evidential than causative" ("Matthew," *Expositor's Bible Commentary,* ed. F. E. Gaebelein [Grand Rapids: Zondervan, 1990], comments on Matt 25:34–40). Craig S. Keener, however, understands Jesus's siblings in v. 40, who are treated kindly by the righteous, as his disciples and gospel messengers. See *The Gospel of Matthew: A Socio-Rhetorical Commentary* (Grand Rapids: Eerdmans, 2009), 605–6. R. T. France agrees that the "brothers and sisters" are disciples, though not necessarily missionaries (*The Gospel of Matthew,* New International Commentary on the New Testament (Grand Rapids: Eerdmans, 2007), 958.

40 Blomberg, *Matthew,* 379.

41 Jack J. Blanco, *The Clear Word: An Expanded Paraphrase to Build Strong Faith and Nurture Spiritual Growth* (Hagerstown, MD: Review and Herald, 2003), 996.

42 Blomberg, *Matthew,* 379.

43 See Thomas R. Schreiner, *New Testament Theology: Magnifying God in Christ* (Grand Rapids: Baker, 2008), 84, 87.

44 J. I. Packer, "Universalism: Will Everyone Ultimately Be Saved?" in *Hell Under Fire,* ed. C. W. Morgan and R. A. Peterson (Grand Rapids: Zondervan, 2004), 183.

45 Horst Balz, "*aiōnios,* eternal, everlasting," *Exegetical Dictionary of the New Testament, Volume 1,* ed. H. Balz and G. Schneider (Grand Rapids: Eerdmans, 1990), 46–47.

46 Schreiner, *New Testament Theology,* 88. Also see G. K. Beale, *A New Testament Biblical Theology: The Unfolding of the Old Testament in the New* (Grand Rapids: Baker, 2011), 948–49.

47 France, *The Gospel of Matthew,* 206.

48 Luke 12:5, the parallel verse, does not specify what is thrown into hell, although the CSB supplies "people."

49 D. A. Carson, "Matthew," comments on Matt 10:28.

50 Keener, *The Gospel of Matthew,* 327.

51 Head, "The Duration of Divine Judgment," 224–25.

52 David Hilborn (ed.), *The Nature of Hell. A Report by the Evangelical Alliance Commission on Unity and Truth among Evangelicals (ACUTE).* (Carlisle: Paternoster Press, 2000). This is cited from Yarbrough, "Jesus on Hell," 85.

53 Henry George Liddell and Robert Scott, *An Intermediate Greek-English Lexicon founded upon the Seventh Edition of Liddell and Scott's Greek-English Lexicon* (Oxford: Clarendon Press, 1889).

54 Thomas R. Schreiner, *1 & 2 Peter and Jude,* Christian Standard Commentary (Nashville: Holman, 2020), 399–401.

55 Schreiner, *1 & 2 Peter and Jude,* 540.

56 Schreiner, *1 & 2 Peter and Jude,* 543.

57 Schreiner, 1 & 2 Peter and Jude, 402–403.

58 Moo, *2 Peter, Jude,* 116.

59 Norman Hillyer, *1 & 2 Peter, Jude,* Understanding the Bible Commentary (Grand Rapids: Baker, 1991), 242.

60 Jack M. Sasson, *Jonah,* Anchor Bible (New York: Doubleday, 1990), 184.

61 Allen P. Ross, *A Commentary on the Psalms, Volume 2 (42–89)* (Grand Rapids: Kregel, 2013), 525.

62 Jubilees was written in Hebrew and translated into Greek, Syriac, Latin, and Ethiopic, the only version that has substantially survived. English versions are translated from Ethiopic. See James H. Charlesworth, ed., *The Old Testament Pseudepigrapha, Volume Two* (Peabody, MA: Hendrickson, 1983), 41–42.

63 G. K. Beale, *The Book of Revelation,* The New International Greek Testament Commentary (Grand Rapids: Eerdmans, 1999), 493.

64 Beale, *The Book of Revelation,* 502–3.

65 Thomas R. Schreiner, *The King in His Beauty: A Biblical Theology of the Old and New Testaments* (Grand Rapids: Baker, 2013), 618.

66 Beale, *The Book of Revelation,* 684.

67 Beale, *The Book of Revelation,* 588.

68 Beale, *The Book of Revelation,* 864.

69 For a survey of options, see Darrell L. Bock, ed., *Three Views on the Millennium and Beyond* (Grand Rapids: Zondervan, 1999).

70 R. G. MacMullen, trans. *From Nicene and Post-Nicene Fathers*, First Series, Vol. 6, ed. Philip Schaff. (Buffalo, NY: Christian Literature Publishing, 1888.) Revised and edited for New Advent by Kevin Knight. Accessed March 15, 2023, http://www.newadvent.org/fathers/160367.htm.

71 Herman Bavinck, *The Doctrine of God* (Grand Rapids: Baker, 1951), 13.

72 Darrell L. Bock, *Luke*, 2 Volumes, Baker Exegetical Commentary on the New Testament (Grand Rapids: Baker, 1994). Kindle.

73 Moo, *2 Peter, Jude,* 117.

CHAPTER 15

BON VOYAGE:
ON DEATH AND DYING

We began our guidebook to the afterlife by comparing the experience of going there to the process of immigrating to a foreign country. Our goal has been to learn as much about the destination as possible. One reason is that our citizenship is already there (see the introduction, titled "Orientation"). We wrestled in chapter 1 with the misinformation available and established how to distinguish between what is true and what's not. We discussed the nature of heaven and earth in our chapter on geography (chapter 2). Then I described the beauty and fearfulness of the afterlife as divine fire and holy light in chapter 3. Only the vicarious sacrifice of Jesus Christ at the cross makes the wonder and beauty of God's dwelling place accessible—just as the platforms and walkways at Yellowstone are essential for the safety of anyone visiting the wonders of the hydrothermal areas without being boiled alive by the mudpots, hot springs, and geysers (chapter 4).

We next dove into the question of whether the afterlife is a celestial experience (chapter 5), or a terrestrial one in a new heaven and new earth (chapter 6). This was followed by more examination of the access to the afterlife. Jesus Christ, I pointed out, is the only vehicle that can get us there, but what powers our journey and our life there? Is there something beyond solar, hydroelectric, combustion, and nuclear? We found it in Jesus's bodily resurrection (chapter 7). But how can we really believe in such a thing? We had to examine the evidence in chapter 8.

My next task was to turn the spotlight on us and ask, What's a person? What is it exactly that makes the move to the afterlife? Is it a soul, a spirit, some kind of body, or the whole person? That took us through chapter 9, the content of which spilled over into chapters 10–11. In these we investigated whether the individual's immigration to the afterlife will be a one-stage event, or a two-stage process. A direct flight? Or one with a layover in an intermediate state? We found that our definition of a person and the nature of this journey are interrelated. And we had to consider a lot of clues, first from the Old Testament (chapter 10), then from the New Testament (chapter 11).

This was followed by an unpleasant but necessary look at certain unseemly regions or features of the "afterlife." We had to reckon with the fact that not all of God's creatures wish to "get on the train" and spend eternity with our Creator and Lord. This includes both natural people and some of the supernatural beings or angels that God created. Where are these, and what will happen to unbelievers? I devoted three chapters to taking us on a "tram-ride" over regions with names like Sheol, Hades, hell, the Pit, Gehenna, Tartarus, the abyss, and the lake of fire to find out. Along the way, we heard dubious descriptions of Hades by people claiming to have been there (chapter 12), considered the view that Christ went to Hades after the cross (chapter 13), and ended up observing the final destinations of all who refuse God's offer of everlasting bliss with him (chapter 14).

That brings us in this final chapter to step back and acknowledge that elephant in the room I mentioned in our introduction. For most believers, immigration to the afterlife, whether to heaven or the new creation, involves something called death. I think it's important to say something about it.

> *For most believers, immigration to the afterlife, whether to heaven or the new creation, involves something called death.*

Pastor Tim Keller, in his book *On Death,* talks about Mark Ashton, an Anglican vicar, who found in 2008 that he had inoperable gallbladder cancer. His "faith and joy in Christ" allowed him to show remarkable "confidence in the face of dying and even a sense of anticipation. . . . During the next fifteen months, [Ashton] talked with virtually everyone he met about his coming death with ease, eloquence, and poise. But this unnerved many people, who found not only his attitude but even his presence difficult to take."[1]

People certainly talk about death, read about it, and even watch its simulated arrival on TV and in movies. But being around dying people is different. Thinking and talking about one's own death is also different. It is natural for a culture that sees nothing beyond death to do whatever it takes to avoid facing it. Retirement is bad enough on the ego; death passes final judgment on my worth as a human being.

In the early chapters of *The Histories,* Herodotus tells us about Croesus, king of Lydia. When Solon of Athens, the famous Greek teacher and lawgiver, visits him in his capital at Sardis, Croesus asks him, "Who is the happiest man you have ever seen?" When Solon names several others, Croesus is offended and asks, "What of my own happiness?" Solon replies that one's life cannot be judged until it is known whether that person "died happily."[2] There is some wisdom in this.

Interior of the Mamertine prison where Paul was imprisoned at one time. It is beneath the church of Giuseppe dei Falegnami in modern Rome. This lower chamber was probably initially a cistern and dated to the sixth century BC.

We often look at various people who excel greatly, and we applaud them and judge them worthy. But then when they disappoint us, as they often do, we trash them despite all their accomplishments and positive attributes. Ours, in fact, is called "the cancel culture." Nobody wants to be cancelled.

People in the Bible talked about their deaths. For instance, elderly Jacob blessed Joseph and his two sons and pointed out that he was about to die. Then he summoned his other sons and blessed them and gave instructions on where he was to be buried. Then "when Jacob had finished giving charges to his sons, he drew his feet into the bed, took his last breath, and was gathered to his people" (Gen 49:33). In the next chapter Joseph calls for his brothers, tells them he is about to die, and instructs them to take his bones back to Canaan (50:22–26).

Moses warned Israel not to turn from the Lord after his own approaching death and then sang them a song and blessed the tribes (see Deut 31:24–30, 32:48–33:1). Later, before he died, Joshua, who was "old, advanced in age" (stated twice in Josh 23:1–2) testified to the people of Israel, saying, "I am now going the way of the whole earth, and you know with all your heart and all your soul that none of the good promises the LORD your God made to you has failed. Everything was fulfilled for you; not one promise has failed" (23:14). King David also acknowledged his approaching death and instructed his son Solomon to "be strong and be a man, and keep [his] obligation to the LORD" (1 Kgs 2:1–3).

Of course, no one spoke about his or her upcoming death as much as Jesus did, especially on the Passover night before he was arrested (John 13–17). And then there was Paul, whose words about his coming death we have examined in this book (see Phil 1:21–26). He also wrote this to his protegé Timothy as he, in what may have been Paul's last letter, passed to him the baton of ministry: "I am already being poured out as a drink offering, and the time for my departure is close.

I have fought the good fight, I have finished the race, I have kept the faith. There is reserved for me the crown of righteousness, which the Lord, the righteous Judge, will give me on that day, and not only to me, but to all those who have loved his appearing" (2 Tim 4:6–8). Paul

"I am already being poured out as a drink offering, and the time for my departure is close."

did not die a pleasant death. He was executed in Rome, most probably by beheading. To that point, he had not lived a peaceful life but experienced imprisonment, beatings, stoning, multiple shipwrecks, plus danger from the elements and especially from enemies (see 2 Cor 11:23–28). He even wrote to Timothy while in chains in a dungeon (see 2 Tim 1:16; 2:9), yet his testimony from there is full of courage, encouragement, patience and humility in suffering, confidence in God's power, and gratitude for God's faithfulness and grace.

Although he was soon to die, Paul was completely convinced that Christ had "abolished death and has brought life and immortality to light through the gospel" (2 Tim 1:10). How could he talk like that under such

Christ had "abolished death and has brought life and immortality to light through the gospel."

circumstances? Well, although the devil, death, and Hades will not be obliterated until Christ returns (see Rev 20:14), for the believer death has lost its sting (see 1 Cor 15:54–56) at the cross. "Condemnation" was eliminated (Rom 8:1) when our "certificate of debt" was erased, the forces of evil were "disarmed" (Col 2:12–15), and we were set "free" from "the fear of death" too (Heb 2:14–15). For God's child, there is no longer anything to fear on the other side of death's door. It's there we'll find the smiling face of Jesus Christ, bringing to us all

For God's child, there is no longer anything to fear on the other side of death's door.

the fullness of life and immortality promised throughout Scripture. No wonder Paul considered his death to be "gain" and longed to "depart and be with Christ"; indeed, it would be "far better" than anything this life could offer (Phil 1:21–23). As Tim Keller points out, ultimately "[i]n every set of arms we [mortals] are seeking God's arms, in every loving face we are seeking God's face, in every accomplishment we are looking for God's approval."[3] Paul knew that many had judged him guilty and deserving of execution, but that "the Lord, the righteous Judge," had reversed that verdict. The approval he sought was the one we already have in Christ, which Paul knew was "reserved" for him, "the crown of righteousness"—and not just for him, but for "all those who have loved [Christ's] appearing" (2 Tim

"In every set of arms we [mortals] are seeking God's arms, in every loving face we are seeking God's face, in every accomplishment we are looking for God's approval."

4:8). As Keller says, "When at last you see the God of the universe looking at you with love, all of the potentialities of your soul will be released and you will experience the glorious freedom of the children of God."[4]

Paul was certain he had lived the life God had called him to, having fought the good fight, finished the race, and kept the faith. But how did Paul live the difficult life he did and die with such dignity and peace? One essential ingredient was prayer; he prayed "night and day" (1:3). Another was remembering that he was an apostle "by God's will" and had "a holy calling" to be "a herald" and "teacher" of the gospel "entrusted to" him (1:1, 9, 11–12). He also humbly relied on "the Holy Spirit who lives in us" (1:14). Paul was focused as well, doing his best to avoid distractions (2:3, 14). Another essential ingredient of his faithful diligence was his total trust in and commitment to God's Word (2:10, 15; 3:15–17; 4:2, 13).

Another essential ingredient of his faithful diligence was his total trust in and commitment to God's Word.

The actor Tommy Lee Jones appeared in commercials for Ameriprise. In them he asked questions like these. "In retirement, will you outlive your money?" or "Can you keep your lifestyle in retirement?" We may be asking, "How many items on my bucket list will I be able to cross off before I die?" and "How much will I be able to accomplish during the last few years of my life?"

But thinking about Paul, his life, and his last words may change our question to something like, "Is it possible for me to live so that I can die with dignity and peace like Paul?" Or if you are a "senior citizen" like me, you may pray things like this: "Lord, I don't know when or how I am going to die, but you do. Please teach me to "number [my] days" carefully so that I "may develop wisdom" in my heart (Ps 90:12) and prove fruitful in my old age."

Please teach me to "number [my] days" carefully so that I "may develop wisdom" in my heart.

In his book on dying and caring, Henri Nouwen asks this: "Is it possible to befriend our dying gradually and live open to it, trusting that we have nothing to fear? Is it possible to prepare for our death with the same attentiveness that our parents had in preparing for our birth? Can we wait for our death as for a friend who wants to welcome us home?"[5] In other words, he urges us to ask, "How can I die well?" And here is one answer Nouwen gives: "A good death is a death in solidarity with others. To prepare . . . for a good death, we must develop or deepen this sense of solidarity."[6] One way to do this is to make our deaths a gift to others. What do I mean? Well, while only Jesus could live a truly redemptive life and die a redemptive death, we can live and die as a testimony to that redemption. In fact, dying, Nouwen says, can be "the way to everlasting fruitfulness. Here is the most hope-giving aspect of death. Our death may be the end of our success, our productivity, our fame, or our importance among people, but it is not the end of our fruitfulness." The beauty of life, he says, it that "it bears fruit long after life itself has come to an end."[7]

"Our death may be the end of our success, our productivity, our fame, or our importance among people, but it is not the end of our fruitfulness."

We can all think of people, living or dead, who have become a big part of who we are. For me, one such person is Dr. Bruce Waltke, my mentor and friend. I met him in 1971 when I was asking God to show me where I should attend seminary. Our meeting provided God's answer. I and tens of thousands of others have studied Hebrew and Old Testament with him either in class or through his writings all these years. But his influence far outreaches anything he's done professionally. Even in his nineties, the man still radiates a humble love for the greatness and goodness of God, for the gospel of Jesus Christ, for the intricate beauty and wisdom of God's Word, and a sacrificial love for people—whether those to whom he is united in the Spirit or those in need of the Savior.

In 2019 I had the tremendous privilege of joining a group of former students of Waltke's in Seattle, where he lives, to study again under his guidance for several days. He led us through several of the Psalms in Hebrew. In those sessions, I felt myself almost lifted to the third heaven, reinspired and reinvigorated not only by God's Spirit working through him, but also by the spiritual fellowship of those godly men—most of whom I'd not met before.

I mention this not only to help illustrate what an impact one's life can have on others, but to share something I learned at that meeting. Psalm 92 was one of the psalms we studied. Here is its last stanza:

> The righteous thrive like a palm tree
> and grow like a cedar tree in Lebanon.
> Planted in the house of the LORD,
> they thrive in the courts of our God.
> They will still bear fruit in old age,
> healthy and green,
> to declare, "The LORD is just;
> he is my rock,
>   and there is no unrighteousness in him." (Ps 92:12–15)

"They will still bear fruit in old age, healthy and green."

"The righteous" are believers, all those who have joined together in solidarity to trust, love, praise, and serve the God of our salvation. We delight in declaring His "faithful love [his *chesed*] in the morning" and His "faithfulness at night"—in other words, all the time (v. 2). We have all been blown away by the "magnificent" works of His hands and His "profound" (unfathomably deep) "thoughts," plans, and purposes He has demonstrated in the world, His church, and in our individual lives (vv. 4–5). But we are more than just grateful audience or even choir members. He has brought us, His children, into the very courts of the house of

Dr. Bruce Waltke (center, wearing hat) and his disciples (personal photo).

the Lord and planted us so that we may "thrive" there under His protection and "still bear fruit in old age, [being] healthy and green."

That's a picture of the eternal life that begins even while we are still living here. It's abundant, fruitful life! But there is more. God has given us the privilege of testifying to others, of bearing witness to all His persistent, faithful acts of loving mercy in our lives even into our old age. You and I get to tell about how He chased us down when we went our own way, how He picked us up when we fell out of weakness and discouragement, about the times when He put the pieces of our broken hearts and lives back together, and when He forgave and cleansed us for His purposes. Our gracious God has privileged and empowered us to declare, "The LORD is just; / he is my rock, / and there is no unrighteousness in him" (v. 15). All that he does is right and good. In his last sermon before he died on January 31, 1892, Baptist preacher Charles Spurgeon declared of Christ, "If there is anything that is gracious, generous, kind, and tender, yea lavish and superabundant in love, you always find it in him. These forty years and more have I served him, blessed be his name! and I have had nothing but love from him."[8]

God has given us the privilege of testifying to others.

At the end of Psalm 92 in my CSB I was carrying at the time (along with my Hebrew Bible) I wrote these words:

> This is my job.
> 9–19–2019

Indeed, that will always be my job. That is the job of each of his children.

In Todd Billings's wonderful book, *The End of the Christian Life: How Embracing Our Mortality Frees Us to Truly Live,* he includes this example of "how Christians can bear witness to Christ's kingdom as they face their own deaths."[9] He writes that when a certain pastor entered a hospital room, a man named Claude was struggling to breathe through a ventilator, surrounded by family and close friends. They were each telling Claude how much they loved him. As the pastor began to speak, Claude removed the ventilator, freeing his mouth to recite something he had learned as a child. It was from the *Heidelberg Catechism* (1563), Question 1:

> What is your only comfort in life and in death?
> That I am not my own, but belong—body and soul, in life and in death—to my faithful Savior Jesus Christ.

These words . . .

> trailed off as Claude's final breaths quietly punctuated his last earthly moments. . . . In an ordinary hospital room, with no video cameras or journalists, he embraced his weakness. . . . In the boldness of his weakness, he commended his own body and soul to the King of the kingdom, the priest of the temple, the crucified and risen Savior, the One who embodies true flourishing in his very person.[10]

My friend Kenneth Mathews recently shared with me a quote from Puritan Pastor Thomas Brooks (1608–1680), which I think is a fitting anthem with which to end our guidebook. It is from a funeral sermon he preached in 1561 entitled "A Believer's Last Day is His Best Day." Referring to the Christ-follower's final day in earthly bondage he said this in a funeral sermon: "In that day [Christians] shall find that God . . . will make good all those golden and glorious promises He has made to them." Then Brooks concluded with these triumphant words: "Then your dying-day shall be to you as the day of harvest to the farmer, as the day of deliverance to the prisoner, as the day of coronation to the king, and the day of marriage to the bride. Your dying-day shall be a day of triumph and exaltation, a day of freedom and consolation, a day of rest and satisfaction!"[11]

NOTES

[1]   Timothy Keller, *On Death* (London: Penguin, 2020), 12.

[2]   *Herodotus: The Histories,* trans. Aubrey de Sélincourt, rev. A. R. Burn (New York: Penguin, 1972), 51–53.

[3]   Keller, *On Death,* 58.

[4]   Keller, *On Death,* 63.

[5]   Henri Nouwen, *Our Greatest Gift: A Meditation on Dying and Caring* (New York: HarperOne, 1994), xiii.

[6]   Nouwen, *Our Greatest Gift,* 24.

[7]   Nouwen, *Our Greatest Gift,* 36.

[8]   Charles Haddon Spurgeon, "The Statute of David for the Sharing of the Spoil," The Spurgeon Center. Accessed March 17, 2023, https://www.spurgeon.org/resource-library/sermons/the-statute-of-david-for-the-sharing-of-the-spoil/#flipbook/.

[9]   J. Todd Billings, *The End of the Christian Life: How Embracing Our Mortality Frees Us to Truly Live* (Grand Rapids: Brazos, 2020), 145–46.

[10] Billings, *End of the Christian Life,* 145–146.

[11] *The Complete Works of Thomas Brooks* (Edinburgh: James Nichol, 1866) 394–408

ART CREDITS

Holman Bible Publishers is grateful to the following persons and institutions for the graphics in the *Ultimate Guide to Heaven and Hell*. Where we have inadvertently failed to give proper credit for any graphic in the Bible, please contact us (customerservice@lifeway. com), and we will make the required correction in subsequent printings.

Clendenen, Ann: 167

Clendenen, E. Ray: pp. 40, 41, 131, 262.

Cornell University Library: p. 19.

Getty Images: pp. 34, 37, 38, 48, 51, 53, 54, 56, 61, 70, 76, 78, 84, 95, 101, 102, 113, 123, 125, 136, 186.

Holman Bible Publishers: pp. 45, 72, 173, 231, 252.

iStock Photos: p. 25.

Lifeway Christian Resources: pp. xii, 116, 150, 234, 243, 246, 259.

Met Museum: pp. 209, 215, 226.

Pixabay: p. 133.

Sluder, Brooklyn: p. 21.

Twilights Warden Blog: p. 23 (https:// twilightswarden.wordpress. com/2011/01/03/book-the-pilgrims-progress/)

Unsplash: pp. xi (Ben Lee), xiv (Annie Spratt), 1 (Ibrahim Asad), 2 (JESHOOTS. COM), 3 (Ben White), 9 (Chastagner Thierry), 12 (NOAA), 29 (Kyle William), 58 (Artem Sapegin), 66 (Chris Slupski), 81 (Stephanie Bergeron), 91 (Paul Zoetemeijer), 97 (Brandon Morgan), 122 (Caspar Rae), 138 (Strauss Western), 140 (Steve Sharp), 145 (Stormseeker), 148 (Kenny Orr), 159 (Tom Delanoue), 161 (Geoffroy Hauwen), 168 (Den Harrson), 177 (Patrick Hendry), 180 (Sangia), 184 (Ben White), 188 (Austin Neill), 189 (Manny Moreno), 191 (Kevin Andre), 223 (Everyday basics), 238 (guile pozzi), 257 (K Hsu).

Wikiart: p. 212.

Wikipedia/Commons: pp. 6, 15, 27, 85, 87, 89, 93, 103, 108, 111 (2X), 143, 152, 154, 157, 171, 175, 194, 201, 203, 205, 218, 221, 250.